Maneuvering Time and Place:
The Poetry of Manuel Maples Arce

By Diane J. Forbes

2022

Copyright © Diane J. Forbes
of this edition © Stockcero 2022
1st. Stockcero edition: 2022

ISBN: 978-1-949938-16-6
Library of Congress Control Number: 2022937210

All rights reserved.
This book may not be reproduced, stored in a retrieval system, or transmitted, in whole or in part, in any form or by any means, electronic, mechanical, photocopying, recording, or otherwise, without written permission of Stockcero, Inc.

Set in Linotype Granjon font family typeface
Printed in the United States of America on acid-free paper.

Published by Stockcero, Inc.
3785 N.W. 82nd Avenue
Doral, FL 33166
USA
stockcero@stockcero.com

www.stockcero.com

Maneuvering Time and Place:
The Poetry of Manuel Maples Arce

By Diane J. Forbes

Acknowledgements

I wish to thank the many people who have supported my work on this book, especially Mireya Maples, also the RIT Department of Modern Languages & Cultures and the College of Liberal Arts at RIT for sabbatical leave and travel funds. For early research doña Blanca V. de Maples, the UNAM Centro de Estudios Literarios, Dr. Aurora Ocampo, Dr. Guillermo Sheridan, and Dr. Leon Lyday. For help with lodging and libraries, Dr. Kenneth Monahan, Dr. Merlin Forster, Dr. Janet Zehr, Dr. Linda Ledford-Miller, Mrs. Joan Bannister, Mrs. Alva Fagrell, and Mr. José Kozer. Thank you to the other friends who encouraged me along the way, and my family. Sincere thanks to Stockcero and don Pablo Agrest Berge for publishing this book that I hold very dear.

TABLE OF CONTENTS

Acknowledgements 5
Introduction 9
Manuel Maples Arce: Biographical Information 15
Works by Manuel Maples Arce 17
Chapter One: Estridentismo and the Avant-Garde 19
Chapter Two: The Prism: Fragmented Reality, *Andamios Interiores*, 1922 75
Chapter Three: The City in Clamor and Reflection, *Urbe*, 1924 177
Chapter Four: Poet in the Transitory World, *Poemas Interdictos*, 1927 229
Chapter Five: The Search for Permanence, *Memorial de la Sangre*, 1947 287
Chapter Six: Self-Portrait with Memories, *Poemas No-Coleccionados*, 1919-1980 355
Chapter Seven: Conclusion, *The Seeds of Time* 398
Works Cited 407
Other References 417

Introduction

2021 marks the one-hundredth anniversary of Estridentismo, Manuel Maples Arce's avant-garde movement in Mexico, an energetic rupture from the past, which brought the Mexican Revolution to all of the arts and brought the Mexican literary community into the 20th century. Manuel Maples Arce was a driving force in the modernization of Mexican poetry in the 1920s, and his complete work, spanning more than six decades, is of a value that should create for him a respected place among the most prominent Latin American poets of the twentieth century. Although a thorough reading of his work confirms this evaluation, the literary world and academia have yet to consider Maples Arce's complete work as a whole, rather than concentrating only on his vanguardista period, Estridentismo. Much was written about Maples and Estridentismo in the 1920s, followed by a carry-over of period polemics after his 1940 anthology of modern Mexican poetry. All of this has been discussed again in recent criticism, with a more contemporary point of view. The 1947 publication of *Memorial de la Sangre* brought many reviews from international friends. Luis Mario Schneider and Kenneth C. Monahan wrote their important studies in the 1970s. The 1981 publication of Maples' complete poetry as *Las semillas del tiempo* brought a bit more attention, as did the reprint in 2013, along with several anniversary retrospectives. More recently, quite a lot has been written (mainly in Mexico and mainly in Spanish) about Estridentismo, mostly about the manifestos, the people, and the aims of the movement. These are from refreshingly new perspectives, but constitute quite a lot of repetition. Still needed is a serious textual analysis of Maples Arce's complete poetry, a close look at the poems themselves, from 1922 to 1981, and how they all fit together. The goal of the present study is to provide that analysis and, through such, to demonstrate the transcendence and lasting value of Maples Arce's poetry.

In this study, historical literary references and connections are made to aid the reader in placing Maples Arce's work in relevant context to gauge Maples Arce's merit and to justify his place in Hispanic letters. An introduction to the historical avant-garde is given to provide the necessary background and context, especially for the English-language readership, and an overview of *Estridentismo* is included both for the sake of information and to rectify errors and omissions in some past criticism. It is the aim of this study to illustrate the cohesiveness and the trajectory of Maples Arce's complete poetry.

Chapter One presents an introduction to *Estridentismo* in the context of the historical avant-garde and modern poetry. Chapter Two analyzes Maples' first volume of poetry in the Estridentismo period, *Andamios Interiores* (1922), in which Maples Arce shows us his style and outlook and presents the basic problem dealt with in all of his poetry. The persona in these poems, the "yo," appears to be a poet, and may or may not be an autobiographical representation of Maples Arce. I will use the terms "protagonist" and "persona" throughout the study to refer to this voice. In a world where nothing seems to last, where everything seems to slip through his hands, the protagonist of the poems strives to overcome separation and transitoriness, to achieve union and permanence: this is the main issue in Maples Arce's poetry. The poems present in a variety of ways the protagonist's situations of loneliness and separation from a loved one, and often a sense of dissociation from some ideal harmonious world, even in the midst of exciting modernity. By merging elements of content and form (e.g. the exhilaration he feels from the new "modern" inventions, plus formal manipulation of the structure of the poem to support and reflect that content) and the act of recording images and emotions in the form of a poem, union and permanence are achieved, not in the "story" of the poem but in the poem itself. These Cubist poems involve the reader, who has to reconstruct the puzzle of shattered images in the poems, which together tell of the death of postmodernismo and the arrival of the jazz age and how it affects the protagonist's life.

Chapter Three discusses *Urbe* (1924), in which Maples Arce gives the urban techno-socio-political context of the problem of separation vs. union and transitoriness vs. permanence (workers' rights struggles, industrialization, the lingering violence of the Revolution, political corruption, amid the dynamism of the city alive with new inventions). The poet observes this city in revolution, as if from his balcony. Chapter Four shows Maples Arce explaining the poet's place in that context and in the world in general, in *Poemas Interdictos* (1927), the protagonist now going out into that world and participating. Examining *Memorial de la Sangre* (1947), Chapter Five illustrates how Maples Arce delves into the eternal crux of the problem (separation/union, transitoriness/permanence, destruction/creation) experienced in the context of war and history, and suggests a solution (which is hinted at in the previous volumes) in poems written during his years in Europe. Chapter Six considers the previously uncollected poems (mostly 1948-1981) included at the end of *Las semillas del tiempo*, in which the poet meditates on the innermost personal dilemmas and implications of the problem of transitoriness vs. eternity. In Chapter Seven some conclusions are made as to how Maples Arce achieves an artistic solution to the problem, how his career as a poet progresses in logical order, and how the complete work functions as a whole.

I believe that a close study of the poems, with textual analysis, is absolutely necessary in order to gain a true understanding of Maples' contribution to modern poetry. My analysis of the poems presents the idea of a destruction/creation dichotomy or cycle which spans Maples Arce's poetic work. Existing criticism tends to look at only the *estridentista* period or, separately and to a much lesser degree, the period covered by *Memorial de la Sangre*, without connecting the two or making any major observations about the trajectory of Maples Arce's complete works. I suggest that the destruction-creation cycle does continue throughout his career, and that there is present in all of the poems (from the 1922 *Andamios Interiores* through the group of previously uncollected poems, which contains many written in the last years of Maples' life) a search for union and permanence in a transitory world. An examination of the complete poetry, as collected in *Las semillas del tiempo*, shows how this thematic thread runs through all of the poems and explains the continuity which exists from beginning to end of Maples Arce's career. The study shows the maturation and evolution of an accomplished poet, whose work has withstood the test of time and belongs among the best of the century.

Manuel Maples Arce: Biographical Information

Manuel Maples Arce was born May 1, 1900 in Papantla, Veracruz, Mexico, son of Manuel Maples (lawyer and poet) and Adela Arce. He spent his childhood in Tuxpan, Veracruz, where he attended the Escuela Cantonal Miguel Lerdo. He later attended the Preparatoria (after one year of study in Jalapa) in the city of Veracruz, followed by the Escuela Libre de Derecho in Mexico City, from which he received his law degree in 1925. In 1930-31 he studied French literature and Art History at the Sorbonne in Paris. He began writing poetry as a teenager and published his first poem in 1919.

In his native state of Veracruz, Maples Arce held several judicial and political posts: judge (*Juez Primero de Primera Instancia*) and Secretary General of the Government of the State of Veracruz (both in Jalapa and beginning in 1925), Interim Governor, and representative to the state legislature (1928). He was also consulting attorney for the State Departments of the Treasury and Government, technical consultant for the State Department of Education, and Head of the Editorial Department of same.

In 1932 Maples Arce was elected representative to the Federal Congress in Mexico City and in 1935 he joined the Mexican Foreign Service as Secretary of the Embassy in Belgium, where he was also *Encargado de Negocios*. In Warsaw and Rome he was *Encargado de Negocios* until the outbreak of World War II, when he was sent to London (with duties also in Lisbon) as Consul General and representative of Mexico to the governments in exile of Belgium, Czechoslovakia, Holland, Norway and Poland. In 1944 he was appointed Ambassador to Panama, later to Chile (1950) and then Colombia (1951). In 1952, Maples Arce was sent to renew diplomatic relations with Japan as the first Ambassador from Mexico to Japan, after which he was Ambassador in Canada (1956), Norway (1959), Lebanon and Pakistan (1962). Some of the diplomatic appointments stated here also included minor representation in other countries. For professional reasons and as a tourist, Maples traveled over most of the world.

Though an energetic and untiring representative of Mexico in the diplomatic corps and champion of Mexican cultural promotion, Maples Arce considered his main profession to be that of poet. He had an avid interest in literature from an early age, and wrote poetry from his teens to the year of his death. Poetry was his way of life and it, along with his appreciation of art, profoundly influenced his work as cultural ambassador.

Maples Arce was a contributing author to most of Mexico's major periodicals, as well as to those of several foreign countries. Maples' work has received critical commentary in numerous periodicals and other publications in Mexico and throughout the world, including countries where he served in the diplomatic corps and in the United States.

Maples Arce married Blanche Vermeersch in Belgium on August 12, 1936, and they had two children, Manuel and Mireya. Upon retirement from the diplomatic corps in 1967, Maples returned to Mexico and continued to write poetry and essays, in addition to his three volumes of autobiography. He died on June 26, 1981 in Mexico City.

Works by Manuel Maples Arce*

Poetry:

Andamios Interiores, México: Editorial Cultura, 1922.

Urbe, México: Andrés Botas e Hijo, 1924.

Poemas Interdictos, Jalapa, Veracruz: Ediciones de Horizonte, 1927.

Memorial de la Sangre, México: Talleres Gráficos de la Nación, 1947.

Las semillas del tiempo: obra poética 1919-1980, México: Fondo de Cultura Económica, 1981.

Editorial/Criticism:

Antología de la Poesía Mexicana Moderna, Rome: Poligráfica Tiberina, 1940.

Siete Cuentos Mexicanos, Panamá: Biblioteca Selecta, 1946.

Essay:

Modern Mexican Art (El Arte Mexicano Moderno). London: A. Zwemmer, 1943.

El Paisaje en la Literatura Mexicana. México: Librería Porrúa Hnos. y Cía., 1944.

Peregrinación por el Arte de México. Buenos Aires, 1951.

Incitaciones y Valoraciones. México: Cuadernos Americanos, 1956.

---

* Maples Arce dismissed his early modernista book, *Rag, tintas de abanico* (1920), written when he was young, and asked that it not be included in his complete poetry. I have honored that request, the same for his teenage poems.

Ensayos Japoneses. México: Editorial Cultura, 1959.

Leopoldo Méndez. México: Fondo de Cultura Económica, 1970.

Memoirs:

A la orilla de este río. Madrid: Editorial Plenitud, 1964.

Soberana juventud. Madrid: Editorial Plenitud, 1967.

Mi vida por el mundo. Veracruz: Universidad Veracruzana, 1983.

Literary Magazines:

Collaboration on many literary magazines, including: Zig-Zag, Revista de Revistas, El Universal Ilustrado, Irradiador, Horizonte.

References

Maples Arce, Manuel. *Las semillas del tiempo: Obra poética (1919-1980).* México: Fondo de Cultura Económica, 1981.

Monahan, Kenneth C. *Manuel Maples Arce and "Estridentismo."* Diss. Northwestern University, 1972. Ann Arbor. Michigan: UMI, 1973. 73-10,260.

Schneider, Luis Mario. *El Estridentismo: o una Literatura de la Estrategia.* México: Ediciones de Bellas Artes, 1970.

Chapter One: Estridentismo and the Avant-Garde

"¡CHOPIN A LA SILLA ELÉCTRICA!"
"¡VIVA EL MOLE DE GUAJOLOTE!"
ESTRIDENTISTA MANIFESTOS 1 & 2

The historical avant-garde, or *vanguardismo*,[1] as it is known in Spanish, was an artistic phenomenon that occurred roughly between 1907 and the end of the 1920s in virtually all of Western art and literature. The avant-garde was composed of a series of movements that worked to renovate artistic and literary expression in order better to reflect life in the twentieth century and modern sensibility. The avant-garde's proponents intended to shock the public into awareness, and attempted to destroy tradition and the bourgeois concept of art. This revolution consisted of a series of expressions. Pablo Picasso's first Cubist painting, "Les Demoiselles d'Avignon," dates from 1907. Italian Futurism began in 1909, Dadaism in 1916 and Surrealism in 1924 (though it was building from 1919), dates corresponding to their first manifestos. These avant-garde "-isms" flourished in the teens and twenties in Europe and had similar expression in the Americas, though starting later there. The avant-garde was most prolific in the Americas in the twenties, with a few important works from the late teens (e.g. T. S. Eliot's *Love Song of J. Alfred*

---

1   Please note that the term *vanguardismo* (or avant-garde) is used here in its specific sense, denoting a particular historical period in the arts, rather than solely in its general sense of that which is always in the forefront, revolutionary, unorthodox, experimental work in any period.

Prufrock, 1915; Vicente Huidobro's *El espejo de agua*, 1916, *Ecuatorial*, 1918, *Poemas árticos*, 1918, and some of his volumes in French). It is important to note that Latin American vanguardismo is, for the most part, a mixture of the tendencies which found separate (though not mutually exclusive) expression in Europe–Cubism, Futurism, Dadaism, followed later by Surrealism.[2]

Some sources generalize that the avant-garde covers the

---

2   These four movements will be discussed in detail later. When addressing the international avant-garde, there is a possibility for confusion in the terminology regarding poetry movements. The following chart shows approximate correspondences in vertical columns, in both time period and style.

Spanish America	Modernismo (Darío, et al)	Post-modernismo	Vanguardismo (various -ismos)	Postvanguardismo
Brazil	Simbolismo Parnasianismo		Modernismo (Mário Andrade, Osvald de Andrade, et al)	Postmodernismo Surrealismo
Europe in general (excluding Spain)	Symbolism Parnassianism Impressionism		Avant-garde (Cubism, Italian Futurism, Dada, Russian Futurism, German Expressionism)	Surrealism
Spain	Modernismo (J.R. Jiménez, M. Machado, F. Villa-Espesa, Valle-Inclán)		Ultraísmo Creacionismo (G. Diego) Catalán avant-garde	Postvanguardismo Surrealismo Gen. '27
United States	formative stage of Modernism		Modernism (many independent writers: Pound, Eliot, Hart Crane, W.C. Williams, W. Stevens, e.e. cummings)	Late Modernism (late Eliot, late W.C. Williams, Frost, Roethke, Lowell) (Post-modernism is later)
Great Britain	Decadents (Wilde, Pater, Symons)	Hardy, Yeats	Vorticism (Pound, Eliot, W. Lewis, Gaudier-Brzeska)	30s Left (Spender, Auden, C. Day Lewis, MacNiece)

years between the two World Wars, but by the 1930s Sur realism dominates and the mood is different, more appropriately termed postvanguardismo in Latin America. In a sense, the poetry of the avant-garde accomplished its mission in the twenties, and in the thirties and forties, poetry was ready to continue evolving and progressing along with the changing world. The avant-garde is revolutionary and violent in its mission—a new vision that abruptly opens the door to new possibilities for all literature that follows. From its accomplishments emerges the great freedom of expression that has produced the 20th century's masterpieces. The literary avant-garde is a transitional stage, but one with significant worth in its own right. The same is true for the corresponding work in painting, sculpture and music.

Ezra Pound's phrase "make it new" expresses a common goal of all of the avant-garde -isms. There was a desire to express the condition of modern life in the new century, and to renovate both thematics and aesthetics. Accelerated time, space, movement, dynamism, speed, communication, modern machines, transportation, and man-made beauty were newly-important issues for the poet, as was humankind's place in that new world. The poet expressed our joy in the rush of modernity, our senses constantly bombarded by stimuli, but also spoke to our ultimate loneliness, paralysis, sense of being lost, lack of personal communication, and to the social injustice of the bourgeois-controlled system. Latin American vanguardismo is cosmopolitan and universal, but at the same time it places much importance on national identity (this is especially true in Mexico, a new nationalism having been created by the 1910-1920 Mexican Revolution).

The avant-garde wanted to create a literature that

would better reflect the spirit and state of mind of the modern world. It wanted to make all artistic expression independent of the constraints of traditional realism. It is often non-representational, anti-sentimental, anti-anecdotal, anti-rhetorical, anti-rationalist, and it rejects the old thematics. The poem (or other work of art) is seen as an object in itself, without necessary ties to any exterior subject. It does not represent; it *is*. Form and the word are set free. Thus form and content are more organically united. There is a great deal of experimentation, including the use of neologisms and creative typography to reflect the content. The concrete form of the written word itself and its placement on the page are used conscientiously (letters, lines, shapes and images they form).

The combination of time and space (the 20th century awareness of their interaction and mutual influence) is a major theme as well as an element of form in both poetry and painting (the spatialization of time, the temporalization of space, the combination of reading's linear time—duration—with the visual instant). There is a movement towards abstractionism, away from the realistically represented object (although the creative work is still based in reality). The avant-garde seeks to express perceived reality rather than apparent reality; that is, the simultaneous multiplicity of perspectives with which one perceives reality and not just one isolated, artificial plane.

The image is all-important, and there is total freedom in its creation. The traditional distinction between image and metaphor virtually disappears and the terms often may be used interchangeably. There is a real avant-garde cult of the metaphor. At the same time there is interesting use of metonymy, often the structuring device and sole key to a poem (e.g. Jean Arp's "Poux Fardés"). The possibilities of association and suggestion are multiplied in the new combinations found in metaphors: juxtaposition of opposites, or other unexpected combinations.

There is a penchant for originality, surprise and novelty. There is much word-play, punning, verbal incoherence (reflecting the state of human communication), and often a strong note of humor and sarcasm designed to attack blatantly the mask of seriousness with which the bourgeois always cloaked its art. "Épater le bourgeois" was a major goal of the avant-garde–this became evident not only in the poetry but also in the public spectacles created by the avant-garde, especially the Dadaists and Futurists, and, as we shall see in Mexico, the estridentistas. In general, the avant-garde was a reaction against nineteenth-century tradition.

During this period, art increasingly emphasizes form more than theme (or one could say that form becomes essentially *the* theme). Wylie Sypher has said that Cubism is painting about painting; one may assert that vanguardista poetry is poetry about poetry. The new century required a new aesthetic. In avant-garde literature we see a fragmentation of syntax, causing concentration on the individual word. There are many kinds of insistent repetition (the best example of which is Gertrude Stein's prose style), and an abstract relationship grows between words. In the image/metaphor there is often a union of two different semantic fields. The constant use of fragmentation and unexpected combinations has to do both with new ideas about perception and with new stimuli to be perceived. Language is the medium by which things are realized (perceived) in the adult human mind; the poet plays with our perception as well as offering new meaning. Ernest Hemingway's prose certainly may not seem avant-garde to most readers, but he was an avid student of Gertrude Stein, and his descriptive paragraphs[3] demonstrate an inscape, an inner sense of the thing described, a spiritual vision of it, thus linking the writer's perception of the stimulus to the literary (verbal) expression of it. The resulting relationship between subject and object (the observer and the thing observed) makes the writing Art. Our manner of perception determines our sense of reality.[4]

Two things happen when the literature and art deal with the explosive first quarter of the twentieth century in the Western world: the profusion of modern phenomena causes the writer/artist to be caught emotionally between extremes of great intensity while physically surrounded by a dynamic whirlwind, and the aesthetic expression of this experience produces a work so apparently hermetic that the traditional reader/viewer often feels incapable of understanding. One sees, however, that there is a need for writers/artists to express modern life, and the reader/viewer, in order to understand, must not only discard traditional expectations but also participate in the re-creation of the work of art and thus in the experience.

A brief summary of what these new phenomena of the twentieth century were may be of use: mechanization, industrialization, Einstein's theory of relativity, Heisenberg's theory of uncertainty, the Mexican Revolution, World War I, the Russian Revolution, Marxism, Socialism, Com-

---

3   Excellent examples are found in the stories "Now I Lay Me" and "Fathers and Sons" (*The Short Stories of Ernest Hemingway,* New York: Charles Scribner's Sons, 1966). Hemingway also studied Cézanne, as did Picasso.
4   A clear example of this is found in the four distinct perceptions and consequent narrations of one situation in William Faulkner's *The Sound and the Fury* (New York: Random House, 1929).

munism, Freud's theories about dreams (psychoanalysis, lunacy, cause and effect), the first surgical interventions, anesthesia, x-rays, the discovery of radioactivity and the effects of light, atomic and nuclear physics (nuclear reaction theories, atomic and molecular theories, atomic model), black holes, quantum theory and mechanics, fission of heavy nuclei, electromagnetism, photography, cinema, translation of Darwin's "Origin of the Species" (still controversial in the public sphere), brain physiology, pavement, cement, more railroads and steamboats, ocean liners, airplanes, helicopters, cars, bicycles, motorcycles, telegraph, telephone, trans-Atlantic cable, microphone, phonograph, radio, jazz, electricity, battery, blast furnace, hydraulic crane, steel bridges, oil wells, oil and gas for cars, vulcanization, McCormick reaper, electric light, typewriter, Eastman-Kodak camera, evaporated milk, canning, dynamos, war machines (tanks, submarines, dynamite, torpedoes, machine guns, mass-production of rifles, revolvers, big ships, dredges, airplanes), man-made fabrics, and so on. Some of these phenomena date from the late 19th century but are still new to the general public in the early 20th century.

The technological advances become the trademarks of modernity. The scientific theories (especially Einstein, Heisenberg and Freud) become distorted popular ideas and cause paranoia among the general public: I can never be sure if I exist or not (Heisenberg); an assertion of anything is no longer possible after Einstein's theory of relativity—this gives a certain freedom to art—"this is round" only because that's how I perceive it in this time and space. "It's all relative." These common preoccupations influence modern thought and the relationship of humans to the environment. The old mysticism is replaced by a new scientific mysticism; the brain is now the central object. In addition, the rise of the bourgeoisie and Positivism in the 19th century and the resultant oppression of the proletariat brought a strong reaction in the 20th century.

Stephen Spender explains the artistic reception of these new scientific and technological concepts in his essay "The Making of a Poem":

> A world of external impersonal forces must be sacrificially reinvented as the poet's inner personal world, so that, for his reader, the impersonal modern world may be personalized in poetry... What I am concerned with is his awareness of a contemporary situation which affects personal relations and art itself, and which is different from past situations...
>
> What writers may fruitfully know is that which they can experience with their sensibility. So it is not so important that they should know the second law of thermodynamics as that they should perceive the subtle changes effected in the rhythm of language by the environment resulting from inventions and its influence on human behavior and modes of feeling. It is not scientific knowledge but its effects which become part of the experience of modern life.[5]

Crucial here: the reader of a poem that expresses the effect of modernity on life is required to decipher the code and then re-create the poem—thus adding, by the way, to its dynamism. Hugh Kenner notes how exciting that can be, referring to an Ezra Pound poem:

> Printed as he prints it, and unpunctuated, the delicacies this scansion obliterates are set out for the mind to discover, the run of live breath checked by eager nerves, played against the units of attention. Make it

---

5   Stephen Spender, *The Making of a Poem* (London: Hamish Hamilton, 1955) 32, 37.

new; its last word is 'revived'.⁶

To conclude this introduction to the avant-garde and return to Latin America specifically, it is useful to look at Andrew P. Debicki's summary comparing Modernismo and Vanguardismo:

> Simplificando demasiado, pudiera decirse que los modernistas trataron de encarnar artísticamente sus temas por medio de un lenguaje especial, que elaboraban y aplicaban a la descripción o a la anécdota para extender su valor. Su esfuerzo se centraba, por tanto, en el enriquecimiento de una realidad exterior. Los vanguardistas en cambio evitan descripción y anécdota, y crean la experiencia más directamente, por medio del lenguaje y de la imagen. Dan un paso más– un paso muy importante–en el alejamiento de la poesía del mensaje y de la confesión personal de su autor. (López Velarde puede considerarse, en este esquema, figura transicional entre el Modernismo y la Vanguardia.) El así llamado 'hermetismo' de la poesía vanguardista se debe en muchos casos a la falta de organización anecdótica o lógica; una vez que el lector deja de buscar tal organización y se fija en la experiencia creada directamente en el poema, éste no le parece extraño.⁷

Estridentismo: A Revolution in Poetry

Manuel Maples Arce's formative years as a poet (teenage years) coincidieron with the periods of Modernismo and Postmodernismo in Mexico. Even though his earliest poems and first published book (*Rag. Tintas de abanico*, 1920, prose poems) were modernistas, Maples felt an in-

---

6   Hugh Kenner, *The Pound Era* (Berkeley and Los Angeles: University of California Press, 1971) 543.
7   Andrew P. Debicki, *Antología de la Poesía Mexicana Moderna* (London: Tamesis Books Limited, 1977) 20.

creasing need for change, the need to renovate and modernize the state of poetry in Mexico. Postmodernismo had reached a point of stagnation and its traditional 19th century/turn-of-the-century perspectives were no longer valid for the new 20th century.

> Yo perseguía un arte que correspondiera a mi propio gusto y no al halago de los demás. Promovía algo nuevo. Las modalidades líricas del modernismo y aun del postmodernismo me parecían [pretéritas], y había que renovarlas. Interesábanme las imágenes enigmáticas que no pudieran formularse racionalmente... Yo preconizaba un cambio en la expresión, pero sobre todo en las imágenes, de las que hacía depender el misterio de la poesía en aquellos años. Cada verso debería encerrar una imagen para pasar a otra, enlazada virtual o explícitamente, fundida en los términos de la comparación. Desaparecían las relaciones visuales, para transformarse en algo prodigioso... Yo había pensado reiteradamente en el problema de la renovación literaria de manera inmediata, en ahondar las posibilidades de la imagen, prescindiendo de los elementos lógicos que mantenían su sentido explicativo. Inicié una búsqueda apasionada por un nuevo mundo espiritual, a la vez que trabajaba por difundir, entre la juventud mexicana, las novísimas ideas y los nombres de los escritores universales vinculados al movimiento de vanguardia, al que México había permanecido indiferente.[8]

Maples began to experiment, as well as to talk with other artists concerned about the need for change. His poem "Esas rosas eléctricas" is the first published manifestation of his new vein of poetry. The poem was rejected by *Revista de Revistas*, one of the three most prestigious literary magazines in Mexico City at the time,[9] but was accepted for publication in *Cosmópolis* (No. 34) in Madrid, Spain. This publication

---

8   Manuel Maples Arce, *Soberana Juventud* (Madrid: Editorial Plenitud, 1964) 120-122.
9   Revista de Revistas, El Universal Ilustrado, Zig-Zag.

was not only a boost to Maples' new style, but provided him with important connections with the Ultraist poets of Spain (who also had connections with Chilean Vicente Huidobro), thus opening a channel of correspondence and a way to receive news of the latest European poetry. In the meantime, Maples Arce planned his strategy:

> "Esta gente está durmiendo—me decía–, hay que despertarla de su sueño profundo, para lo cual es indispensable gritar, sacudirla y darle de palos si es necesario." Explicar las finalidades de la renovación implicaba un largo proceso. La estrategia que convenía era la de la acción rápida y la subversión total. Había que recurrir a medios expeditos y no dejar títere con cabeza. No había tiempo que perder. La madrugada aquella me levanté decidido, y... me dije: "No hay más remedio que echarse a la calle y torcerle el cuello al doctor González Martínez."[10]

Maples Arce wrote his first manifesto, "Actual No. 1, Hoja de Vanguardia, Comprimido Estridentista de Manuel Maples Arce," in December 1921. It contained fourteen points that blasted the traditionalists ("¡Chopin a la silla eléctrica!",[11] "¡Muera el cura Hidalgo!"), exalted everything new and dynamic, and included a photo of Maples Arce and at the end a list of the names of more than 200 international writers and artists whom Maples considered avant-garde. The manifesto was an attack on the Mexican literary establishment and a call to arms.

Printed on brightly-colored paper, the manifesto was

---

10 Maples Arce, *Soberana Juventud*, 123.
11 This trademark of Maples Arce is related to F. T. Marinetti's call for the assassination of moonlight and Rafael Cansino-Asséns call for the liquidation of dry leaves, to rid modern poetry of the overworked clichés of the past. See Luis Mario Schneider, *El Estridentismo: o una Literatura de la Estrategia* (México: Ediciones de Bellas Artes, 1970) 38; and Kenneth C. Monahan, *Manuel Maples Arce and "Estridentismo,"* Dissertation, Northwestern University 1972. Ann Arbor, Michigan: UMI, 1973. 73-10, 260: 41.

posted overnight next to bullfight and theater posters, in the business district of Mexico City, and especially on prominent walls in sections of the city frequented by literary and university people. The manifesto was also distributed to newspapers and sent to various people in Mexico and abroad. The next day it was received with shock, and with extreme reactions in favor and against. It provoked the scandal that Maples Arce hoped it would.

Actual No. 1 is a combination of attention-getting shock phrases, modern references, crashing put-down of the bourgeoisie, and serious literary theory. In it are both Maples Arce's own ideas and some borrowed from the few European manifestos and reviews he had seen. "Toda técnica de arte, está destinada a llenar una función espiritual en un momento determinado. Cuando los medios expresionistas son inhábiles o insuficientes para traducir nuestras emociones personales,—única y elemental finalidad estética,—es necesario, y esto contra toda la fuerza estacionaria y afirmaciones rastacueras de la crítica oficial, cortar la corriente y desnucar los 'swichs.' "[12]

> Es necesario exaltar en todos los tonos estridentes de nuestro diapasón propagandista, la belleza actualista de las máquinas, de los puentes gímnicos reciamente extendidos sobre las vertientes por músculos de acero, el humo de las fábricas, las emociones cubistas de los grandes trasatlánticos con humeantes chimeneas de rojo y negro, anclados horoscópicamente—Ruiz Huidobro—junto a los muelles efervescentes y congestionados, el régimen industrialista de las grandes ciudades palpitantes, las blusas azules de los obreros explosivos en esta hora emocionante y conmovida: toda esta belleza del siglo ...[13]

---

12 Manuel Maples Arce, Actual No. 1: Comprimido Estridentista de Manuel Maples Arce (Mexico, 1921) pt. II.
13 Maples Arce, *Actual No. 1,* pt. IV.

Point VII of the manifesto proposes a quintessential and purifying synthesis of all of the modern vanguardist tendencies, not because of a false wish for conciliation, but because of a strong aesthetic conviction and spiritual urgency. The idea of a synthesis of the avant-garde is one of the most original contributions of Estridentismo and, correspondingly, of Maples' first manifesto. When one considers the fact that Estridentismo stated clearly at its outset in 1921 its desire to unify the various avant-garde movements, all critics' accusations that Maples Arce and his group "imitated" the Futurists and Dadaists are instantly invalid. In addition, Maples does not want to change different tendencies to become one; rather he says they are all basically the same thing, organically similar, and the only real problem (mutual, but dealt with differently) is technique. Together they could "[iluminar] nuestro deseo maravilloso de totalizar las emociones interiores y sugestiones sensoriales en forma multánime y poliédrica."[14]

Point VIII, importantly, affirms that humanity is not a mere uniform piece of systematic clockwork mechanism but a being of emotion. Sincere emotion is a form of "suprema arbitrariedad y desorden específico," and in the past poets have failed because they have tried to express only one aspect of it, when emotion is really "originaria y tridimensionalmente esférica." The new poetry—that of the vanguardia—should illustrate the complex of emotion as it exists in the modern world; "los nuevos procedimientos técnicos ... cristalizan un aspecto unánime y totalista de la vida."[15]

Point X asks Mexicans to become more cosmopolitan. The avant-garde's concentration on life in the city is in

---

14 Maples Arce, *Actual No. 1*, pt. VII.
15 Monahan, MMA and "Estridentismo," 42.

part a reaction against the ruralistic tendency of Postmodernismo. It also reflects the avant-garde's emphasis on the new technology and other modern innovations, all of which were seen first in the big cities.

Point XI says that artistic delimitations must be set. Art should be made from elements in one's own environs. This is a move away from the exotic, away from the modernista interest in orientalism, toward the immediate, the here and now. The manifesto says that the artist should create new values and destroy falsely modern interpretive theories. The artist should make pure poetry, excluding every element exterior to it (description, anecdote, perspective). Maples Arce echoes the call made by Huidobro and Creacionismo not to imitate nature but rather use it as an example to create something new in the poem. In point XII, Maples Arce specifies that it is the present he is concerned with —no retrospection, no futurism, just the individual caught up in the stupendous apex of the present moment. "Hagamos actualismo." In point XIII, Maples Arce defines Estridentismo (and what it has in common with Dadá) as "una fuerza radical opuesta contra el conservatismo solidario de una colectividad anquilosada."

Maples Arce's entrance into the literary community with *Actual No. I* was a brave, bold step, which received some negative criticism but eventually accomplished its goal. "Whether or not they approve of Maples' ideas, most critics concede that he was the first to bring Vanguardism to Mexico, in the form of his personal invention which was to be called estridentismo. As a young man barely twenty-one years old, he challenged the world of Mexican poetry to enter the twentieth century and, as a result, he faced alone the writers and critics of the day."[16]

One of the most important positive reactions that the manifesto caused, especially when combined with the subsequent publication of Maples' first volume of avant-garde poetry, *Andamios Interiores* (1922), was the contact made with other young writers, most notably Arqueles Vela and later Germán List Arzubide, Salvador Gallardo and Miguel Aguillón Guzmán. Vela, who was working at *El Universal Ilustrado*, read *Andamios* as soon as it was out, and met Maples shortly after. At once they became friends and comrades in the struggle to revolutionize literature. List Arzubide and Gallardo (together with the younger Miguel Aguillón Guzmán, their friend in Mexico City), poets with a similar desire to renovate Mexican poetry, contacted Maples from Puebla to arrange a meeting. Maples, Vela and List Arzubide subsequently became the nucleus of the estridentista group, which took its name from the first manifesto.

A second manifesto was circulated from Puebla on New Year's Day 1923, and while it was a continuation of the same ideas as the first manifesto, it was shorter, more succinct, less detailed, and more explicit in its attacks on the bourgeois establishment. This document was signed by the principal members of Estridentismo and also by many of their followers. Meanwhile, Maples' *Andamios Interiores* was provoking additional extreme reactions and commentaries.

The estridentista group gained allies (as well as enemies) and eventually a third and fourth manifestos were published by the Congreso Nacional de Estudiantes in Zacatecas and in Ciudad Victoria, respectively. The Zacatecas

---

16 Monahan, 37.

manifesto (#3)[17] copies much from the two earlier documents but adds in upper case letters strong slogans: "¡MUERA LA REACCIÓN INTELECTUAL Y MOMIFICADA!", "HAY QUE REBELARSE CONTRA EL MANDATO DE LOS MUERTOS", "EL CLICHÉ ES LA SOGA DE LAS IDEAS". It is dated July 12, 1925, and signed by Salvador Gallardo, Guillermo Rubio, Adolfo Ávila Sánchez and Aldegundo Martínez. The manifesto from Ciudad Victoria (#4) is long, exaggerated, ambitious, includes some poems, calls for literary renovation and is a general statement of solidarity with the estridentistas. Headed "CHUBASCO ESTRIDENTISTA" and declaring "Nos hemos levantado en armas contra el aguachirlismo literario en México," it is signed by scores of students, led by Miguel Aguillón Guzmán, and dated January 1926. These later manifestos were mainly votes of sympathy by a large number of young writers and students. Maples Arce did not intend to attract followers into a formal literary movement or school, but rather to incite other writers to renovate the state of Mexican literature. As he clarifies in an article summarizing the state of Estridentismo at the end of 1922: "El estridentismo, no es una escuela, ni una tendencia, ni una maña intelectual, como las que aquí se estila; el estridentismo es una razón de estrategia. Un gesto. Una irrupción."[18]

The nucleus of the group met regularly in cafés to share ideas on writing and painting, and to plan their continued attack on the bourgeois art establishment. Maples also often

---

[17] The second, third (and fourth) manifestos are not to be confused with *Actual No. 2* and *Actual No. 3*; only the first manifesto was in *Actual*, of which there were three issues, in 1921-22.

[18] Manuel Maples Arce, "El movimiento estridentista en 1922," *El Universal Ilustrado* 28 diciembre 1922: 25.

recited his poems to his friends during these gatherings. The manifestos were part of their attack but there were also a number of social-artistic "events" in the manner of the European Dada movement, including plenty of shouting, denouncing, provocative statements, and modern visual statements (a fire truck on the steps of a building), as well as poetry readings. The most important of these estridentista "events" (much like the "happenings" of the 1960s, or the work of "performance artists" in the 70s and 80s in the U.S.) was an art exhibit, attended by invitation, held in the Café de Nadie—the favorite estridentista hang-out. (The Café de Nadie was an almost abandoned café formerly known as the Café Europa in the Colonia Roma on Avenida Jalisco, the street now called Avenida Álvaro Obregón. The café was discovered by chance by Maples Arce and adopted as the group's meeting place, because it was quiet and they could do as they pleased there, as well as for its anomaly of being rather abandoned—one could sit for hours without seeing a waiter. It seemed not to be run by anyone in particular—it was, therefore, "de nadie". Arqueles Vela produced an intriguing short avant-garde novel, *El Café de Nadie*, based on this meeting place.) The art exhibit featured recent works by estridentista artists, poems were read, and "estridentista music" was played. The event, as well as being typically scandalous, provided a good forum for artists to show their (serious) work. It was the first event of its kind in Mexico, and prominent artistic and literary figures were invited, including Rafael López, who later proved to be a valuable ally.

 The name Estridentismo may seem unusual, but it is very fitting —strident, noisy, screeching, shocking. The group's aim was to wake up the public, slap them into consciousness, and pull them out of their postmodernista daze and into the booming twentieth century. Maples Arce knew that change through printed poems alone would be too slow; the social attack was crucial to getting attention, to achieving change, and to winning the artistic revolution. In fact, it was a major aim of Estridentismo to apply the ideals and goals of the Mexican Revolution to the arts, which had lagged behind the political and social spheres in renovation and modernization. The well-known muralist painters of Mexico developed their ideas and techniques alongside the estridentistas; Ramón Alva de la Canal was a major muralist, along with Fermín Revueltas (brother of composer Silvestre Revueltas). Diego Rivera also worked with the estridentistas for a while and was a close comrade. Photographers Tina Modotti and Edward Weston collaborated in the estridentista magazine *Horizonte*, and artists Jean Charlot and Fernando Leal worked with the group. Estridentismo was an effort to unite and revolutionize all of the arts in Mexico. In the process, the estridentistas related the arts to what was going on in the rest of world society. Some critics mistakenly call Maples Arce's work socially or politically committed poetry–a categorization that is really not true, and is an exaggeration based on superficial reading of the 1924 *Urbe*.[19] His work was, rather, an

---

19   The social/moral aspect of Surrealism, Dada, Cubism, and *Estridentismo* is not the same as the political commitment and propaganda of "social literature" or "committed literature." It is art, concerned with the state of the world, but it is not political statement, even considering the great interest at the time in Socialism and proletarian revolution. The Mexican murals were committed, the poetry was not. (See chapter on *Urbe*.) There were a few small socially committed -isms in Latin America–*agorismo*, for one–which did not achieve high literary quality, perhaps because the message got in the way. Discussion of the social/moral aspect of Surrealism and Dada is available in Mary Ann Caws, *The Poetry of Dada and Surrealism: Aragon, Breton, Tzara, Eluard & Desnos* (Princeton, N J: Princeton University Press, 1970) 6, 12n, 20, 38, 91. In the opening section of the chapter on Aragon, Caws says: "There could, from one point of

attempt to bring the present moment into art, to reflect in art man's predicament in the modern world, his joy and anguish. The "happenings" of Estridentismo were the strategy to effect change: a call to arms for writers and artists, an attempt to "épater le bourgeois" in order to set the stage for the artistic and literary revolution needed in Mexico. Aside from the strategy and the "happenings," the creative works produced by the estridentistas were valuable in their own right as serious artistic expression.

Maples Arce was the acknowledged leader of Estridentismo and his work received the bulk of critical attention, but the other members also produced interesting, important works, and deserve to be studied more than they have been to date. Arqueles Vela was the prose writer of the group, noted for his vanguardista novels *El Café de*

---

view, be no more striking contrast than that between Dada and surrealist aesthetic theories on the one hand and a Marxist aesthetics on the other. At the outset, both the Dada and the surrealist movements were highly antipolitical, even if certain members did eventually become involved in political commitment. Neither movement would seem to have anything whatsoever to do with 'socialist realism' of any variety since, though they attacked bourgeois principles, they appealed neither to the lower classes nor to the 'realists.' Dada, in attacking everyone and everything, in its deliberate provocation of the 'gens de goût,' could not conceivably help to form a constructive society after destroying the old. Surrealism, with its continued emphasis on the dream, its horror of *le travail* and of *le métier* and its latent appeal to a certain leisured class (the same class which can afford to purchase surrealist works) can scarcely be thought of as a valuable discipline for the 'anticapitalist' mind. While it is true that Breton, for example, was always aware of the paradox implied in surrealism as a sort of parasite on wealthy society (see his letters at the time of his employment by Doucet) and always took a strictly 'liberal' view of political events, that awareness in no way excuses him in the eyes of the 'realists' for whom Aragon speaks. In any case, the distinction between surrealism and realism is a clear one: and though Aragon admits, in *J'abats mon jeu*, that his present style has been to a degree formed by his surrealist past, he never fails to point out the great difference between the content of his present writings and the content of surrealist works." (38-39). It should be noted here that the estridentista magazine *Horizonte*, which the group published in Jalapa, contained several essays on specific social, political and economic issues of the day. This is different from the poems.

Nadie and *La Señorita Etc.* As previously mentioned, Vela was on the staff of *El Universal Ilustrado*, arguably the most important literary supplement of the 1920s in Mexico, when he was introduced to Maples Arce by a mutual friend also on the staff. Editor Carlos Noriega Hope became a loyal supporter of the estridentistas and by publishing their work, feature articles, and special weekly pages edited by them, provided them with a vehicle to gain the attention of a wide readership. *El Universal Ilustrado* played, thus, a very important role in the life of Estridentismo: it became the movement's voice and forum for dialogue with the public.

As for the other members of Estridentismo's inner circle, Germán List Arzubide wrote poetry, prose and essay and was the most socially committed member of the group. He remained an estridentista writer throughout his career, one of the few in the group to do so, though in his later years he also wrote a number of essays on varied topics for Mexican newspapers. A key historical-critical work on the movement is List Arzubide's *El movimiento estridentista*, published in 1927, with a later version in 1967.

Ramón Alva de la Canal was the group's leading painter and an accomplished muralist. His murals attracted scant attention, however, as he was so overshadowed by the more public figures Rivera, Orozco and Siqueiros. Alva de la Canal is perhaps best known by the populace for his portraits. Like many other painters of his generation, he was trained at the Escuela de Pintura al Aire Libre in Coyoacán, just outside of Mexico City, in the post-Velasco (landscape artist), pre-pollution days. Many of the great modern painters came out of this school and later developed their own techniques. Maples Arce often went to the school in Coyoacán to observe the various painters' work and to discuss it with them. He had a serious interest in painting and studied it throughout his life.

Fermín Revueltas was perhaps the most estridentista of the group's painters, noted for infusing mazes of telephone poles and wires into landscapes. Leopoldo Méndez was mainly a graphic artist, and his greatest estridentista contributions were advances in woodblock print techniques (a medium very popular at the time). Illustrations by the three artists mentioned above and by Jean Charlot are included in many of Maples Arce's books. Germán Cueto was the sculptor of the group and a well-known late work of his currently stands near an entrance to UNAM, the National University in Mexico City.

Luis Quintanilla, writing under the pseudonym Kyn-Taniya, was the most experimental poet of the group, and Salvador Gallardo Dávalos, a medical doctor from Aguascalientes, was perhaps the most subdued and serious. Writer Miguel Aguillón Guzmán was younger than the rest and played a minor role in the group.

Estridentismo, in addition to being the first movement to introduce the avant-garde to Mexico, lasted longer (from the end of 1921 through mid-1927) and produced more books than any other vanguardista group in Spanish America or Spain,[20] and in effect, helped to change the state of Mexican letters. According to Luis Mario Schneider, Estridentismo initiated in Mexico the most drastic and scandalous renovation that can be observed throughout the history of Mexican literature, and made possible, directly and indirectly, the revision of aesthetic values in general in Mexico. In a 1924 newspaper article,

---

20 Schneider, *El Estridentismo*, 209.

one of Maples Arce's contemporaries said that the Revolution had one great painter: Diego Rivera, one great poet: Maples Arce, and one great novelist: Mariano Azuela.[21]

In their attempt to renovate Mexican poetry, the estridentistas became notorious for their attacks on the modernista and postmodernista poets. A particular target was Enrique González Martínez, who was a primary source of inspiration for the *Contemporáneos* group. But the estridentistas were just as enthusiastic in their support of poets they did admire: Maples Arce was the first to voice strong support and recognition of the value of the work of Ramón López Velarde (now recognized by many as the leading transitional figure between postmodernismo and vanguardismo). The estridentistas encouraged Rafael López (but did not pressure him, as some believe) not to accept a seat on Mexico's Academia de la Lengua, which they viewed as a stagnant body of bourgeois traditionalists, and in which they felt López did not belong. Indeed, Rafael López finally refused the position and continued to be a loyal ally of the estridentistas. José Juan Tablada was a literary generation older than the estridentistas but truly avant-garde from the beginning of his career. He was an individualist who evolved continually with each new age. His poetry progresses from modernista and postmodernista verse, to avant-garde calligrams (composed at about the same time as those of Apollinaire in Europe), and the first haiku written in Spanish. Tablada was a supporter of the estridentistas, and they of him.

There was significant correspondence between the estridentistas and other avant-garde poets both in Europe

---

21 Luis Mario Schneider, *Ruptura y continuidad: la literatura mexicana en polémica* (México: Fondo de Cultura Económica, 1975) 159, 161.

and in the rest of Latin America, and poetry by these correspondents frequently appeared on the estridentista pages of *El Universal Ilustrado* and also in their magazines *Irradiador* and *Horizonte*. Unfortunately, mail shipment was very slow in those days, so news of foreign poets was slow to arrive, brought most often by friends who travelled. Texts were also difficult to acquire because they were typically published in a small number of copies.

The work of the estridentista movement occurred in two phases: the first in Mexico City from December 1921 until March 1925, the second in Jalapa (capital of the state of Veracruz) from early 1925 until mid-1927. In the first phase, the estridentistas accomplished the strategic work of tearing down the barriers to modernization, shocking the population awake, and energizing the artistic community with a jolt of electric current. The second phase produced a fine-tuning of estridentista poetry (e.g. Maples' publication of *Poemas Interdictos*), and the important work of the estridentista press (*Ediciones Horizonte*) and the magazine *Horizonte*. The magazine often treated issues of a social nature, printing articles on politics, economics and social themes as well as literature and avant-garde photography. The *Horizonte* press published the first book-form edition of Mariano Azuela's *Los de abajo* (previously printed in newspaper serial form) as part of the estridentista's *Biblioteca Popular* series, which was committed to making the classics readily available to the general public. Their *Biblioteca de Estudiante* printed various works about Mexico. The estridentistas also participated in making plans for the founding of the Universidad Veracruzana and for a large stadium in Jalapa.

The estridentista group moved to Jalapa in 1925 when

Maples Arce, after receiving his law degree, was appointed judge (and later State Secretary General) by General Heriberto Jara, governor of the state of Veracruz. Jara became the mentor of the estridentistas and provided them with a forum in which to put their social ideologies to work; they in turn did significant publication work for the State of Veracruz. Maples Arce, along with performing his judicial and governmental duties, wrote several articles on social and economic themes. He alternated his administrative duties with his literary activities, and also taught at the Escuela de Leyes del Estado.[22] During this time, the group formed its idea of the model city of the future, "Estridentópolis," as seen in many wood-block prints and engravings from the period. The *estridentistas* worked fervently on *Horizonte*; it was their life and purpose. The Jalapa phase of Estridentismo was a cultural movement with revolutionary aims.

The break-up of the group in 1927, when they were forced to leave Jalapa, was rarely understood or explained in early criticism. Up until recent times, only Maples Arce in *Soberana Juventud* and José Emilio Pacheco gave detailed explanations of what happened. Pacheco writes:

> El arte mexicano ha vivido siempre como hongo en los sótanos del Estado y sujeto por tanto a los sismos de la política. El general Jara se opuso a la tentativa reeleccionista de Obregón y asiló en Jalapa a dos gobernadores perseguidos: Francisco J. Mújica y Aurelio Manrique. Cuando el Jefe Máximo exterminó a Serrano y a Gómez, Jara fue desplazado del gobierno veracruzano. Su caída en 1927 dio fin al movimiento estridentista, no a la amistad entre sus componentes ni a la continuación de sus trabajos personales.[23]

---

22   Monahan, 3, referring to Maples Arce, *Soberana Juventud*, 14.
23   JEP [José Emilio Pacheco], "Manuel Maples Arce (1900-1981) (Segundo

In *Soberana Juventud,* [24] Maples Arce explains the growing schism between the Jara government in Veracruz and the federal government, in addition to various other new enemies of Jara. The State of Veracruz had an impressive program of social and material improvements, but due to manipulation either by jealous enemies of Jara or by enemies of Veracruz, the federal government suddenly cut off funds previously committed to these programs. More bad feelings were caused by Jara's aid to those opposing Obregón in reelection, and especially, as Pacheco stated, by General Jara's protection of Governor Múgica (of Michoacán) and Governor Manrique (of San Luis Potosí), who were enemies of the federal administration. The lack of incoming federal funds to Veracruz caused state treasury problems, which then provoked a split in the local legislature between those remaining faithful to Jara's government and those who named a new governor from among the ranks. This dual isolation of General Jara occurred at a time of great political violence (mid-1927) and there was constant fear of armed assault. The rebel generals Serrano, Arnulfo Gómez and Adalberto Palacios were publicly executed by the federal administration. Even Maples Arce, whose record was clean, was accosted at a street corner near his house one day by two armed henchmen who intended to seize him and, if he resisted, kill him. Fortunately, just at that moment a friend of Maples' came on the scene and brandishing his pistol, threatened the attackers into retreat and whisked Maples off to safety in his car. Maples spent the next several days in secret hideaway.

---

y último artículo)–'Así en la paz como en la guerra,'" *Proceso* 13 julio 1981: 48.
24 Maples Arce, *Soberana Juventud,* 207ff.

Jara was forced to leave office in September of 1927. His estridentista colleagues left with him. A new governor was appointed: Professor Abel S. Rodríguez, an independent. Rodríguez invited Maples Arce to stay on, but Maples declined, out of loyalty to Jara and to the work his administration had done. Maples also disliked the increasing instances of violence and backstabbing that pervaded Veracruz politics. He preferred to go back to Mexico City.

In 1928 Maples did return to government work. For a short while he promoted the Obregón campaign (ironically) among the working class. Later he was elected to a two-year term in the state legislature. Another period of violence caused his disillusion with politics, and he left Mexico to visit New York and Europe. While in Paris he took classes at the Sorbonne. Thus Maples Arce was able to fulfill a long-time desire to travel and to study art and literature.

The break-up of Estridentismo in 1927 was not solely forced by the political situation: it was a timely event that propitiated a split that probably would have happened sooner or later. Arqueles Vela had left for Europe in 1926, Maples Arce had a growing desire to travel, and the group's members were each developing their own individual ideas. The fact that List Arzubide felt it was time to summarize the movement's ideas at the end of 1926 in his *El movimiento estridentista* (published in early 1927) signaled a sense of conclusion of the group work. All of them needed to pursue their individual careers, to tackle new adventures. Maples was then 27 years old, his cohorts were of approximately his same age, and it is natural that they would be changing, maturing, looking toward farther horizons. Each went his own way to develop his own career but, as Pacheco affirmed, their friendship continued.

The estridentistas should be remembered and judged for having produced a serious body of literature and art, and not recalled only for their strategy of Dadaist-Futurist style manifestos, public spectacles, and their efforts to demythify the popular postmodernista demi-gods of the time. Unfortunately, few critics do detailed analyses of the poems. Many early articles copied erroneous second- and third-hand accounts of the poems, even copying lines incorrectly, without looking far enough beneath the surface of the poems' verses. This situation, along with personal grudges held by other writers, has resulted in the movement not receiving the critical acclaim it deserves over the decades until recent renewed interest has sprung up about Estridentismo in the 21st century.

One major conflict, and curious phenomenon, managed to overshadow for many years any attempt in published criticism at objective consideration of Estridentismo: the anthology battle between estridentistas and Contemporáneos—the bitter rivalry between the two major poetry movements in Mexico between the two World Wars. Their polemic has been one of the liveliest in modern Hispanic letters, also one of the most bitingly personal. It is an unfortunate polemic of the 1920s mindset in Mexico that should not have existed, but it did, nonetheless, and needs to be addressed, as it involves the dangerous practice of mixing life with art and the growing pains of modern society. Perhaps we should be careful not to project our 21st century mindset related to diversity onto the society of a hundred years ago.

During the same years of the height of estridentista activity, another group of somewhat younger poets began to write in Mexico, though in a more conservative vein, continuing and modifying the tradition of the *Ateneo* poets and especially the work of Enrique González Martínez. These writers: Jaime Torres Bodet, Salvador Novo, Xavier Villaurrutia, José Gorostiza, Carlos Pellicer, Bernardo Ortiz de Montellano, Jorge Cuesta, Gilberto Owen, and a few others, have now become the acknowledged modern "classics," the mainstays of Mexican literature in the first half of the twentieth century. They were only recognized as a "group" in 1928 when they collaborated in the publication of the magazine *Contemporáneos*, which ran from 1928 to 1931, but they had been writing individually for a few years before that (their work of those previous years largely recognized as postmodernista). This "grupo sin grupo," Contemporáneos, was readily accepted by the literary public, since they took a more conservative, non-political route than the estridentistas. Because both groups wrote at more or less the same time (the Contemporáneos had their forte period later), and both considered themselves innovators, they became —inevitably, perhaps— rivals, even enemies. This rivalry is given voice in the literary criticism of the period, but more explicitly so in a series of opinion polls in the literary supplement *El Universal Ilustrado* and in the two anthologies edited by the rival groups, identically titled *Antología de la poesía mexicana moderna*, of 1928 and 1940. The second anthology can be seen as an attempt to replace the first one. Although these anthologies state their function essentially as one of *difusión cultural*, they are used as a forum to express mutual dislike, insult and vengeance between the estridentistas and the Contemporáneos. The biases expressed corrupt the literary information given to the reader supposedly in good faith.

Jorge Cuesta, the Contemporáneos member whose main genre is criticism, signs the 1928 anthology as editor, but acknowledges in his preface that the edition is the result of group work. Cuesta's anthology includes twenty-two poets, including six modernistas, seven postmodernistas, and nine from his contemporary period. The nine of his contemporary period were all Contemporáneos members except for Maples Arce. This fact would give the impression that Cuesta and colleagues held Maples' work in high esteem —and certainly no one can deny Maples' place as an active force in Mexican poetry of the 1920s— until one reads the critical commentary which precedes Maples Arce's poems (first Cuesta lists Maples' birthdate incorrectly as 1898 instead of 1900, and continues):

> Manuel Maples Arce ocupa, dentro del "grupo de soledades" que alguien ha creído advertir en la poesía nueva de México, un sitio aparte, más que solitario, aislado. Esta isla que habita y que bautizó —en un alarde de "acometividad pretérita", romántica— con el nombre injustificado de *estridentismo*, le ha producido los beneficios de una popularidad inferior, pero intensa. Entre cierta porción de la actual literatura hispanoamericana, Maples Arce representa una de las conquistas de vanguardia. El marco de socialismo político en que ha sabido situarse le ha sido, para estos fines, de la mayor utilidad.
>
> La poesía de Maples Arce intenta una fuga de los moldes formales del modernismo pero incurre, con frecuencia, en deplorables regresiones románticas. El tono mismo del alejandrino que prefiere —y que desarticula con escasa agilidad— lo ata a esa tradición que continúa precisamente cuando más la ataca.
>
> La cohesión de su esfuerzo y la forma directa de la

existencia industrial y fabril como la que describe, son sin embargo a nuestro juicio—aun descontando el pretexto del éxito transitorio que alcanza—razones suficientes, válidas, para hacerlo figurar en esta Antología.²⁵

Cuesta doesn't recognize what Octavio Paz later said, that all modern literature is romantic, and neither does he see Maples' verse manipulation and skill that we will examine here in Chapter Two. One might compare Cuesta's commentary with Torres Bodet's introduction to Maples Arce in his *Perspectiva de la literatura mexicana actual 1915-1928:*

> Con menos limpidez irónica que en la de Novo y un vigor menos significado que en la de Pellicer, se advierte ya, en la obra de Maples Arce, una generosa inquietud de renovación que, aunque no modifica sino la superficie de sus *poemas interdictos*, acabará muy pronto por destruir los *andamios interiores*, románticos, sobre cuyo esqueleto sentimental el lector atento había visto esbozarse su demasiado rápida construcción. Todo cabe, todo—hasta la poesía—en la impaciencia laboriosa de este poeta. Pero la temperatura que circula en las arterias de sus alejandrinos lo salva en el preciso punto en que lo compromete, ligándolo—al que hubiera querido aterrizar de un salto hermoso, brusco, sobre el litoral de un mundo nuevo—con la misma tradición de melancolías que el programa lírico de su escuela: el *estridentismo* hace profesión de abominar.²⁶

Xavier Villaurrutia makes a similar evaluation of Maples Arce in his Biblioteca Cervantes lecture, but in a sly, low-key tone, that makes it even more biting. Obviously, Cuesta and Torres Bodet could have omitted Maples Arce from their studies if they considered his work

---

25 Jorge Cuesta, *Antología de la poesía mexicana moderna* (México: Contemporáneos, 1928) 130.
26 Jaime Torres Bodet, *Perspectiva de la literatura mexicana actual 1915-1928* (México: Ediciones de Contemporéaneos, 1928) 32.

barely worth including. It seems clear that the Contemporáneos used their publications as a chance to take another jab at their rival.

Cuesta's anthology is accused of partiality, of Contemporáneos' narcissistic propaganda, and of leaving out too many important poets (especially postmodernistas). Critics at the time worried that international readers were receiving a partial or false view of modern Mexican poetry. With regard to the impression that Cuesta's anthology gives of Maples Arce's poetry, Ermilo Abreu Gómez says: "... los grupos literarios no fueron justos con Manuel Maples Arce. Jorge Cuesta –hombre de indiscutibles prejuicios estéticos y políticos– le juzgó mal; le entendió peor y le sentenció con encono, muchas veces condenado por mí."[27]

Maples was accused by Cuesta of being both overly romantic and too socialist. However, Cuesta does not include any part of Maples' only really social volume, *Urbe* (1924), in the anthology, and misinterprets the idea of being a romantic. Octavio Paz notes that it was the fashion for a while to criticize Maples harshly, and speaks of the latter's supposed *romanticismo* as follows: "La crítica revela cierta miopía: Apollinaire y Mayakowski fueron románticos y el surrealismo se declaró continuador del romanticismo."[28] Luis Melgar clarifies further the tie with Romanticism in his statement about the avant-garde in Mexico: "Une a esas escuelas artísticas el rechazo a la tradición clásica, al racionalismo y al realismo; el afán experimental, así en las

---

27 Ermilo Abreu Gómez, "Sala de Retratos: MMA" [*Revista Mexicana de la Cultura*, Sup. de *El Nacional* c.1947]: 3, 8. N.B.: Many of the newspaper clippings in Doña Blanca de Maples Arce's large collection, which I read, unfortunately do not include the name of the newspaper or any other publication information. I will refer to them as "unidentified," and when possible, estimate the year.

28 Octavio Paz, *Poesía en movimiento: México 1915-1966* (México: Siglo Veintiuno Editores, 1974) 17.

formas como en las significaciones. Vienen del romanticismo, sobre todo en la reivindicación del yo, de la subjetividad y de la emoción."[29]

Socio-politically, the two groups were at opposite poles, the Contemporáneos being conservative traditionalists and the estridentistas rebellious iconoclasts. Many critics (including the later group, *Taller poético*) have never forgiven the Contemporáneos for their self-imposed isolation from *el pueblo* and for not having any real connection with the Revolution or the aspirations of the Mexican people. On the other hand, many people have never forgiven the estridentistas for being linked with social causes and their association with people like Narciso Bassols, a socialist educator, and Heriberto Jara, progressive governor of Veracruz.

The Contemporáneos were taken under the wing of José Vasconcelos and given good jobs in the *Secretaría de Educación*. With this support they were free to work on their own publications (instead of publications for the government) and in fact used government funds to publish the 1928 anthology and government mail to distribute it. The Contemporáneos were also able to keep poets they disliked out of possible jobs in the *Secretaría de Educación*.

Maples Arce published his *Antología de la poesía mexicana moderna* in 1940 while in Rome. The book is widely praised for its vindication and restoration of many poets omitted from the Cuesta list, for the broader spectrum of postmodernistas represented (though the presence of two in particular is questioned), for the inclusion of a group of young poets, and for the excellent critical commentary on the work of the poets who were not part of the Contem-

---

[29] Luis Melgar, *Historia de la Literatura Mexicana, #11: Las Vanguardias* (México: Cultura/SEP/Editorial Somos, [1982]) 4-5.

poráneos. One curiosity is that Maples Arce did not include any of his fellow estridentistas in his anthology and did not comment as to why.

The crux of the problem in the anthology dialogue between Maples Arce and the Contemporáneos is that personal grudges caused them to include biased commentary on each other's work. Both anthologies belittle their rival/enemy's literary talent, and even extend the disparaging comments to allusions about personal matters. In his 1940 volume, Maples took revenge on the Contemporáneos for the way he was presented in their 1928 anthology, and for a difference in lifestyle that had influenced the polemic for years: the Contemporáneos were supposedly gay and the estridentistas did not consider homosexuality socially acceptable at the time in Mexico, at least in their personal opinion, and that the Contemporáneos' writing did not fit in to the 1920s nationalistic debate about "literatura viril." A reading of Maples Arce's prologues to the *Contemporáneos* poets in his anthology and comments over the years from other estridentistas makes it very clear that the main attack was not because of the difference in writing style but in lifestyle, not literary preferences but sexual preferences. Ramón Alva de la Canal said in a 1981 interview: "Por último, un recuerdo de los Contemporáneos. Esos afeminados fueron nuestros enemigos. Bueno no, no enemigos, pero sí estábamos separados. No nos llevábamos. A nosotros nos gustaban las muchachas y a ellos no."[30]

According to Efraín Huerta, in the letter that accompanied Maples Arce's anthology when it was sent to

---

30 Ramón Alva de la Canal speaking to Miguel Angel Morales, "Viva el Mole de Guajolote," *Diorama* [Sup. de *Excelsior*) 6 diciembre 1981: n. pag.

several critics, Maples explained his intentions saying that, "en el extranjero se ha divulgado la idea de que la literatura mexicana, es una literatura afeminada, débil y de un bajo *pastichismo*, gracias a la propaganda de un grupo que no representa, felizmente, más que una porción insignificante de ella."[31]

Years before, during the 1920s, Julio Jiménez Rueda had started a debate in Mexican newspaper literary supplements about virility in Mexican letters. One finds innumerable references to "una literatura viril," "poesía de varón" and similar expressions, without this tendency ever being precisely defined in a literary context. The debate continued for years, with many writers commenting.

In his anthology,[32] Maples Arce includes from the Contemporáneos group Torres Bodet, Pellicer, Gorostiza, Ortiz de Montellano, González Rojo, Novo and Villaurrutia. Of these, Pellicer and Gorostiza get glowing reviews; González Rojo is also treated well. The other four are attacked with calculated language spoken with a very sharp tongue. It seems that every word was carefully chosen for its scathing *double entendre* possibilities. Bernardo Ortiz de Montellano got the worst and most unfair treatment. This "literatura viril" debate and the anthology battle have been commented on extensively in recent criticism and there is no real need to repeat it here. The reader is referred to those other commentaries (some referenced here).[33]

---

31 Efraín Huerta, "Una antología de forcejeos," *Taller* XII (enero-febrero 1941): 68-70.
32 Manuel Maples Arce, *Antología de la poesía mexicana moderna* (Roma: Poligrafia Tiberina, 1940).
33 Miguel Bustos Cerecedo, *La creación literaria en Veracruz* II (Xalapa: Editora del Gobierno, 1977) 238-39.
Alí Chumacero, "Una antología," *Tierra Nueva* I.6 (nov.-dic. 1940) 353-

Obviously, many years have passed since the time of this polemic, and now we see it with a modern liberal sensibility. However, one must remember that the polemic took place roughly from 1921 to 1942 in Mexico, when homophobia was common. Critical response to the 1940 (Maples Arce) anthology can be divided into four perspectives: foreigners who are unaware of the polemic and are only mildly piqued by the fiery exaggerations in these four introductions; those who see absolutely no way to forgive Maples Arce; those who think the Contemporáneos got what they deserved; and those who see the conflict objectively, reproach the editor for it, and offer intelligent suggestions as to what an anthology of poetry should and should not do.

One mistaken statement, in my opinion, is made by Alí Chumacero who, while applauding the inclusion of Carmen Toscano in the Maples Arce anthology, states: "Maples hace resaltar, inteligentemente, la importancia de Carmen Toscano que –mientras la América entera se encuentra plagada de pequeñas ibarbourous– alza la voz con un sentimiento nunca viriloide, sino femenino y poético siempre."[34] This is exactly the same prejudiced game the estridentistas were playing with the Contemporáneos, set in a women's situation –equally unfair.

56.
Enrique Díez Canedo, "Poetas en antología," *Letras de América*. Colección Estudios Literarios 3. (México: El Colegio de México y Fondo de Cultura Económica, 1944) 251-57.

Evodio Escalante, *Elevación y caída del Estridentismo*. México: Consejo Nacional para la Cultura y las Artes / Edición Sin Nombre, 2002.

Eduardo Mejía, "Más allá del estridentismo," *La Guía* [Supl. De *Novedades*] 24 (domingo 14 marzo 1982).

Elissa J. Rashkin, "La poesía estridentista: vanguardismo y compromiso social," *Intersticios sociales* 2012, No. 4.

34 Chumacero, "Una antología."

Both anthologies received intense praise and intense criticism, both deservedly. Both claimed in their prefaces to be impartial in selection, and that personalities did not figure in to the critical commentaries. Both failed to keep these promises, because life was allowed to be confused with art. One can say that Maples Arce committed the worst offense. And it seems that Maples Arce and Estridentismo suffered afterwards far more for this confusion or prejudice than did the Contemporáneos. There are two reasons for this: the estridentistas were always harshly judged for their iconoclasm and rebellion; their strategy to get attention was confused with their literary production. Thus there were relatively few critical statements against the Cuesta anthology's treatment of Maples Arce. Also, the effect of Maples' judgements of the Contemporáneos was worse because Maples was the only estridentista singled out in the Cuesta anthology, while he included several of the Contemporáneos group in the later anthology. Luis Mario Schneider insists that we probably should not even compare the two groups' poetry, since the Contemporáneos are really not vanguardistas.[35] Octavio Paz agrees. The Contemporáneos are more aptly compared with Spain's Generation of '27.

The sad fact is that a rich body of national literature has been forcibly split in two, each half demanding exclusive attention, when in fact we need to examine and appreciate the positive contributions of both. One hopes that future histories of modern Mexican poetry will resolve this polemic and return to a system of objective analysis.

Controversial as it was, Estridentismo filled a need of the times: it brought the Mexican Revolution to the arts;

---

35 Schneider, El Estridentismo.

at the same time, it expressed the state of literary life in 1920s Mexico. The movement's importance is affirmed in several statements by prominent critics. Miguel Bustos Cerecedo has stated that Estridentismo was not an incidental literary movement merely imitating other avant-garde models, as some would like to categorize it, "sino la consecuencia lógica de un estado social producido por la Revolución y las asechanzas de la burguesía nacional y extranjera, tan evidentemente metidas en su remolino."[36] He adds that because of its "corriente impetuosa," the movement managed to attract the sympathy and interest of many writers of the old guard, such as José Juan Tablada —and Bustos Cerecedo notes the estridentistas' early signaling, before others recognized it, of Tablada's uniqueness as a constant innovator. Other supporters included Rafael López, Julio Torri, Mariano Silva y Aceves, Francisco González Guerrero, and Genaro Estrada. Maples Arce echoes: "Es evidente que aun los poetas ya formados no fueron insensibles a estas manifestaciones de renovación, y como una electricidad que está en el ambiente, percibieron señales, aunque fueran furtivas. Algo nuevo se había descubierto efectivamente y sería fácil señalar los indicios de curiosidad e insatisfacción lírica que siguieron al movimiento."[37]

Francisco Borja Bolado explains the age's anxieties and why it was difficult for some of the older generation to accept the changes attempted by the estridentistas and other avant-garde movements:

> Todo intento de renovación, pero principalmente
> el que persigue cambiar valores literarios y dar nuevos

---

36 Bustos Cerecedo, *La creación...*
37 Maples Arce, *Soberana Juventud*, 136.

rumbos a la forma, trae consigo la gritería de los consagrados.

El 'estridentismo,' con ser también un intento, resulta en la hora desconcertante en que vivimos, algo que responde ya a nuestras ansias. Sentimos que se nos derrumba toda una tradición mentirosa y artificial; que se nos muere todo un viejo sistema del color, de la palabra, de la línea. Presentimos pero resistimos. Las cifras inmutables van perdiendo su vieja autoridad aparatosa y nos hallamos (los educados en el rigorismo del sistema métrico de la idea) en uno de esos momentos críticos que desimantan la brújula y extravían los caminos. Deseamos lo nuevo, pero lo tememos.[38]

Maples Arce explains that the anxiety felt is symptomatic of society's needs at the time. He believed that the postmodernista literature being written then was insufficient. He sought drastic renovation in order to produce a literature that would match the times (modern, post-revolutionary Mexico).

... toda técnica de arte está destinada a llenar una función espiritual en un momento determinado... Cuando los medios de expresión son insuficientes para satisfacer una necesidad espiritual, recurrimos a una rebusca de nuevos elementos y sistemas. A un nuevo estado de espíritu, corresponde necesariamente una nueva técnica de arte... Muchas cosas que eran consideradas como bellas, hoy han dejado de serlo, justamente, en todo aquello en que no se identifican con nosotros, en todo aquello en que no logran captar nuestro interés emocional... Del principio analítico hemos emigrado hacia una idea sinóptica. La tendencia del esfuerzo contemporáneo... es hacia la supresión de las antítesis... En arte, no se trata de probar algo; basta con justificar una necesidad espiritual.[39]

---

38 Francisco Borja Bolado, in Oscar Leblanc, "¿Qué opina Ud. del estridentismo?" *El Universal Ilustrado* 8 marzo 1923: 33-34.
39 Maples Arce, "La Sistematización de los Movimientos Literarios," *El Universal Ilustrado* 10 julio 1924: 57.

Maples goes on to say in the same article that the full development of the individual (like that of society) involves education on the one hand, and on the other, the dynamic influence of the epoch ("[la] explosión simultaneísta de los panoramas mecánicos, acercamiento de las perspectivas internacionales"), which together form the new state of intelligence: "Una Conciencia Universal. Y un mundo inmediato de 4 dimensiones."

The Rise of Vanguardismo in Latin America

As stated above, from about 1907 through the end of the 1920s, Western culture witnessed the rise of a wealth of "-isms," or artistic movements, each espousing a certain (iconoclastic, revolutionary, modernizing) theory or perspective toward art, collectively referred to by the historical term "avant-garde." Because Hispanic American Modernismo was so strong a period and was still in vogue (though diminishing in strength) and Postmodernismo was on the rise[40] when the earliest European avant-garde movements began, there was a short lapse before the ideas of Cubism, Futurism and Dadaism took hold in Latin America. Another factor in information exchange at the time was slow transoceanic communication and transport. As a result, these three -isms occur simultaneously in Hispanic America, and are fused into one vanguardismo. Estridentismo is a perfect example of this combination.

---

40 Rubén Darío's *Cantos de vida y esperanza,* signaling a change of style and attitude for Darío, was published in 1905. Imitators were still writing classic *Modernismo.* Enrique González Martínez's "Tuércele el cuello al cisne," calling for an end to *Modernismo,* was published in 1910. *Vanguardismo* covered approximately 1920-1928/30. (In Brazil, "Modernismo" is the name of the avant-garde movement there.)

The situation may be compared to the way European Symbolism and Parnassianism, two literary generations earlier, were combined in a unique way in Hispanic America, with local modification, to form Modernismo.

In spite of this convergence of trends that had surfaced a bit earlier in Europe, I believe that the rise of vanguardismo in Latin America was, to a large degree, a natural process, and would have been realized even if it hadn't happened previously in Europe.[41] Latin America was ready for change (just as Europe and North America were), and its artists were searching for a way to express the new modern sensibility. As Gustavo Pérez Firmat has affirmed (cf. footnote #41), "... the defining characteristics of these authors' works issue from a common source–a diffuse epochal mentality that molds the literary preferences of foreign and Hispanic writers alike... 'The tone of this kind of [literature] is required and provided by the spirit of the age.' " In this study, therefore, I consider the

---

41 Compare Gustavo Pérez Firmat's reference to an article printed in *Ulises*, the Mexican periodical, which refutes Salazar y Chapela's statement that Benjamín Jarnés was Jaime Torres Bodet's model: "The claim that Jarnés [a Spaniard] was Torres Bodet's [a Mexican] professor did not sit well, however, with those on the other [i.e. the Mexican] side of the Atlantic. In a spirited reply to Salazar y Chapela published in the short-lived Mexican periodical *Ulises*, such a connection is disavowed. There is no need, says the review, to resort to Jarnés or Giraudoux to account for [Torres Bodet's 1927] *Margarita de niebla*, for the defining characteristics of these authors' works issue from a common source–a diffuse epochal mentality that molds the literary preferences of foreign and Hispanic writers alike... 'The tone of this kind of prose is required and provided by the spirit of the age.'" Gustavo Pérez Firmat, *Idle Fictions: The Hispanic Vanguard Novel 1926-1934* (Durham, NC: Duke University Press, 1982) 17. See also 9, 32, 33.

In an August 12, 1986 interview on National Public Radio, the organizer of the 1986 Venice Biennale, which had as its theme that year the connection between art and science, affirmed that Picasso and Einstein both discovered the relativity of point of view at about the same time, without (it seems virtually certain) knowing each other. My point is that it is not imitation, but intertextuality or synchronicity, which links Maples Arce to the Italian Futurists and the other European avant-garde movements.

similarity of the avant-garde movements in Europe and the Americas as being more or less synchronous related developments rather than influence or imitation.

Some critics have accused Maples Arce of simply copying trends of the European avant-garde.[42] Nevertheless, the fact is that there is virtually always a precedent for any artistic movement. Western culture and Art seem so related between countries that once a new trend starts in one place, it spreads to the other countries. As Pérez Firmat stated, the trend is dictated by the spirit of the age. There is therefore no relevant basis for critics to say that Estridentismo is merely a copy of Italian Futurism (the most frequent accusation, and not correct). Pointing out intertextualities is a valid observation, but reducing criticism to an accusation of imitation is shortsighted and insults the creativity of all artists. A survey of the international poetry of the time reveals many similarities in virtually all Hispanic countries.

The move to the avant-garde in literature (especially poetry) occurred in virtually all Latin American countries in the 1920s. It was a period of great creativity. Some of the major centers of vanguardista literary expression were: Mexico City (Estridentismo, José Juan Tablada's haiku and calligrams, the vanguard novel of the estridentistas and of the Contemporáneos); São Paulo (Brazilian Modernismo—Mário de Andrade, Osvald de Andrade, et al, and their magazine *Klaxon*); Buenos Aires (Argentine Ultraísmo—Borges, Macedonio Fernández, Ricardo Güiraldes, Leopoldo Marechal, Ricardo Molinari, Oliverio Girondo; and the Martinfierristas); Havana (Mariano Brull, Manuel Navarro-Luna, the magazine *Avance*);

---

42 Cf. Monahan's (op cit) summary of the critical reception of *Estridentismo*.;

Lima (Alberto Hidalgo, Magda Portal, Serafín del Mar, Juan Parra del Riego, Luis de la Jarra, César Vallejo in his volume *Trilce*, Mariátegui and the magazine *Amauta*, the magazine *Tartura*); Santiago de Chile (Vicente Huidobro and Creacionismo, the runrunistas, Pablo de Rokha, Jorge Moraga Bustamante, Apolo de Roca and *Dínamo*, Pablo Neruda in some poems of surrealist tendency); Colombia (the Piedracielistas–Luis Vidales, Jorge Rojas, E. Carranza, A. Camacho Ramírez, Aurelio Arturo; Los Nuevos–León de Greiff, Rafael Maya, Germán Pardo García); Uruguay (Alfredo Mario Ferreiro, Delgado, Fusco Sansone, Pereda Valdes, Silva Valdes); Venezuela ("el grupo del 28" and the magazine *Válvula*); Puerto Rico (the *diepalismo* of Isaac de Diego Padró and Luis Palés Matos), Ecuador (Hugo Mayo), and groups in Asunción, Tegucigalpa, Santo Domingo, among others. Some say the group movements that produced the most lasting work in poetry were Estridentismo, Huidobro's Creacionsimo, and the Argentine Ultraísmo.[43]

Some of the European Dadaists visited New York City, and a New York Dada group was formed with such figures as Francis Picabia, Robert Desnos, and photographer Alfred Stieglitz. Work from the first half of William Carlos Williams' career (especially *Spring and All*) is highly influenced by Dada. Writer and painter Wyndham Lewis, sculptor Henri Gaudier-Brzeska, poet Ezra Pound, and poet T. S. Eliot formed the Vorticism (or Vortex) movement in London, publishing their magazine

---

43 See Nelson Osorio, "El estridentismo mexicano y la vanguardia literaria latinoamericana,"*El estridentismo: memoria y valoración*, ed. Esther Hernández Palacios (México: Fondo de Cultura Económica, 1983) 51. I will reiterate here that I do not consider the poetry of the Mexican *Contemporáneos* to be truly *vanguardista*. Cf. Schneider, *El Estridentismo*.

Blast from 1914-1919. These poets were extremely important in renovating American and British poetry, and together with the exiled writers of the Lost Generation cast the mold for modern literary expression in North America. The flood (almost a pilgrimage) of artists going to Paris in the first decades of the century allowed many close contacts between writers and painters from North and South America and Europe.

The Major Avant-Garde Movements in Europe

The following is a general summary of the major avant-garde movements in Europe. This reference will be helpful to clear up the confusion manifested in previously published criticism of Estridentismo regarding the various avant-garde styles.

1907–CUBISM (mainly in France, with principal artists Picasso, Braque, Gris, Léger, Delauney): an attempt to break down the apparent reality of traditional representational art into its components by viewing an object from many planes or points of view simultaneously. The Cubists contended that traditional representational art froze time to depict an object, seen from only one perspective. Cubism tried to show the object from many perspectives in fluid time, as these artists believed illustrated true reality. This breaking down of the component elements of an object and of our perception of it, strives ultimately to arrive at the essence of the object. The work of art then reconstructs (recreates) the (reality of the) object. Cubism was an exploration of perception processes, and also of image construction processes.[44]

---

44   *The Harper Dictionary of Modern Thought* defines Cubism as follows:
"An artistic movement often regarded as the most revolutionary and influential of the 20th century. Led by Picasso and Braque, the Cubists, while attempting to represent what the eye sees, aimed to render objects more essential and tangible by means of stylized forms and symbols.

"Three phases are commonly distinguished. The first may be dated from the completion early in 1907 of Picasso's *Les Demoiselles d'Avignon*, whose angular, distorted shapes reflected the growing interest in primitive sculpture and the work of Cézanne. In the next two years Picasso and Braque depicted familiar objects by means of interlocked geometrical figures, abandoning traditional perspective and chiaroscuro.

"The second, 'analytical' phase (1910-12) is notable for the development of the techniques of presenting different facets of an object simultaneously, superimposed or side by side. Guitars, bottles, pipes, and written words appear regularly in the paintings of Picasso and Braque at this time. Other artists associated with Cubism included Gris, Léger, Delaunay, Metzinger, and Gleizes; the latter two published a theoretical work, *Du Cubisme* (1912), though their own painting tended merely to 'cubify' their subject-matter in harmonious designs, without any radical restructuring.

"In May 1912 Picasso included a piece of printed cloth, representing a chair seat, in a painting–a significant moment in the history of collage; in September of that year Braque incorporated strips of wallpaper in his work, and he, Picasso, and Gris soon developed the new medium of *papier collé*, which (they felt) introduced a fresh element of 'reality' into their art. This concern with textures led them to experiment with sculpture: Cubist sculpture, again pioneered by Picasso, was to reach its peak during World War I in the work of Archipenko, Laurens, and Lipchitz (forerunners of Constructivism).

"In the final, 'synthetic' phase (1913-14), Cubist painting tended to become more complicated and colourful, employing multiple repetitions of forms and a language of visual signs. But by this time it was less easy to discern a single Cubist school; moreover, the influence of Cubism had spread abroad, affecting Expressionism, Futurism, Dada, Vorticism, Orphism, Suprematism, *De Stijl*, etc. The Armory Show (New York, 1913) included a Cubist contingent. The Purists, on the other hand, presently joined by Léger himself, reacted against Cubism in returning to undissected shapes and a severe machine-like precision.

"Cubism had affinities with the new European interest in jazz; and in 1923 Léger designed Cubist sets for Milhaud's negro jazz ballet *La Création du Monde* . Indeed, works of art in several other fields have been called 'Cubist', either because they were directly inspired by Cubist painting (as was some of the poetry of Apollinaire and Cendrars) or because of their fragmented, multiple-image structure (Stravinsky's *Petrushka* of 1911, Satie's *Parade* of 1916, Joyce's *Ulysses* of 1922)." Patrick Conner, *The Harper Dictionary of Modern Thought*, eds. Alan Bullock and Oliver Stallybrass (New York: Harper & Row, 1977) 147-148.

This dictionary was chosen because it offers excellent concise, accurate, brief definitions of the avant-garde movements, written by various autho-

1909–ITALIAN FUTURISM (in Italy, with Marinetti, Boccioni, Carrá, Russolo, et al). A revolt against the outdated bourgeois system, Italian Futurism idealized movement, dynamism, speed, rejected the past and wanted to shock the bourgeoisie. Futurist manifestos were published in newspapers and presented in public concerts or "happenings." Works included experimentation with sound, machine-age noise, typography, free verse, simultaneity, kinetics, images of motion and force, and unusual image combinations.[45]

---

rities in the field, which are useful to our purpose here. Book-length studies have proven to give book-length definitions which are difficult to synthesize as cited support for my own comments.

45 "Futurism. Italian movement in the arts, originating as a purely literary doctrine with F. T. Marinetti's 'Futurist Manifesto' in *Le Figaro* , Paris, 20 February 1909; subsequently extended to the other arts, then after 1922 partly assimilated in the official ideology of Fascism, to peter out in the mid-1930s. Its principles, asserted in a loud succession of manifestos, were dynamism, the cult of speed and the machine, rejection of the past, and the glorification of patriotism and war. Techniques put forward and practised to these ends included (1) in literature, free verse, phonetic poetry, and a telegraphic language without adjectives or adverbs or much syntax ('words in liberty'); (2) in the visual arts, Neoimpressionism, pictorial dynamism ('lines of force'), simultaneity, and the interpenetration of planes; (3) in music, a bruitisme evolved by Francesco Pratella and Luigi Russolo, and based on the noises of the modern industrialized world; instruments were also to be made which would divide the octave into 50 equal microtones.

"These largely new methods were demonstrated and tested by, e.g., the painter-sculptor Umberto Boccioni, the painter Ardengo Soffici, and the architect Antonio Sant'Elia (notably in his 1914 series of architectural drawings, *Città Nuova*), while the movement's shows and lecture-demonstrations from 1912 to 1914 had some influence in France (on Apollinaire, Léger, and Delaunay), England (Vorticism), and the U.S.A., making a real contribution in Russia (Rayonism, Ego-Futurism, and Cubo-Futurism) and affecting German Expressionism via *Der Sturm* . Its impact on Dada from 1916 on was even more profound, not only through the new techniques, but still more by Futurism's blurring of the frontiers between different arts, and its conscious exploitation of the mass media's power to publicize any adroitly staged piece of cultural provocation. It thus paved the way both for such artistic developments as concrete poetry, concrete music, and kinetic art, and for the concept of art as a more or less sensational event." John Willett and Antony Hopkins, *The Harper Dictionary*, 251-252. (It became an advocate of violence only near the end, perhaps because of

1916–Dada (in Switzerland, Germany, and France, with Ball, Arp, Tzara, Hülsenbeck, Grosz, Ernst, Schwitters, Picabia, Duchamp, and later a group led by Breton): a revolt against the senseless state of things, against the state of violence and war, against the meaningless state of contemporary language (especially as manifested in journalism of the day), against the accepted form of bourgeois Art. It was a search for the primal roots of language and expression. It was important to express rebellion, destroy the old (nihilism), and create a new order. The movement accomplished the expression of revolt and the destruction of the old, but never really achieved the creation of a new order. Work was done in theater, poetry, photography, art, and emphasized the destruction of traditional expectations for artworks, the expression of senselessness, and employed the concept of art as "happening."[46]

---

the tremendous psychological effect of World War I and the death of some of the members of the group while in combat.)

46 "Dada (-ism, -ists). International movement in the arts originating in Zurich in 1916 from a sense of total disillusionment with the art-loving public, the role of the creative artist, and, finally, with art as such; famous consequently more for its spirit of artistic flippancy, bourgeois-baiting, and nihilism than for its purely formal methods, most of which were borrowed from Cubism and Futurism. Its name was 'found in a lexicon–it means nothing. This is the meaningful nothing, where nothing has any meaning'. Its founders were mainly German–the theater director Hugo Ball, the artist Hans Arp, and the poet Richard Hülsenbeck–plus the Romanian Tristan Tzara, while its adherents at one time or another over the next few years included Georg Grosz and John Heartfield (both in Berlin), Max Ernst (Cologne), and Kurt Schwitters (Hanover; [his own technique 'Merz']); the Cuban [in France] Francis Picabia and the Frenchman Marcel Duchamp (both of whom had previously experimented in a comparable nihilism in New York ... [with] readymades); and finally a literary group centred around André Breton's Paris review *Littérature* (1919-24).

"By 1924 the various groups had either stagnated, transferred loyalties, or merged into Constructivism or Surrealism; after which the movement's characteristic methods–phonetic poetry ([cf.] concrete poetry), bruitisme, collage, and nonsense dialogue, as well as its two original contributions, the

A related movement is German Expressionism, occurring at about the same time (1910-1924), which sought to destroy the old and create a new form of expression that would be more true and valid. In their poetry, the Expressionists experimented with perspective: they disrupted the normal, conventional perspective by combining words and images that usually do not go together, thus changing/challenging the established spatial relationships between things and people. They also worked with the absolute metaphor, where a poem seems to be a series of images with no apparent connection, which the reader must put together to form the whole picture. This use of perspective and of metaphor and metonymy is present in virtually all avant-garde poetry.[47]

---

photogram and photo-montage—were hardly again recognized as such till the publication in New York in 1951 of Robert Motherwell's *The Dada Painters and Poets*, the consequent Fluxus revival, and the rise of pop art. In this new context Dada, like its Futurist precursors, became relevant above all for its basic, if unformulated, conception of art as happening or manifestation, and an exercise in public relations." John Willett, *The Harper Dictionary*, 153.

47 "Expressionism... Virtually the whole modern movement in the arts in Germany and Austro-Hungary between 1910 and about 1924, subsuming all local manifestations of Fauvism, Cubism, and Futurism, and constituting the origins of Dada and Neue Sachlichkeit. Though subsequently extended backwards to cover, e.g., the paintings of the Norwegian Edvard Munch or the early work of the Brücke, the formula 'Expressionism' entered Germany from France in 1910 and thereafter became used to describe the German movements first in art, then in literature, the theatre (from 1918), music, architecture, and the cinema. Its hallmarks accordingly were theirs: distortion, fragmentation, and the communication of violent or overstressed emotion.

"With *Der Sturm* and *Die Aktion* as its organs, it embraced *(a)* in painting, the Brücke and the Blaue Reiter; *(b)* in literature, the poetry of Georg Heym, Georg Trakl, and Franz Werfel, and the prose of Alfred Döblin and Franz Kafka; *(c)* in the theatre, the plays of Georg Kaiser and Ernst Toller; *(d)* in music, the early works of Arnold Schönberg and Alban Berg; *(e)* in architecture, Erich Mendelsohn's Einstein Tower and the utopian projects of Bruno Taut; *(f)* in the cinema, Robert Wiene's *The Cabinet of Dr. Caligari* (1920).

"German Expressionism's predominantly Pacifist and Socialist political aims, crystallizing in the wartime movement of Activism, were frustrated by such post-war developments as the suppression of the Spartacists and

1924–SURREALISM (in France, with Breton, Aragon, Soupault and Éluard in literature; de Chirico, Miró, Tanguy, Magritte, Dalí in art; also some Dada converts): a moral revolt against the state of the world; a social revolution of the arts. The Surrealists tried to (re-)capture the source or means of true artistic creation (i.e. not traditional patterns) by tapping the subconscious. A goal was to get at the innate workings of language and visual images. Importance was given to freedom of image and of expression. Only a few writers opted for an "automatic writing" style—most were studied workers—though the movement likes to explore its possibilities, likes the idea of it. The Surrealists wanted to go beyond the apparent surface to a higher (or deeper) reality: not conscious but subconscious reality. Dreams were seen as expressions of a deeper, subconscious reality, and ergo more natural and true, unconditioned by social restrictions and traditional art patterns. The Surrealists wanted to open up the possibilities of expression and of the image. Many Dada writers became members of the Surrealist group, continuing their efforts in a slightly different vein; the Surrealist manifesto is dated 1924.[48]

---

the Munich Soviet; and it was superseded by the more pragmatic Neue Sachlichkeit—on which, as on the Bauhaus, it left a distinctive mark. Though Nazism suppressed all three movements as degenerate, it was again influential in the revival of the arts in Germany after 1945." John Willett, *The Harper Dictionary* 223-224.

[48] "Surrealism. French literary movement evolving from the Paris wing of Dada during 1920-23, thereafter establishing itself also in the visual arts, theatre, and cinema, to become the last (to date) of this century's great international modern currents. Though the name had been coined in 1917 by Guillaume Apollinaire, the true spiritual ancestors of the movement were Rimbaud, the newly rediscovered poet Lautréamont, the German and other late-18th-century Romantics (including de Sade), and the Symbolists. Its animator was the poet André Breton, who in 1919 founded the review

Littérature with his friends Louis Aragon and Philippe Soupault, joined later that year by Paul Éluard, and there published his first experiments in *automatic writing* : a random stream of words coming from that subconscious which the movement now deliberately set out to explore. Already aware of the manifestos and activities of Zurich Dada, as well as Tzara's poems, in the winter of 1919-20 Breton joined forces with Picabia and Tzara himself to create a comparable succession of Parisian shocks and scandals, whose aggressive, continually newsworthy tactics thenceforward became an integral part of his movement. In 1924, with Dada outside France effectively dead and his new allies discarded, Breton and his friends formally constituted the Surrealist group. Its manifesto, proclaiming the inferiority of realism to 'psychic automatism' and and 'previously neglected forms of association' of a magical, irrational, hallucinatory sort, appeared that October; its new, politically-tinged review *La Révolution Surréaliste* two months later.

"Though visual art was neglected in the manifesto and its place at first far from clear, a distinctive Surrealist art gradually developed. Its main model was the metaphysical painting of de Chirico, with its disquieting perspectives and poeticizing of the banal, but the more Dadaist work of Arp, Ernst, Duchamp, and Picabia also contributed and some attempt was made to annex Picasso and Paul Klee. In 1923 André Masson began to make 'automatic drawings' (or largely random doodles), influencing the lighthearted biomorphic art of Joan Miró who, with Arp, represented the more abstract wing of the movement. But the surreal poetry of de Chirico's pictures—a blend of strikingly dead subject-matter, at once familiar and improbable, with a smoothly academic technique—was not developed further until the emergence, during the second half of the 1920s, of such artists as Yves Tanguy, the Belgians René Magritte and Paul Delvaux, and finally the Spaniard Salvador Dalí, who settled in Paris at the end of 1929. Basing himself on a 'paranoiac-critical method' (delirium tempered by a Meissonier-like meticulousness), Dalí depicted soft watches, decomposing human limbs, and other glutinously biomorphic props lost in endless arid landscapes. By a mixture of technical skill and brilliant self-projection he became, for the public of the next two decades, the quintessential surrealist.

"As a literary movement, Surrealism spread mainly to those areas where French cultural influence was strong, e.g. Latin America, the Middle East, Spain, and Eastern Europe, though it had its followers (such as David Gascoyne) in England, while there was an important group in pre-1939 Czechoslovakia. As a political force, dedicated to a concept of revolution that became increasingly Trotskyist, it was always negligible, its pretensions, which were largely those of Breton himself, leading only to disagreements (hence the secession of Aragon and Éluard in 1932 and 1938 respectively) and mystification. In the visual field, however, as also in Antonin Artaud's theatre of cruelty and Luis Buñuel's films, it had a world-wide impact, particularly as a result of the London Surrealist Exhibition of June 1936, of Dalí's window-dressing and happenings in New York of 1939, of the posters of A. M. Cassandre and other epigones, and finally of the arrival in the U.S.A. of Breton, Ernst, Masson, Tanguy, and other refugees from German-occupied France. Gimmicks apart—and certainly it had these—Surrealism acted throughout the second quarter of this century as a universally intelligible plea for a revival of the imagination, based on the unconscious as revealed by psychoanalysis, together with a new emphasis on magic, accident, irrationality, symbols, and dreams. Not the least of its

All of these movements held in common: (1) a dissatisfaction with traditional (representational) artistic expression. Traditional art was no longer able to express contemporary reality (the early 20th century brought with it previously unknown complications: a boom of dynamism, an awareness of the intermingling of time and space, and an awareness of the relativity of perception). Therefore, the avant-garde movements searched for a new mode of expression to communicate their world, and also to explore the possibilities of Art. A freedom of expression opened up. There was much experimentation. Creativity and originality were rewarded within the avant-garde group. (2) They had a moral disagreement with and rebellion against the contemporary social situation—the tight and constipated control of everything by the bourgeoisie: Art, business, money, fashion, tastes, politics. The avant-garde championed the proletariat and admired eccentrics and individualists. There was a profound influence (especially in Europe, for obvious reasons) left by the wars and the absurd politics of the period. The bourgeoisie was by the time of the rise of the avant-garde corrupt and self-serving, to the exclusion of the proletariat. Everything bourgeois, therefore, had to be attacked and overthrown. The avant-garde promoted nonconformism to break the control of the conformist bourgeoisie. There was a joy in shocking the conservative moral and artistic standards of the bourgeois establishment. There was a corresponding reassertion of the individual (cf. nonconformism), which one might historically compare to the Romantic swing away from Neoclassicism. Although the avant-garde was a re-

---

achievements was that it led to a major revaluation of comparable romantic movements in the past." John Willett, *The Harper Dictionary* 614-615.

bellion against the traditional norms and morés that society held regarding the arts, the creative works themselves were not politically committed. Indeed, part of the new freedom of expression included the importance of the art object in and of itself, free of any necessary attachment to the outside world, unlike traditional representational art and politically committed art.

The reader will have noted that a large part of the preceding discussion of the avant-garde movements has centered on the plastic arts as much as on literature, and some of the interpretation which follows in later chapters will also refer to that aspect. This approach is justified in several ways. For one, many more studies have been written about avant-garde painting than about avant-garde poetry or fiction. Those commentaries, nevertheless, are also applicable to the literary avant-garde. It is often helpful to use a visual illustration of a concept, especially a complex, abstract one, to explain its verbal parallel. One of the aims of *Estridentismo* was to unite all of the arts, and also to synthesize all of the avant-garde tendencies or movements. Avant-garde theory is applicable to all of the manifestations it yields, whether literary, artistic, musical, or architectural. Mary Ann Caws justifies the use of uniting avant-garde literature and the plastic arts in critical studies of either when she writes:

> In his autobiography, Louis Aragon [a writer] says of himself: 'I am an ordinary Frenchman and like all my countrymen I have a passion for painting, an *irrational* passion for painting. Nothing can so excite us in this so-called country of moderation.' All the writers dealt with here share his love of art, and none of them make any distinction between the theory of poetry and that of plastic art. When they speak of one they speak for the other; they are passionate about both. Since any

attempt on the part of a nonsurrealist and a nonpoet to theorize about the nature of surrealist (or ex-surrealist) poetry and art is necessarily at a remove from the poet's own view of his art and of art in general, and since we are fortunate enough to have the reflections of these poets on their own work as well as the writings and paintings of others, their opinions make an obvious starting point. The major themes which they discover and elaborate when they are judging or theorizing are at the same time the focus of their own poetic work: in other words, these particular themes are *constants* in their criticism, their manifestos, and their poetry.[49]

Maples Arce's passion for painting (he was a lifelong avid student, collector, and critic of painting) fortifies the connection even more. Estridentismo was composed of poets, writers of prose, painters, sculptors, illustrators and, for a time, musicians and photographers, all working with a common idea.

Theory of Estridentismo

The theory of Estridentismo as written by the estridentistas —when not declared nonexistent (i.e. saying this is not a movement, so there is no theory; cf. Tzara's "Dada ne signifie rien")— is difficult to decipher. It is generally written in an elevated style, with complex terminology and an air of abstraction that evades being pinned down by any concrete examples. This style is evident in Maples Arce's first manifesto and in his remarks in magazine interviews in the early 1920s, in List Arzubide's history of the movement, and in much of Vela's discussion of Estridentismo. Three terms that are repeated frequently, though almost never

---

49   Caws, 3-4.

defined, seem to be the building blocks of estridentista writing. They are *la imagen equivalentista* (also known as *la figura indirecta compuesta*), *la imagen doble*, and *abstraccionismo*. Importance is also given to *emoción*. The best available definitions of these terms (*abstraccionsimo, figura indirecta compuesta/imagen equivalentista, imagen doble*) are provided by Arqueles Vela in his article in the second issue of the group's magazine *Irradiador*.[50] In this article, Vela

---

50 The complete passage from Vela's article to be summarized below, reads as follows:

"El comprimido estridentista de Manuel Maples Arce, publicado en la primera hoja de 'ACTUAL', no hace especulaciones sobre un arte estridentista. Incita a los intelectuales jóvenes a hacer un arte personal y renovado, fijando las delimitaciones estéticas. A destruir las teorías equivocadamente modernas. A hacer poesía pura. Sin perspectivas pictóricas. Sin anecdotismo. Una poesía sincera, sin ordenar la emoción que es siempre desordenada. Las tendencias antiguas sujetaron la emoción a una esquema, a un itinerario para presentarla como una obra de equilibrio arquitectónica, de orfebrería y no como una obra imaginal y emocional. Toda esa literatura está basada en una ecuanimidad que no tiene la vida. Lo real y lo natural en la vida es lo absurdo. Lo inconexo. Nadie siente ni piensa con una perfecta continuidad. Nadie vive una vida como la de los personajes de las novelas románticas. Nuestra vida es arbitraria y los cerebros están llenos de pensamientos incongruentes. El ensueño no tiene la plasticidad, la claridad de los poemas de los novecentistas.

"La teoría abstraccionista, no es una teoría, sino una insinuación de afirmar la personalidad. De crear un arte puro y sin repujaciones. Un arte en que el sincronismo emocional tenga una equivalencia con ese ritmo sincrónico del ajetreo de la vida moderna.

"En su poema 'Prisma', Maples Arce logra ensamblar su inquietud interior con esa inquietud que flota en unas pestañas, en la calle toda llena de inquietudes eléctricas y de humo de fábricas, con imágenes diametralmente opuestas y yuxtapuestas con una fuerte hilación ideológica.

"¿Quién no ha sentido en sus recuerdos desordenados, las miradas de las 'mujeres telescopiadas en catástrofes de recuerdos' del poema de la 'MUJER HECHA PEDAZOS' de José Juan Tablada? Los que no comprenden la belleza del poema de Tablada es porque han tergiversado completamente la visión estética. Su falta de sinceridad los ha obligado a tener un concepto diferente de la emoción. Los que interpretan con más exactitud ese estado absurdo del espíritu que es la emoción, han sido siempre los poetas incomprensibles y por lo mismo, los más sinceros.

"Las innovaciones del grupo estridentista: la figura indirecta compuesta y las imágenes dobles—no dobles a la manera creacionista—han revolucionado no sólo la forma, que es lo menos importante en una renovación, sino la ideología, la manera de interpretar la armonía del universo. La poesía está en esa música luminosa desenrrollada por la rotación de las esferas. Y esa si-

notes that Maples Arce encourages young poets to "hacer un arte personal y renovado ... hacer poesía pura ... sin ordenar la emoción que es siempre desordenada." Regarding emotion, Vela observes:

> Las tendencias antiguas sujetaron la emoción a una esquema, a un itinerario para presentarla como una obra de equilibrio arquitectónica, de orfebrería y no como una obra imaginal y emocional. Toda esa literatura está basada en una ecuanimidad que no tiene la vida. Lo real y lo natural en la vida es lo absurdo. Lo inconexo. Nadie siente ni piensa con una perfecta continuidad. Nadie vive una vida como la de los personajes de las novelas románticas. Nuestra vida es arbitraria y los cerebros están llenos de pensamientos incongruentes.[51]

To define *"la teoría abstraccionista"*, Vela says that it is "un arte en que el sincronismo emocional tenga una equiv-

---

multaneidad de armonías logradas sin tiempo, ni espacio, sin sujeto, es lo que hace nuestra teoría abstraccionista.
"La figura indirecta compuesta es una visión, lograda con dos sugerencias desiguales sintácticamente, y que ensambladas ideológicamente establecen una relación incoercible:
'... y el pentagrama eléctrico
de todos los tejados
se muere en el alero del último almanaque'
(de Maples Arce)
"La imagen doble interpreta simultáneamente la actitud espiritual y la actitud material:
'... Y me alejé hacia el lado opuesto de su mirada...'
(de 'La Srita. Etc.')
"Esta síntesis exegética del estridentismo–la primera irrupción subversista que suscitó la pasividad ambiente–y la teoría abstraccionista, –la primera manifestación renovadora–es una interpretación personalista. No teorizamos sobre el abstraccionismo porque no es una teoría. Y porque nosotros no limitamos la fuerza creadora como los impulsionistas–teoría cientifico-filosófica–, los paroxistas–teoría neobaulerina–, los neoparoxistas–teoría tridimensional–, Etc. y las demás tendencias que circunscriben la emoción." Arqueles Vela, "El estridentismo y la teoría abstraccionista," *Irradiador* 2 (octubre 1923): n. pag.
51   Vela, "El estridentismo...," *Irradiador* 2.

alencia con ese ritmo sincrónico del ajetreo de la vida moderna ... En su poema 'Prisma,' Maples Arce logra ensamblar su inquietud interior ... con esa inquietud ... en la calle ... con imágenes diametralmente opuestas y yuxtapuestas con una fuerte hilación ideológica." Vela believes that the innovations of Estridentismo have revolutionized not only form but also ideology, "la manera de interpretar la armonía del universo. La poesía está en esa música luminosa desenrrollada por la rotación de las esferas. Y esa simultaneidad de armonías logradas sin tiempo, ni espacio, sin sujeto, es lo que hace nuestra teoría abstraccionista." We see here similarity with Cubism's attempt to capture the essence of an object in fluid time from many simultaneous perspectives, to approach human perception. Estridentismo adds an affective or spiritual dimension: the emotion felt by the person as s/he contemplates the object, thus joining the interior and exterior realities of a situation.

The *figura indirecta compuesta* and the *imagen doble* are accomplished through a similar construction: 1) the union of opposites (or elements not commonly associated with each another) through juxtaposition and "ideology" or poetic vision in the *figura indirecta compuesta*, and 2) the simultaneous expression of the spiritual level and the material level of an image complex or a situation. Arqueles Vela explains: "*La figura indirecta compuesta es una visión, lograda con dos sugerencias desiguales sintácticamente, y que ensambladas ideológicamente establecen una relación incoercible,*" and he gives a verse from Maples Arce as an example: "y el pentagrama eléctrico / de todos los tejados / se muere en el alero del último almanaque." Vela continues: "*La imagen doble interpreta simultáneamente la actitud espiritual y la actitud material,*" and quotes an image from his own novella, *La Señorita Etcétera.* , "Y me alejé hacia el lado opuesto de su mirada."⁵²

To summarize, the three main poetic devices of Estridentismo to express life in the modern world are 1) union of the interior and exterior worlds (*emoción/abstraccionsimo*), 2) normally unassociated ideas united by poetic vision (*imagen equivalentista/figura indirecta compuesta*), and 3) union of the spiritual and the material (*imagen doble*).

While it is true that Maples Arce and the other writers of Estridentismo were able to combine the above-mentioned elements in such a way as to create a unique and distinct image, those elements are present in other ways in avant-garde poetry in general, especially the union of apparent opposites (cf. Huidobro) and the importance given to emotion. William Carlos Williams defined the poetic image as a complex of emotion in an instant of time. Mary Ann Caws asserts that a poem recreates an emotion, and that "for surrealism, poetry is the precise equivalent of passion." She also notes that since the avant-garde was against institutions, they were therefore against definitions, thus the difficulty in explaining their theory.⁵³

---

52 Vela. All quotes in this section are taken from the same article in *Irradiador* 2. I have added italics for emphasis and clarification of the main points.
53 Caws, 4, 9.

Chapter Two: The Prism: Fragmented Reality, *Andamios Interiores*, 1922

> "Art gives form and harmony to what in life is chaos and discord."
> Isadora Duncan

Maples Arce's 1922 volume *Andamios Interiores* contains a uniform, cohesive group of poems of Cubist structure in which form reflects and reports theme. In the situation of the protagonist separated in one way or another from his beloved, the dichotomy of union vs. separation is presented and vanquished in each poem, reunion being achieved in the structure and images of the poem above and beyond the verbal thematic meditation; that is, the poet creates a timelessness within time and salvages the situation in the work of art. The Cubist mode is the right choice for these poems, since it works with the same problems and finds resolution in the same way as the particular situation of the protagonist in Maples Arce's *estridentista* volumes.

> ... en el cubismo, al igual que en el creacionsimo, las imágenes se van sucediendo hasta fundirse en una situación final donde [se] ve no aparecen la perspectiva ni las distancias y se pierden los tiempos del ayer y del mañana, donde una imagen o un poema engloban todos los tiempos y todos los planos en un solo instante.[54]

---

54   A. Maack, "Huidobro, Picasso, y la correlación de las artes," *El Sur* [Con-

> ... Es decir, que los excitantes interno y externo se reducen a uno solo, al tiempo que la inteligencia va fatigándose.⁵⁵

Poems written in this mode, in order to be deciphered and understood, require active involvement on the part of the reader. These poems are not easy to read. One must find the connections between images, consider the poem as a whole, and reconstruct the total image. Most published criticism of *Andamios Interiores* falls victim to the danger of seeing only isolated images, never reaching a total picture. Frank Rutter speaks to this situation when he explains the problem and the necessary method of approaching a Cubist poem:

> ... existe un predominio de lo ilógico y lo irracional, resultado inevitable de la casi eliminación de elementos narrativos o descriptivos. El lector, entonces, utiliza sus facultades imaginativas para evocar su propia visión interior, construyendo así una 'totalidad' a partir de un poema que consiste sólo en imágenes aparentemente inconexas. En la mayor parte de los casos esta totalidad se registra en la mente del lector únicamente después de un esfuerzo intelectual posterior a la lectura. En la pintura cubista se observa un paralelo semejante... exigía un concepto intelectual de cómo todas las partes formaban la totalidad del objeto de arte. Esto conllevaba una visión de la que el observador se hacía partícipe en la construcción de la totalidad por medio de sus poderes de imaginación e intelecto. Por eso el arte moderno no permite una rápida mirada superficial... El tema principal o la totalidad del poema ["Vide," de Vicente Huidobro] es tradicional, es decir, se trata del dolor y sufrimiento de una

---

cepción, Chile] II (19 agosto 1984): n. pag. (Referring to Estrella Busto Ogden's study of Vicente Huidobro's poetry.)

55 Luis Marín Loya, *El meridiano lírico* (México, 1926) n.pag.

persona que ha perdido el objeto de su amor; la presentación, sin embargo, es distinta. La omisión de descripciones, narraciones y de un orden cronológico oculta el leitmotif poético que se revela sólo después de un análisis del conjunto de las imágenes que compone el poema.[56]

The process Rutter describes is precisely the key to interpreting Maples Arce's *estridentista* (Cubist) poems, and will be used throughout this study. Rutter has made an excellent observation, and his explanation of how modern art and modern poetry work, as stated in the above quotation, delineates the fundamentals of understanding and interpreting such works.

Similarly, in his 1923 review of *Andamios Interiores*, the Mexican novelist Gregorio López y Fuentes explains that one cannot approach these poems in a traditional way, since they are not immediately linear or representational.

> El procedimiento que sigue Manuel Maples Arce es un procedimiento que requiere una constante gimnasia mental porque él no toma la imagen como la cámara fotográfica, en línea recta, sino que el objetivo llega al cristal receptor, podría decirse, mediante una combinación de espejos cóncavos y convexos: cuando los espejos han modificado la imagen, marcando poderosamente los rasgos característicos, él la traslada al lienzo; por eso a sus temas no se puede ir en línea recta: debe desandarse la línea quebrada que él siguió sobre los cristales reflectores.[57]

Poet and reader both follow a decipherization or reduction-reconstruction process (like Maples Arce's de-

---

56 Frank Rutter, "La estética cubista en 'Horizon carré' de Vicente Huidobro," *Bulletin Hispanique* 80 (1978): 129-131.
57 Gregorio López y Fuentes, review of *Andamios Interiores* by Manuel Maples Arce, *El Heraldo* 16 marzo 1923: 3.

struction-creation cycle) in the first three of Maples Arce's books, much as the Cubist and Dada painters (and viewers of their work) did, taking the total image apart, separating its components and eliminating all but the essential elements in order to get to the essence (identity), to then, in a Cubist manner, reconstruct that image anew. The reader must take the puzzle pieces that are presented in the poem and put them together to form the complete picture. Recreation is the dynamism of this process and it preserves motion, eternalizing the present moment in a kind of timelessness within time. As each individual reader tries to decipher and reconstruct the story, multiple interpretations may occur, each valid as long as it is justified, and rather than detracting, this adds to the dynamic quality of the poem.

The following characteristics of *Estridentismo* in general, as noted by Luis Mario Schneider, can be observed in the poems of *Andamios Interiores*: "una dirección de lenguaje ... emotivo, ... pirotecnias verbales, ... imágenes y metáforas por lo general de raíz cubista, yuxtapuestas, pero motivadas todas por una sola idea, ... una musicalidad, y un vértigo espiritual que se produce por el cultivo excesivo de los sentidos." Schneider also points out the unique use of perspective and mood in *Andamios Interiores*: "Por medio de acendrado subjetivismo que muchas veces conduce a un desarraigo, al derrotismo o a un estado de soledad, crea atmósferas que están más sugeridas que declaradas."[58]

Most of the poems of *Andamios Interiores* treat the same basic theme and situation and contain similar elements of

---

[58] Luis Mario Schneider, *Mele* (Carta Internacional de Poesía/International Poetry Letter) ed. Stefan Baciu [Special issue on *Estridentismo*] agosto 1980: 10-11.

Maples Arce's poetic vocabulary –a series of words which, used over the course of his career, signal his poetic vision of the world. This vocabulary consists of groups of words which designate space, time, certain objects and states of being, and these particular words appear in most of Maples Arce's poems. Maples Arce's vocabulary or vision can be reduced to the dichotomy of creation and destruction–a major preoccupation throughout his career as a poet– along with other expressions of the same basic conflict: life/death, spring/autumn, light/dark, sound/silence, union/separation, permanence/transitoriness. The poet is witness to the effect of the creation-destruction cycle on humankind in the twentieth century. As mentioned above, the protagonist of Maples Arce's poems, while exhilarated by modernity, is plagued by a feeling of separation from others and a sense that nothing good lasts. In *Andamios Interiores*, his lover has left him or cannot communicate with him, or he feels alone in a society that is still living in the past. In *Urbe*, what was good in the Revolution has now gone bad. *Poemas Interdictos* adds the idea that nothing is permanent in the modern world. In his introduction to *Las semillas del tiempo*, Rubén Bonifaz Nuño explains: "Así comenzamos a verlo: un vasto panorama espacial corre hacia su propia ruina por los caminos voraces del tiempo. Y para el espíritu del poeta vigilante–insomne–y memorioso, todo se condensa en una visión de adiós desesperado a sí mismo y a todas las cosas."[59] Through the creation of the poem, however, the poet can transcend time and escape total destruction. In Maples Arce's poems, the tran-

---

[59] Rubén Bonifaz Nuño, Estudio preliminar, *Las semillas del tiempo*, by Manuel Maples Arce (México: Fondo de Cultura Económica, 1981) 24. (All subsequent quotes from RBN's preface will be cited by page number parenthetically in the text.)

sitory nature of the positive elements of the dichotomy is transformed into a dynamic permanence within the successful poetic expression of their essences as the poet achieves a vision of timelessness within time. In "reality," the process is usually creation followed by destruction in the world, but in his poetry, where Maples Arce adds the dimension of imagination, he makes it a process of destruction followed by (re)creation; the art renews, saves, creates.

Maples Arce's use of the imagination as a filter through which to see and express his world and his emotions creates innovative images and is a catalyst for the destruction-creation process. What he does is similar to the approach advocated by American poet William Carlos Williams in his 1923 book of theory and poetry, *Spring and All*. Williams contends that the traditional rules for art must be destroyed, and that the force needed to create a new, viable art is the imagination. In the prose sections of *Spring and All*, Williams explores and expounds a personal *ars poetica* for modern poetry, which he then employs in the poems of the same book.

> The imagination, intoxicated by prohibitions, rises to drunken heights to destroy the world... Then at last will the world be made anew... Yes, the imagination, drunk with prohibitions, has destroyed and recreated everything afresh in the likeness of that which it was. Now indeed men look about in amazement at each other with a full realization of the meaning of 'art.'[60]

In the same text, Williams refers to art as a phoenix-like bird turned to stone and born again into a "prismatically plumed bird of life." He says that the imagination,

---

60 William Carlos Williams, *The Collected Poems of William Carlos Williams, Volume I, 1909-1939*, eds. A. Walton Litz and Christopher MacGowan (New York: New Directions, 1986) 179, 181.

once freed from the rules and restrictions of traditional art, takes the lead. The role of the artist, according to Williams, is not to copy nature but to imitate the creative process that nature uses; the product is a separate entity, something nature could not have produced. The poet must "employ correctly those 'sympathetic pulses at work' within himself and [also employ] the 'aid of the imagination.' If he employs them correctly he focusses external reality through the lens of his total personality, and in doing so creates a work of art."[61] The poet should try "to perfect the ability to record at the moment when the consciousness is enlarged by the sympathies and [by] the unity of understanding which the imagination gives."[62] In a statement similar to the *estridentistas*' belief in the importance of the expression of emotion in poetry, Williams explains how prose and poetry express emotion differently: "prose has to do with the fact of an emotion; poetry has to do with the dynamisation of emotion into a separate form,"[63] which is achieved through the use of the imagination. Maples Arce's protagonist is able to create a kind of unity and permanence in the writing of a poem, even though in the story or situation about which he writes he has been a victim of destruction (separation from a lover, loneliness, alienation from society, and so on).

> It is a work of the imagination. It gives the feeling of completion by revealing the oneness of experience; it rouses rather than stupefies the intelligence by demonstrating the importance of personality, by showing the individual, depressed before it, that his life is valuable–when completed by the imagination.

---

61 Geoffrey H. Movius, *The Early Prose of William Carlos Williams, 1917-1925* (New York & London: Garland Publishing, Inc., 1987) 96.
62 Williams, 206.
63 Williams, 219.

And then only. Such work elucidates—[64]

In Maples Arce's *estridentista* poetry, there is a destruction of the traditional expectations (or rules) for poetry and of the traditional connections between images. Through the filter of the imagination, a new kind of poem and new images are created. To the traditional objects of poetry, objects of the modern city are added and new connections are made between the two groups. New images are made often by means of innovative adjectivization, metaphor, juxtaposition of disparates or opposites, unusual subject-verb combinations, or personification of inanimate objects, especially when placed in a modern context.

"Prisma"

Yo soy un punto muerto en medio de la hora,
equidistante al grito náufrago de una estrella.
Un parque de manubrio se engarrota en la sombra,
y la luna sin cuerda
me oprime en las vidrieras.
                 Margaritas de oro
                 deshojadas al viento.

La ciudad insurrecta de anuncios luminosos
flota en los almanaques,
y allá de tarde en tarde,
por la calle planchada se desangra un eléctrico.

El insomnio, lo mismo que una enredadera,
se abraza a los andamios sinoples del telégrafo,
y mientras que los ruidos descerrajan las puertas,
la noche ha enflaquecido lamiendo su recuerdo.

El silencio amarillo suena sobre mis ojos.

---

64 Williams, 194.

¡Prismal, diáfana mía, para sentirlo todo!

Yo departí sus manos,
pero en aquella hora
gris de las estaciones,
sus palabras mojadas se me echaron al cuello,
y una locomotora
sedienta de kilómetros la arrancó de mis brazos.

Hoy suenan sus palabras más heladas que nunca.
¡Y la locura de Edison a manos de la lluvia!

El cielo es un obstáculo para el hotel inverso
refractado en las lunas sombrías de los espejos;
los violines se suben como la champaña,
y mientras las ojeras sondean la madrugada,
el invierno huesoso tirita en los percheros.

Mis nervios se derraman.
                    La estrella del recuerdo
naufraga en el agua
del silencio.
            Tú y yo
                coincidimos
                en la noche terrible,
meditación temática
deshojada en jardines.

Locomotoras, gritos,
arsenales, telégrafos.

El amor y la vida
son hoy sindicalistas,

y todo se dilata en círculos concéntricos.

The poem "Prisma" holds the place of honor of opening both Maples Arce's 1922 volume *Andamios Interiores* and his 1981 complete poetry, *Las semillas del tiempo*.

"Prisma" was the last poem of *Andamios* to be written, but it is placed at the beginning as the key poem of the volume and rightly so, because it achieves the most complete structural and thematic realization of the group.

"Prisma" is structured around two manifestations of Maples Arce's destruction/creation dichotomy, which are darkness vs. light and separation vs. union. The protagonist, abandoned and in darkness, is transfixed by images of light, the ultimate distillation of which becomes a symbol for both his departed lover and their relationship, and for the poem itself—or Poetry. During this trance-like state, the protagonist experiences a "moment of illumination."[65] Though in the exterior world of time the protagonist is separated from his beloved, by means of art he saves their relationship and achieves union through the structure of the poem. "Prisma" is a somewhat hermetic poem that invites multiple interpretations, but this possibility of various interpretations, together with the reconstruction or participation required of the reader, contributes to the poem's dynamic quality. In addition, the poem is saved from abstraction and sentimentality by the constant use of concrete images and motion, which link it to the exterior world.

"Prisma" opens with an image which situates the poetic voice in cosmic space and time: "Yo soy un punto muerto en medio de la hora, / equidistante al grito náufrago de una estrella." Inanimate objects are personified, and images are spatialized and temporalized. From the beginning we are presented with the ideas of timelessness within time, the combination of apparent opposites—especially of sky and sea images—and destruction. The narrator is a still point at

---

[65] A moment of enlightenment, similar to Joyce's "epiphany."

the center of the hour, like T. S. Eliot's still point at the center of the turning world in his *Four Quartets*, and similar images throughout centuries of literature: Dante's vision of God, the mystics' idea of the soul, Juan Ramón Jiménez's essence in time, to name a few.

The protagonist sees a falling star, whose cry is like that of Vicente Huidobro's Altazor, falling infinitely from zenith to nadir. The persona, being on Earth, is equidistant from zenith and nadir and from the star,[66] as it and he both fall eternally, like a system of atoms, the galaxies, or the universe, through space, in a continuous *naufragar* towards the abyss (where perhaps, as if at the bottom of the sea, its light would be extinguished).

The persona, "yo," begins to identify with the star, and relates its situation to his own. He contemplates their fate at the hands of the Creator who makes the universe revolve, comparing man to a *pequeño dios* who in turn makes the microcosms of the world revolve: "Un parque de manubrio se engarrota en la sombra" (note that action stops in this poem with lack of light). A similar image to this hand that makes the world go round (a metonymic extension of the image of an organ grinder's hand, or the grip on handlebars that make a bicycle go around) is found in another poem of *Andamios Interiores*, "Al margen de la lluvia": "Deduzco de la lluvia que esto es definitivo. / ¿Quién está en el manubrio? Hay un corto circuito." The park that the protagonist was contemplating freezes in time when he becomes transfixed by the image of the moon–timeless, eternally returning light suspended in the night sky–and he continues to stare out the window.

---

66 Note that the configuration of zenith-nadir (up-down), Earth/protagonist-star (side-side) is like a diamond-shaped prism. Cf. Borges' labyrinths in "La muerte y la brújula," which also continue infinitely.

Golden daisies in the park below are plucked off and scattered by the wind, as in a lover's gesture of "she loves me, she loves me not," another image of separation and of the destruction of something precious at the hands of higher forces in the cold, dark, rainy winter night. The wind, in like action to the lover saying "she loves me, she loves me not," establishes a connection between the poetic voice and the outer world, or the interior and exterior realities of the poem.

After this connection, we are presented with the work of humankind's creation, the modern city. The city rises up against the night and rebels against the threat of darkness, employing its incessant lights and flashing signs. In the city, time is measured out in comprehensible parcels (cf. Eliot's Prufrock, whose life is measured out in coffee spoons) by calendars which divide it into days and months and years, and daily events which establish an assuring routine, like the scheduled passing by of a streetcar, all controlled by man. ("La ciudad insurrecta de anuncios luminosos / flota en los almanaques, / y allá de tarde en tarde, / por la calle planchada se desangra un eléctrico.")

The combination of words in this second strophe creates highly kinetic images, giving the idea of the city moving both vertically and horizontally through space and time. The streetcar passes along the wet, flat, paved street, its headlight beaming out into the shadows at dusk. The light is also reflected on the wet pavement, extending the image along the street as if its life force, like blood, were trailing out. The streetcar is a positive image of movement, modernity and communication, but the use of *se desangra* is negative and deathlike.

The allusion to insomnia ("El insomnio, lo mismo que

una enredadera") brings the first break in the heptasyllabic rhythm found in all of the lines of the poem up to this point. The caesura comes at the comma after *insomnio*, thus breaking the established cadence (seven syllables plus seven syllables) and thereby giving a great deal of emphasis to the word. The protagonist's state of insomnia is a key aspect of the poem, because it is both his reason for *meditación* and ultimately the creative energy for the making of the poem. A rhythm break is also appropriate here to reflect the break in the normal sleeping/waking pattern. His insomnia echoes the poet's role as witness and keeper of vigil while others sleep unaware.

During his insomnia, the protagonist is searching, reaching out –like the image in the poem of a vine which climbs a telegraph pole– for a method of communication with his beloved. The telegraph pole is referred to as scaffolding ("los andamios sinoples del telégrafo") and the vine climbs it like a builder climbs scaffolding on a building. Given the title of this book, *Andamios Interiores*, the idea of the poet building his poem is also implied. In this image, the green color of the vine blends in with the green color (sinople) of the pole, and the two become one. Similarly, the insomniac protagonist's *meditación temática* eventually becomes the poem before us, which is the means of communication finally found. Here again there is a connection between the inner and outer worlds. While this tremendous effort at reunion is being made by the persona, the night passes. Rubén Bonifaz Nuño suggests that "los ruidos descerrajan las puertas" means that "el silencio [del insomne] cobra voz y trata de resquebrar las puertas de la casa donde ella duerme" (p. 15). This is possible, but they could also be the noises that an insomniac hears (Thurber's "things that go bump in the night") which are exaggerated by the stillness of the night and made by the darkness to seem like invaders or burglars. The image that closes strophe three, "la noche ha enflaquecido lamiendo su recuerdo," indicates that the night passes by in insomniac meditation as the protagonist remembers past days with his beloved. The last part, "lamiendo su recuerdo," is a melancholic, almost self-pitying caress, like an animal licking a wound to make it feel better.

The richly synaesthetic image found in the next line, "El silencio amarillo suena sobre mis ojos," is described by Bonifaz Nuño as "un silencio que suena como bajar de hojas otoñales encima del tejado de los párpados" (p. 15), a beautiful description which gives one possible explanation of the verse. However, in addition to its autumnal connotations, *amarillo* is generally a negative term in Maples Arce's poetry, as in the phrase "amarillismo gris" from the poem "A veces con la tarde." In general (except in "Y nada de hojas secas," where he is talking about morning), yellow has two manifestations in this poetry, one depicting autumn or late afternoon, both times of pensive reflection, and the other representing a melancholy, depressed mood, even to the extreme of infirmity. The first case is a dark, grayish yellow that is used in Maples Arce's work to signal a time of day for reflection, thinking, nostalgia. It is the quality of light during a transitional period (e.g. from afternoon to evening). Many of Maples Arce's poems are set in the late afternoon. In *Soberana Juventud*, Maples Arce says this was a time of day that he set aside for walking to his favorite parks for quiet reflection, which often engendered verses for his poems. Here, in strophe four of "Prisma," the use of yellow and the idea of transition has to do with the protagonist's being transfixed by the images of light (seen earlier in the poem: the star, the moon, the electric signs, their reflections in the window and mirror) which have transfused themselves into his consciousness, so much that the "lighting" of the poem moves from darkness and shadows to yellow, and then suddenly in the second line of strophe four to "¡Prismal, diáfana mía, para sentirlo todo!" There is a gradual progression from darkness into light, to translucent vision and the prism (cf. title), with its magical ability to reveal all the richness and component color of light, and its double identity as both clear and multicolor. The prism is the agent through which the moment of illumination is possible. This verse ("¡Prismal ...") is the most positive image of the poem and contains total experience, sensing, understanding: "para sentirlo todo!" The prism is another still point, at which luminous intellection is possible and from which energy emanates —it is center and circumference, maximum in minimum, unity and multiplicity. The adjectives in the line ("diáfana mía") equate the beloved with the prism, and both are essentially equated with the poem itself, or poetry in general. This line embodies a semi-climax of the poem. As the first of two major points of union, it is symmetrically placed in the poem, in line 17, with the second point of union after 17 more lines, with the remaining verses functioning as a dénouement.[67] The vision or moment of illumination is only momentary, of course (like Eliot's moment in the rose garden in "Burnt Norton," from his *Four Quartets*). Then

---

67 If the heptasyllabic and shorter lines are combined into groups of fourteen syllables, this first point of union is placed in the fourteenth full line and the second point of union is fourteen full lines later, followed by the dénouement.

the protagonist is taken back in memory, now more specifically, to the scene of the *despedida* and his lover's departure.

Opening strophe five, the verse "Yo departí sus manos" combines the ideas of the protagonist gently talking with his beloved and their holding hands, an understanding "conversation" between hands as well as one with words. The line is expressed in the preterite tense (*departí*), referring to the day of her departure ("en aquella hora / gris de las estaciones") and implying that the separation of the couple is definite, permanent. The last three lines of this strophe contain some interesting images. In the verse "sus palabras mojadas se me echaron al cuello" there is an effective synaesthetic combination of auditory and tactile images in a compact form that is original and at the same time efficient, in that we understand easily what it means: the woman was crying while saying goodbye to her lover, the protagonist, and threw her arms around his neck in a strong embrace. Then, the train took her away from him. The violent image of "la arrancó de mis brazos" in juxtaposition with the above embrace is made even stronger by the description of the train as "sedienta de kilómetros," conveying the urgency of the departure. The visual effect on the page of two long lines surrounding a short line reflects the embrace, the woman's arms reaching for and surrounding the man's neck:

> sus palabras mojadas se me echaron al cuello,
> y una locomotora
> sedienta de kilómetros la arrancó de mis brazos.

The moment of separation is reflected in the structure

of the poem at this point. The inverted assonantal rhyme of the line endings (a-o, o-a, o-e, e-o, o-a, a-o) caused by the separated hemistichs echoes the reversal in the thematic situation that occurs in this strophe (union/separation). Also at this point of separation, the first of two major displacements in the established syllable/line structure occurs. Up to this point, all lines have been either full fourteen-syllable verses or heptasyllables (verses of seven syllables, equal to half a normal line) grouped in pairs (totaling fourteen syllables in each pair). Strophe five begins with a line of seven syllables ("Yo departí sus manos"), then adds another of seven syllables ("pero en aquella hora") which is semantically linked to the next line of seven syllables ("gris de las estaciones"). The first two lines combine to form fourteen syllables, but the next possible pair is interrupted by a full line of fourteen syllables ("sus palabras mojadas se me echaron al cuello"). Jumping over this interjection, the two heptasyllabic lines that combine to form fourteen syllables are "gris de las estaciones" and "y una locomotora" –the place and agent of the "crime," the separation. "Sus palabras mojadas se me echaron al cuello" is the desperate and tearful embrace interjected between these two heptasyllables, a sudden rush of emotion when the train whistle blows and the woman knows she has to leave. The embrace also prolongs the last moment of being together; it delays the moment when the train takes her away. As noted above, the two hemistichs surrounding the longer line reflect the lovers' embrace, her arms around his neck (and probably his arms around her). The hemistichs that are paired sequentially to complete the syllable count of a full *alejandrino* line are not the same lines as the semantically-linked pairs. The resulting pattern creates a woven effect that adds particular structural strength to this section of the poem. The intertwined verses represent the physical embrace and they also link past (union of the lovers) with future (separation). Thus, the present moment seems to stop time or unite all time, and the lovers' embrace is made "permanent" (timeless, eternal) in the actual lines of the poem. This meaningful displacement of structure occurs at the mid-point of the poem ("y una locomotora" is line 22 in this 44-line poem).

The next strophe (six) returns to the cold and lonely night when the protagonist is staring out into the dark sky. Now, there is only the memory and echo of the sound of his beloved's words, which seem cold because they are so distant and because the protagonist feels abandoned ("Hoy suenan sus palabras más heladas que nunca"). These feelings in strophe six are related to strophe seven's images that express the coldness of the night, and also to the loneliness they imply. The second verse of strophe six implies that the electric light bulb ("¡Y la locura de Edison a manos de la lluvia!") gives light but provides no heat or dryness against the cold, wet night, unlike an old-fashioned fireplace would do. A typical symbol of the modern man-made city, the light bulb here cannot defeat the higher natural forces.

The poem "Prisma" contains a series of images, especially images of light, that are reflected and refracted on various surfaces or are seen through the window glass. The light images are multiplied by these reflections either in mirrors or in water (the rain and the sea), and thus acquire a simultaneous multiplicity and unity through the union of extremes or opposites, such as sky and sea, and a certain permanence through the infinite reflections. This union links all of the light images to the prism and to the still point.

The protagonist is trying to escape from darkness, abandonment, separation, death –all of the negative forces– and trying to reach light, life, clarity, union. Perhaps for this reason he is transfixed by all of these images of light. The union of extremes, zenith and nadir, will help him in this pursuit, as was told in the eighth point of the tablets of the mythical gnostic Hermes Trismegistus (quoted here in a Spanish translation): "Sube de la tierra al cielo y de nuevo desciende a la tierra, y trae al regreso el poder de las cosas superiores e inferiores. Así tendrás la gloria del mundo entero. Por esta causa huirá de ti la oscuridad."[68]

Rubén Bonifaz Nuño refers to the above principle of Trismegistus in his introduction to *Las semillas del tiempo*, saying that, as the poet places the problem in a universal context, man's situation in cosmic time and space finds a correspondence in his own innermost time and space; in his heart, as we say. "Empieza el poeta por exponer su situación en ámbitos universales. La situación del hombre en el espacio y el tiempo cósmicos que, en última instancia, hallan correspondencia, como en la imagen de un espejo vivo, en el tiempo y el espacio de la interioridad humana. Es el principio guardado por las tablas de esmeralda de Trismegisto: 'como es arriba es abajo' " (p. 12). A modified phrasing of "as above, so below" for this case would be "as in the exterior world, so too in the interior world of each person," or "como es afuera, es adentro." This ideal correspondence between man's outer and inner realities is referred to many times in Maples Arce's poetry. The union

---

[68] Emma Susana Speratti-Piñero, *El ocultismo en Valle-Inclán* (London: Tamesis Books Limited, 1974) 175-176.

of interior and exterior is something that the protagonist desires to achieve. It is a vanquishing of the modern feeling of abandonment or isolation (cf. Eliot's *Prufrock*) and discontinuity from the past (cf. Eliot's *Wasteland*). For Maples Arce, the discontinuity is from an ideal harmonious world. For him, the transitoriness and consequent condition of separation in the modern world need to be replaced by permanence and union in order to regain harmony. What the story of Trismegistus teaches is that union, specifically uniting the powers of zenith and nadir, will make the darkness go away ("por esta causa huirá de ti la oscuridad") and thus, we infer, bring us into the light, along with all of its positive connotations.

In "Prisma," the windows of the room are mirrors into the protagonist's past and into his soul, providing another connection between the outer world and his inner reality. Strophe seven begins, "El cielo es un obstáculo para el hotel inverso / refractado en las lunas sombrías de los espejos." The hotel across the street, reflected in the mirror, is pushing up in its height against the resisting force of darkness. The poem contains multiple and infinite reflections of the moon, the star, the park scene, and the hotel. They are seen through the window, in the mirror, and possibly even in the raindrops on the window, each reflecting in the other, as with two facing mirrors, spreading the image, multiple now, to each reflecting surface. This refraction is also shown in the structure of the images and of the entire poem. The infinite series of reflections is linked to the concentric circles referred to at the end of the poem.

The next verse of strophe seven, "Los violines se suben como la champaña," is probably the recollection of a bar or restaurant that the couple went to before going to the train station. As the protagonist remembers it or possibly hears it now, the music goes to his head just as the champagne has gone to his head. Along with a synaesthetic image complex that includes the latent sound of the music, the restaurant, and the champagne, plus the feel and taste of the bubbly champagne, there is an appropriate break in the rhythm of the very line that alludes to the distorted perception experienced in drunkenness. The first half of line 28, "los violines se suben," seems like a typical heptasyllabic hemistich for this poem, but when the remainder of the line is added, "como la champaña," the diphthong in *violines* must be broken in order to extend the syllable count to fourteen, thus creating hemistichs of eight and six syllables rather than the previous seven-seven pattern. This conscious upset of rhythm, though minor, is accentuated by the metonymic use of violins for music, and the connection of music to rhythm, at the precise point where the break in rhythm occurs.

Back to the present moment in strophe seven, perhaps feeling somewhat inebriated (the multiple images therefore dizzying), the protagonist looks at himself in the mirror and notices the dark circles under his eyes, which are a measure of how late it is and of the effect of his insomnia. He is reminded of the coldness of the night, expressed in the image of empty coat hangers rattling in the closet (maybe he gets his coat) like shivering little skeletons, echoing the loneliness of being there alone in that room: "y mientras las ojeras sondean la madrugada, / el invierno huesoso tirita en los percheros." The dark "u" sound in *madrugada* and *huesoso* echoes the abundant u-a rhyme of the previous strophe: "Hoy suenan sus palabras más heladas que nunca. / ¡Y la locura de Edison a manos de la lluvia!" Both sound and theme are dark and cold, and at the end of strophe seven (line 30), the protagonist has reached the lowest point of the poem.

However, as for Heraclitus, the mystic San Juan de la Cruz and T. S. Eliot in his *Four Quartets*, "the way up is the way down," and suddenly at this lowest point the protagonist reaches a state of total release, letting-go, fatigue, giving in to it: "Mis nervios se derraman." There is at this point a connection between the exterior and interior worlds, seen in the protagonist's subsequent recalling of the image of the falling star, and at the moment in which his own nerves let go, spill over, the star hits the water and sinks. The liquid image of *derraman* connects with *el agua* and they foreshadow the concentric circles seen at the end of the poem. "Mis nervios se derraman. / La estrella del recuerdo / naufraga en el agua / del silencio."

This moment of exterior/interior connection (plus the union of zenith and nadir by the star), and the protagonist's state of mind when it occurs, lead to the climax of the poem. Curiously enough, it is "el agua del *silencio*" which appears precisely before the climax in the next line. This is significant if one remembers that earlier "el *silencio* amarillo suena sobre mis ojos" came just before the verse "¡Prismal, diáfana mía, para sentirlo todo!" (the first moment of clarity and vision and emotional climax). Both moments of silence seem to be like the calm, peaceful, state of grace (or Eliot's "grace of sense") which is achieved just before the moment of illumination or revelation, when one arrives at the still point at the center of the turning world, timelessness within time. If one notes the protagonist's condition as "a still point at the center of the hour" at the beginning of the poem, and his ultimate illumination near the end, it seems clear that the poem as a whole achieves timelessness within time, as the total prismatic vision takes place in a single instant, but an instant that lasts for what seems an entire night. Maples Arce structures "Prisma" in such a way that the thoughts and images that lead to the moment of illumination are gradually interspersed with "sparks" of light, and thus creates another allusion to the multiplicity-plus-unity of the images.

During the above-mentioned silence or calm, the state of grace, the ultimate point of union is reached; it is also the structural and thematic climax of the poem: "Tú y yo / coincidimos / en la noche terrible." This is the moment of illumination, the vision, in which the protagonist captures essence in time, and where he also achieves direct communication with his beloved, signaled by the use of "tú" for the first time in the poem. Bright sounds also appear with the inclusion of the "i" sound several times from here to the end of the poem. This climax is symmetrically placed in relation to the first vision ("¡Prismal ...") and, as at the earlier moment of separation ("arrancó"), the moment of union here is emphasized by the second structural displacement of lines from the established pattern. If one combines the short lines to reach seven syllables, then to the end of the poem there is a smooth pairing of seven- plus seven-syllable groups and a final verse of fourteen syllables. However, in order to have seven syllables at the point of union in strophe eight, there must be an overlapping of lines, using "Tú y yo" twice (with "del silencio" and with "coincidimos") in order to complete the pattern. The various combinations that result throughout strophe eight reinforce the bond between the exterior and interior worlds, and the word "coincidimos" is particularly appropriate.

The achievement of total union —the two lovers, the outer and inner worlds— brings the whole poem together. The protagonist, the star, the woman, the prism, and the poem are ultimately joined, all one and the same thing, brought together in the poet's "meditación temática" —that is, united in the poem itself. It is the "meditación temática / deshojada en jardines" (the last two lines of strophe eight) which joins the insomniac thoughts, the park scenes, the flowers, the woman, the contemplation of the lovers' relationship, and the poem. The complete sentence is "Tú y yo / coincidimos / en la noche terrible, / meditación temática / deshojada en jardines." This sentence is a synthesis of the protagonist's thoughts.

The remaining lines of the poem are a dénouement, recapitulating some of the images seen previously out the window, summarizing the situation. The poem concludes by saying, "El amor y la vida / son hoy sindicalistas, / y todo se dilata en círculos concéntricos." Rubén Bonifaz Nuño comments:

> Y el poema se cierra con una reflexión sobre la vida moderna, con sus luchas, sus uniones, su necesidad de organización social, predominante sobre los deseos individuales; vida que se dilata desde el centro del hombre, ese punto en medio de la hora, equidistante al naufragio de las estrellas en el silencio, que, como una piedra que cae en la superficie líquida, engendra en sí mismo la magnitud sin término de lo existente (p. 17).

This last sentence of "Prisma" functions as an epilogue to the poem and conveys the feeling that the protagonist seems to have at the end of his "meditación temática." He feels that love and life are so difficult, to the point that some days it seems like there is a lobby against a person's success in them. The last verse reminds the reader that this difficulty has tested humans throughout time, and that we are all connected somehow in the larger design. Yet, even if the lovers cannot be together in the outside world, they can be together in the world of the poem, there transcending time and place. The verse "Y todo se dilata en círculos concéntricos" embodies the idea of multiplicity and unity. The image illustrates the creative energy which emanates from the still point infinitely outward, and radiates back again each time it connects with an object within the infinite circumference. When a pebble falls into a pool of water, it sends out concentric circles that are its own image reproduced and radiating outward. The energy of that action is sent out through both space and time, and it energizes other objects it meets. All things are thus connected. The same thing happens in "Prisma" when the star falls into the sea (or appears to) and when the protagonist's "nervios se derraman." This idea of concentric circles radiating out from a point of energy is found in many works of literature, each with its own particular variation of the same theme, as occurs with the idea of the still point. The center still point and the circumference are both ultimately the same thing. They are also associated with the creator, life, light, energy, essence, and consciousness, as well as the interrelatedness of all being.[69] The prism is a similar concept; it is at once unity and multiplicity, and therefore ultimately denies separation. It is both still point and circumference, pure light and component colors, the multiple

---

69 Cf. Emily Dickinson's poem "Circumference" (and others), Walt Whitman's "Sparkles at the Wheel," chapter VII of William Faulkner's *Absalom, Absalom!*, Dante's vision of God and the rose circle in *Paradiso*, John Donne's *"No man is an island"*.

possibilities of an image, all and one.

The entire poem "Prisma" works as a prism does. The images in it exist in a dynamic state–they are spatialized, kineticized and temporalized–often uniting opposites and thus creating a third reality in their union. Within that union is contained the multiplicity and simultaneity of all things. As light goes through a prism, it is refracted, split up, bent, distorted, and angled to reveal its component parts, much as a Cubist painting shows a scene simultaneously from many different angles or on many different planes at the same time. Images of time and space are juxtaposed or combined in the poem to exist in a dynamic (and therefore modern) state. The dynamic quality of the experience extends to the reader being required to reconstruct the situation and thus participate in the experience.

It is possible to analyze the poems of *Andamios Interiores* by separating word groups and showing how those groups interrelate and work together toward an end point which is the culmination of the poem, equal to the thematic climax and the structural point of union. In "Prisma," for example, using only the fragment "Mis nervios se derraman. / La estrella del recuerdo / naufraga en el agua / del silencio," significant word categories are, nouns: *nervios, estrella, recuerdo, agua, silencio*; verbs: *se derraman, naufraga*; time: *recuerdo*; space: *se derraman, naufraga*; up: *estrella*; down: *naufraga*; horizontal: *se derraman*; liquid: *agua, se derraman*; motion: *se derraman, estrella, (recuerdo), naufraga, (nervios)*; stasis: *agua, silencio*. Of the five nouns, three are imagistically involved in motion in the poem (*nervios, estrella, recuerdo*). The other two nouns are the receptors (*agua, silencio*) of the first three and also of the two verbs (*se derraman, naufraga*–actions done by the first three nouns). That is, the nerves spill out, the star falls, memory goes back to the past. The nerves and the star both become or fall into water images (liquid). The star and memory fall into silence. *Se derraman* and *naufraga* are both associated in this fragment with water and silence. The element of time gains spatial qualities due to the motion verbs, and gains concrete shape due to the visual images moving through it. The two liquid images are related to each other not only by their nature but also by the implied connection between the nerves letting go and the star hitting the water at the same moment. Both liquid images have motion possibility, but one (*agua*) takes on stasis and one (*se derraman*) takes on motion. The image of upwardness (star) moves down, and what is concentrated (tense nerves) spreads out. All of the words involved with motion finally move toward (the signals of) stasis. At this moment of stasis comes the point of ultimate union, "Tú y yo coincidimos," the climax of the poem. In other words, in the poem everything is in a process of moving toward the point of union. This happens both in the content and in the form, as we have seen already, and also at the level of signs or interrelated word (meaning) groups.

The motion is all initiated and contained in the phenomenon of the poem and the protagonist's insomniac meditation. Outside forces do not figure in (he is awake, the rest of the city is asleep); it all happens within the work of art. Arqueles Vela describes this situation, speaking of Maples Arce's *Andamios Interiores* as a whole: "Su libro parece un jardín a la media noche, todo encendido de frutos incandescentes y policromados. Solitario. Sonoro. Múltiple. Las siluetas de los paseantes se han estatizado como árboles. Las voces de los paseantes se han congelado en las fuentes. Un jardín en donde las sombras de las cosas no se sabe si se proyectaron. Si se van a proyectar..."[70]

After "Prisma," the remaining nine poems of *Andamios Interiores* are divided into three groups, titled "Flores aritméticas," "Voces amarillas" and "Perfumes apagados." Many of the themes and structural devices of "Prisma" continue throughout the volume. These include the scenario of the melancholic protagonist contemplating the loss of love, the absence of a lover, or the lack of a common outlook on life shared by himself and the woman he loves. One unique and interesting aspect of the majority of these poems is the representation of the poetic attitude of the late nineteenth century as exhibited by the decadents: feelings of *mal du siècle*, neurasthenia, spleen, world-weariness and despair plague the women of *Andamios Interiores*.[71] The

---

70 Arqueles Vela, "Los 'Andamios Interiores' de Maples Arce," *El Universal* 31 agosto 1922, segunda edición: 8.

71 *Mal du siècle* = disquietude, pessimism, melancholy, lack of confidence in the future. *Neurasthenia* = a state of excessive fatigue and irritability, due to emotional conflict. *Spleen* = the spleen was believed to secrete black bile, too much of it causing depression, gloom, melancholy (from the Greek, *melan* - black, *cholé* - bile). *The New Lexicon Webster's Dictionary of the English Language, Encyclopedic Edition*, 1987 ed.

Avoir le spleen = (Fr.) to be in the dumps. *Cassell's New Compact French Dictionary*, 1975 ed.

Decadence = "In literature, an aspect and offshoot of the 19th-century Symbolist and aesthetic (Art for Art's Sake) movements. Arising from the bohemian protest against bourgeois society in France from the 1840s onward, *decadence took and emphasized the febrile, neurasthenic, and world-weary element in the Symbolist presumption about the poet,* and also dramatized its belief in the essential amoralism of art. As in much Symbolism, it was a subject-matter and an imaginative response enacted as a life style. The motto of its exponents (known as the decadents) was Rimbaud's: 'The poet makes himself a seer by a long, intensive, and reasoned disordering of all the senses.' Intensified by a sense of cultural anomie, a high-style dandyism, and a fin de siècle despair, it has particular associations with the 1880s and 1890s, e.g. Huysman's *À Rebours* (1884) and in England Swinburne, Wilde, Aubrey Beardsley (artistic director of The Yellow Book), Ernest Dowson, and Lionel Johnson. With the Wilde-Queensberry trial in 1895 the public display of decadence suffered a setback. However, as a poetic sensibility it has remained important in modern writing..." Malcolm Bradbury, *The Harper Dictionary of Modern Thought*, 157.

protagonist considers this attitude to be outdated. This "amarillismo" is part of the old poetics that Maples Arce wants to replace with a new, revitalized, modern sensibility. Even though the protagonist is somewhat melancholy and nostalgic at times, his attitude is not that of the women who appear in the poems of *Andamios Interiores*, especially those in the "Voces amarillas" section, who display a hopeless *fin de siècle* despair, are ill or want to die. Their neurasthenia and *mal du siècle* and the morbid actions of characters or objects around them are things that the protagonist observes but does not espouse. The avant-garde relishes the shock of expressions such as "se atraganta un pájaro los últimos compases," but *Estridentismo* opposes phrases like "me quisiera morir." Perhaps the old, ill, world-weary attitude is shown principally in the women of these poems (as opposed to men) in order to emphasize the fact that the protagonist is looking for "una mujer estridentista" but he has not found one yet. He seems to find her (or his true poetic muse) in *Poemas Interdictos*, especially in the car-ride poem, "80 H.P.," during the height of *Estridentismo*.

As sub-groups of *Andamios Interiores*, "Flores aritméticas" presents the decadent/illness/death imagery in groups of people or in the city in general; "Voces amarillas" shows it in dialogues between the protagonist and a woman or women. "Perfumes apagados" laments the loss of a compatible lover and confronts the difficulty of separation. Perhaps "Prisma" (which does not deal directly with this issue) is the most ideal poem of the volume; it was written last and is the signal work of the 1922 book. A tally of vocabulary in these poems of *Andamios Interiores* reveals an almost even number of modern/affirmative words vs.

illness/death/negative words, except in "Por las horas de cuento" and "En la dolencia estática," which are dominated by the darker side.[72]

The subtitle of *Andamios Interiores* is "Poemas radiográficos"–x-ray poems. When Maples Arce was writing these poems (1919-1922), he wanted to show readers that Mexican poetry was "ill" and in need of acute medical care in the form of modernization. By exposing the skeletal and organic ills of the poetry of the day and of the public's outdated attitude toward literature, at the same time as he suggested a new "interior scaffolding" for poems (e.g. "Prisma"), Maples Arce paved the way for a rejuvenation and modernization of Mexican poetry. If the poems treating this theme in *Andamios Interiores* are the diagnosis, *Estridentismo* is a form of shock treatment, and *Poemas Interdictos* is the cure.

"Esas rosas eléctricas…"

Esas rosas eléctricas de los cafés con música
que estilizan sus noches con "poses" operísticas,
languidecen de muerte, como las semifusas,
en tanto que en la orquesta se encienden anilinas
y bosteza la sífilis entre "tubos de estufa".

Equivocando un salto de trampolín, las joyas
se confunden estrellas de catálogos Osram.
Y olvidado en el hombro de alguna Margarita,
deshojada por todos los poetas franceses,
me galvaniza una de estas pálidas "ísticas"
que desvelan de balde sus ojeras dramáticas,
y un recuerdo de otoño de hospital se me entibia.

---

72 "Prisma," "Al margen de la lluvia," "Tras los adioses últimos" and "Como una gotera" do not treat this theme overtly.

Y entre sorbos de exóticos nombres fermentados,
el amor, que es un fácil juego de cubilete,
prende en una absurda figura literaria
el dibujo melódico de un vals incandescente.

El violín se accidenta en sollozos teatrales,
y se atraganta un pájaro los últimos compases.

Este techo se llueve.
La noche en el jardín
se da toques con pilas eléctricas de éter,
y la luna está al último grito de París.

En la sala ruidosa,
el mesero académico descorchaba las horas.

The poem "Esas rosas eléctricas" is akin to a party at Jay Gatsby's mansion or something of a macabre farce in the style of Charles Addams' "Addams Family." This poem is a good example of how Maples Arce's destruction-creation cycle functions much like that spoken of in the prose sections of William Carlos Williams' *Spring and All*, as discussed above. In both works, the new takes over the old and recharges it with energy. Similarly, *Vanguardismo* took over what had been the realm of *Postmodernismo* and brought poetry up to date with the modern world. *Vanguardismo* infused life into what was moribund, destroying the old in order to create the new. The images of "Esas rosas eléctricas" are unusual, morbose, brass. The poem is an assault on the poetic images of *lo viejo*. As Maples Arce said, it was time to "torcerle el cuello al Dr. González Martínez."

The scenario of "Esas rosas eléctricas" can be interpreted as follows: the "rosas eléctricas" are women in a café, nightclub, or party, sitting in studied dramatic poses as they listen to the orchestra play. Sparkles of light from the women's jewelry flash about the room. Forgotten by his old-fashioned date ("olvidado en el hombro de alguna Margarita, / deshojada por todos los poetas franceses"), the protagonist's attention is suddenly caught by another woman —one of the *rosas eléctricas* stares at him: "me galvaniza una de estas pálidas "ísticas" / que desvelan de balde sus ojeras dramáticas." The adjective "electric" effectively modernizes the rose of traditional poetry, and galvanization is a modern invention, but the protagonist's attraction to the woman does not last (this is hinted at by the reference to her as a "pálida 'ística' "). The "y" at the beginning of line 12 might more appropriately be "pero," because the protagonist says his emotions are soon cooled by "un recuerdo de otoño de hospital." The death/illness image complex overpowers and extinguishes any spark of amorous interest there might have been. From this line onward, it seems clear that the protagonist considers himself apart from the rest of the people in the café, somehow distanced, and we begin to see how this poem illustrates one characteristic of *Andamios Interiores*: a lack of communication, or a difference in perspective on the world, between the protagonist and the other people in the café. He represents the modern world and he desires to express it in poetry; they represent the outdated 19th-century poetic attitude. The modern words in the poem express the point of view or interpretation of the protagonist ("esas rosas eléctricas," "estrellas de catálogos Osram"–a reference to an electric lightbulb company, "vals incandescente," "pilas eléctricas de éter"). Those words contrast with the stale, decadent, sickly images with which the 19th-century minded characters present themselves ("poses' operísticas," "languidecen de muerte," "bosteza la sífilis," "desvelan de balde sus ojeras dramáticas," "sollozos teatrales").

Strophe one contains some interesting visual images, described from the point of view of the protagonist. The women, perhaps leaning back with their elbows on tables or with their arms outstretched in operatic poses, look like musical notes on a staff. Men are wearing stove-pipe hats. The orchestra is playing some explosively emotional, sentimental music, which, interestingly, is described with mostly visual rather than auditory images ("en la orquestra se encienden anilinas;" aniline is an oily poisonous liquid chemical used in making dyes, medicines and explosives. It might be a metaphor for the orange-blue glow of lighting a cigarette or it might refer to "explosive" musical notes). Strophe two contrasts light and dark: the sparkling jewel/star/electric light image complex mentioned above and the women's pale faces juxtaposed with the dramatic dark circles under their eyes and the dark feeling of "un recuerdo de otoño de hospital." Also contrasted are attention and abandon (being stared at by one woman vs. being forgotten by another).

In strophe three, the protagonist mentions the exotic cocktails served at the café, and refers to the music again, saying that love, which is a game of chance, sets the melody to the lyrics. He calls the lyrics an absurd literary form—seemingly negative—but refers to the song as an incandescent waltz—a traditional rhythm updated by a modern-world adjective, which we must assume was attractive to him. It is possible that in strophe three the protagonist is writing a love poem and imagining a melody, while sipping cocktails at his table. The melodramatic sounds in strophe four bring him back to the "reality" of the café. He describes the orchestra's music as overly dramatic, almost suicidal: "El violín se accidenta en sollozos teatrales, / y se ataganta un pájaro los últimos compases." This seems to be the crisis point of the poem, the lowest point; but here the form is creative: the waltz rhythm of the music is echoed by the frequent use of *esdrújulas* here and throughout the poem, and the bird (singer?) and violin of strophe four are described in shocking, unusual images, similar to many expressions used in the *estridentista* manifestos. In these two verses (strophe four), the "old" dies—chokes on the music—making way for the "new."

Strophe five accentuates the separation of the protagonist from the rest of the people in the café, as he goes outside to the terrace and gazes at the night sky. That open-air scene feels like a breath of fresh air to the reader after the stifling "bosteza la sífilis" atmosphere inside the nightclub. "La noche en el jardín / se da toques con pilas eléctricas de éter, / y la luna está al último grito de París." The stars twinkle like battery-powered lights in the upper spheres of space, giving new life to the night,[73] and the moon is dressed in the latest fashion —they foreshadow the fresh new world that *vanguardismo* will bring. This night sky is like the twigs in William Carlos Williams' poem (#I) "Spring and All," also known as "By the Road to the Contagious Hospital," at the moment of change from late winter to early spring, as the plants "grip down and begin to awaken." In a prose section, Williams declares, "destruction and creation are simultaneous," "suddenly it is at an end. THE WORLD IS NEW."[74]

Regarding structure, the protagonist's spiritual and

---

[73] "Ether" in this sense refers to the upper regions of space. In those years, it was thought that the gas ether filled space (cf. "ethereal").
[74] Williams, 182, 183, 213.

physical separation from the nightclub crowd is accentuated in strophe five (while he is outside on the terrace) by an off-center division of the hemistichs in line 22 (5+9 syllables rather than 7+7): "y la luna está al último grito de París." This irregular division or rhythm signals another important point: separation from the crowd and the interior (self)/exterior world connection achieved between the protagonist and the night sky as he stands out on the terrace. The outside-world images here are all zenith (moon, stars), no nadir, and therefore very positive images to the protagonist. This section is the climax of the poem. It gives a feeling of hope for the future, for a fresh, new beginning. The final strophe of the poem serves as a dénouement or epilogue, showing the somewhat stiff, formal waiter inside the noisy café uncorking wine bottles as the hours pass (literally, "uncorking the hours"), as if merely marking time. In that decadent café society, there is no sense of movement toward the future, only a stagnation. In contrast, the protagonist is attracted to the expanse of space, fresh air, lively modern imagery and innovative poetic style. The separated and unpaired hemistichs near the end of the poem that refer to the terrace (lines 19 and 20) and the inside of the café (line 23) emphasize this separation of the protagonist from the café world.

Earlier in the poem, a pause caused by punctuation upsets the normal hemistich division of line six, which refers to the pieces of jewelry as if they had bounced off by a jump on a trampoline and mixed with the stars in the sky, glowing like a conglomeration of electric lights, form thus reflecting content: "Equivocando un salto de trampolín, las joyas / se confunden estrellas de catálogos Osram." Punctuation similarly changes the normal hemistich division in line 14 after "el amor," where love is referred to as chance or a dice game. The jumbling of the structure is justified by the implied reference to the shaking and rolling of dice. The first total line break (separation of hemistichs onto different lines) occurs when the protagonist goes out to the terrace alone (lines 19 and 20).

The key to the transformation from old to new is the way Maples Arce combines words and word groups, creating original images and fresh ways of looking at the typical subjects of poetry. The subtitle of the section of *Andamios Interiores* that begins with "Esas rosas eléctricas" is "FLORES ARITMÉTICAS." This is the most difficult and most experimental section of *Andamios*. Flowers traditionally have appeared in poems (the rose as a symbol of love, for example) but here they are different, they are *aritméticas*. The title combines two worlds that usually do not meet in poetry: nature and numbers (mathematics). The poet does not directly destroy the traditional images, but he subverts tradition by putting words together in an energized way in the poem. In "Esas rosas eléctricas," in effect, he electrifies or electrocutes everything. As Williams says in *Spring and All*, you can make things new, make them your own, by adding your attitude, your perspective, how you see the world differently. Maples Arce effects change by means of creative adjectivization and contrasting semantic groups in this poem.

Some of the semantic groups found in "Esas rosas eléctricas" are: illness or death and destruction (twelve images), motion (ten), music (nine), electrical images (six), modernity (five), and stillness (two). Interestingly, although the main scenario described in the poem is one of a *mal du siècle*-suffering café society, that vision is sabotaged by the intervention of images of modernity and motion. The modern, dynamic images outnumber the images of illness, death and stillness by a ratio of more than 2 to 1. The most subtle subversion occurs in the inclusion of words like *semifusas* (64th notes) and *deshojada*, which indirectly imply abrupt motion, in verses that refer to stasis ("languidecen de muerte, como las semifusas") or to old-fashioned sentimentality ("deshojada por todos los poetas franceses"). The most obvious subversion is found in the combination of traditional poetic images (*rosas, el amor, vals, la noche en el jardín, la luna, el violín, un pájaro*) with modern adjectives ("rosas eléctricas," "vals incandescente") or with modern adjectival or verbal phrases ("el amor, que es un fácil juego de cubilete," "la noche en el jardín / se da toques con pilas eléctricas de éter," "y la luna está al último grito de París," "el violín se accidenta," "se ataganta un pájaro"). This kind of adjectivization (traditional noun + modern adjective; or modern noun + traditional adjective) and use of verb phrase (traditional noun + modern or non-traditional verb; or modern noun + traditional verb) is the most frequent and most identifying characteristic of Maples Arce's *estridentista* poems. This technique imbues "Esas rosas eléctricas" with a sense of imminent change. The old world is being subverted to invent the new. Destruction and creation are simultaneous. By the road to the contagious hospital (Williams), the roots grip down, getting ready for spring.

"Todo en un plano oblicuo..."

En tanto que la tisis –todo en un plano oblicuo—
paseante de automóvil y tedio triangular,

me electrizo en el vértice agudo de mí mismo.
Van cayendo las horas de un modo vertical.

Y simultaneizada bajo la sombra eclíptica
de aquel sombrero unánime,
se ladea una sonrisa,
mientras que la blancura en éxtasis de frasco
se envuelve en una llama d'Orsay de gasolina.

                    Me debrayo en un claro
                    de anuncio cinemático.

Y detrás de la lluvia que peinó los jardines
hay un hervor galante de encajes auditivos;
a aquel violín morado le operan la laringe
y una estrella reciente se desangra en suspiros.

Un incendio de aplausos consume las lunetas
de la clínica, y luego —¡oh anónima de siempre!—
desvistiendo sus laxas indolencias modernas,
reincide –flor de lucro—tras los impertinentes.

                    Pero todo esto es sólo
                    un efecto cinemático,
porque ahora, siguiendo el entierro de coches,
allá de tarde en tarde estornuda un voltaico
sobre las caras lívidas de los "players" románticos,
y florecen algunos aeroplanos de hidrógeno.

En la esquina, un "umpire" de tráfico, a su modo,
va midiendo los "outs", y en este amarillismo,
se promulga un sistema luminista de rótulos.

Por la calle verdosa hay brumas de suicidio.

The beginning of the poem "Todo en un plano oblicuo" again contrasts the world of "lo viejo," the old century and Bohème-like heroines suffering from *tisis* (tuberculosis, consumption), with the protagonist and his modern outlook. The poet transforms the old-fashioned elements by modifying them with modern adjectives: the *tisis* is "paseante de automóvil," the *tedio* is "triangular." Everything is seen "en un plano oblicuo." Geometrization is combined with avant-garde images and words referring to the modern world ("me electrizo en el vértice agudo de mí mismo") in a lively structure full of metrical elision and jumps across punctuation. The way the second, third and sixth strophes of this poem are placed on the page gives a hint of the triangularity and obliqueness referred to in the poem. The geometrical words provide a visual sense of movement along a plane (*vértice, vertical, triangular, oblicuo*). As the poem continues, a series of traditional poetic images (sunset, perfume, rain, gardens, lace, violin, star) become dynamic as they are combined with modern expressions, creating a poem rich in visual, auditory and kinetic imagery. What was dying is rejuvenated; what was about to become stasis is reactivated.

The middle section of the poem (strophes four and five) presents a complicated medical/cinematic metaphor–describing a movie theater as if it were a surgical theater (operating room)–whose main effect in the context of the total poem is to compare illusion to reality. This medical metaphor continues the illness/death imagery as seen in "Esas rosas eléctricas": "a aquel violín morado le operan la laringe / y una estrella reciente se desangra en suspiros," "la clínica," "desvistiendo," "reincide."

The story line of the poem seems to go as follows: the protagonist is out driving as afternoon turns into evening. As the sun sets and darkness falls ("la sombra eclíptica / de aquel sombrero unánime"), the protagonist sees a woman, she smiles at him, and as she walks (or drives) by him the scent of her perfume mixes with that of the car's gasoline fumes. Enraptured, the protagonist is both figuratively and literally thrown out of gear: his car stops in the light of a movie marquee. Here Maples Arce takes the French verb *débrayer* (to throw out of gear, to disengage, to declutch –to let the clutch out; in Spanish, *desembragar*) and conjugates it in the first person singular in Spanish: "me debrayo." (This practice of creating new words is not uncommon in Maples Arce's work.) The verse, "Me debrayo en un claro / de anuncio cinemático," is set off to the right side of the page as a separate strophe. This lineation reflects the abrupt stop –the car probably stalls– and emphasizes the dramatic effect the woman has on the protagonist. He gets out and follows her into the movie theater. The movie is a romantic love story with melodramatic music. Finally, the last scene fades into darkness and the movie ends. The audience breaks into applause. The protagonist looks for the woman but, in the confusion and activity, he cannot find her. There is another wave of applause, and suddenly he sees the woman through a pair of opera glasses. There is a word play here with *lunetas*, referring to both the lenses of the opera glasses (*los impertinentes*) and to the theater stalls. The movie theater is referred to as a clinic, as part of the medical metaphor, and in that context the applause seems to acknowledge a successful operation (cf. "le operan la laringe"). In the medical/cinematic image complex, this moment coincides with the end of the movie (applause), which signals the protagonist's chance to find the woman again. At first he despairs when he cannot locate her, feeling he will never meet her ("¡oh anónima de siempre!"). However, the "relapse" or second burst of applause coincides in this multi-level strophe with the "reappearance" of the woman as he finds her with the opera glasses. This moment ("flor de lucro," he exclaims) is the climax of the poem.

Unfortunately, the protagonist does not get together with the woman. Strophe five ends with the image of her seen through the opera glasses, and strophe six begins with an observation (set off to the right side of the page and thus emphasized), that all this is only a cinematic effect, an illusion, an elusive image. Strophes six, seven and eight function as an epilogue to the rest of the poem, commenting on life and the game of love. Outside, the long line of cars moving slowly through the street as the movie theater empties reminds the protagonist of a funeral cortege. Another intense visual image echoing the earlier light from the movie marquee (a moment of heightened emotion when he first saw the woman) finishes strophe six: from time to time "a voltaic sneezes" —that is, sparks fly from a short circuit on a streetcar wire, and the arc of light illuminates the faces of the people below (making them look pale– "lívidas"). These people are "los 'players' románticos' " —players in the game of love. That flash of light might illuminate the faces of two potential lovers seeing each other for the first time, a modern-day Romeo and Juliet. Strophe six ends with the image of some zeppelins ("aeroplanos de hidrógeno") in the sky, an ultra-modern invention, which are also illuminated by the flash of light. These illuminated images recall the film seen in the movie theater. In the movies of the period (e.g. a Rudolph Valentino film), actors' faces were pale, camera cuts were often abrupt, the projector flickered, dialogue for silent films was written in white on a black background and was interjected between the brighter light of acting scenes, and as always the darkened theater contrasted to the light images on the screen. This play between black and white and gray is illustrated in the series of light and dark images in Maples Arce's poem.

Strophe seven compares a policeman directing traffic on the corner to an umpire of a baseball game. As he points and waves and moves his arms in the various directions, it is as if he were "midiendo los 'outs'" of the game—in this case, not baseball but romance. Such is the scene there amid the signs and flashing lights of the commercial district of the city. Take your chances, play the game, see if you get a "green light."

The one verse which comprises strophe eight reminds the reader that, this time, the protagonist lost the game— he did not get together with the woman. The verse brings back the dark side of the issue, the loneliness and despair expressed so often by the protagonist in Maples Arce's works: "Por la calle verdosa hay brumas de suicidio." It is a dark night, and many people are alone, just as he was in "Prisma." Perhaps this is another motivation for the illness/death images: often winning and losing at love seems like life and death to us. The cinema image complex effectively communicates the elusive quality of the chance of finding love. The illusion on the movie screen cannot be held on to, it is there and then fades away; it is another example of transitoriness. What Maples Arce accomplishes is to capture this dynamic process in a poem. Like the movie, the romance game is active and "now," but it does not last, is not permanent. The same is true of a baseball game. However, the poem fixes the ideas and illusory moments in written form, and the dynamism is included in the poem's images and structure, thus achieving timelessness within time.

In the metrical structure of the poem, the frequent occurrence of elision (synalepha) reflects the continuous motion of the movie film, the line of cars, and the game of love that repeats and repeats in a continuous connecting cycle. The jumps over punctuation and the frequent *esdrújula* rhythm also contribute to the flowing movement. In contrast, the inclusion of a few breaks and interjections echoes the car being thrown out of gear and the isolated glimpses of the woman ("–todo en un plano oblicuo–," "–¡oh anónima de siempre–," "–flor de lucro–").

It is interesting to note the large number of geometric shapes and allusions to motion. They are a manifestation of the protagonist's emotions, swirling around in an interior vortex. They are also related to his interest in perspective, modernization, and the idea that everything depends on the way one looks at things. One shape, the triangle, as usual in Maples Arce's poetry, becomes the connection between the protagonist and the object of his contemplation, in this case the woman in the crowd who attracts his attention. He and she are two points of the triangle, and their union in the poem forms the third point or angle, thus completing the triangle. That is, a connection is achieved between the protagonist and the woman in the structure of the poem, even though they are not permanently united in the story of the poem. The protagonist loses in the game on the street, but in a way, he wins in the poem; there, they are together forever.

"A VECES, CON LA TARDE..."

A veces, con la tarde luida de los bordes,
un fracaso de alas se barre en el jardín.
Y mientras que la vida esquina a los relojes,
se pierden por la acera los pasos de la noche.

    Amarillismo
    gris.

Mis ojos deletrean la ciudad algebraica
entre las subversiones de los escaparates;
detrás de los tranvías se explican las fachadas
y las alas del viento se rompen en los cables.

Siento íntegra toda la instalación estética
lateral a las calles alambradas de ruido,
que quiebran sobre el piano sus manos antisépticas,
y luego se recogen en un libro mullido.

A través del insomnio centrado en las ventanas
trepidan los andamios de una virginidad,
y al final de un acceso paroxista de lágrimas,
llamas de podredumbre suben del bulevar.

Y equivocadamente, mi corazón payaso,
se engolfa entre nocturnos encantos de a 2 pesos:
amor, mi vida, etc., y algún coche reumático
sueña con un voltaico que le asesina el sueño.

Sombra laboratorio. Las cosas bajo sobre.
Ventilador eléctrico, champagne + F. T.
Marinetti = a
    Nocturno futurista
    1912.
Y 200 estrellas de vicio a flor de noche
escupen pendejadas y besos de papel.

The last poem of the "FLORES ARITMÉTICAS"

section, "A veces, con la tarde," is centered around these phrases: "la ciudad algebraica," "siento íntegra," "a través del insomnio," "amor, mi vida, etc.," and the reference at the end to the writing of poetry. The poem is set in the afternoon. As he often does, the protagonist is sitting on his balcony looking out over the city. The afternoon sun shines on the city, reflecting off metal and glass, casting long angular shadows at the end of the day. Something startles some birds that were near the balcony and they take off suddenly in flight (the use of "fracaso" cleverly breaks a solid image into pieces, a Cubist technique). The protagonist thinks about how life's daily activities square off, sectioning the day as the hours go by, like the hands of a clock forming angles and geometric shapes on the clock face. It is late afternoon turning into evening, which will turn into night.

> A veces, con la tarde luida de los bordes,
> un fracaso de alas se barre en el jardín.
> Y mientras que la vida esquina a los relojes,
> se pierden por la acera los pasos de la noche.

As is often the case, in this poem Maples Arce writes about twilight, the hour of transition and of magical possibilities. While afternoon turns into evening (cf. the last line of strophe one), one sign of the transition is the change of activities out on the street (e.g. from work to entertainment) as people walk by. Strophe two, offset and emphasized: "Amarillismo gris," gives the color and feeling of late afternoon, the long rays of the sun and long afternoon shadows. As the hours pass, the air gradually looks thicker, gray-mauve, and the sky turns twilight colors as the sun sets. It seems that here the sky is not purple and pink and orange; it is grayish yellow, a more urban, industrial, melancholic color. Correspondingly, the main mood words of the poem tend to be negative images: *fracaso, se pierden, subversiones, se rompen, ruido, quiebran, trepidan, mullido, insomnio, paroxista, podredumbre, equivocadamente, reumático, asesina, sombra, vicio, escupen, pendejadas.*

In strophe three, the protagonist looks out over the city and contemplates the shapes of the buildings and the streets (geometric, algebraic). The shop windows (displays) are subversive because they try to entice passersby to enter the stores. A streetcar goes by and, after it has passed, reveals behind it signs on the front of buildings, the names of stores, advertisements.

> Mis ojos deletrean la ciudad algebraica
> entre las subversiones de los escaparates;
> detrás de los tranvías se explican las fachadas
> y las alas del viento se rompen en los cables.

The presence of cables or telegraph wires is a frequent image in *estridentista* art (the work of Fermín Revueltas, for example), and they appear here in strophes three and four. Criss-crossing the city skyscape, they are a constant reminder of modern technology. The last line of strophe three describes the wind blowing between the rows of wires as if it were a bird maneuvering through man-made obstacles in the sky.

The fourth strophe begins, "Siento íntegra toda la instalación estética / lateral a las calles alambradas de ruido," an important phrase which carries force contextually, rhythmically, and in its placement. It is a conclusion drawn from what the protagonist has observed. The first three strophes of the poem show us what he sees (description), and then strophe four comments on it. The same process occurs with strophes five and six as description and strophe seven as conclusion. In this statement, "Siento íntegra ... ," the protagonist feels the elements of the scene and his place in it come together, he sees it all ("toda la instalación estética") as a coherent whole. The picture the protagonist paints of an algebraic, geometric, sun-reflecting, busy, alive, dynamic city in the grayish-yellow dusky twilight, is his world, his environment, the place in and out of which he moves.

Maples Arce's image of buildings rising up on each side of the busy city street is much like Mário de Andrade's triangle-forming street image in "Rua de São Bento," from *Pauliceía Desvairada*:

> Triângulo.
> Ha navios de vela para os meus naufrágios!
> E os cantares de uiara rua de São Bento ...
> Entre estas duas ondas plúmbeas,
> as minhas delícias das asfixias da alma!
> ...
> Entre estas duas ondas plúmbeas de casas plúmbeas,
> vê, lá nos muito-ao-longes do horizonte,
> a sua chaminé de céu azul![75]

Andrade echoes this triangular shape in the design on the costume (diamond shapes) of the Harlequin, the character in *Pauliceía Desvairada* who functions as the adventurer into society, linking the poet to the city and uniting all of the poems of the volume. Andrade looks out his window at the city (as he explains in the preface) and projects his alter-ego (Harlequin) onto the street scene. Maples Arce's equivalent to the Harlequin is the character I refer to as the protagonist.

---

75 Mário de Andrade, *Hallucinated City: Pauliceía Desvairada*, trans. Jack E. Tomlins (Kingsport, TN: Vanderbuilt University Press, 1968) 28.

In some notes he prepared for an interview, Maples Arce quotes Pedro Salinas on the use of a new kind of metaphor in poetry, which, by uniting two disparate elements, creates a new third reality in their combination.

> A su vez, Pedro Salinas, al estudiar la metáfora en la poesía de Jorge Carrera Andrade, dice: 'Hoy vemos la metáfora como un acto poético puro, forma nueva de percepción poética, que brota de la aproximación de dos objetos que a veces no tienen semejanza alguna entre sí. Fue Vico quien llamó a la metáfora un mito en pequeño. Y sabemos que la metáfora, para vivir, necesita subyugar o matar. Cuando se encuentra a sí misma, creando una tercera realidad, lo hace alzándose sobre las ruinas de las dos cosas comparadas que quedan esfumadas o muertas junto a la nueva y radiante cosa poética.'
>
> Este tipo de metáforas no fue percibido por los poetas de aquel entonces que siguieron jugando con los tradicionales artificios literarios.[76]

This kind of metaphor is similar to the triangle mentioned above. The triangular process creating a new third reality happens not only in the geometrical images in Maples Arce's poems but also in the typically avant-garde word combinations seen in his work, such as "vals incandescente," "parques afónicos," "cafés insomnes," "estrellas de vicio," "besos de papel." The unexpected combination of two previously unrelated elements creates a third image which exists uniquely in the poem. This combination of two opposing points to form a third point is represented by the triangle. What is achieved in the poem in that third reality is a permanent capturing of the union, timelessness within time. R. Gómez Robelo speaks of this phenomenon

---

76 Manuel Maples Arce, typescript notes for an interview, c. 1971, n. pag.

in his article about the Egyptian pyramids, which was published in the first issue of the *estridentista* magazine *Irradiador*:

> ... realizando la más noble empresa de la especie humana: la de fundir las dos formas antitéticas del conocimiento en la obra de arte.
> Dos son las misiones supremas de la suprema actividad estética: eternizar el momento; inmovilizar la eternidad.
> Los árabes dicen: 'Todo teme al tiempo, el tiempo sólo teme a las pirámides.' Porque en el triángulo de las pirámides, el tiempo ha quedado inmóvil.[77]

Several other poets and artists have used the same concept in their work. The painter Vasily Kandinsky wrote in his article "On the Spiritual in Art" of the acute-angled triangle as the life of the spirit (the life image, the life source). Comparable to the *estridentistas*' emphasis on emotion, Pablo Picasso said that a picture should be the pictorial equivalent of the emotion produced in the artist. Photographer Alfred Stieglitz and painter Georgia O'Keefe were concerned with the feeling an image gives. They noticed and took advantage of the vertical convergence effect caused when using old cameras to photograph two or more tall buildings surrounding another–this is the triangle street image found in Maples Arce's and Mário de Andrade's poems discussed above. A similar image appears in O'Keefe's oil painting of the Brooklyn Bridge, in which arches are formed by vertical cables, closely recalling (perhaps intentionally quoting) Sheeler and Strand's film "A Day in New York" and the photo "Manhatta." O'Keefe's goal was not realism but the reality that

---

[77] R. Gómez Robelo, "Las Pirámides," *Irradiador* 1, eds. Manuel Maples Arce y Fermín Revueltas (México, septiembre de 1923): n. pag.

we perceive.[78] This seems to be Maples Arce's goal, as well.

American poet Wallace Stevens, in his poem "The Idea of Order at Key West," works with the triangle form in his image construction. For Stevens, the union of "the thing" and "the song" about it in the poem creates "the Art." The perception of this combination leads to a heightened consciousness; the combination itself creates a new reality. Art orders reality. In Stevens' poem, the woman's song does not change the actual existence of the thing she sings about (the sea), but it does change Stevens' perception of it. The only reality humankind can know is the one it perceives. So too, the poetic image influences the reader's perception of the objects described.

> It was her voice that made
> The sky acutest at its vanishing.
> She measured to the hour its solitude.
> She was the single artificer of the world
> In which she sang. And when she sang, the sea,
> Whatever self it had, became the self
> That was her song, for she was the maker. Then we,
> As we beheld her striding there alone,
> Knew that there never was a world for her
> Except the one she sang and, singing, made.[79]

Similarly, William Carlos Williams combines elements of the objective world (things, the objective universe) with the subjective world (the universe of the mind: Ideas, imagination) to form the word (the poem), which is the

---

[78] Sarah Whitaker Peters, "Georgia O'Keefe and Photography: Sources and Transformation," lecture, Memorial Art Gallery, Rochester NY, March 8, 1988.

[79] Wallace Stevens, from "The Idea of Order at Key West," *Chief Modern Poets of Britain and America, Volume II: Poets of America*, eds. Gerald DeWitt Sanders, John Herbert Nelson, M. L. Rosenthal (London: Mac-Millan, 1970) II-145.

new third reality created by the union of the other two. T. S. Eliot discusses a similar idea in his dissertation, saying that the union and mixture of subject (personal feelings, the psyche) with object (thoughts, intellect, epistemology) together form our perception of immediate experience.[80]

Returning to Maples Arce's poem "A veces, con la tarde," the last two lines of strophe four ("Siento íntegra toda la instalación estética / lateral a las calles alambradas de ruido, / que quiebran sobre el piano sus manos antisépticas, / y luego se recogen en un libro mullido") suggest the opening and closing of a business day in the city: a fresh start every morning, hours of hustle and bustle, then tallying up and closing the books at the end of the work day. There is a sense of the work day as a coherent unit, noisy but ordered, recalling the verse "la vida esquina a los relojes" from strophe one.

In strophe five it is night, the protagonist is suffering his habitual insomnia and staring out the window. Similar to events in Alfred Hitchcock's movie "Rear Window," some of the scenes observed out the window are unpleasant: innocent young women being taunted to the point of tears by aggressive men, giving the observer the feeling that "llamas de podredumbre suben del bulevar." The architectural imagery of previous strophes (*la acera, la ciudad algebraica, los escaparates, los tranvías, las fachadas, los cables, las calles alambradas*) continues in skillful metaphors in strophe five, applying the concrete images of *andamios* and *un acceso* to abstract emotions felt by people in other apartments and in the street ("trepidan los an-

---

[80] Sanford Schwartz, "Eliot and the Objectification of Emotion," conference paper, T. S. Eliot Centennial conference, University of Maine at Orono, 18-20 August 1988.

damios de una virginidad," "al final de un acceso paroxista de lágrimas").

Strophe six turns from the observed to the observer. The protagonist says that he gets involved in "nocturnos encantos de a 2 pesos: / amor, mi vida, etc.,"–romantic dreams or misplaced affection–but eventually he is brought back to reality by some mundane noise or event that shatters the illusion ("y algún coche reumático / sueña con un voltaico que le asesina el sueño").

Strophe seven comments on the observations made in strophes five and six. The first line of strophe seven, "Sombra laboratorio. Las cosas bajo sobre," suggests that the events of nighttime street life (or of an insomniac's revelries) are like experiments in a lab and our destiny is a mystery unknown to us, like the contents of a sealed envelope. The rest of the strophe gives the formula for an ideal evening: an electric fan, champagne, and F. T. Marinetti –these add up to a futurist evening, 1912 style (the date would refer to the heydey of Italian Futurism). This seems to sound attractive, but just as the "coche reumático" brought the protagonist back to reality at the end of strophe six, the last two lines of strophe seven bring him out of his dream about a perfect futurist evening. These lines either make fun of romantic poetry (cf. "Y nada de hojas secas"), or demonstrate a lack of self-confidence on the part of the protagonist and a feeling that the poems he tries to write as he stares out his window are stupid, useless dreams, because he is still alone. "Y 200 estrellas de vicio a flor de noche / escupen pendejadas y besos de papel."

Structurally, "A veces, con la tarde" has a pattern of introduction (strophe one), mood set (strophe two), observation of city (strophe three), comment/conclusion (strophe four), observation of other people (strophe five), observation of self (strophe six), comment/conclusion (strophe seven). There are two points of major emphasis: "Amarillismo gris" (strophe two) and "Nocturno futurista / 1912," which are set off to the far right side and right of center, respectively. Both of these emphasized points give a dual sensation when read in context. First, the reader feels that the expression is an apt label for the descriptive passage immediately preceding it, and then a contrary emotion is evoked by the expression's juxtaposition with the verses that follow it. "Amarillismo gris" sums up the feeling of strophe one, but contrasts to the affirmation of strophes three and four. "Nocturno futurista / 1912" is the result of the equation formulated in lines two and three of strophe seven: "Ventilador eléctrico, champagne + F. T. / Marinetti = a / Nocturno futurista / 1912." The reader supposes this equation to be an affirmative expression, but when seen later in the context of the two lines that follow it and end the poem, the feeling given is one of depression, frustration and loneliness. This ambivalence is another manifestation of the duality felt by the protagonist in his world: a positive attraction to modernity and dynamism, but a feeling that those same qualities are too transitory and elusive.

The innovative use of mathematical symbols and numerals in strophe seven (+, =, 1912, 200) adds visual impact to the poem and hints at the typographical creativity of Italian Futurist and Dadaist poetry. One "optical illusion" that results from this typography is that the verses (e.g. "Marinetti = a" and "1912") look very short. When the verses are read, however, the words form typical seven-syllable hemistichs ("Ventilador eléctrico, champagne 'más efe te' / Marinetti 'es igual' a / Nocturno futurista / 'mil novecientos doce' "). This attention adds further emphasis to the middle of strophe seven and these verses become the most intense and concentrated part of the poem. With the detailing of natural, urban and human elements, the first six strophes of the poem lead up to the formula for a "nocturno futurista." The form reinforces and echoes the content.

The poem "A veces, con la tarde" contains several images that combine the concrete and the abstract by pairing words normally not associated with each other: "tarde luida de los bordes," "un fracaso de alas," "la vida esquina a los relojes," "ciudad algebraica," "subversiones de los escaparates," "se explican las fachadas," "las alas del viento se rompen," "instalación estética," "alambradas de ruido," "los andamios de una virginidad," "un acceso paroxista," "llamas de podredumbre," "coche reumático," "algún coche ... sueña," "un voltaico ... asesina," "sombra laboratorio," "estrellas de vicio," "besos de papel." The majority of these images unite a concrete object with an abstract concept. This union both concretizes the abstract element and abstracts the concrete; their combination forms a new third reality or the apex of the triangle, as mentioned above.

This process of combining words that normally are not paired can be compared to Mário de Andrade's theory of the use of melody, harmony and polyphony (ultimately achieving simultaneity) in poetry, as explained by him in the preface to *Paulicéia Desvairada*:

> I consider melodic verse the same as musical melody: a horizontal arabesque of consecutive tones (sounds) which contain intelligible thought. Now, if instead of using only verses which are horizontally melodic ... we have words follow each other without any immediate connection among themselves, these

words, for the very reason that they do not follow intellectually and grammatically, overlie one another for the gratification of our senses, and no longer form melodies but rather harmonies... Harmony: combination of sounds... These words have no connection. They do not form a series. Each one is a phrase, an elliptical period, reduced to the telegraphic minimum... Since it does not belong to a phrase (melody), the word calls our attention to its detachment and it continues to vibrate, waiting for a phrase which will give it meaning, a phrase which DOES NOT FOLLOW. [The second word] gives no conclusion whatever to [the first word]; and under the same conditions, as we are not made to forget the first word, it continues to vibrate along with the other word. The other voices do the same. Thus: instead of melody (grammatical phrase) we have an arpeggiated chord, harmony—the harmonic verse. But, if instead of using only disconnected words, I use disconnected phrases, I get the same sensation of overlay, not now of words (notes) alone but of phrases (melodies). Hence: poetic polyphony. Thus in *Hallucinated City* are employed melodic verse: 'São Paulo is a stage for Russian ballets'; harmonic verse: 'Pack of dogs... Stock Market...Gambling...'; poetic polyphony (one and sometimes two and even more consecutive verses): 'The gears palsy... The mist snows...'[81]

Critic Wilson Martins has explained this process in poetry as follows: "Simultaneity is the coexistence of things and events at a given moment. *Polyphony* is the simultaneous artistic union of two or more melodies which have the fleeting effect of clashing sounds as they contribute to a *total final effect*."[82] This idea of a total final effect underscores the importance of considering each image as part of the whole poem rather than merely pointing out isolated words or verses.

---

81 Andrade, 12-13.
82 Wilson Martins, *The Modernist Idea*, trans. Jack E. Tomlins (New York: New York University Press, 1970) 37.

The addition of harmony and polyphony to melody brings a new dimension to the possible images in poetry. Sensorial images combined in polyphony become synaesthetic or multiple. The modern world has caused this expansion:

> Modern-day inventions have transformed our senses. Man no longer has merely five senses: he has hundreds and thousands. The speed of modern life forces the artist to depict quickly what he felt quickly, before the intellect intervenes. From that condition was born the synthetization of modern art. Time! ... Besides cinematographic synthetization, the dizzying whirl of modern life also creates in the artist a facility of close analysis produced by the multiplicity of different facts which occur over a short space of time, almost simultaneously.[83]

Thus one finds in modern poetry unexpected or unusual combinations of words and the surprising union of images, actions or emotions which seem at first to be incompatible. New expressions are invented to describe new sensations. The realms of time and space are often united in modern literature. Modern music is influenced by city life, and in turn the new music influences the sound of poetry. The basis for all of these expressions is humanity's perception of the modern world, just as the protagonist in Maples Arce's poetry contemplates the world around him and his place in it.

---

83 Martins (quoting Rubens Borba de Moraes), 32.

"Y NADA DE HOJAS SECAS..."

(La mañana romántica, como un ruido espumoso,
se derrama en la calle de este barrio incoloro
por donde a veces pasan repartiendo programas,
y es una clara música que se oye con los ojos
la palidez enferma de la súper-amada.)

(En tanto que un poeta,
colgado en la ventana,
se muere haciendo gárgaras
de plata
electrizada,
subido a los peldaños de una escala
cromática,
barnizo sus dolencias con vocablos azules,
y anclada en un letargo de cosas panorámicas,
su vida se evapora lo mismo que un perfume.)

—Mi tristeza de antes es la misma de hoy.
—Tú siempre con tus cosas.
      —¡Oh poeta, perdón!

(En el jardín morado
se rompe el equilibrio fragante de una flor.)

—Sol, blancura, etc., y nada de hojas secas.
—La vida es sólo un grito que se me cuelga al cuello
lo mismo que un adiós.
      —Hablemos de otra cosa,
te lo ruego.

     (Su voz
tiene dobleces románticos de felpa
que estuvo mucho tiempo guardada en naftalina,
y duerme en sus cansancios ingrávidos de enferma,
la elegancia de todas las cosas amarillas.)

(Y mientras la mañana, atónita de espejos,
estalla en el alféizar de la hora vulgar,
el dolor se derrama, lo mismo que un tintero,
sobre la partitura de su alma musical.)

The poem "Y nada de hojas secas" begins the section of *Andamios Interiores* called "VOCES AMARILLAS." Each poem of this section is a dialogue surrounded by a prelude and a postlude (or introduction and epilogue). As in the first two poems of the "FLORES ARITMÉTICAS" section ("Esas rosas eléctricas" and "Todo en un plano oblicuo"), there are two contrasting perspectives on life represented in the poems of "VOCES AMARILLAS." The dialogues bring the opposing points of view into sharp contrast by juxtaposition and direct statement. In the dialogues, the protagonist voices the active, life-affirming view of 1920s modernity, while his lover represents the neurasthenic feelings of *mal du siècle, spleen* and *ennui* of the late nineteenth century and turn-of-the-century decadents that have been discussed above. The prelude and postlude surrounding their dialogue comment on the coexistence of the opposing attitudes and how the protagonist and his lover try to cope.

The protagonist's lover is stuck in a world of tedium, sadness and depression. Her world is "incoloro," a quality that is reflected in the "palidez enferma" of her face, as indicated in the prelude (strophe one). The protagonist tries to lessen his lover's sadness and neurasthenia with his poetry and his positive point of view. The protagonist is in favor of "sol, blancura, etc., y nada de hojas secas." He promotes life, not death. The title of this poem recalls Spanish *ultraísta* poet Rafael Cansino-Assens' call for the liquidation of dry leaves, one of the avant-garde cries to end *Postmodernismo*.[84]

Maples Arce's poem "Y nada de hojas secas" is set in the

---

[84] Cf. Mexican *postmodernista* Enrique González Martínez's poem "A veces una hoja desprendida."

early morning, as bright sunshine begins to pour into the streets of the neighborhood. Dawn is a more positive transition time than twilight (the latter is the more common setting of Maples Arce's poems), and it is an appropriate time for this poem. As in "Esas rosas eléctricas," the protagonist in "Y nada de hojas secas" has a different perspective on life from the other participant(s) in the poem. The protagonist's view on life is very affirmational about the present and hopeful about the future. Frequently in other poems he is melancholic, distressed about the transitory nature of modern activities, and feels lonely and separated from a loved one. Here, in "Y nada de hojas secas," he is the strong character who tries to encourage and cheer up his depressed lover. The protagonist's typical melancholy and frustration come in to play in the postlude of the poem, which tenderly expresses his love for the woman at the same time as it communicates the futility of his efforts to brighten her spirit. The spiritual difference between the characters seems unbridgeable, and it is a frustrating "separation."

In "Y nada de hojas secas," the protagonist is looking out the window, spiritually connected to the vibrant city outside. The references to the street, a garden, a flower, and the many images of light are associated with him. These images are part of a consistent extended metaphor which works well in this poem: the protagonist represents what is exterior–fresh air and sunshine, all that is bright, a new day, the garden and the city streets. The woman represents that which is interior–all that is stuffy, dark, musty, old, infirm, pale, yellowed, tired and sad. The protagonist is presented in upward-moving images (except for "colgado," but even that is reaching out to the city and is at a window): "subido," "escala cromática." He is also associated with words full of action: "espumoso," "se derrama," "electrizada," "se rompe," "estalla," "atónita." The woman is shown in static images: "la misma [hoy que antes]," "siempre," "equilibrio," "se me cuelga al cuello," "anclada," "letargo," "lo mismo," "guardada en naftalina." She will not let herself be freed of the *ennui*. It seems that she almost wants to suffer. The protagonist wants change: "— Hablemos de otra cosa, / te lo ruego." He is at the windowsill–the ledge, the border between the interior and exterior worlds, the point of transition. He is the new dawn, the new day. She is the past. For her, life always stays the same. The words of positive connotation found in the poem refer to the protagonist's actions, his feelings, or his commentary ("la mañana romántica," "la súper-amada," "barnizo," "vocablos azules," "sol," "blancura"). The words of negative connotation refer to the woman ("palidez enferma," "dolencias," "tristeza," "hojas secas," "cansancios," "enferma," "cosas amarillas," "el dolor"). A few words have a double connotation (that is, they can be either positive, negative, or both): "romántica," "se derrama," "música," "escala"; these are moments of union and attempts at communication between the lovers. The woman is romantic, elegant, and beautiful, but in an outmoded way. Now there is a new, dazzling, electric, bright kind of beauty, which the protagonist knows and to which he is attracted.

In the poems of *Andamios Interiores*, Maples Arce uses the *alejandrino* line, popular since *Modernismo*, but he does creative things with it at key moments. His modified use of this form may at first seem too traditional, but upon closer inspection one sees how Maples Arce's manipulation of the standard form shows ingenuity and provides more intense focus on certain elements of the poem which would not be as evident in a freer structure. As Frederick J. Hoffman observes with regard to Ezra Pound, in Hoffman's book on American writing in the 1920s,

> Finally, "As regarding rhythm, to compose in the sequence of the musical phrase, not in the sequence of the metronome." Whatever Pound may have meant by this, he did *not* mean a wholesale sponsorship of "free verse"; nor did Eliot believe that there was such a thing as *vers libre*, in spite of the fact that the most lively controversy in modern poetry had to do with the question of free verse. In his essay on "Arnold Dolmetsch" (*New Age*, January 1915), Pound made his position on this matter clear: 'Any work of art is a compound of freedom and order. It is perfectly obvious that art hangs between chaos on one side and mechanics on the other. A pedantic insistence on detail tends to drive out 'major form.' A firm hold on major form makes for a freedom of detail."[85]

Hoffman includes another observation that is applicable to Maples Arce: "While the external form may be quite traditional, the poetic values are achieved almost as if independently of it."[86] These thoughts from Pound and Hoffman are enlightening when one remembers the numerous attacks on Maples Arce made by his adversaries for using the *alejandrino* line, suggesting that he treated it in the same way that the *modernistas* did. On the contrary, he liberated it. In addition, as noted in Chapter One above, the seven-syllable hemistich and the fourteen-syllable line are the natural rhythm in which Maples Arce heard verse as he composed it mentally, and also the rhythm of some of his prose writing.

---

85 Frederick J. Hoffman, *The 20's: American Writing in the Postwar Decade* (New York: The Free Press; London: Collier MacMillan Publishers, 1965) 200-201.
86 Hoffman, 203.

At the beginning of the second strophe of "Y nada de hojas secas," "un poeta" literally drinks in the new morning and all of its brightly reflecting light:

> (En tanto que un poeta,
> colgado en la ventana,
> se muere haciendo gárgaras
> de plata
> electrizada,

The division and placement of these lines on the page reflects the content in a subtle way: the short lines descending in a column visually suggest the vertical length of the throat of the character gargling. The dominance of the sound of the vowel "a" is a possible echo of the "ah" sound of gargling. The use of "se muere" in "se muere haciendo gárgaras" seems to be an expression of extremism (as in "me muero de hambre," "nos morimos de la risa") or scandal (akin to the death references in "Esas rosas eléctricas": "languidecen de muerte," "se accidenta," "se atraganta"), rather than actually signifying death. While one might die from gargling electrified silver, the image is a metaphor for taking in the sunshine and light that is reflected on metal and glass surfaces.

The mid-section of strophe two[87] contains a beautiful synaesthetic image complex:

> subido a los peldaños de una escala
> cromática,
> barnizo sus dolencias con vocablos azules,

---

[87] In the original edition of *Andamios Interiores*, there was a space after "electrizada," and "subido a los peldaños de una escala" started a new strophe. In the *Semillas* edition, that space has been omitted. The wide double spacing of the original text made it somewhat difficult to distinguish line separation from strophe separation, and some editing errors resulted in the printing of *Semillas*.

This image is visually concrete enough to be a Ziegfeld Follies stage set, and at the same time it is so abstract (especially the third line) that it is almost impossible to separate the visual, auditory, tactile and emotional references. In this passage, as well as in strophe one and in the postlude, it is clear that the protagonist loves the woman very much. His attempts to make her feel better are tender, respectful and sincere.

Nevertheless, the dialogue between the protagonist and his beloved, which forms the body or central portion of the poem, is tense, somewhat cold, almost combative, and shows no true communication between the two people. Each barely listens to what the other says:

—Mi tristeza de antes es la misma de hoy.
—Tú siempre con tus cosas.
                    —¡Oh poeta, perdón!

(En el jardín morado
se rompe el equilibrio fragante de una flor.)

—Sol, blancura, etc., y nada de hojas secas.
—La vida es sólo un grito que se me cuelga al cuello
lo mismo que un adiós.
                    —Hablemos de otra cosa,
te lo ruego.

In the middle of this tense interchange there is a short strophe of parenthetic commentary, interrupting the dialogue while at the same time forcing a break in both the form and the content. "(En el jardín morado" is the first unpaired hemistich of the poem, occuring right before the words (in the next line) "se rompe el equilibrio" and just after the woman's sarcastic counter, "¡Oh poeta, perdón!" This break in the flow of the poem signals not only the communication and spiritual gaps between the two lovers, but also the protagonist's desire to break away from traditional poetry, to modernize it. The idea of a break with the past is reinforced in the protagonist's next line as the dialogue starts up again: "Sol, blancura, etc., y nada de hojas secas." The woman continues speaking in the same negative vein in which she spoke before, and the man pleads for a change of subject for their conversation: "—Hablemos de otra cosa, / te lo ruego."[88] The woman does not respond, and her silence ends the dialogue section of the poem. The next two strophes form the postlude or epilogue.

The end of the dialogue and the beginning of the postlude contain a significant manipulation of form. The presumably contrary thoughts involved in the protagonist's begging to change the topic of conversation and his tender contemplation of the quality of his lover's voice, lines ending the dialogue and beginning the postlude, respectively, are forced together by metrics. These lines are an important moment of thematic climax and, appropriately, they are also the point of most structural union and

---

88   Some typographical errors in both the original published version of "Y nada de hojas secas" in *Andamios Interiores* and in the version printed in *Las semillas del tiempo* have caused a few slight differences in form and punctuation. The last sentence of the dialogue, "Hablemos de otra cosa, / te lo ruego," should be preceded by a dash to indicate speech, as in the original, but the dash was left out in *Las semillas*. This dash seems clearly necessary to indicate a change of speaker. The *Semillas* version adds more parentheses to the prelude and postlude: now included are parentheses at the end of strophe one and at the beginning of strophe two, as well as at the end of strophe six and the beginning of strophe seven, so that each strophe of the prelude and postlude is enclosed in parentheses rather than just one set of parentheses enclosing the entire two-strophe sections. This addition of parentheses was not done to the other two poems of the "VOCES AMARILLAS" section, however. Such editorial inconsistencies and discrepancies are frustrating to the Maples Arce student, but none of the changes are really significant, with the exception of the text of "En la dolencia estática," the next poem to be discussed.

overlap. The fragment "te lo ruego" must be combined with the first line of the next strophe (quite a jump), "su voz," in order to reach seven syllables. The union of these two fragments is interesting because in a sense, it joins the two people together: it is the protagonist who begs that they change the topic of conversation, and it is the woman's voice to which the companion line refers ("su voz"). The second line of strophe six describes her voice in a loving way: "tiene dobleces románticos de felpa." This line must be combined with the previous, "su voz," which has already been counted once, in order to reach fourteen syllables (one must count it as if there were no line break after "voz"). The previous hemistich of combined lines ("te lo ruego. / (Su voz") must be left unpaired, thus adding even more emphasis to the content at that point. This intertwining of verses recalls the "tú y yo / coincidimos" section of "Prisma." The remaining lines of "Y nada de hojas secas" are each complete fourteen-syllable verses, each with punctuation at the end. The pauses caused by that punctuation establish not only the relative independence of each line (most are commas rather than full stops) but also a definite separation from the previous linking pattern.

In addition to the prelude - dialogue - postlude format, the strophes of "Y nada de hojas secas" are further balanced by a 1 - 2 - 3 - 2 - 1 content order. Content #1 is a description of the morning sun as seen by the protagonist (two verses), followed by a description of the infirm condition of the woman. This is the content of the first and last strophes of the poem. Content #2 is more personal: first, strophe two contains an attempt by the protagonist to wipe away the cares and troubles of the woman he loves. Similar in tone, strophe six is a description from the man's point of view of the beauty of his lover's voice and the elegance of her old-fashioned spirit. Content #3 is the dialogue between the lovers (two short strophes separated by a short parenthetical comment), quite tense in feeling, clearly showing their opposing views of life. The sharpness of the dialogue is toned down by the soft, understanding quality demonstrated in strophe six ("Su voz ..."). Strophe seven functions as an epilogue, restating the separate perspectives of the man and the woman, giving the feeling that they will continue to be of opposite spirit. In this last strophe, however, after the poem has been written and "vocablos azules" have been spoken, the protagonist seems more accepting of his beloved's character, even though it is different from his own. Their duality is echoed in the balanced structure of the poem (with the exception of the emphasized point "En el jardín morado / se rompe el equilibrio ...," as discussed above), in the frequent assonantal rhyme, the numerous synaesthetic images, and the series of light/dark image contrasts in this highly visual poem. The protagonist is symbolized by action and blazing sunlight ("Y mientras la mañana, atónita de espejos, / estalla en el alféizar de la hora vulgar") and the woman is characterized by "la palidez enferma," "cansancios ingrávidos de enferma," "cosas amarillas," sadness, and insistent pain ("la vida es sólo un grito que se me cuelga al cuello / lo mismo que un adiós"). The protagonist will change poetry, but he will still love this woman. They are separate in spirituality but they are brought together by their love in the poem.

"En la dolencia estática"[89]

(En la dolencia estática de este jardín mecánico,
el olor de las horas huele a convalecencia,
y el pentagrama eléctrico de todos los tejados
se muere en el alero del último almanaque.

Extraviada en maneras musicales de enferma
inmoviliza un sueño su vertical blancura,
en tanto que un obscuro violín de quinto piso
se deshoja a lo largo de un poema de Schumann,
y en todos los periódicos se ha suicidado un tísico.)

—Hoy pasan los entierros, como un cuento de ojeras,
lo mismo que en otoño.
                        —Ese tema, no es tema
de primavera. Ya ves lo que dice el médico!)

(En el jardín hay 5 centavos de silencio.)

—Entonces, quiero un poco de sol azucarado.
—Ya vuelves con tu acústica.
                        —Pues mírame las manos.
Mis dedos caligráficos se han vuelto endecasílabos.

(Y meditando un lento compás de 3 por 4:)

—¡Oh tus cosas melódicas!
                        —¡Soy un frasco de música!

(Y en esta tarde lírica
                    85-74, señorita ...
la primavera pasa como en motocicleta,
y al oro moribundo, historiada de cintas,
lo mismo que un refajo se seca mi tristeza.)

---

[89] Original version as published in *Andamios Interiores*, 1922. The text of "En la dolencia estática" as it was originally published will be analyzed first, followed by discussion of the changes in the version published in *Las semillas del tiempo*.

"En la dolencia estática" presents a problem of stasis and paralysis where there should be movement. The key to interpreting this rather hermetic poem lies in the reference in line 8 to the German Romantic composer Robert Schumann. Another point to support the Schumann-related interpretation is the poem's reference to the speaker's stiff hands and fingers in the latter part of the dialogue. While experimenting with unorthodox ways to improve his piano technique, Schumann paralyzed one of his fingers and thus ended his virtuoso playing career; he then turned to composing. This event will be discussed in detail later. The poem may be seen in general as a discussion of Schumann and his career in music. A Romantic composer may seem an unlikely topic for a poem by jazz-age avant-gardist Maples Arce, but Schumann was an iconoclast in his time, and his behavior was often radical.

Like the *estridentistas*, Schumann considered emotion an important catalyst for art. He, too, felt limited by traditional forms. In order to attain a higher level of expression, he had to create revolutionary new forms. "It was an approach to the unattainable, a description of the ineffable. It was music *about* something. At its best it was the triumph of the intimate personal expression over the imperatives of the academy."[90] Schumann invented new and unusual uses of harmony, counterpoint and complex rhythms, constantly trying to improve technique, with unexpected changes in tone and harmony, "'sheer revelings in strangeness' in the aphoristic and fragmentary piano pieces,"[91] chord combi-

---

[90] James Lyons, ed., *The American Record Guide*, jacket notes, *Arabeske, Nachstücke, Romanzen, The Prophet Bird*, by Robert Schumann, Guiomar Novaes, pianist (Vox PL11.990, 1961).

[91] Jacket notes, *"Lieder" from the Spanish and from "Myrtle,"* by Robert Schumann (Deutsche Grammophon LPM18655, Oct. 1960).

nations, games, contradictions, contrasts and experiments with the style of writing notes on the page.

Maples Arce's poem, "En la dolencia estática," achieves musicality through abundant vowel sounds, assonantal rhyme, and the rhythmic patterns formed by several *esdrújulas*. Again Maples Arce uses the *alejandrino* line, with some modifications. The poem is rich in synaesthetic images and typically Maplesian unusual word combinations. The general structure of the poem is similar to that of a Schumann song (*lied*). It begins with a prelude (lines 1-9), presented in parentheses. A dialogue forms the middle section, and the poem concludes with a postlude (lines 22-26), in parentheses. As in the other two poems of the "VOCES AMARILLAS" section of *Andamios Interiores*, the prelude and postlude are commentary separated from the dialogue. This kind of structure was used frequently in Schumann's songs: "The long prelude which gave rise to the voice, and the long postlude in which it disappeared, were quite new in the field of the *lied*, and delineated the contours of this perfected romantic universe."[92] A similar structure is seen clearly in "My Soul is Dark," which is patterned on Byron's "Hebrew Melodies" and included in a collection of Schumann's songs entitled "*Lieder* from the Spanish and from 'Myrtle'" (dialogue between voice and piano).

The conversation in Maples Arce's poem could be a dialogue between any one of several possible couples. The word *señorita* in the second half of line 23 indicates that one of the speakers is a woman. She could be Clara, Schumann's wife, who was also a pianist, composer, and

---

92 André Boucourechliev, *Schumann* (London and New York: John Calder Ltd. and Grove Press Inc., 1959) 100.

daughter of Schumann's teacher. Schumann and Clara had a long friendship before marrying, during which time they frequently wrote letters to one another. Clara would be the second person of the poem's dialogue, the speaker of lines 12, 13, 16 and 20. The conversation could also be a dialogue between the piano and the voice of the song:

> The piano was too intimate an expression of Schumann's ego not to be, when placed so close to the voice and on its identical level, 'another character' who conversed with and sometimes even absorbed and dominated it. This unity of voice and piano, both as independent and necessary to one another in dialogue as in dramatic conflict, was essentially Schumannesque.[93]

Another dialogue possibility is that between Florestan and Eusebius, characters invented by Schumann in order to express the two sides of his personality, the negative and positive. Other possible dialogue pairs (representing the same negative/positive dichotomy) are death and life, autumn and spring, or the impossible and the possible. The conversation works on all of these levels, and no matter which pair of speakers is chosen, it illustrates Schumann's life.

There are several references in Maples Arce's poem to the paralysis of Schumann's hand. This is perhaps the most important image of the poem, since the event changed the course of Schumann's life.

> Schumann worked relentlessly. The piano was not obedient enough, technique was tiresome, and slow to come. Obsessed by the great example of Paganini and impatient to press on, he evolved the absurd notion of assuring the independence of his fourth finger by working with his middle finger kept immobile by a string.

---

93   Boucourechliev, 100.

In the spring of 1832 his hand was paralysed. Driven to distraction, Robert kept his accident hidden from his family, and took his hopes from one doctor to another, even having recourse to quacks. His house was transformed into a chemist's shop. Would he have to give up music? Right up to March 1834, he tried all the treatments with a fierce and desperate obstinacy, and hoped for a miracle. But his [third] finger remained paralysed, and Schumann would never be a virtuoso.

This accident, which the biographers call providential, since it removed Schumann from the destructive fascination of a virtuoso career and obliged him to devote himself entirely to his loftiest and most personal vocation, made him suffer cruelly for a long time.[94]

The lines in Maples Arce's poem that refer specifically to this injury are : "Extraviada en maneras musicales de enferma / inmoviliza un sueño su vertical blancura" (l. 5-6), "Ya ves lo que dice el médico!" (l. 13), "Pues mírame las manos. / Mis dedos caligráficos se han vuelto endecasílabos") (l. 17-18).

Strophe one reads: "(En la dolencia estática de este jardín mecánico, / el olor de las horas huele a convalecencia, / y el pentagrama eléctrico de todos los tejados / se muere en el alero del útlimo almanaque." The "dolencia estática" is the physical and emotional pain that Schumann feels. The adjective "static" applies to the paralysis of his finger and the termination of his career as a pianist. "El jardín mecánico is the piano, perhaps also the city. The hours smell of convalescence: Schumann spent a long time trying to cure himself. "El pentagrama eléctrico" is either the metronome on top ("en el tejado") of the piano, which stops being used when he stops playing, or the lines of a

---

94 Boucourechliev, 42.

musical staff on sheet music. The part of the piano that holds the sheet of music looks like the eaves on a house ("alero"), and the electrical wires that run from poles to buildings look like a musical staff (this image has been used by Maples in other poems). "El último almanaque" means either recently or that time has run out.

The rest of the prelude continues: "Extraviada en maneras musicales de enferma / inmoviliza un sueño su vertical blancura, / en tanto que un obscuro violín de quinto piso / se deshoja a lo largo de un poema de Schumann, / y en todos los periódicos se ha suicidado un tísico.)" "La vertical blancura" represents the piano keys ("su" refers to the "jardín mecánico") or a musical scale. Schumann's dream ("sueño") of being a great pianist was destroyed by the experiment to make his fourth finger more independent (by immobilizing ["inmoviliza"] the third finger, in order to perfect technique), something which was "extraviada en maneras musicales de enferma." "Inmoviliza un sueño" is also the defeat of the dream to do the impossible, go beyond the usual, achieve new modes of expression, surpass traditional limitations. The "violín de quinto piso" means a violin playing very high musical notes. The word *deshojarse* is interesting here, especially in combination with the references to spring and fall, and may refer to the unfolding musical piece played by the violin or the piano and voice.

Line 8 says "un poema de Schumann." The autobiographical and personal qualities of Schumann's music often led him to use intimate and diminutive forms, such as art songs and chamber music:

> This creative self-reflection necessarily leads from the large scale works of Beethoven to more intimate

miniature forms. Musical ideas which, with the Viennese classicists, were often used merely as impersonal structural material that gained in individual form by being developed in the larger framework of the total musical architecture, were allowed by the Romantics to exist in their own right as essential elements of the music.[95]

"Un poema de Schumann" could also refer to Schumann's interest in literature. His father worked in literature, and when Schumann was young he had to make a career choice between music and literature. Because of his interest in literature, it was always present in some way in his music. He read a great deal, and many of his musical compositions, especially the songs, were inspired by works of his favorite authors. Poetry inspires the work of Schumann just as the music of Schumann inspires this particular poem by Maples Arce.

Line 9 of Maples Arce's poem reads, "Y en todos los periódicos se ha suicidado un tísico." In 1826, when Schumann was sixteen years old, his nineteen-year old sister Emilie, who had been mentally and physically ill, committed suicide. Schumann's father was ill at the time and the shock of Emilie's suicide aggravated his condition; he died shortly thereafter. Schumann himself tried to commit suicide at least twice. During the period of the paralysis of his hand (1832-34), he jumped out a window. Later, when he was showing signs of mental derangement, he threw himself into a river. Some strangers rescued him and took him home. Within a week, he entered the sanatorium where he spent the last two years of his life.

The dialogue in "En la dolencia estática" begins: "—

---

95 Alfred Beaujean, jacket notes, *Waldszenen*, op. 82 by Robert Schumann (N.p.: n.d.).

Hoy pasan los entierros, como un cuento de ojeras, / lo mismo que en otoño" (l. 10-11).

> One evening in late March of 1839, just before his return to Leipzig, Schumann was sitting at the piano, absorbed in composition, when suddenly he was overcome by an unmistakable presentiment of death, and his mind was flooded by visions of 'funerals, coffins, and unhappy, despairing faces.' It is a fact that his beloved brother Eduard was fatally stricken at precisely that time.[96]

Schumann was writing his work "Nachstücke" ("Nocturnes") that night. The presentiment of death that he felt is expressed in lines 10 and 11 of Maples Arce's poem. The presentiment of death was "como un cuento de ojeras," like a ghost story, typically told late at night. An alternative reference for lines 10-11 would be Schumann's work "Der arme Peter," opus 53, with a text taken from Heine, a piece in which the typical contrasts and ironies of both Schumann and Heine are evident. "Der arme Peter" speaks of suicide motivated by love problems, and the music alternates light and lyrical feelings with the horror of death in a dialogue between piano and voice (which rises higher and higher, like the "violín de quinto piso," in a trajectory of torment).

Death is symbolized in the autumnal image in line 11, "lo mismo que en otoño." Throughout "En la dolencia estática," the dichotomies of spring/autumn, movement/stasis, music/silence, and life/death are present. Lines 12 and 13 confirm the dominance of the dark side of these dichotomies: "ese tema, no es tema / de primavera." Schumann's own problem exists on several levels: the paralysis of his hand, his split personality, his suicide at-

---

[96] Lyons.

tempts.

Line 14 is a parenthetical comment that creates a pause after the first exchange of dialogue between the two speakers: "(En el jardín hay 5 centavos de silencio.)" The comment alludes to the silence of the piano during the paralysis and also to the pause in the dialogue. "5 centavos" seems to mean it is only a brief pause. After the pause, the Schumann character says, "Entonces, quiero un poco de sol azucarado," a synaesthetic image that communicates the desire for something positive, a cure, medicine that tastes good, something of springtime. The image of the sugared sun is similar to the title of Schumann's last work, "Songs of the Dawn." In line 16, "tu acústica" refers to Schumann's music. The reference to the paralysis of Schumann's finger is next, in lines 17-18: "Pues mírame las manos. / Mis dedos caligráficos se han vuelto endecasílabos." The change from calligraphic to hendecasyllabic could mean from special to ordinary, from creative hands to hands like those of everyone else. In general, it is a change from flourishes to traditional form. This section of the poem is outstanding for its rhythm, produced by the *esdrújula* words. In line 19, "un lento compás de 3 por 4: " could refer to any of several works written in 3/4 time (the colon leads to the next line of the poem and is also the symbol that appears on a musical staff after the time signature), or it could simply mean the Schumann character is humming a waltz tune. In line 20, "tus cosas melódicas" is his music in general, or a specific reference to his use of melody in songs. As line 21 tells the reader, Schumann felt an integral relationship between his life and music: "— ¡Soy un frasco de música!—" This affirmation of Schumann's identification with music is very strong, and it ends the dialogue of Maples Arce's poem.

Line 22 starts the postlude. "Often the voice part ends on a note of the dominant chord ... and the piano is left to bring the music back to the tonic key."[97] Frequently there is a summary or epilogue at the end of a song or at the end of a cycle of songs, which is played on the piano.

The numbers in line 23, "85-74," probably refer to the opus numbers of some of Schumann's works: Opus 85 are four piano duets and Opus 74 are the Spanish Love Songs. The use of numerals in the poem (here and in two other verses) is notable for their visual effect on the page, and for the play between the visual and the auditory aspects of those words, a technique of which avant-garde poets were fond. Schumann plays similarly with letters (names of notes) and notes (their shape) in his works "Abegg" and "Sphinxes." He uses the letters of a word or of someone's name as inspiration for a melody and creates harmonies and various themes around those notes, for example: A, B, E, G, G. "Sphinxes" presents more extreme play, as in it he invents new shapes for notes, creating pieces that, like the title, are an enigma. Anagrams were very popular in Germany in Schumann's time, and he incorporated them creatively into his music.

As a return to the tonic key brings resolution in a musical composition, the postlude or epilogue in lines 22-26 brings resolution to the poem "En la dolencia estática":

(Y en esta tarde lírica
                    85-74, señorita ...
la primavera pasa en motocicleta,
y al oro moribundo, historiada de cintas,
lo mismo que un refajo se seca mi tristeza.)

---

[97] Joan Chissell, *Schumann* (London: J. M. Dent and Sons, Ltd., 1948) 141-142.

The afternoon of this poem is "lyrical," because the poem is about poetry and music, because it is melancholy, and because of the sunset. Lines 13 and 24 tell us it is springtime; one imagines flowers, fresh air. In line 25, "El oro moribundo" is the setting sun. "Historiada de cintas" refers to the colors of the sunset spread out across the sky. The protagonist's feelings are colored by the afternoon and by his thoughts. He is very sad, but the vision of the sunset makes him feel better. This is the "sol azucarado" he wished for in line 15. His sadness "dries up," fades, like the colors of old ribbons. A petticoat can be adorned with colored ribbons, and here it is a beautifully original metaphor for the sunset. With the passing of time, a petticoat loses its stiffness, becomes worn and thin and the colors of the ribbons fade. Another Mexican usage of "refajo" refers to the beer drink (English "shandy") of beer plus lemonade or soda water or grenadine, or especially the foam on top of it. The lemonade or grenadine would form the ribbons of color. The foam gradually disperses and disappears with time. As the Schumann character hums a waltz melody and contemplates the spring afternoon and sunset, he is no longer at the height of his anger and frustration, but in a melancholy, nostalgic reminiscence of a lost dream.

Although the version of "En la dolencia estática" published in *Las semillas del tiempo* includes many changes from the original, I believe that the original version achieves a superior poetic realization, and have therefore used it in this analysis. The reader should note that in his 1983 anthology, *El estridentismo*, for UNAM's "Cuadernos de Humanidades" series and his 1985 anthology, *El estridentismo, México 1921-1927*, published by UNAM's Instituto de Investigaciones Estéticas, Luis Mario Schneider chose to print the original versions of all of the poems and not include the changes found in *Las semillas del tiempo* (1981). "En la dolencia estática" was changed more for *Las semillas* than any other of Maples Arce's poems (as we know, poets sometimes change their mind during recitals). Following is the version printed in *Las semillas*:

>(En la dolencia estática de este jardín mecánico,
>el olor de las horas huele a convalecencia,
>y el pentagrama eléctrico de todos los tejados
>se muere en el alero del último almanaque.
>
>Extasiada en maneras musicales de enferma
>inmoviliza un sueño su vertical blancura,
>en tanto que un obscuro violín de quinto piso
>se deshoja a lo largo de un poema de Schumann,
>y en todos los periódicos se ha suicidado un tísico.)
>—Hoy pasan los entierros
>lo mismo que en otoño.
>   —Ese tema no es tema
>de primavera.
>
>(En el jardín hay cinco centavos de silencio.)
>
>—Quiero un poco de sol azucarado.
>—Tú pides imposibles.
>   —Mira mis manos mustias,
>mis dedos casi yertos ...
>(Mientras medito un lento compás de 3 X 4)
>
>—¡Oh virgen supertónica!
>   —Soy sólo una quimera,
>se dijo murmurando.
>(Y en esta tarde lírica
>   85-74, señorita ...
>la primavera pasa en motocicleta,
>y al oro moribundo, historiada de cintas,
>lo mismo que un refajo se seca mi tristeza.)

There are changes in fourteen lines, most of which either involve several words or alter the rhythm or meaning of the verse significantly (only two are punctuation changes). In line 5, *extraviada* changes to *extasiada*. In line 10, "—Hoy pasan los entierros, como un cuento de ojeras," the second phrase is omitted in the new version. The comma in line 12 is taken out. In line 13, "de primavera. Ya ves lo que dice el médico!", the second phrase is left out in the revision. The new line 14 spells out *cinco* instead of using the numeral, and omits the period of the original line, but the latter is most likely a typographical error. Line 15, "Entonces, quiero un poco de sol azucarado," loses "Entonces" in the new version. Line 16, "—Ya vuelves con tu acústica," changes to "—Tú pides imposibles." Line 17, "—Pues mírame las manos," is changed to "—Mira mis manos mustias," and line 18, "Mis dedos caligráficos se han vuelto endecasílabos," becomes "mis dedos casi yertos..." Line 19, "(Y meditando un lento compás de 3 por 4:)," changes slightly to "(Mientras medito un lento compás de 3 X 4)." The new line 20 changes "¡Oh tus cosas melódicas!" to "¡Oh virgen supertónica!" Line 21 changes from "—Soy un frasco de música!—" to "—Soy sólo una quimera," and a new line is added: "se dijo murmurando" (line 22 in *Las semillas*). Line 24 of the original changes slightly, from "la primavera pasa como en motocicleta" to "la primavera pasa en motocicleta" (line 25 in the revision). While the changes found in the new version in most cases (not all) maintain more or less the same meaning as the original lines, they do alter the rhythm and the syllable count, and they omit important references (e.g. *médico, acústica, endecasílabos, cosas melódicas, música*). The syllable count in the new lines

13, 15 and 25 cause them not to fit into the pattern. One could justify their standing out from the others (they speak of *primavera* and *sol azucarado*), but they are not set apart in a definite or organized way.

The change in line 20 is significant because it changes the speaker: while the original verse was spoken by the woman to the Schumann character or the man/composer/protagonist, in the new version the feminine adjective indicates that it is said by the man to the woman. This would be parallel to the other dialogues of the "VOCES AMARILLAS" section, with the woman as the speaker of negative views and the man (the protagonist) as the speaker of affirmative views. It is indeed possible to apply that pattern to this poem, in both versions, making the woman a neurasthenic musician and the protagonist the lover that tries to cheer her up, but the result is a poem of less depth and specific images without particular referents. As always, multiple interpretations are possible.

One can only guess why Maples Arce changed "En la dolencia estática" so much. His notes reveal that he reworked the poem several times (not a common practice for him after publication), writing changes in by hand over an already modified typescript. Either interpretation of the meaning and of the speakers works, but structurally and rhythmically, the original poem seems to be the best version.[98]

---

[98] At least one anthology has incorrectly printed an additional line at the end of "En la dolencia estática." The line "derramada en silencio sobre mi corazón," which is in reality the final line of the poem "Tras los adioses últimos" (*Andamios Interiores*), appears at the end of "En la dolencia estática" in the anthology *La poesía hispanoamericana desde el modernismo*, edited by Eugenio Florit and José Olivio Jiménez (NY: Appleton-Century Crofts, 1968) 245. Often when one anthology makes a mistake, it is copied as such incorrectly by later anthology editors who do not consult (or perhaps have no access to) the original.

"Por las horas de cuento..."

Por las horas de cuento de estos parques sin rosas,
ambulan, un diptongo de ensueño, nuestras sombras.

Y en tanto que algún piano fantástico, desvela
los bemoles románticos de un estudio sin luna,
sus ojos se adormecen en un cansancio de felpa,
como si estuviera muriendo de blancura.

(Y después, quedamente:)
                    —¿Amor, oyes las hojas?
—¡Si no es eso!
            —¿Entonces?
                    —Tal vez es una enferma
que llora con Beethoven...

(Y seguimos del brazo nuestro obscuro diptongo,
por los parques afónicos,
lacrimeantes de oro...)

—¡Me quisiera morir!
                —¡No digas esas cosas
que me hacen tanto mal!
                —¡Si la vida es tan triste!
—Pero no pienses eso.
                —¡Si la vida es tan triste!
—Me duele el corazón cuando tú estás así.
Doblaremos la hoja.
            (Y sobre el mismo tema,
su voz, casi ojerosa:)
                —¡Me quisiera morir!
¡Me quisiera morir!

(Y en el cloroformado cansancio de la sombra,
nuestras 2 vidas juntas, por el parque sin rosas,
se pierden en la noche romántica de otoño
ambulando en silencio la teoría de un diptongo.)

"Por las horas de cuento" is the third and last poem of the "VOCES AMARILLAS" section of *Andamios Interiores*. As in the other two poems, "Por las horas de cuento" has a prelude and postlude (the prelude is not enclosed in parentheses in this case, but the postlude is) surrounding a dialogue between two speakers of opposing viewpoints, one positive and one negative, representing life and death. All three poems have to do, in one way or another, with music and parks and gardens. These images are subtly balanced in "Y nada de hojas secas." Music dominates "En la dolencia estática," and the park image is predominant in "Por las horas de cuento."

The principal image of "Por las horas de cuento" is that of a couple walking in a park late at night. The shadow of them walking together is called "un diptongo de ensueño"; this is the image that opens the poem, appears at mid-point, and closes the poem.

> Por las horas de cuento de estos parques sin rosas,
> ambulan, un diptongo de ensueño, nuestras sombras. (l. 1-2)
> (Y seguimos del brazo nuestro obscuro diptongo,
> por los parques afónicos,
> lacrimeantes de oro...) (l. 13-15)
> (Y en el cloroformado cansancio de la sombra,
> nuestras 2 vidas juntas, por el parque sin rosas,
> se pierden en la noche romántica de otoño
> ambulando en silencio la teoría de un diptongo.) (l. 28-31)

The image of two shadows blending into one unites the two lovers visually and symbolizes their love, even though they are individuals of contrary spirit. The diphthong, two vowel sounds joined in one syllable to form one speech sound, is the union of disparate elements in a compatible environment—so too are the lovers as they walk arm in arm through the park this romantic autumn night.

The phrase "por las horas de cuento" probably means late at night, the hours when ghost stories are told. Line 30 says it is a "noche romántica de otoño." There is no moon ("un estudio sin luna"), and therefore the shadows are not caused by the moonlight of nineteenth-century Impressionism but rather the streetlight of the modern city of the twentieth century. The lateness of the hour is conveyed by the references to being tired and to staying up late: "desvela," "sus ojos se adormecen en un cansancio felpa," "su voz, casi ojerosa," "en el cloroformado cansancio de la sombra." It is autumn, and for that reason it is a "parque sin rosas." The woman asks, "—¿Amor, oyes las hojas?" and lines 14-15 say that the parks are "lacrimeantes de oro," a metaphor for yellow leaves falling from the trees.

Musical images and references found in the poem are "algún piano fantástico, desvela / los bemoles románticos de un estudio sin luna" and "—Tal vez es una enferma / que llora con Beethoven..." (l. 3-4, 11-12). Sound and silence are represented by "quedamente," "oyes las hojas?", "llora," "diptongo," "los parques afónicos," "su voz, casi ojerosa," "ambulando en silencio," and the spoken dialogue. Whatever sound there actually is, including the dialogue, is hushed ("quedamente," "afónicos," "su voz, casi ojerosa"). The feeling of quiet is almost palpable. The sounds the couple hears or believes they hear are either unidentifiable ("—¿Amor, oyes las hojas? / —¡Si no es eso! / —¿Entonces? / —Tal vez es una enferma / que llora con Beethoven...") or illusion–part of the whole dreamlike setting of the poem ("Por las horas de cuento," "un diptongo de ensueño," "algún piano fantástico," "cloroformado cansancio," "se pierden en la noche romántica de otoño").

As we have seen in the other poems of *Andamios Inte-*

riores, one character of "Por las horas de cuento" (probably a woman) represents the neurasthenic, *mal du siècle*, world-weary feelings of late nineteenth-century decadentism. She repeatedly laments, "¡Si la vida es tan triste!" and "¡Me quisiera morir!" For her, this autumn night is sad and depressing. The other character, the protagonist of Maples Arce's poems, has a different outlook on life. When his lover says that she wants to die, he tells her not to say that kind of thing, and that it hurts him to hear her say it. When she says that life is so sad, he asks her not to think that way. They each repeat their feelings, and the protagonist says "Doblaremos la hoja" (perhaps more correctly expressed, "Doblemos la hoja"), suggesting that they change the topic of conversation ("let's turn the page") or that they make a fresh start, turn over a new leaf, in their life. The woman, however, continues in the same vein as before, repeating "—¡Me quisiera morir!"

The postlude follows, summarizing the scene (lines 28-31 cited above) of the couple walking in the park on a romantic autumn night, their shadows blending into one, "nuestras 2 vidas juntas ... / ambulando en silencio la teoría de un diptongo." Ending the poem in this way gives a cinematic effect, as if it were the final scene of a movie, when the couple walks off into the fog in the distance ("se pierden en la noche romántica de otoño"). The feeling is that they will continue in the same way. One point of structure, however, hints at a possibility for change: the line "Doblaremos la hoja" is the only unpaired hemistich of the poem and as such, stands out. Whether attitude changes or not, a sense of union does pervade the poem, in the repeated image of the diphthong/shadow as they walk together, in the use of the numeral 2 in line 29 to reinforce the idea of two things combined in one symbol, the many synaesthetic images, the pairing of hemistichs, and the frequent elision of vowels in the metrical structure. It seems that the couple will stay together; at the least, they are united eternally in the poem as it paints this romantic scene.

As is the case with "Prisma," the sense of love and union is much stronger in the three poems of the "VOCES AMARILLAS" section than in the "FLORES ARITMÉTICAS" and "PERFUMES APAGADOS" sections. The dialogue format requires the actual presence of the beloved, rather than just the memory of her, and this in itself enables her character to be perceived as more immediate and closer to the protagonist. The overall sense of union rather than duality in "Por las horas de cuento" neutralizes the opposing (negative and affirmative) viewpoints. Isolation of the woman and her extremely negative outlook would be fatal for her; the positive attitude and affection of her lover help her, just as he and she support each other walking arm-in-arm ("Y seguimos del brazo nuestro obscuro diptongo").

"AL MARGEN DE LA LLUVIA..."[99]

Al margen de la lluvia en los cafés insomnes,
los perfiles se duermen en las láminas sordas.
Y es ahora que todo coincide en los relojes:
mi corazón nostálgico ardiéndose en la sombra.

---

99   I have included the spaces after line 17 and after line 21, and the upper case "E" beginning line 22 from the original publication of this poem in *Andamios Interiores*. These are omitted in the *Semillas* edition, but I believe them to be typographical errors ("e") and difficulty determining the spacing distinctions in the original. These are the only discrepancies in the two versions of this poem.

Después de los vulgares asombros del periódico
en que sólo se oye el humo de las pipas,
florecen a intervalos las actitudes lívidas
retropróximamente de los paraguas cónicos.

Deduzco de la lluvia que esto es definitivo.
¿Quién está en el manubrio? Hay un corto circuito.

La trama es complicado siniestro de oficina,
y algunas señoritas,
literalmente teóricas,
se han vuelto perifrásticas, ahora en re bemol,
con abandonos táctiles sobre el papel de lija.

Explotan las estrellas
eléctricas en flor.

Pero más que todo esto, en el sintaxicidio
de unos cuantos renglones desgarrados de adioses:
¡oh su carne amarilla!
¡mis dedos retroactivos!
                (En el piano automático
                se va haciendo de noche.)

Y en el mismo declive del interior romántico,
me interrumpo en un faro de automóvil, en tanto,

—-bohemios romboidales—mi corazón se llueve;
la tarde en las vidrieras traquetea como un tren,
y mi dolor naufraga, definitivamente,
en la literatura de todos los "ayer."

The last section of *Andamios Interiores* is called "PERFUMES APAGADOS." In the three poems of this section, the protagonist laments being separated from his beloved, recalling with anguish their goodbye: "Deduzco de la lluvia que esto es definitivo," "Pero más que todo esto, en el sintaxicidio / de unos cuantos renglones de adioses: / ¡oh su carne amarilla! / ¡mis dedos retroactivos!" (from "Al margen de la lluvia"); "¡oh dolorosa mía, / tú estás lejos de todo," "Locomotoras últimas / renegridas a fuerza de gritarnos adiós" (from "Tras los adioses últimos"); "Aquel adiós, el último, / fue un grito sin salida" (from "Como una gotera").

"Al margen de la lluvia" is the first poem of the "PERFUMES APAGADOS" section. In this poem, the protagonist is sitting in a café on a rainy afternoon, writing and watching the other people in the café and outside in the street. The café is always busy—only the pictures on the wall seem to sleep. To the protagonist it is a familiar place, always the same, and being there brings back memories of the past: "Al margen de la lluvia en los cafés insomnes, / los perfiles se duermen en las láminas sordas. / Y es ahora que todo coincide en los relojes: / mi corazón nostálgico ardiéndose en la sombra" (l. 1-4). Some customers read the newspaper, others come and go; the protagonist notices the newspaper headlines, the smoke of someone's pipe, umbrellas closing or opening as people enter or leave the café. At one table, a group of women share office gossip while idly filing their fingernails. The rain seems endless. It gets dark out, and the electric lights come on.

The protagonist has been sitting alone, in the shadows, thinking about the past and watching other people go about their business. The café seems to be a kind of safe harbor for the protagonist, at least momentarily. But there are many references in the poem to endings and things being ill or damaged or otherwise wrong (*insomnes, sordas, lívidas, corto circuito, siniestro, re bemol, sintaxicidio, desgarrados, adioses, dolor, naufraga, definitivo, definitivamente*). There are also several words that refer to the past (*relojes, nostálgico, retropróximamente, retroactivos, ayer*). Among the many geometrical shapes in the poem's images are a number of lines of downward direction that imply negativity (*lluvia, declive, naufraga*). The protagonist has been sitting there in the café, watching others and thinking about his own past. It seems that in particular he has been thinking about a love recently lost and trying to write a letter or a poem of goodbye. He is unable to express in writing what he wants to say, and in his anguish and frustration he wishes he could turn back time: "Pero más que todo esto, en el sintaxicidio / de unos cuantos renglones desgarrados de adioses: / ¡oh su carne amarilla! / ¡mis dedos retroactivos!" As it gets dark, the lights come on inside the café ("Explotan las estrellas / eléctricas en flor"), and when the protagonist looks out the window and notices the darkness of the evening outside, the headlights of a car shine on him. Suddenly he feels alone, isolated, exposed. "(En el piano automático / se va haciendo de noche.) / Y en el mismo declive del interior romántico, / me interrumpo en un faro de automóvil, en tanto, / —bohemios romboidales—mi corazón se llueve." Throughout "Al margen de la lluvia," there are contrasting images of light and dark: "mi corazón nostálgico, ardiéndose en la sombra," "florecen a intervalos las actitudes lívidas / retropróximamente de los paraguas cónicos," "Hay un corto circuito," "Explotan las estrellas / eléctricas en flor," and the above-cited nightfall and automobile headlight. Sitting in the shadows, remembering pleasant times of the past, was safe and not too painful ("mi corazón nostálgico ardiéndose en la sombra"), but being suddenly caught in the bright headlight reveals everything, and his pain crashes to abysmal depths. He sees that life goes on as usual for everyone else, but there he is, alone, isolated, lonely, and the absence of his lover is unbearable.

–bohemios romboidales–mi corazón se llueve;
la tarde en las vidrieras traquetea como un tren,
y mi dolor naufraga, definitivamente,
en la literatura de todos los "ayer".

One could conceivably argue that at this point the protagonist's sadness is revealed as self-pitying and melodramatic, and he casts it aside along with "la literatura de todos los 'ayer.' " There are no structural irregularities in the poem to support that change, however–none of the usual Maplesian clues of formal manipulation of the content. I see the burst of light from the headlight as a spotlight, a blow that snatches the protagonist out of his safe haven and causes him to feel the depth of his despair. "Al margen de la lluvia" laments the loss of love and days gone by like the Beatles' song "Yesterday" does. What the poem captures are the protagonist's feelings while in the café on that rainy evening, much like César Vallejo's poem "Piedra negra sobre una piedra blanca": "Me moriré en París con aguacero, / un día del cual tengo ya el recuerdo. / ... jamás como hoy, me he vuelto, / con todo mi camino, a verme solo..."[100]

Both interpretations show an outcome (the protagonist forgetting his loneliness or falling completely into despair) that is the result of a union of exterior and interior, with the automobile headlight as the catalyst or agent. Before the flash of light, the protagonist has been isolated inside the café–isolated from the "business as usual" exterior world and also from the other customers of the café. He has

---

100 César Vallejo, "Piedra negra sobre una piedra blanca," (*Poemas humanos*, 1939) in Florit and Jiménez, eds., *La poesía hispanoamericana desde el modernismo* 293-294.

observed the other people, but there has been no interaction between himself and them. The light connects him with the exterior world and, in one possible interpretation of the poem, saves him from his loneliness. In the other interpretation discussed here, the flood of light exposes his vulnerability and plumbs the depth of his emotions.

"Tras los adioses últimos..."

Tardes alcanforadas en vidrieras de enfermo,
tras los adioses últimos de las locomotoras,
y en las palpitaciones cardíacas del pañuelo
hay un desgarramiento de frases espasmódicas.

El ascensor eléctrico y un piano intermitente
complican el sistema de la casa de "apartments",
y en el grito morado de los últimos trenes
intuyo la distancia.

A espaldas de la ausencia se demuda el telégrafo.
Despachos emotivos desangran mi interior.

Sugerencia, L-10 y recortes de periódicos;
¡oh dolorosa mía,
tú estás lejos de todo,
y estas horas que caen amarillean la vida!

En el fru-fru inalámbrico del vestido automático
que enreda por la casa su pauta seccional,
incido sobre un éxtasis de sol a las vidrieras,
y la ciudad es una ferretería espectral.

      Las canciones domésticas
      de codos a la calle.

(¡Ella era un desmayo de prestigios supremos
y dolencias católicas de perfumes envueltos

a través de mis dedos!)

Accidente de lágrimas. Locomotoras últimas
renegridas a fuerza de gritarnos adiós,
y ella en 3 latitudes, ácida de blancura,
derramada en silencio sobre mi corazón.

The poem "Tras los adioses últimos" is composed of a series of memories—small fragments of scenes from the past—that are tied together by their common subject, the departure of the protagonist's beloved. The short scenes depict the couple saying goodbye at a train station, the sounds in an apartment building, a train whistle, the sound of the woman walking around her house, a sunset, street sounds, and the goodbye scene again. Interspersed throughout the poem are expressions of the loneliness felt by the protagonist in the absence of his beloved.

Especially effective are the train station scenes, in which the trains are given human qualities to communicate the lovers' emotions: "tras los adioses últimos de las locomotoras," "en el grito morado de los últimos trenes / intuyo la distancia," "locomotoras últimas / renegridas a fuerza de gritarnos adiós." The wave of a handkerchief symbolizes the woman saying goodbye from the train: "y en las palpitaciones cardíacas del pañuelo / hay un desgarramiento de frases espasmódicas." The emotion of the moment is conveyed in the references to repeated words of goodbye and to crying: "los adioses últimos," "un desgarramiento de frases espasmódicas," "accidente de lágrimas," "gritarnos adiós."

Other verses express how much the protagonist misses his beloved now that she has gone away, how painfully lonely and melancholic he feels: "tardes alcanforadas en vidrieras de enfermo," "oh dolorosa mía," "estas horas que caen amarillean la vida," "ácida de blancura, / derramada en silencio sobre mi corazón." The use of yellow imagery (e.g. "estas horas que caen amarillean la vida") is frequent in Maples Arce's poems, usually with a melancholic, negative connotation, in settings such as lonely afternoons, and can be compared to the yellow fog in T. S. Eliot's "Love Song of J. Alfred Prufrock":

> The yellow fog that rubs its back upon the window-panes,
> The yellow smoke that rubs its muzzle on the window-panes
> Licked its tongue into the corners of the evening,
> Lingered upon the pools that stand in drains,
> Let fall upon its back the soot that falls from chimneys,
> Slipped by the terrace, made a sudden leap,
> And seeing that it was a soft October night,
> Curled once about the house, and fell asleep.[101]

It seems that the protagonist receives no word from the woman after she leaves ("A espaldas de la ausencia se demuda el telégrafo") even though he writes passionately to her ("Despachos emotivos desangran mi interior"). The geographical distance between the lovers is expressed in the verses "y en el grito morado de los últimos trenes / intuyo la distancia," "tú estás lejos de todo," and "y ella en 3 latitudes." The length of time she has been gone (actual and perceived time) is conveyed in the references to her silence (no telegrams, "derramada en silencio"), in the feeling that the protagonist has spent long days waiting to hear from her while staring sadly out the window ("Tardes alcanforadas en vidrieras de enfermo," "las canciones domésticas / de codos a la calle," "y estas horas que caen amarillean la vida"), and in the use of the past tense

---

[101] T. S. Eliot, from "Love Song of J. Alfred Prufrock," *"The Waste Land" and Other Poems* (New York: Harcourt, Brace & World, 1934) 1-9.

in strophe seven ("¡Ella *era* un desmayo de prestigios supremos / y dolencias católicas de perfumes envueltos / a través de mis dedos!"). The woman's absence is felt in the apparent emptiness of the apartment building, where now all that is heard is the sound of an elevator operating and occasional piano music from another apartment. This almost palpable, lonely silence evokes a memory in the protagonist: he recalls the sound of the woman's dress swishing as she walked from room to room in the past, a lovely detail that exemplifies the small things (a perfume, an idiosyncrasy, a particular sound) that a person identifies with a loved one: "el fru-fru inalámbrico del vestido automático / que enreda por la casa su pauta seccional."

The dual meaning of the word "espectral" —referring either to the colors of the spectrum or to a ghostly image— complicates the meaning of the second half of strophe seven. As the protagonist remembers fondly the sound of the woman walking around the apartment, he looks out the window and sees a breathtaking sunset. The dramatic panorama of the city at sunset that day either fills the protagonist with a sense of awe and beauty or strikes him as a ghostly, impersonal, lonely place (cf. images of the sky in *Urbe*). One could say that in the past, when the woman was present, such a sunset was beautiful to the protagonist, but now that she is gone, it gives him a feeling of distance and loneliness.

Two verses stand out in "Tras los adioses últimos" because of their placement in the poem: "intuyo la distancia" (line 8) and "a través de mis dedos" (line 23) are the only unpaired hemistichs of the poem. These lines, especially due to their isolation, emphasize the separation of the lovers. In addition, line 13 includes the only direct statement to the woman in this poem, using second person instead of third person: "tú estás lejos de todo." This use of "tú" together with the most extreme reference to distance in the poem ("lejos de todo") intensifies the feeling of separation.

The final strophe of "Tras los adioses últimos" works both as a summary of the preceding strophes and as a poematic union of the protagonist and his departed lover:

> Accidente de lágrimas. Locomotoras últimas
> renegridas a fuerza de gritarnos adiós,
> y ella en 3 latitudes, ácida de blancura,
> derramada en silencio sobre mi corazón.

The full stop between hemistichs in line one of this last strophe emphasizes the finality of the woman's departure. The short phrases separated by punctuation in lines one and three echo the couple's repeated uttering of goodbye. The woman's departure and subsequent distance ("y ella en 3 latitudes") from the protagonist are painful to him, like an acid spilled on his heart. The feelings of separation and loneliness eat away at him. At the same time, there is a kind of union in the last two lines of the poem (the third and fourth lines of the strophe quoted above), as the "ácida de blancura," which represents the departed beloved, spills silently over the protagonist's heart: it is a type of contact and it is now a permanent image in the poem. Though separation and temporality dominate in the couple's lives, their mutual affection is captured in the poem. Typical of *Andamios Interiores*, "Tras los adioses últimos" exemplifies the process of emotion as the originator of a poem. Emotion is the energizing force; it is what generates expression. Such use of emotion is one of the primary tenets of *Estridentismo*.

"Como una gotera..."[102]

Como una gotera de cristal, su recuerdo,
agujera el silencio
de mis días amarillos.

Tramitamos palabras
por sellos de correo,
y la vida automática
se asolea en los andamios de un vulgar rotativo.

Las canciones florecen
a través de la lluvia,
en la tarde vacía, sin teclado y sin lágrimas.

Los tranvías se llevaron las calles cinemáticas
empapeladas de ventanas.

Mis besos apretados
florecían en su carne.

Aquel adiós, el último,
fue un grito sin salida.

La ciudad paroxista
nos llegaba hasta el cuello,
y un final de kilómetros subrayó sus congojas.

¡Oh el camino de hierro!

        Un incendio de alas
        a través del telégrafo.

        Trágicas chimeneas
        agujeran el cielo.

        ¡Y el humo de las fábricas!

---

102 I have used the spacing of lines 21-25 as in the original version: a space after line 20, after line 22, and after line 24, separating this section into three strophes. These spaces were omitted in the *Semillas* version.

> (Así, todo, de lejos, se me dice como algo
> imposible que nunca he tenido en las manos.)
>
> Un piano tangencial se acomoda en la sombra
> del jardín inconcreto; los interiores todos
> se exponen a la lluvia –selecciones de ópera—.
> En las esquinas nórdicas hay manifiestos rojos.

The last poem of the "PERFUMES APAGADOS" section and of *Andamios Interiores* is "Como una gotera." As in "Tras los adioses últimos," in "Como una gotera" the protagonist laments the departure of his beloved. The rhythm of this poem is similar to that of the rest of *Andamios Interiores*, but here a special visual effect is achieved due to the separation of the *alejandrino* verses into hemistichs placed on separate lines in most of the poem. These short lines descending the page mirror the drops of water dripping down that are referred to in the lovely simile of the first strophe: "Como una gotera de cristal, su recuerdo, / agujera el silencio / de mis días amarillos." This first strophe summarizes the protagonist's thoughts after the departure of the woman he loves: the memory of her penetrates his lonely, melancholy days, tugs insistently at his heart strings. He goes on to say that he and the woman write letters to each other, but life is just a boring daily routine devoid of meaning since she left. The emotion and dynamism of the past are now gone.

> Tramitamos palabras
> por sellos de correo,
> y la vida automática
> se asolea en los andamios de un vulgar rotativo.
>
> Las canciones florecen
> a través de la lluvia,
> en la tarde vacía, sin teclado y sin lágrimas.

Los tranvías se llevaron las calles cinemáticas
empapeladas de ventanas.

Four strophes at the middle of the poem are written in the past tense, in contrast to the present tense of the strophes surrounding them at the beginning and ending of the poem. Strophes four and six are in the preterite tense, indicating abrupt change ("Los tranvías se llevaron las calles cinemáticas / empapeladas de ventanas") and finality ("Aquel adiós, el último, / fue un grito sin salida"). Strophe five is expressed in the imperfect tense, illustrating the couple's relationship in the past ("Mis besos apretados / florecían en su carne"). Strophe seven begins in the imperfect and ends in the preterite, showing a situation in the past and how it ended ("La ciudad paroxista / nos llegaba hasta el cuello, / y un final de kilómetros subrayó sus congojas"). The move from present tense to past tense and back to present tense over the course of the poem simulates the protagonist's lapse into thoughts of the past. The raindrops (or water drops) and rain mentioned at the beginning and end of the poem take the protagonist and the reader into and out of the flashback scenes of the middle of the poem. A rainy afternoon is conducive to daydreaming, and is an appropriate objective correlative for the protagonist's sadness.

After strophe seven presents the stress-filled, anguished situation of the departure and the time just preceding it, strophe eight compresses the distress into an exclamation of blame aimed at the agent of separation, the train (and train tracks): "¡Oh el camino de hierro!" This same line in another Maples Arce poem might praise the dynamism and power of the train as a modern machine, but here it gives a negative feeling, reinforced by the phrases surrounding it: "un grito sin salida," "la ciudad paroxista," "sus congojas," "trágicas chimeneas."

Lines 21 through 25 serve multiple purposes. They continue the intensity and to a certain extent the negativity of line 20 ("¡Oh el camino de hierro!"). They make the transition from the flashback to the scene of the narrative present (perhaps the birds taking flight in lines 21-22 "wake up" the protagonist from his reverie). These verses introduce upward-moving images ("Un incendio de alas," "chimeneas," "cielo," "humo") that contrast to the dripping water (but continue the up-down line) and connect to the exteriorization of the final strophe. In addition, they include images (flight, smoke) related to the elusive qualities discussed in lines 26 and 27. To give added emphasis to this group of verses (21-25) which might otherwise appear unimportant at first glance, the poet sets them off to the right side of the page, the only verses so placed in this poem.

> Un incendio de alas
> a través del telégrafo.
>
> Trágicas chimeneas
> agujeran el cielo.
>
> ¡Y el humo de las fábricas! (l. 21-25)

Following the above-quoted verses is the next-to-last strophe of "Como una gotera," the most important lines of the poem: "(Así, todo, de lejos, se me dice como algo / imposible que nunca he tenido en las manos.)" These two lines (26-27) express the frustration of the protagonist regarding the elusive, transitory nature of things in the modern world. This image of not being able to hold on to anything appears throughout Maples Arce's poetry (e.g. "¡Dios mío! / Y de todo este desastre, / sólo unos cuantos pedazos / blancos / de su recuerdo, / se me han quedado entre las manos" –from *Urbe*; "y el paisaje entreabierto se me cae de las manos"–from "Canción desde un aeroplano"; "sobre olas de ausencia y polvosos mirajes"–from "Mensaje"). Lines 26-27 serve as a commentary not only for the loss in "Como una gotera" but for all the loss felt in the ten poems of *Andamios Interiores*. The persistence of the problem is illustrated in the pacing of line 26 ("Así, todo, de lejos ...") –the short, slow phrases echoing the dripping water of strophe one ("Como una gotera de cristal, su recuerdo, / agujera el silencio / de mis días amarillos").

The final strophe of "Como una gotera" follows that commentary. These last four lines continue the idea of the problem of elusivity and also suggest a possible recourse through exteriorization of the pain.

> Un piano tangencial se acomoda en la sombra
> del jardín inconcreto; los interiores todos
> se exponen a la lluvia –selecciones de ópera—.
> En las esquinas nórdicas hay manifiestos rojos.

The first phrase of this strophe, "Un piano tangencial se acomoda en la sombra / del jardín inconcreto," at first suggests escape by hiding in the dark or hiding in a corner. The indefinite adjective used to modify *jardín* here continues the feeling of elusivity from the previous strophe. The continuation of the verse, however, indicates an opening up to the exterior elements: "los interiores todos / se exponen a la lluvia." This apparently voluntary exposure leaves the subject ("un piano tangencial," but possibly also the protagonist by extension) totally vulnerable.

It seems to be a moment of despair, of giving in, the lowest point of the poem. But as we learned in "Prisma," "the way up is the way down." In "Prisma," the sinking of the star ("la estrella del recuerdo") at the same moment the protagonist's nerves collapsed produced the greatest point of union in the poem: "Tú y yo / coincidimos ..." In "Como una gotera," as the piano settles down into the shadows, its interior is exposed to the rain. Rather than rotting the wood, the rain beating on the piano chords creates a beautiful song, "–selecciones de ópera–." This emotional, operatic music is the expression of the protagonist's pain. Before this exteriorization, as he marked time through empty days, the only music was "sin teclado y sin lágrimas" (l. 10). The rain that produces this wonderful operatic music at the end of the poem is a beautiful evolution of the "gotera de cristal" from strophe one. Both images and both sounds are generated by the memory of the protagonist's beloved.

The implied course of action is to exteriorize one's grief rather than holding it inside. There is a reaching out to the world for help in the last part of the poem, hinted at earlier in the images of lines 21-25: birds, telegraph, smokestacks, factories. If an abstract sentiment is made evident in concrete objects of the exterior world, the ineffable has been expressed. This is similar to the effect of putting feelings into words, whether in speech, poetry or song. The last line of "Como una gotera," "En las esquinas nórdicas hay manifiestos rojos," suggests such an exteriorization and expression: a protest of the current situation. This line foreshadows Maples Arce's 1924 poem *Urbe*, where the protagonist joins the workers in the street in the spirit of their cause. Somehow in this process there is a feeling of hope for the future at the end of "Como una gotera," appropriately the closing poem of *Andamios Interiores*. This poem is, in many ways, a summary of all of the poems of *Andamios Interiores*, and the writing of the poems has been the exteriorization of the protagonist's inner feelings.

One of the most overt and obvious innovations of Maples Arce's *Andamios Interiores* is the inclusion of urban vocabulary (previously extra-poematic) along with traditional poematic vocabulary in his poems. Although the poems of this 1922 volume retain many characteristics of pre-*vanguardista* poetry, such as the *alejandrino* line, there is sufficient modification and manipulation of content and form to merit placement in the category of "new" poetry. Maples Arce's work unquestionably has great innovation in imagery and metaphor. Just as the modern city is beginning to grow, its own blueprints and scaffolding still in use, Maples Arce shows us his construction plans for a new kind of poetry. In *Andamios Interiores*, the modern "ciudad paroxista" is used as the stage or backdrop for romantic drama and meditation.

The yearning for love, permanence and union in a world of transitoriness and separation is a constant in *Andamios Interiores* that continues in Maples Arce's later volumes of poetry. The very introspective protagonist of the balconies, parks and cafés of *Andamios Interiores* increasingly moves outward in the subsequent volumes, following the lead suggested at the end of "Como una gotera," walking the post-Revolution streets and plazas of *Urbe*, speeding across town and across the country in *Poemas Interdictos*, and travelling to foreign lands in *Memorial de la Sangre*.

Chapter Three: The City in Clamor and Reflection, *Urbe, 1924*

"...the street cars go by singing to themselves
I am iron "
      W. S. Merwin, "Touching the Tree,"
      The Rain in the Trees

"–One Song, one Bridge of Fire! Is it Cathay,
Now pity steeps the grass and rainbows ring
The serpent with the eagle in the leaves...?
Whispers antiphonal in azure swing."
      Hart Crane, *The Bridge*

The above quotations illustrate the dual character of Maples Arce's 1924 book-length (228 lines) poem *Urbe*. This poem is at once a Whitmanesque song of praise to the modern city and a record of the gradual corruption of a revolution that dreamed of utopia. The rapid growth of modern technology in the early twentieth century coincided with Mexico's 1910 revolution and its hopes for the future. Young writers and artists in the early 1920s in Mexico felt an electric surge of optimism, produced by the exciting new technological inventions world-wide, the improvement in transatlantic communication, the creative boom in the arts, the attempt to put the goals of the Revolution into practice and into a new government, and by the writers'/artists' own brash youth. In Maples Arce's poetry, we see the effect of the above-mentioned phenomena most clearly in *Urbe* and in *Poemas Interdictos*. These volumes are indeed the product of their times, filtered through the poet's vision and sensibility.

In his November 1, 1981 Public Television program, "The Shock of the New," Robert Hughes noted the effect of modern art and literature on life, and vice-versa. He explained that the avant-garde of engineering had something in common with the avant-garde of art: the conquering of horizontal and vertical space. The new machines brought heightened notions of motion and speed. They changed man's perspective on the world: the blurred vision of rapid motion through space past static objects is captured in many paintings of the Italian Futurists, as well as in Maples Arce's poem about an automobile ride, "80 H. P." The view of the ground from the top of the new Eiffel Tower in 1899 was a turning point in human consciousness, as was the view from an airplane some years later (on her first airplane ride, Gertrude Stein remarked that what she saw below reminded her of Picasso's paintings), and can be compared to the sight of Earth from the moon in our own times, after the 1969 lunar landing. Such a new view of the universe inevitably altered man's concept of identity and existence. More and more, Einstein's theory of relativity became evident to the public. Hughes noted Cezanne's emphasis on the process of perception, and Picasso's attempt to compress the inspection of an object—a perception which, because of the object's tridimensionality, normally requires linear time to complete—into one single moment on the canvas. In addition to the idea of perception through dynamism and from new angles, people were fascinated by the machine.

The new technology meant a brighter future, and it was man-made beauty as well as power. The tremendous optimism involved in humankind's esteem for wondrous mechanical feats such as the Brooklyn Bridge, the Eiffel Tower, transatlantic ships, the automobile and the airplane, is much like the optimism found in the early stages of a revolution. The Russian Revolution of 1917 gave the Russian avant-garde its image of dynamism; it was the hope for the future. The same applies to the 1910 Mexican Revolution and the *estridentistas*: they wanted to carry the Revolution to the arts, and they did so with great energy. The apogee of their efforts was in their work in Jalapa. *Urbe* was published at the very beginning of that period of combined literary and social activism. Indeed, it was a sort of catalyst or springboard for the *estridentista* move to Jalapa and the subsequent addition of a social and political orientation to the movement.[103]

The impetus for the Russian avant-garde was, however, "the future that never came," in Hughes' words, and likewise in World War I, when modern machinery was turned against its inventors and its children. The dream destroyed itself; this also happened in Mexico. The Mexican Revolution succeeded in ousting elitist dictator Porfirio Díaz in favor of agrarian reform and more rights for the proletariat. Unfortunately, however, in the 1920s, while trying to put together a new government, the former rebels, now political bosses, fought for power amongst themselves and the Revolution became corrupt. In the process, the ideals of the Revolution became secondary concerns to the officials, even though the *pueblo* still

---

103 Luis Leal, *Panorama de la literatura mexicana actual* (Washington, DC: Unión Panamericana, Secretaría General de la OEA, 1968) 41-42.

marched for labor unions and equal rights. This is the atmosphere that produced Maples Arce's *Urbe*.

Maples recounts in *Soberana Juventud* the violent political situation in Mexico City during the 1920s:

> La vida del México de aquellos años se encontraba tensa de dificultades y de potenciales estallidos militares. Después de cada elección presidencial sólo había una pausa, relativamente breve, de tranquilidad pública, y volvían otra vez a agitarse los círculos políticos y los elementos militares a pretender conquistar el Poder. Esto daba origen a horas de inquietud, de agitación parlamentaria y de violencia armada. De esta suerte, reinaba siempre un estado de angustia que impresionaba a todos los espíritus y que no dejaba de tener resonancias psicológicas en la vida de los jóvenes.[104]

Maples Arce often attended sessions of the House of Representatives (Cámara de Diputados) to listen to the speeches–probably not uncommon for a law student–and on one such occasion a flurry of pistol shooting broke out among the arguing representatives. The shooting caused two deaths and many injuries while observers and politicians alike scattered for refuge. The poet comments, "Después me encaminé a pie hasta mi casa, pensando con amargura en el fracaso político de nuestra democracia y en la violencia que dominaba nuestras instituciones;" and later, "Yo seguía los acontecimientos en los diarios y con amigos de las más diversas orientaciones, y sentía la trágica realidad de nuestra historia."[105] Several rebellions and violent skirmishes followed. The implications of this situation for Mexican society as a whole, especially with regard

---

[104] Manuel Maples Arce, *Soberana Juventud* (Madrid: Editorial Plenitud, 1967) 144.
[105] Soberana Juventud 145-146.

to the goals of the Revolution, became clearer to Maples Arce in a quasi-"revelation" he experienced while walking home and observing a May Day march. This revelation produced the poem *Urbe*.

> Un primero de mayo, por la tarde, regresaba de Mixcoac a pie, pues no había servicio de transportes, totalmente paralizados por la manifestación obrera. El viento arremolinaba el polvo de las barriadas y grupos proletarios regresaban cargando sus pancartas y calicós con lemas reivindicadores y banderas rojas y negras. Oleadas de obreros vestidos de mezclilla se sucedían constantemente y se escuchaban vítores a sus líderes y confederaciones. No obstante la fatiga de la caminata, me interesaba ese movimiento de masas humanas. Sentía la impresión de lo que estaba pasando y la fiesta de los trabajadores llegaba como una apoteosis hasta mi corazón. Me parecía bello aquel desfile interminable bajo el sol deslustrado de la tarde. Mi espíritu, lleno de las inquietudes del instante, me sugería esas resonancias. Así, me fui pensando y soñando a través de la ciudad, integrado a la marcha gloriosa de los obreros. Las disensiones sindicales, las agitaciones políticas y las amenazas de la guerra civil se cernían sobre nuestros destinos. En la Cámara de Diputados, la razón de los discursos se trocaba sorpresivamente en un relámpago de pistolas. Los entorpecedores del progreso de México fanatizaban a grupos de militares y políticos para adueñarse del poder, los obreros desfilaban en manifestaciones de alerta, y por mi parte, miraba estos espectáculos y reflexionaba sobre las circunstancias y responsabilidades de los hombres que podrían influir en los destinos nacionales. Cuando llegué a mi casa, bajo las fuerzas estimulantes, me puse a escribir un canto en que latía la esperanza y la desesperación. Vi más claramente la necesidad de dar una intención estética a la Revolución, y en *Urbe* junté mi emoción íntima y el clamor del pueblo. Todos estos elementos, acompañados de mis reacciones emotivas,

constituían el cuerpo vivo del poema. Los sentimientos que lo animaban, la audacia de las imágenes y la novedad de la expresión literaria eran la revelación de un hondo sentido de la existencia, de sus trances y de sus culminaciones. Si se advierten en él ciertos contrastes, débense a circunstancias amargas que aniquilaban la alegría... En medio de mis preocupaciones sufrí los desgarramientos de nuestra vida civil, y sus hondas vibraciones repercutieron en mi emoción. Así era la vida mexicana, y, en mi juventud, yo me sentía su profeta.[106]

As we examine the lines of *Urbe* we will see that Maples Arce succeeded in putting into verse the complex of the above phenomena. The situation recalls Mário de Andrade's writing of *Pauliceia Desvairada*, in a rush of emotion after intensely observing São Paulo. *Urbe* is indeed a "pauliceia desvairada" (in addition to the accepted translation "Hallucinated City," Andrade's title could be translated as "agitated, frenetic city," full of the clashing, strident voices of the complex times). Luis Marín Loya provides a helpful insight into the structural and stylistic way that Maples Arce achieves in *Urbe* the poetization of the impression that the bustling city, full of high-pitched emotion, made on him as he observed it. In his extensive and elsewhere largely impressionistic comment on the poem, Marín Loya explains (I have added italics to distill and clarify):

> El poeta ha puesto en marcha la formidable maquinaria de su técnica poética, con la que logra fijar para siempre su genésico *anhelo constructivo*. Así encontramos en su obra, riquísima de imágenes, una *variabilidad continua y diferencial*, que presta una simultánea virtud a la *sensación*. Este *fenómeno impulsionista*

---

[106] Soberana Juventud 147-149.

es genuino de Maples Arce. Sería un alarde estéril querer conquistarlo. Maples Arce ha logrado *apuntar en la belleza desordenada de los elementos modernos, la belleza subjetiva de ese gran panorama interior*, estableciendo, así, una *relación diferencialista*, para obtener una *nueva sugerencia insospechada. Al impulso dinámico* todo ritmo espiritual y audacia, *se aduna una gran exaltación suprasensible*. Esta realización encierra toda la manera peculiar de su *técnica abstractiva*.[107]

The "relación diferencialista" may be explained with the metaphor of an automobile, as the equal rolling of different (opposite) wheels, simultaneous and equal power and movement in two or more different parts. Thus in the poem, for example, these pairs of simultaneous but different phenomena operate in conjunction: dynamism + sensation; modernity + expression of wonderment; technology + emotion; the phenomenon of city/revolution + effect on people; action + reception. Luis Marín Loya calls this Maples Arce's "técnica abstractiva". We recall from Chapter One of this study Arqueles Vela's explanation of the "teoría abstraccionista": "La teoría abstraccionista, no es una teoría, sino una insinuación de afirmar la personalidad. De crear un arte puro y sin repujaciones. *Un arte en que el sincronismo emocional tenga una equivalencia con ese ritmo sincrónico del ajetreo de la vida moderna.*" [108] If we see the "relación diferencialista" as explained above, then the *estridentista* "teoría abstraccionista," as well as the "imagen equivalentista" (often concrete noun plus abstract adjective) and the repeated emphasis on emotion, all begin to make more sense. It is an *equivalencia* of the objective and the subjective (the subjective is materialized and the objective is animated).

---

107 Luis Marín Loya, *El meridiano lírico* (México: n.p., 1926), n. pag.
108 Arqueles Vela, "El estridentismo y la teoría abstraccionista," *Irradiador* 2 (octubre 1923): n. pag. Italics are mine.

In his essay, Arqueles Vela asserted that real life is incongruous and absurd, unordered, unconnected, arbitrary, illusionary (a mirage), not the balanced and perfectly ordered picture of the literary tradition. Vela says that emotion is the absurd condition of the spirit. He also writes that "la imagen doble interpreta simultáneamente la actitud espiritual y la actitud material." This image ("la figura indirecta compuesta," "la imagen doble," "la imagen equivalentista"), Vela suggests, has not only revolutionized form but also ideology, or "la manera de interpretar la armonía del universo." "La poesía está en esa música luminosa desenrrollada por la rotación de las esferas. Y esa simultaneidad de armonías logradas sin tiempo, ni espacio, sin sujeto, es lo que hace nuestra teoría abstraccionista." Vela recalls the combination of interior and exterior in *Andamios Interiores*: "En su poema 'Prisma,' Maples Arce logra ensamblar su inquietud interior con esa inquietud que flota en unas pestañas, en la calle toda llena de inquietudes eléctricas y de humo de fábricas, con imágenes diametralmente opuestas y yuxtapuestas con una fuerte hilación ideológica."

In this context, Emile Malespine's article on *cenestesia* and *sinestesia* in *Irradiador* 3 has a strong connection with the *estridentista* image. On *cenestesia* he writes:

> Cada sentido pide ayuda a los otros sentidos. Entre ellos una relación estrecha existe. Su punto de contacto es pues la parte obscura de nuestro ser (sensación interna, cenestesia) y rehúye a todo análisis. Todo lo que se puede decir, se resume en algunas palabras. Una sensación no es jamás neutra. Nos afecta de alguna manera. En nosotros un cambio se produce, especie de impregnación sutil que colora en alegría o tristeza nuestro yo. Es el coeficiente cenestésico. Dos sensa-

ciones que teñirán nuestro yo de una cenestesia semejante van a ligarse entre sí. La una llama a la otra. Así nacen las correspondientes.[109]

The reason for including this passage on *cenestesia* here is that the same relationship exists between the "actitud material" and the "actitud espiritual" in the "imagen equivalentista" through the "relación diferencialista." The previously mentioned (see Chapter Two) essay on the pyramids and the triangle emphasizes the same basic point: "fundir las dos formas antitéticas del conocimiento en la obra de arte;" "la unidad en la dualidad, y la creación, su fruto, constituyeron la divina triada."[110]

Luis Marín Loya, after his explanation of the stylistic process found in *Urbe*, quotes a section of Maples Arce's *Actual No. 1* and adds to the process *actualismo* (and in it we see Maples at the May Day rally): "Todo el mundo allí, quieto, iluminado maravillosamente en el vértice estupendo del minuto presente; atalayado en el prodigio de su emoción inconfundible y única; sensorialmente electrolizado en el 'yo' superatista, vertical sobre el instante meridiano, siempre el mismo y renovado siempre."[111] This combination of the "teoría abstraccionista" or "imagen equivalentista" in a "relación diferencialista" (dynamism plus sensation, modernity plus emotion, the material plus the spiritual) with *actualismo*, creates the vortex that is the same thing Picasso was trying to capture when he attempted to compress the time-dimensioned perception of an object into one single moment on the canvas. The

---

109   Emile Malespine, "La audición colorida y las sinestesias en los ciegos," *Irradiador* 3 (noviembre 1923): n. pag.
110   R. Gómez Robelo, "Las Pirámides," *Irradiador* 1, 2 (septiembre, octubre 1923): n. pag.
111   Maples Arce, *Actual No. 1*.

process involves the typically modern spatialization of time and temporalization of space. What Maples Arce achieves by this process is also similar to Mário de Andrade's theory of melody, harmony and polyphony (simultaneity) (see Chapter Two). Marín Loya believes that it is in *Urbe* that the *estridentista* aesthetic is finally set and achieved.

The various groups forming the international avant-garde of the 1920s had much in common, including basic roots in Marinetti's Italian Futurism[112] and a Cubist approach to the image. Much has been written elsewhere on Futurism and Cubism and the other major European avant-garde movements. What surfaces in a comparative reading of such studies is that *Estridentismo* was somewhat unique in that it had a social ideology: it showed solidarity with the goals of a political revolution, as did the Mexican muralists. In addition, *Estridentismo* was unlike the other Hispanic vanguard movements in the importance given to emotion—not whining sentimentality but rather the bounding energetic force of emotion, a kind of dynamism in itself.[113] This politization or socialization did not happen in Spain; there the avant-garde of the 20s was apolitical and intellectual (poetry as calculated form), rather than emotional.[114] The Ultraists of Spain and Argentina

---

112   This is very well documented and substantiated in Juan Cano Ballesta's book on the avant-garde in Spain, *Literatura y Tecnología: Las letras españolas ante la revolución industrial, 1900-1933* (Madrid: Editorial Orígenes, 1981), especially chapter two.

113   It is useful to recall here Ezra Pound's previously mentioned definition of poetry as an "emotional complex in an instant of time," and his statement that "emotion is the source of form in poetry." (See A. David Moody reference in the Bibliography below.) Compare also this comment by Arqueles Vela on *Urbe*: "La pasión por su tiempo enciende la poesía de Maples Arce. Todo estado neutro es anti-artístico. Sólo es digno de la vida lo que es capaz de arder. La frialdad es ajena al arte. En la poesía de Maples Arce palpita la ignición de la sociedad transformándose." (Arqueles Vela, "MMA, Poeta de la Revolución," unidentified magazine, n.d.: n. pag.)

were motivated by their sense of humor and playfulness when confronting the machine world. The difference in Mexico is, of course, explained by the historical and political setting. In the 1920s Mexico had just experienced a revolution, and was grappling with building a new nation. Spain would not reach its crisis point until the 30s, and then literature changed accordingly. Argentina's next moment of social upheaval was perhaps in the early Peronist years (1940s-50s), with Eva Perón standing by the *descamisados*. The subsequent literature reflected the times. These are only two examples. At the beginning of change, there is hope and optimism: most of the avant-garde movements have this characteristic (Huidobro does not despair until *Altazor*). When corruption, war, and disillusion grow in the decades following the 1920s, Western literature turns to surrealism, then existentialism, and then absurdism.

For the *estridentistas*, Mexico is still at a very high, optimistic point. Yet, as *Urbe* shows and as Maples Arce explained in *Soberana Juventud*, the Revolution was already becoming corrupt and implementation of the idealistic goals was failing on many counts. In 1924 Maples Arce was spiritually balancing on a highwire over Mexico City. He was uplifted by the wonders of modern technology, inspired by the Revolution, but teetering at the sight of gunfights in Congress, and gripping tightly to his hope for the future and the thrill of today.[115] The fact that Maples Arce chooses to address the state of the Revolution in *Urbe*,

---

114 Cano Ballesta, 93, 127, 129.
115 A parallel motivation might be found in the Expressionist period in Germany, given the social and political unrest there between the two world wars.

rather than just continuing to "revolutionize" poetry, sets *Estridentismo* apart: "en el momento en que adopta la ideología social de la Revolución Mexicana y la incorpora a su literatura, el movimiento adquiere solidez, organización, y de alguna manera se separa del resto de la vanguardia internacional."[116] This is also the period (just after *Urbe*) when Maples Arce joins Jara's government and moves with the other members of *Estridentismo* to Jalapa, Veracruz. As Schneider goes on to clarify, the *estridentistas* did not write politically-committed literature (with the possible exception of List Arzubide at times), and it was not a literature of the proletariat. They are much better characterized as young middle-class liberals in love with the idea of rebellion and subversion (as are all the avant-garde) than as political activists. It happened that they coincided with an environment of social change, they admired the Revolution, and they chose to correspond in spirit. They supported the cause best in their editorial work: the *Editorial Horizonte* published a series of classics, *Biblioteca Popular*, in order to make them easily accessible to the Mexican populace, the most notable book of the series being Mariano Azuela's *Los de abajo*. The group also produced the magazine *Horizonte*, which included articles of social orientation as well as literature. This publishing was complemented by work for the city of Jalapa, and by teaching. In all, there remained as a constant the role of art in life. It was a sustaining force and inspiration for the *estridentistas*, and was Maples Arce's heartfelt hope as a plausible solution to the problems of separation and transitoriness.

---

116 Luis Mario Schneider, *El estridentismo*, 206.

Luis Mario Schneider explains in his book *El estridentismo: o una literatura de la estrategia*, the integral role of art in life and society as felt by the *estridentistas*:

> For them, Art became the principal action in human life... This action was not only a desire for freedom in the creative process, but also the only liberating system of the human race, enabling the artist to break away from society's moral norms, prejudices and dogmas. The *estridentistas* felt that Art and time were almost one and the same. They availed themselves of the rhythm of the times and fused it with the mission that Art has, according to them, in the destiny and development of history. They were essentially renovators... Their union of the messianic spirit of Art with a principle of originality and continual renovation brought as a consequence a transformation of the creative attitude of the writer and of the general context of Mexican literature.[117]

Arqueles Vela expresses his view of this process, or the role of the Revolution in Maples' poetry and the role of Maples' poetry in the Revolution, in his article on *Urbe*, titled "Manuel Maples Arce, Poeta de la Revolución". To paraphrase Vela's thoughts, the shakedown of the social stratification provoked by the insurrectional contingents brought out the reversibility of things. As behind every po-

---

[117] Schneider, 207-208. Translation and paraphrase mine. The original quote is as follows:
  El arte pasa a ser la principal acción de la vida humana, y se cree en él, no sólo como anhelo de libertad en el proceso creativo sino, además, como único sistema libertario de la raza humana, ya que así se puede romper con las normas y los prejuicios morales y los dogmas. El arte y el tiempo son casi una misma entidad. Los estridentistas se apoyaron en el ritmo de la época y lo fusionaron a la misión que, según ellos, el arte tiene en el destino y en el desarrollo de la historia. Eran esencialmente renovadores... El espíritu mesiánico del arte unido a un principio de originalidad y renovación continua trajo como consecuencia una transformación en la actitud creativa del escritor y por supuesto, del contexto general de la literatura mexicana.

litical act lies a socio-economic event, so too behind every artistic irruption (as opposed to an art whose style comes from stable aspects of life) burn the problems that move society. The new turmoil in the world of art—rebellion stemming from the feeling that the art of the day was insufficient and that its style no longer corresponded to aesthetic demands, in short, the need for something new and timely—was a product of the Mexican Revolution, "the Revolution that illuminated the factories and shook the plantations of the Mexican countryside." Arqueles Vela says that Maples Arce's poetry rose from that shaking of Mexican society. Maples Arce states in his manifesto: "We have given an aesthetic sense to the Revolution."

Vela continues to illustrate the parallels: the Revolution demanded the return of the land to the people; Maples Arce proposed the return, to the people of today, of the nation's poetry, which Vela says had been buried in "mysticism and triviality" since the times of Amado Nervo.

Vela notes a characteristic of Maples Arce's poetry that we see most clearly in *Urbe*: that the influence of workers on cultural matters of the day is most pure in Maples Arce's work. Vela asserts that the multitude is the character, the artistic subject: a combination of people and occurrences within the process of human activities in social relations. The poet's anguish is not merely that of his lonely solitude but that of a solitude which could not be more deeply entrenched in the multitude. It is a deep solitude that rises from the darkest part of nature ("Ríos de enredaderas que vienen desde el fondo de los sueños"– *Urbe*). Vela concludes that the reality of Maples Arce's poetry is an imagistic commemoration of the events of the day—internal happenings with external motives. The objectivity of his verse, Vela says, comes from feeling so subjectively the subject. The thematics are determined by the times and serve the times. The voice of Maples' poetry is the voice of his times.[118]

In *Urbe*, there is a deepening of thought concerning the modern city and its marvels. The poet not only rejoices at man's technological creation and the dynamism of modern

---

118 Arqueles Vela, "MMA, Poeta de la Revolución." Translation and paraphrase mine. The original states as follows:
El sacudimiento de las estratificaciones sociales, provocado por los contingentes insurreccionales, extraía la reversibilidad de las cosas. Y así como detrás de todo hecho político se esconde siempre un acontecimiento económico-social, así también detrás de una irrupción artística, opuesta a la que ha condicionado su estilo de las formas de vida estables, arden los problemas que conmueven a la sociedad.
La inquietud por el funcionamiento de nuevos elementos expresivos, la rebeldía ante la insuficiencia del arte, el desasosiego por un material estilístico que ya no correspondía a las exigencias estéticas, eran producto de la Revolución que iluminaba las fábricas y estremecía los latifundios de la campiña mexicana.
De ese estremecimiento surge la poesía de Manuel Maples Arce. 'Hemos dado un sentido estético a la Revolución,' dice en uno de sus primeros manifiestos.
...
La Revolución exigía la devolución de la tierra. Maples Arce aportaba la devolución de la poesía soterrada en un misticismo, en una trivialidad descompuesta desde los tiempos de Amado Nervo. Contra la recreación arqueológica del arte y la inspiración pasiva de los intelectuales se pronuncia la estética de Manuel Maples Arce.
Las influencias obreras en los hechos culturales son las más puras en la poesía de Maples Arce y la substancia de su obra. La multitud es el personaje, el sujeto artístico: una combinación de hombres, de acontecimientos dentro del proceso de las actividades humanas en las relaciones sociales.
...
En cuanto surge políticamente una nueva energía social, sirve de representación artística.
...
La angustia del poeta no es la de su soledad sola... es la de una soledad que no puede adentrarse más profundamente en la multitud. Es una soledad honda que asciende de lo más oscuro de la naturaleza:
Ríos de enredaderas que vienen desde el fondo
de los sueños...
La realidad de su poesía es una conmemoración imaginística de los hechos. Sucesos internos con móviles externos. La objetividad de su verso proviene de sentir tan subjetivamente el sujeto. La temática la determina la época y sirve a su época... La voz de su poesía es la voz de la época.

life, he also becomes vitally concerned with the ephemeral quality of those inventions, of that life. There arises a nostalgia for permanence, an anguish over not being able to hold on to anything, to retain anything through time. It all passes by too quickly. All is adventure, but when the adventure ends there is nothing left. The poet, living in the present, also fears the loss and destruction that the passing of time brings. Even the Revolution gradually becomes corrupt, the original ideal lost. It is the Revolution's fall to corruption and failure, as he sees it in the city, that Maples Arce's poem relates. The poet concludes that the Revolution must be kept alive in the memory of the people and in works of art (such as this poem), where it is saved for future generations, future attempts.

Maples Arce's vision of the modern city is always of a double attitude: a positive and a negative perspective. This duality produces a tension evident in all of the poems. The poet is part of the dynamism of the city (as in "80 H. P." and "Canción desde un aeroplano," from *Poemas Interdictos*) but at the same time he is "un punto muerto en medio de la hora" ("Prisma," from *Andamios Interiores*). Since there is a multiplicity and simultaneity of sensations in the city and in the poem, the positive and negative attitudes exist simultaneously in the perception of the poet. This duality is also reflected in the continuous opening and closing of possibility and hope in the poems. Apparent possibility is later snuffed out, all hope lost, only to appear again in another moment.

In order to resolve this anguish-causing duality, the poet presents us with two possible courses of action: either try to capture the present moment and prolong it for as long as possible, live it to the fullest; or create something durable to represent the moment, whether in material, concrete form such as the city, or in artistic form, to preserve the essence of the moment in memory and in art.

The modern city is presented as the place where it may be possible to transcend the transitory. The city is the microcosm created by man (as opposed to the Earth, the work of God or nature). It is where one finds man-made beauty. The city is at the same time the microcosm of art and of poetry, where the poet-magician-"pequeño dios" can create transcendental works. We are constantly at the mercy of time; the only salvation, or transcendence, is found in art.

If we see the modern city ("urbe") as the symbol for this potential and desired transcendence (as well as the setting of the existential conflict that the protagonist suffers and which produces the double perspective), Maples Arce gives us four possible manifestations (or stages) in his poetic work in which this transcendence can occur. The first manifestation is *Estridentópolis*, the ultramodern city invented and dreamed of by the *estridentistas*. It is not really Jalapa (as some critics think) or Mexico City, but an ideal city, usually imagined as a great ocean port full of modernity, dynamism and communication with the rest of the world (depicted in many of the wood-block prints and drawings of the artists of the *estridentista* group). It is here that the protagonist tries to live the present moment to the maximum and prolong it as much as he can, as seen in all of Maples Arce's *vanguardista* volumes but especially in *Poemas Interdictos*.

The second manifestation is found in cities such as Venice and Brussels, and in the pyramids of Egypt (also by extension those of Mexico), where the essence of great cultures of the past has been preserved in art and architecture. This manifestation is found in the poems of *Memorial de la Sangre*. Here there is a shift from one person living in the present moment to a prolongation of that moment for whole civilizations in the timelessness of art and memory.[119] Another (third) related manifestation of possible transcendence, but outside of the microcosm of the city, is that expressed by the Tuxpan River, near which Maples Arce grew up, and which influenced the poet greatly, as shown in some of the previously uncollected poems of *Las semillas del tiempo*.

The final (in an ascending scale of abstraction) manifestation of possible transcendence is found in revolution, and specifically the Mexican Revolution. The poet wonders how to maintain its original ideal, how to keep it alive. This stage is expressed in *Urbe*,[120] and also to a certain extent in some of Maples' last poems, found at the end of *Las semillas*. Where *Urbe* is the expression of this problem on a social or world level, the other poems in *Las semillas* (for example, "A Hamlet") give the same expression on a personal and existential level. While in "A Hamlet," written in the final years of Maples' life, fate and the fear of nothingness dominate, in *Urbe*, an early work, there is still hope for the Revolution in the future; however difficult it may be, society will keep trying.

We experience anguish in the twentieth century in trying to realize this transcendence of the present moment, because it seems more difficult than in the past, the modern world being as it is. In the Maplesian city of the

---

[119] The manifestations dealing with books later than *Urbe* will be discussed further in subsequent chapters.
[120] As mentioned above, the level of *Estridentópolis* is, of course, also found in *Urbe*.

twentieth century, we see the tension between hope and despair, between possibility and futility, between life and death or nothingness. In Maples Arce's poetry, "todo lo efímero, forma los elementos donde querría fundar la eternidad."[121] *Urbe* is an attempt to achieve that transcendence in a literary manner.

"URBE"[122]

I

He aquí mi poema
brutal
y multánime
a la nueva ciudad.

                  Oh ciudad toda tensa
                  de cables y de esfuerzos,
                  sonora toda
                  de motores y de alas.

                  Explosión simultánea
                  de las nuevas teorías,
                  un poco más allá
En el plano espacial
                  de Whitman y de Turner
                  y un poco más acá
                  de Maples Arce.

---

121 Bonifaz Nuño, ed., *Las semillas del tiempo* 30.
122 I have used the spacing and punctuation of the *Semillas* version of "Urbe." Again, the irregularly double-paced original makes it difficult in some places to distinguish regular line space from strophe separation. The exclamation points have been added in *Semillas*. Two verses that were in italics in the original are in plain print in *Semillas* ("Y la fiebre sexual de las fábricas" and "Gallardetes de hurras al viento."

Los pulmones de Rusia
soplan hacia nosotros
el viento de la revolución social.
Los asalta-braguetas literarios
nada comprenderán
de esta nueva belleza
sudorosa del siglo,

                y las lunas
                maduras
                que cayeron,
                son esta podredumbre
                que nos llega
                de las atarjeas intelectuales.
He aquí mi poema:
                ¡Oh ciudad fuerte
                y múltiple,
                hecha toda de hierro y de acero!

Los muelles. Las dársenas.
Las grúas.
        Y la fiebre sexual
        de las fábricas.
        Vrbe:
                Escoltas de tranvías
                que recorren las calles subversistas.
                Los escaparates asaltan las aceras,
                y el sol, saquea las avenidas.
                Al margen de los días
                tarifados de postes telefónicos
                desfilan paisajes momentáneos
                por sistemas de tubos ascensores.

Súbitamente,
¡oh el fogonazo
verde de sus ojos!

Bajo las persianas ingenuas de la hora
pasan los batallones rojos.
El romanticismo caníbal de la música yankee
ha ido haciendo sus nidos en los mástiles.

¡Oh ciudad internacional!
¿Hacia qué remoto meridiano
cortó aquel trasatlántico?
Yo siento que se aleja todo.
Los crepúsculos ajados
flotan entre la mampostería del panorama.
Trenes espectrales que van
hacia allá
lejos, jadeantes de civilizaciones.

            La multitud desencajada
            chapotea musicalmente en las calles.

Y ahora, los burgueses ladrones, se echarán a temblar
por los caudales
que robaron al pueblo,
pero alguien ocultó bajo sus sueños
el pentagrama espiritual del explosivo.

He aquí mi poema:
Gallardetes de hurras al viento,
cabelleras incendiadas
y mañanas cautivas en los ojos.

            ¡Oh ciudad
            musical
            hecha toda de ritmos mecánicos!

Mañana, quizás,
sólo la lumbre viva de mis versos
alumbrará los horizontes humillados.

II

Esta nueva profundidad del panorama
es una proyección hacia los espejismos interiores.

La muchedumbre sonora
hoy rebasa las plazas comunales
y los hurras triunfales
del obregonismo

reverberan al sol de las fachadas.

¡Oh muchacha romántica
flamarazo de oro!

     Tal vez entre mis manos
     sólo quedaron los momentos vivos.
Los paisajes vestidos de amarillo
se durmieron detrás de los cristales,
y la ciudad, arrebatada,
se ha quedado temblando en los cordajes.
Los aplausos son aquella muralla.

—¡Dios mío!
     —No temas, es la ola romántica de las multi-
     tudes.
Después, sobre los desbordes del silencio,
la noche tarahumara irá creciendo.
     Apaga tus vidrieras.
Entre la maquinaria del insomnio,
la lujuria, son millones de ojos
que se untan en la carne.

     Un pájaro de acero
     ha emprorado su norte hacia una estrella.
El puerto:
     lejanías incendiadas,
     el humo de las fábricas.
     Sobre los tendederos de la música
     se asolea su recuerdo.
Un adiós trasatlántico saltó desde la borda.

Los motores cantan
sobre el panorama muerto.

III

La tarde, acribillada de ventanas,
flota sobre los hilos del teléfono,
y entre los atravesaños
inversos de la hora

se cuelgan los adioses de las máquinas.

                      Su juventud maravillosa
                      estalló una mañana
                      entre mis dedos,
                      y en el agua vacía
                      de los espejos,
                      naufragaron los rostros olvidados.

¡Oh la pobre ciudad sindicalista
andamiada
de hurras y de gritos!

                      Los obreros
                      son rojos
                      y amarillos.

Hay un florecimiento de pistolas
después del trampolín de los discursos,
y mientras los pulmones
del viento
se supuran,
perdida en los obscuros pasillos de la música
alguna novia blanca
se deshoja.

IV

Entre los matorrales del silencio
la obscuridad lame la sangre del crepúsculo.
Las estrellas caídas,
son pájaros muertos
en el agua sin sueño
del espejo.

Y las artillerías
sonoras del Atlántico
se apagaron,
al fin,
en la distancia.

　　　　　　　　Sobre la arboladura del otoño,
　　　　　　　　sopla un viento nocturno:
　　　　　　　　es el viento de Rusia,
　　　　　　　　de las grandes tragedias,
y el jardín,
amarillo,
se va a pique en la sombra.
Súbito, su recuerdo,
chisporrotea en los interiores apagados.

　　　　　　　　Sus palabras de oro
　　　　　　　　criban en mi memoria.

Los ríos de blusas azules
desbordan las esclusas de las fábricas,
y los árboles agitadores
manotean sus discursos en la acera.
Los huelguistas se arrojan
pedradas y denuestos,
y la vida, es una tumultuosa
conversión hacia la izquierda.

Al margen de la almohada,
la noche, es un despeñadero:
y el insomnio,
se ha quedado escarbando en mi cerebro.

¿De quién son esas voces
que sobrenadan en la sombra?

　　　　　　　　Y estos trenes que aúllan
　　　　　　　　hacia los horizontes devastados.

　　　　　　　　Los soldados
　　　　　　　　dormirán esta noche en el infierno.

¡Dios mío!
Y de todo este desastre,
sólo unos cuantos pedazos
blancos
de su recuerdo,
se me han quedado entre las manos.

V

Las hordas salvajes de la noche
se echaron sobre la ciudad amedrentada.

La bahía,
florecida
de mástiles y lunas,
se derrama
sobre la partitura
ingenua de sus manos,
y el grito lejano
de un vapor,
hacia los mares nórdicos.

     ¡Adiós
     al continente naufragado!

    Entre los hilos de su nombre
se quedaron las plumas de los pájaros.

Pobre Celia María Dolores;
el panorama está dentro de nosotros.
Bajo los hachazos del silencio
las arquitecturas de hierro se devastan.
Hay oleadas de sangre y nubarrones de odio.

    Desolación.

    Los discursos marihuanos
     de los diputados
salpicaron de mierda su recuerdo.
pero,
sobre las multitudes de mi alma
se ha despeñado su ternura.

Ocotlán
allá lejos.

Voces.
    Los impactos picotean sobre

las trincheras.

La lujuria apedreó toda la noche
los balcones a obscuras de una virginidad.

La metralla
hace saltar pedazos del silencio.

Las calles
sonoras y desiertas,
son ríos de sombra
que van a dar al mar,
y el cielo, deshilachado,
es la nueva
bandera
que flamea
sobre la ciudad.

The general pattern and flow of the poem is as follows. *Urbe*, subtitled "Súper-poema bolchevique en 5 cantos," is dedicated to the workers of Mexico. The poem takes place in one "day." Canto I is the birth of the Revolution and the new city, totally optimistic and caught up in the fervor of social revolution. Man must get rid of the old and create a new society, and a new literature for the new century.[123] The feeling is one of expansion, surpassing limitations, future glory, the joy of everything modern and dynamic. The tone is reminiscent of Walt Whitman's "Song of Myself" and "A Broadway Pageant." As early as

---

[123] Compare William Carlos Williams' 1923 *Spring and All*, a Dadaist work combining prose and poetry. The poems are his most famous and have been widely anthologized. The prose sections that alternate with the poems have largely been forgotten, yet they are what makes the book the creative and original work it is. These passages call for the destruction of the old world (or traditional art and literature) in order to create it anew, though what really changes is the outlook, the perspective from which one sees the world, by adding imagination. The scenes depicted have quite a bit of a common flavor with *Urbe*.

the end of Canto I, however, hints begin to appear that something will be lost, and only the poem will remain:[124] "Mañana, quizás, / sólo la lumbre viva de mis versos / alumbrará los horizontes humillados."

In Canto II we hear the shouting of the crowd in the plazas, and their echo remains later when the plazas are deserted. It is afternoon and the city takes a siesta after the morning's fervent demonstrations. There are indications of communication between this port and the other great cities of the world, plus a transatlantic transmission of the news of the Revolution. However, there is already some feeling of disillusion, as seen in the goodbyes, in the moribund panorama, and in the image "tal vez entre mis manos / sólo quedaron los momentos vivos". Only the poem is left. The protagonist fears that all of this optimism about future glory is just illusion, wishful thinking. By the end of Canto II the excitement of the Revolution begins to fade.

Canto III takes place during the late afternoon, and is characterized by subtle images of a termination of communication, images of destruction, and emptiness. The ideals of the Revolution start to be corrupted. "Hay un florecimiento de pistolas / después del trampolín de los discursos." Now the winds of revolutionary inspiration from Marxist Russia, present from the beginning of the poem, begin to dissipate, and come from lungs that are infected and discharge pus. Several years have passed from the beginning of the two revolutions to the time of the writing of this poem, and there has been a loss of innocence; the Revolution loses its way and becomes corrupt: "perdida en

---

124 Cf. Whitman, "Drum Taps" and "Passage to India," *Leaves of Grass*, eds. Harold W. Blodgett and Sculley Bradley (NY: W. W. Norton & Co., Inc., Comprehensive Reader's Edition, 1965).

los oscuros pasillos de la música / alguna novia blanca / se deshoja". There is an identity connection between the Revolution, the city and the beloved woman throughout the poem. Instead of a city receiving joyous praise, now it is called "la pobre ciudad sindicalista."

Canto IV begins in the evening, and the scene is death, destruction and darkness. The protagonist suddenly recalls a positive image of the early Revolution, and the tone of the poem brightens for a moment, but only to fade again. The night is like a precipice (fear of falling, darkness, the abyss, fear of the unknown), while the protagonist's insomnia (recalling *Andamios Interiores*) keeps digging and poking at his mind. He asks whose voices float in the shadows, and what trains howl off toward the wasteland, and he remarks that tonight the soldiers will sleep in hell. Images of shadows, laments and devastation predominate. The canto ends with the protagonist saying: "¡Dios mío! / Y de todo este desastre, / sólo unos cuantos pedazos / blancos / de su recuerdo, / se me han quedado entre las manos," and he reminds us that the only possible transcendence is through art. There, perhaps, the remaining sparks of the original Revolution can be kept alive, and the poem holds on to the hope of making them glow again in some future time.

Canto V is set in the deep of night. The city is terrified, besieged by "savage hordes." The protagonist remembers the city's former innocence, and a girlfriend, but now only fragments of the past remain. Hope for the future is gone: "¡Adiós / al continente naufragado!" He says to the girlfriend, "el panorama está dentro de nosotros"–perhaps suggesting that it is up to them to continue civilization, or that the imagination must help them to survive (cf. discussion of William Carlos Williams' *Spring and All* in Chapter Two above). The city falls under a destructive silence, and there are waves of blood and dark clouds of hatred. Verse 21 characterizes the situation: "Desolación." The politicians are corrupt and have abandoned their original promises. Nevertheless, the protagonist says, the tenderness of the memory of the past has remained in his soul. Gunfire and corruption continue through the night. The deserted city streets are rivers of darkness flowing into the sea. In contrast to the beginning of the poem, Canto V ends with the image of a shabby, threadbare sky as the new flag that flutters over the city. Although it seems that destruction has triumphed and the city is in ruins, the flag which is the sky (perhaps not belonging to any nation or political ideology) "flamea sobre la ciudad." The verb "flamea" gives not only the image of a flag waving in the breeze but also that of a sky illuminated by the red-orange glow of the fires of destruction in the midst of the black night. Something in that flag flying over the city, though threadbare and ragged, gives a sense of hope, if faint and distant, perhaps the approaching dawn. What we do know is that the ideal of the Revolution persists in the memory of the people, of the poet, and above all in the poem that he has written, where he saves it for future generations.

A closer look at specific verses in each of the Cantos will help to analyze the poem more completely.[125] The function of *Urbe* as a social document to remind future generations of the Revolution's mission influences the tone

---

125 Rubén Bonifaz Nuño, in his introduction to *Las semillas del tiempo*, is one of the few critics of *Urbe* to have substantially and significantly examined the actual lines of the poem rather than just the general idea. Unfortunately, Bonifaz Nuño only discusses Canto I.

and word choice: the highs are high ("súper") and the attacks are harsh ("los asalta-braguetas literarios," "las atarjeas intelectuales"). The subtitle ("Súper-poema bolchevique en 5 cantos") may have provoked as many verbal attacks on Maples Arce as the entire body of the poem, misinterpreting the emphasis on "bolchevique." As stated previously, *Urbe* is not really a politically-committed piece of literature; the allusion to Bolshevism is brought on by the romantic attraction of socialist revolution and the communion the poet experiences with the *pueblo* at the May Day rally.[126] The expression of solidarity with the Mexican Revolution and with the Russian Revolution are the words of the poet as witness to the social environment of his day rather than as preacher of political dogma. Stefan Baciu recalls:

> Lo importante era *épater le bourgeois*, pues eran los seguidores del estilo de Porfirio Díaz, esto sí, haciéndose de manera muy mexicana.
> En lo que respecta al comunismo, tratábase todavía (refiriéndose específicamente a México) de un comunismo romántico, surgido, principalmente, de la mencionada tendencia de *épater le bourgeois*, y no por razones ideológicas.[127]

Bonifaz Nuño adds: "En aquel año ... la revolución rusa estaba presente, y con sus grandes llamas despertaba la conciencia fraternal de los hombres hacia la necesidad de la justicia y la acción."[128] This is supported by Rubén Salazar Mallén, who says, "Lo que Bonifaz Nuño dice ...

---

126 The committed literature of the day, for example that of the *agoristas*, did not generally achieve high literary quality, perhaps because the energy was put into politics rather than art.
127 Stefan Baciu, "Un estridentista silencioso rinde cuentas," *La Palabra y el Hombre*, II (julio-sept. 1968): 453.
128 Bonifaz Nuño, 17.

es cierto. Hubo una época, que quizás se haya alargado hasta 1926, en que la revolución bolchevique fue la gran esperanza del hombre."[129]

Commenting on both his choice of title, "Urbe," and the concept of a Mexican poem about an ultramodern city, Maples Arce recalls the reception of his work:

> Un crítico con cabeza de calabaza dijo que México no era entonces una verdadera urbe 'toda tensa de cables y de esfuerzos, sonora toda de motores y de alas.' Y creo que hasta alegó que no había suficiente siderocemento en su construcción, sin percibir que en las obras literarias mezcladas a la realidad va la imaginación o que puede haber implicaciones de aquella, sin que forzosamente se la reproduzca de un modo material. Así, las ciudades de Verhaeren, no son tal o cual ciudad, sino ciudades que participan del espíritu moderno.[130]

The character of this city is perhaps not as one would expect in a typical *vanguardista* poem (i.e., it is not totally positive regarding modernity). The positive/negative duality explained above brings complications, as does the combination of the exterior world with the interior world of the protagonist. Bonifaz Nuño describes the material as surprising, robust, multiple, noisy and full of tension; the author calls his poem "brutal y multánime." The unexpected characterizations here are *brutal* and *tensa*. "No es, así, una ciudad apacible el objeto del canto. Es la ciudad contemporánea, multitudinaria de almas combatientes, que en su agresivo desenfreno trasminarán el poema que la celebra. Esa ciudad en donde culminan juntamente los

---

129 Rubén Salazar Mallén, "Maples Arce: *Las semillas del tiempo*," *Excélsior* 13 marzo 1982: 7A.
130 Maples Arce, typed notes (20 pp.) for an interview, c. 1971: 13.

resultados de las teorías de la ciencia y de la sociedad."[131] The aggressivity becomes more and more important as the poem progresses.

Bonifaz Nuño notes a contrast between two verbal planes, the new and the traditionally poetic, which are combined in the images of *Urbe*. Examples of these two planes combined in verses at the beginning of Canto I are:

new	traditionally poetic
de cables	y de esfuerzos
de motores	y de alas
sudorosa	belleza

This kind of image combination echoes the "explosión simultánea" of the new social and scientific theories. It is a Cubist perception of the city, seen from multiple perspectives simultaneously, with an *estridentista* combination of modern technology and heightened emotion. It is not the nineteenth-century view of a (New World) urban panorama—Whitman wrote lines such as "Superb-faced Manhattan!" and "O superb! O Manhattan, my own, my peerless! / O strongest you in the hour of danger, in crisis! O truer than steel!"[132]—but he did not see the city with the super-modern eye of the 1920s avant-garde.[133]

---

131 Bonifaz Nuño, 18.
132 Walt Whitman, "A Broadway Pageant," "Drum Taps," *Leaves of Grass* 243, 280. Note also the contrast to a D. H. Lawrence or Miguel de Unamuno-like reaction against the turn-of-the-century industrial city of Europe (coal mines, dirty factories, loss of a pastoral sense of nature).
133 The Romantics were able to provide an original content and add the dimension of imagination, but were as yet unequipped to change the traditional (Renaissance) structural composition of space. "The romantic period ... was given only to renovating themes and manners of handling them, without involving the technical basis of the spatial idiom itself." Pierre Francastel, "The Destruction of a Plastic Space (1951)," *Art History: An Anthology of Modern Criticism*, ed. Wylie Sypher (NY: Vintage Books, 1963) 386. One could say the same idea applies to literature.

Maples Arce continues in *Urbe*:

>>> Explosión simultánea
>>> de las nuevas teorías,
>>> un poco más allá
> En el plano espacial
>>> de Whitman y de Turner
>>> y un poco más acá
>>> de Maples Arce.

The mention of painter J. M. W. Turner here is curious and is ignored in *Urbe* criticism. Masters of the Romantic landscape in England, Turner (1775-1851) and John Constable (1776-1837), preceded the Impressionists in their interest in the conditions of the sky, light, and the atmosphere. Constable tried to paint his perception of those conditions as faithfully as possible, creating works that were, rather than representational landscape scenes, studies of the sky (e.g. "Hampstead Heath"), imbued with sentiment and the forces of nature to which the Romantics were so attracted. Turner used as a starting point views of the sea, mountains, or historical sites, and transformed them through his preoccupation with colored light. Constable described Turner's work as "airy visions painted with tinted steam," and the locations were often unrecognizable in the final versions. Many times Turner added quotations from literature to his paintings for exhibitions, so the cross-over reference is entirely appropriate. What connects most with *Urbe* is Turner's frequent use of quotes from his own unpublished poem, "Fallacies of Hope." "Yet these canvases are the opposite of history painting as defined by Poussin: the titles indeed indicate 'noble and serious human actions,' but the tiny figures, lost in the seething violence of nature, suggest the ultimate defeat of all endeavor–'the fallacies of hope.' "[134] This attitude toward fate seems somehow akin to Maples Arce's sense of the defeat of the Revolution and to his anguish over the lack of permanence and union in the modern world. Moreover, the high-powered emotion of *Urbe* is much in tune with the very emotional quality of Turner's paintings, expressed in the "tinted steam."

Turner was ahead of his time in the use of particular colors, and the orange-red and yellow glow in his painting "The Slave Ship" (1839), one of his most famous works, has a modern feel to it as it rises up out of the brown and gray, probably taking its cue from a sunset, and, given the context of throwing dead slaves overboard before an oncoming sea storm, seems quite possibly similar to the dusk-hour colors over the factories and piers of revolution-torn *Urbe*. The colors recall the above-mentioned passage about the sky as a tattered flag flying over the burning city in the night, as well as other verses: "pasan los batallones rojos," "cabelleras incendiadas," "la lumbre viva de mis versos," "flamarazo de oro," "los paisajes vestidos de amarillo," "lejanías incendiadas," "los obreros son rojos y amarillos," "el jardín amarillo, se va a pique en la sombra," "sus palabras de oro," "hay oleadas de sangre y nubarrones de odio." What is different is that Turner is expressing the force of nature, "the seething violence of nature," and Maples Arce is expressing the force of a man-made city, "brutal y multánime," in its revolution, and its "almas combatientes," "su agresivo desenfreno"[135]–and thus they belong to their respective centuries and *Urbe* is "un poco más acá de Maples Arce." We know that Maples Arce studied art

---

134 H. W. Janson, *History of Art* (Englewood Cliffs, NJ: Prentice-Hall, Inc., and New York: Harry N. Abrams, Inc., 1971) 469.
135 Bonifaz Nuño, 18.

history, and there may also be some influence here from Ramón Alva de la Canal and the other *estridentistas* who had studied painting at the Escuela al Aire Libre in Coyoacán (where Maples frequently visited), and he would have known Turner's work.

In *Urbe*, Maples Arce continues his experimentation with lineation and the use of white space (though it is not extreme). The repeated presentational phrase "He aquí mi poema" is often set off to the left side of the page, as an introduction to the verses that follow, and also to separate this poem from those of the *postmodernista* literary establishment (specifically from lines referring to them). "En el plano espacial" is set off to the side from the verses associated with it, thus giving spatial reality to a spatial reference. Most of the verses of the poem are short, but the placement on the page, approximating left and right vertical columns of available working space, makes even the long lines seem short. This has the effect of adding a quickness of pace–echoing the fever-pitch speed of the city–and also visually reflecting the panorama of skyscrapers, cranes, telephone poles and avenues. Whenever there is a reference to falling, it is reflected in the lineation: short lines descending in a vertical column set off to the side of the page. There is some movement of lines that refer to the shipping docks and machinery of the port, reflecting their shape and how they jut out into space. An airplane ("un pájaro de acero," a bird of steel) takes flight from the city, headed for the stars, and is imitated in the placement of the verses on the page. A section centered on the word *andamiada* (scaffolded) uses a creative structuring of the lines. References to being lost, to distance, to goodbyes, and to desolation, are all set aside in very short verses with white space surrounding them. Lines containing the image of the tattered sky as flag at the end of the poem are also arranged to make form reflect the content. This use of lineation is very tame, almost unmentionable compared to that used by Marinetti or Kurt Schwitters or the German Expressionists, but it comes from a poet who, in his previous book, barely veered from the coupling of *alejandrino* hemistichs (except for extreme emphasis), which was the natural rhythm of language in his head.[136] It seems obvious that he is very conscious here of how he places words on the page, and that he does it deliberately. The rhythm of the poem is important.

The images of the poem may be divided into several categories, the most significant being: positive images of the city, negative images of the city, images of force and energy in the city, images of violence in the city, references to the interior world of the protagonist and/or the blending of his interior world with the exterior world, images of wind, references to a woman, and insults aimed at the bourgeoisie and the literary establishment. These groups (or categories) of images play off each other to create the tension of the poem. Correspondingly, the protagonist's reaction to these images over the course of the poem produces the thematic (and through the act of writing, the formal) resolution of the conflict. There is a

---

136   The reader will recall Maples' practice of memorizing and reciting poems before ever writing them down—rhythm played an important role, and his natural tendency is a 7 / 14 syllable line. It is present in his prose of the 1920s as well. Witness this sentence from a 1921 article: "Y ahora más que nunca [7], entre las sombras cómplices [7] de la ciudad a obscuras [7], el vicio, lo mismo que una enorme flor monstruosa [14], pródigamente crece [7] en los invernaderos [7] laicos en que el ambiente [7] de fenol se disfraza [7] con adorables complicaciones [10] de Roger-et-Gallet [7]." ("Complications" is emphasized by an irregular variation in the phrase's syllable count.) El Duque de Fréneuse [MMA], "Pinceladas de colores: los cabarets," *Zig-Zag* 14 abril 1921: 32-33.

gradual progression from positive to negative, from general to specific, and from abstract to concrete. To a certain degree, there is also a gradual progression from isolation (of self) to interaction (of self with other).

The positive images of the city are at the beginning of the poem and they end before the middle of Canto II, with the exception of the crowd's shouting of "hurrah!" referred to throughout the poem. The positive images are greatly overshadowed (by a ratio of almost 5 to 1) by the negative images of the city, which increase in frequency in each subsequent canto. Included in this negative group are references to goodbyes, separation, departure, distance, death, mourning, and emptiness or void. These positive and negative groups go hand in hand with two other categories, those of images of force and energy in the city, and images of violence (i. e. negative or destructive force and energy). The more positive images of energy occur at the beginning of the poem, almost all of them in Canto I. In Canto II we find "la ciudad, arrebatada," and in Canto IV "desbordan" (echoed metaphorically elsewhere in the poem). The violent images begin in Canto I with "asaltan," "saquea," "subversistas," "batallones," "caníbal." "Escoltas" has a military flavor but is not always inherently violent. Canto II has "millones de ojos / que se untan en la carne," which are "lujuria." Canto III initiates more concrete movement in the images with "Hay un florecimiento de pistolas / después del trampolín de los discursos." Canto IV includes "la obscuridad lame la sangre del crepúsculo," "artillerías," "los árboles agitadores / manotean sus discursos en la acera," "los huelguistas se arrojan / pedradas y denuestos," "la vida es una tumultuosa conversión hacia la izquierda." Canto V brings the largest portion of this category, including "Las hordas salvajes de la noche / se echaron sobre la ciudad amedrentada," "grito lejano," "los hachazos del silencio," "hay oleadas de sangre y nubarrones de odio," "salpicaron de mierda su recuerdo," "los impactos picotean sobre / las trincheras," "la lujuria apedreó toda la noche / los balcones a obscuras de una virginidad," "la metralla / hace saltar pedazos del silencio." There is also in Canto V what may be an echo of "la noche triste" of the Spanish conquest of Mexico City (then Tenochtitlán), when Hernán Cortés and his men, after initial peaceful waiting, launched a surprise attack on the natives one night, a slaughter that filled the canals with blood and bodies: "Las hordas salvajes de la noche / se echaron sobre la ciudad amedrentada." The Aztecs saw the Spanish *conquistadores* as "hordas salvajes" (the Spaniards also considered the Aztecs as such). The conquest had been foreshadowed by numerous bad omens in Tenochtitlán ("la ciudad amedrentada"). The conquest signals the end of the native civilization as it was: "Adiós / al continente naufragado!" The name of the *mexica* Indians is partially preserved in the modern name of the country, and the *quetzal* bird is still present in national symbols, as is the eagle: "Entre los hilos de su nombre / se quedaron las plumas de los pájaros." In this canto the poet links the memory of the conquest with the Mexican Revolution, thus hinting at the Mexican people's continuing struggle for empowerment and search for identity.

The insults aimed at the bourgeoisie and the literary establishment are in Canto I, and although they are an important aspect of the *estridentista* attempt to shock and dethrone the establishment, the idea seems to fade in later cantos in the shadow of the conflict itself. The practice of *épater le bourgeois* is effective in Canto I, but is more evident in the *estridentista* "happenings" than in the poem *Urbe*.

The wind images throughout the poem refer to the inspiration Mexico received from the Bolshevik Revolution in Russia. At first (Canto I), they are positive: "Los pulmones de Rusia / soplan hacia nosotros / el viento de la revolución social," and are connected to the idea of the new city, the new man-made industrial beauty that the nineteenth-century minded literati just cannot comprehend. The next reference to this revolutionary wind from the east is at the end of Canto III, where we find that it is dying out, fading, and the verb implies also a second meaning that the lungs producing that wind are now infected and discharging sickly pus. These verses in Canto III are associated with a loss of innocence: "y mientras los pulmones / del viento / se supuran, / perdida en los obscuros pasillos de la música / alguna novia blanca / se deshoja." The third reference is in Canto IV, indicating darkness and tragedy: "Sobre la arboladura del otoño, / sopla un viento nocturno: es el viento de Rusia, / de las grandes tragedias."

There are numerous references to music in *Urbe*, most of which are positive and function like the labor songs of the '50s and early '60s in the U. S. They are linked to the masses marching through the streets at the May Day rally, calling for labor unions and equal rights. The opposite of that image of music is the powerful reference to silence in the group of images of violence ("los hachazos del silencio"), as well as the silence felt in the deserted city plazas.

Vocabulary and images relating to ship rigging also abound. These remind us that the city is a port and they are part of the verbal plane of the "new," but the images become increasingly complex and negative. The first images involve the idea of leaving, then there are references to trembling and to getting tangled in the rigging ropes (the clanging sound is echoed here), then we see people jumping overboard, and we see shipwrecks. There is also an autumnal reference (the masts look like leafless trees in autumn) linked to the tragedy-plagued revolutionary winds, and there are images of sinking and of being part of a panorama that collapses and is connected to images of departure, distance and death.

References to a woman continue throughout the poem. At first there is "Súbitamente, / ¡oh el fogonazo / verde de sus ojos!," where she could almost be a factory or sparking machine rather than a human. Then Canto II presents "¡Oh muchacha romántica / flamarazo de oro!"–specifically more human, though still very close to the image in Canto I. Canto III brings "Su juventud maravillosa / estalló una mañana / entre mis dedos," which is more concretely corporeal, but could still be a metaphor for the city. The end of that canto includes "alguna novia blanca se deshoja"–impersonal for the "alguna," but obviously referring to a woman, or metaphorically alluding to the Revolution. The verses in Canto IV, ("Súbito, su recuerdo, / chisporrotea en los interiores apagados. / Sus palabras de oro / criban en mi memoria"), noted previously as referring to the Revolution, could also describe a woman. There is also the dialogue in Canto II and "Apaga tus vidrieras," suggesting, as Bonifaz Nuño has noted, a scene with a lover at the woman's apartment or house, looking out the windows, watching the crowds march below on the streets. She doesn't understand what is happening (throughout the poem she is "ingenua," "blanca") and the protagonist tells her not to be afraid, "es la ola romántica de las multitudes." It is curious that he would tell her to close the windows, to shut the scene out, but then all during the night he is unable to sleep and the whole situation haunts him in his insomniac imagination. This continues in Canto IV. In Canto V he finally mentions her name (probably the same woman) and tells her that the future is up to them, that they hold within themselves the memory of the past: "Pobre Celia María Dolores; / el panorama está dentro de nosotros." "*Su* recuerdo" and "*su* ternura" most likely refer to the Revolution. Arqueles Vela gives the best explanation of the presence of the woman in the poem, proposing that she is the city and the Revolution transubstantiated, that is, given human form: "La influencia de la nueva clase—adolescente aún—se manifiesta en *Urbe* como una protesta y en forma lírica transubstanciada en una sombra femenina."[137] This metaphor of city/Revolution transubstantiated into woman works best, because it brings all of the facets of the reference together and makes sense. It is also an appropriate explanation because it connects the references to the city/Revolution with the group of images concerning the interior (or personal) world of the protagonist, which in the course of the poem gradually gains connection with the exterior world (city/Revolution). This union of exterior and interior is the major achievement of the poem. It links self with other, vanquishes the problem of separation (here, self from society) through the union of the two entities in the words of the poem itself, and preserves the memory of the Revolution in a timeless work of art.

The group of images depicting the interior world of the

---

137 Arqueles Vela, "MMA, Poeta de la Revolución."

protagonist begins in Canto II with "espejismos interiores." "Espejismos" are normally connected with the exterior world, and the use of this word implicitly suggests the exterior. Nevertheless, the protagonist at this point is still isolated, not yet connected to the outside. There follows the dialogue between protagonist and lover, questioning the meaning of the spectacle outside, then closing the windows on the scene, saying that night is approaching. Darkness will blot out the street scene so they don't have to deal with it. This idea reminds the reader that the protagonist comes from a bourgeois background, and is as yet unsympathetic to the proletarian cause. However, that night he is haunted by insomniac visions in the darkness, nightmarish hallucinations (or are they real?) of the conflict going on outside.

In Canto III there is a brief recollection of past innocence ("Su juventud maravillosa") but it is followed by a list of references to death, emptiness, and corruption: "en el agua vacía / de los espejos, / naufragaron los rostros olvidados," "perdida en los obscuros pasillos de la música / alguna novia blanca / se deshoja." Then in Canto IV there begins to be evidence of an influence of the exterior on the interior (or of the societal on the personal) worlds: "su recuerdo, / chisporrotea en los interiores apagados," and "sus palabras de oro / criban en mi memoria." In addition, the insomniac visions he suffers are of the exterior world: "ríos de blusas azules," "huelguistas," "voces," "trenes," "soldados." Canto IV ends with the thought that of all this (exterior) disaster only a few bits of its memory have remained, *in my hands*. That is, the memory of the conflict has been recorded in the poem that the protagonist has written ("pedazos blancos" refers to pieces of paper). The sense is that the historical fate of the situation depends on his action. There follows reference to exodus and loss, and the protagonist's realization that, as he says to the woman, "el panorama está dentro de nosotros." Exterior and interior are now fully connected.

The conflict worsens, but (*pero* set off in a line by itself, indicating a great exception) union has been achieved between the interior and exterior worlds. In Canto V, lines 26 and 27 illustrate this union: "sobre las multitudes de mi alma / se ha despeñado su ternura." "Su ternura," and "su recuerdo," refer to the Revolution (and to the modern city, seen in "las arquitecturas de hierro") rather than solely to the woman. In the first verse, "las multitudes" has earlier in the poem referred to the crowds of the exterior world. Here the word refers to the complexity of the innermost part of the protagonist's interior world, "mi alma"–thus the image produces a fusion of exterior and interior, form reflecting content. In the second verse, "se ha despeñado" would normally be a negative image (implying death), referring to jumping off a cliff ("despeñadero" appeared in the Canto IV night insomnia section and jumping overboard was alluded to at the end of Canto II). Here it is the tenderness of the memory of the Revolution, diving onto the vastness and new multiplicity of the protagonist's soul, which is a positive image, and the resolution of the problem of separation and transitoriness. The poet and his poem will be the standard-bearers of the cause of the Revolution and hope for the future.

Ocotlán can be seen in the distance.[138] Voices echo in the night. The use of short verses and space in the lineation here conveys both the quiet and the loneliness of that

---

138 Probably a church in Tlaxcala, or a town to the west.

night. The devastation continues, but there is hope for the future now that the union of interior and exterior has been achieved, and the tattered but undaunted flag which is Mexico (the sky, the land, its natural presence) waves on.

Maples Arce's *Urbe* has much in common with Hart Crane's 1930 book-length poem *The Bridge*. In terms of style, Crane is more traditional, but the two poems are quite similar in theme. In Crane's poem (which is named for the Brooklyn Bridge), there is, as the critic Thomas A. Vogler points out, a quest for mythic vision; "the vision sought is one that will assure a hopeful future in the face of a sorry present." This is similar to the search for unity (a "bridge" for the separation of self and other) in all of Maples Arce's poetry. The geneses of the two poems are also similar: Maples Arce meets the May Day rally while walking home from Mixcoac, and Crane walks between Brooklyn and Manhattan over the bridge:

> Against the background of the daily cycle from Brooklyn to Manhattan and back, essentially a closed and discouraging routine, the poet carries on his quest, ranging into the legendary aspects of the past for elements still viable in the present, and for signs of hope on which to base an affirmative attitude toward the future.[139]

Crane combines his private suffering with that of the rest of society, without any guarantee of finding alleviation, and embarks on a trek through the centuries since Columbus and across American space from shore to shore, in search of unity with the cosmos. It seems at the end of the poem that he has achieved that oneness, but there is an

---

[139] Thomas A. Vogler, introduction (1970) to *The Bridge* by Hart Crane (New York and London: Liveright, 1970) xi.

element of doubt, just as the end of *Urbe* offers tentative, vulnerable hope in the "cielo deshilachado" / "nueva bandera." Vogler explains the poematic importance of this intense yet uncertain quality at the end of *The Bridge*:

> When the poem finally reaches its conclusion in the *Atlantis*, we must be able to hear in the midst of the 'Psalm of Cathay' the tone of doubt that gives it a desperate urgency rather than a triumphant finality. 'Hold thy floating singer late!' he pleads, as if conscious that this vision he is trying to sustain is in danger of disappearing once more into the teeming span. *Is* it Cathay, he asks in the final stanza, that the 'orphic strings' sing? As Orpheus lost Eurydice when he turned to look at her, the poet may lose this vision after the poetic ecstasy of expression passes.[140]

Both Crane and Maples Arce are men of the modern city, both write to attempt to create order out of the chaos around and inside them. Crane chooses the man-made Brooklyn Bridge, a tremendous achievement of modern technology (the first suspension bridge), to use as a metaphor for the union of self and other, a continuity of time past and time present. Maples Arce chooses the man-made wonders of the modern city as the setting of the continuation of the Mexican Revolution into the 1920s. The city experiences the simultaneous explosion of social and scientific theories—workers' rights, new technology, personal freedoms, new inventions, new politics and new philosophies. The Mexican Revolution was the first of the great socialist revolutions of the twentieth century that defeated oppressive dictators. Maples Arce uses the ongoing maintenance of the Revolution's ideals as a metaphor for the connection between individual and society and be-

---

140 Vogler, xiii-xiv.

tween past, present and future. Both *Urbe* and *The Bridge* give us "the revelation ... of a man who through the immediate conduit of his senses experienced the organic unity between his self, the objective world, and the cosmos."[141]

As Luis Mario Schneider points out, *Urbe* was the first book of Mexican poetry (as a complete monograph)–and the first such of all of the Spanish-language *vanguardia*– to be translated into English.[142] The American writer John Dos Passos (*Manhattan Transfer*, 1925), was shown *Urbe* on a visit to Mexico, and he immediately asked Maples for permission to translate it. His version, *Metropolis*, was published in New York in 1929.[143] Dos Passos' translation of *Urbe* is passable in general, though sometimes it is too tame, and some words are translated inaccurately. It was, in any case, a compliment to Maples Arce to have such a prominent writer from the U. S. translate his poem.

An aspect of Maples Arce's works which was virtually ignored in published criticism until recent years is the character of the wood-block prints that illustrate the books, and their relationship to the poems. They are particularly prominent in *Urbe*, and do indeed make a comment on the poetry. All of the wood-block (or "woodcut") prints in *Urbe* were done by French artist Jean Charlot, a member of the *estridentista* group for some time, and they seem to have been conceived as an integral part of the volume. The cover illustration of *Urbe* has "Maples Arce" written at the top in large capital letters in a zig-zag so that the A and E of both words are used only once,

---

141 Waldo Frank, 2nd introduction to *The Bridge* (1932), included in same edition, 1970: xxxvi.
142 Schneider, 100.
143 John Dos Passos, *Metropolis* (New York: T. S. Book Co., 1929).

fusing the two surnames. In the middle are some modern city buildings, and below, "VRBE" in large letters. Underneath are the subtitle and then "Mexico 1924" and a credit to Jean Charlot.[144] In the opening pages, following the list of the author's previous books, is an outline drawing of Maples Arce's head, full-page. Between the dedication and the beginning of Canto I is a wood-block print of two skyscrapers (with many windows) looming over a city street teeming with people, some pointing this way or that, some running. There are a few smaller buildings on the distant horizon, and a hot-air balloon flying over the two skyscrapers.

Canto II is preceded by a curious wood-block print depicting a street with a group of city buildings on a diagonal, a winged horse (probably Pegasus), and what appears to be a huge airplane flying above. The airplane is very abstractly drawn, in a T-shape, with a figure at the cross point of the wings and fuselage that appears to be a dead bird, possibly hit by the airplane. (Or is it Pegasus? In either case the allusion is to the machine—the airplane—replacing the animal after which it was patterned. This recalls Williams' destruction and re-creation in *Spring and All*.) Canto III is preceded by a print of a tall aqueduct with a train steaming across the top of it, a building below, and a woman falling through the air, apparently having jumped off the aqueduct, a handkerchief in her hand. Before Canto IV there is a wood-block print of two ships with large smokestacks (transatlantic steamers or military boats) going across the bay in opposite directions. Mean-

---

144 The title page has at the center a small encircled bust of a woman in profile, head down, a Hindu-like dot on her forehead. This may be a trademark of the publisher, or may be an original to *Urbe*, in which case it would give surprising emphasis to the woman in the poem.

while, two powerful searchlights, one from either shore, beam out into the starry night and cross paths. Preceding Canto V is a wood-block print of a huge ship (probably a transatlantic steamer) entering or leaving the port (buildings on a diagonal at the side), smoke billowing from the stacks, and a man and woman falling headlong from the ship into the water below.

The wood-block prints described above begin with a positive character (the hot-air balloon over the busy modern city), as does Canto I. The print that introduces Canto II shows the domination of machines over nature and Pegasus standing nearby to provide poetic inspiration[145] —still positive, yet now with an ominous quality. We feel the tremendous power of the machines and the city and also of the workers' protest marches, and there is the suggestion that there may be some innocent victims. Canto III is preceded by the wood-block print of the aqueduct, train, and woman falling. This is the first of the suicides depicted in *Urbe's* wood-block prints, thus introducing the sense of despair that is imminent. The woman is perhaps the "novia blanca," and the wave of her white handkerchief communicates both her tears and a mute cry for help. The mysterious ships crossing the bay in the dark of night at the beginning of Canto IV illustrate the growing instance of battle and nightmare. The searchlights, along with the poet, ask: "¿De quién son esas voces ... ?" These are not pleasure boats, there is no dancing or cocktail parties on their decks. These ships seem stealthy

---

145   Pegasus is the mythological winged horse who sprang from the blood of Medusa. When Pegasus' hoof struck the ground of Mt. Helicon, home of the muses, it created the Hippocrene, a fountain that gives poetic inspiration. (*The New Lexicon Webster's Dictionary of the English Language*, Encyclopedic Edition (New York: Lexicon Publications, Inc., 1987 ed.) 741.

and cautious. The poet now refers to the situation described in the poem as a disaster. Canto V is introduced by the wood-block print of the couple jumping overboard from a huge transatlantic ship—more suicides. This is, of course, the canto of destruction and devastation. The protagonist finds a ray of hope at the end of the poem, but many others have succumbed to the battle along the way.

The wood-block print may seem simple or primitive, but it was a very popular medium in the 1920s in both Latin America and Europe. Many of the Merz-Dada publications of Kurt Schwitters were illustrated with wood-block prints, and in those the falling figure is extremely prevalent: human figures falling, arrows or umbrellas falling, other lines curving or pointing downward.[146] Thus, although many of the drawings depict a sense of the power, dynamism and wonderment of the modern city, there is also a sense that something profoundly human and fragile is being lost. The idea of modern man as being alone and abandoned, cut off from the past, and unable to communicate his feelings to others, surfaces increasingly in other literary works of the period (e.g. *Prufrock, Altazor, The Waste Land*, etcetera).

Almost all of the *estridentista* group's books were illustrated (at least the covers) with wood-block prints or other graphic media, done by the artists of the group. The energy and dynamism they show (e.g. the covers of

---

146 Some examples are: the cover of the magazine *Sekunde Durch Hirn* (by Melchior Vischer, Hannover, 1920), *Anna Blume Dichtungen* (Hannover, 1919), *To Anna Blume* (1919), *Sturm-Bilderbücher IV: Kurt Schwitters* (Berlin, 1920), *Die Kathedrale* (Hannover, 1920). The typography in Schwitters' magazine *Merz* is similar to that on the covers of *estridentista* publications. *Merz 18/19* (Jan.-Apr. 1926) has a skyscraper on the cover. (All at the "Kurt Schwitters (Merz-Dada)" exhibit at the Museum of Modern Art, New York, 10 June-1 October 1985.) The covers of the German Expressionist magazine *Der Sturm* are similar.

Germán List Arzubide's *Viajero en el vértice* and *Esquina*, or Kyn-Taniya's *Avión* and *Radio*) exhibit similarity to the work of international futurist artists. Especially akin to *Urbe* are several works by Italian futurist Umberto Boccioni, others by Boccioni's compatriots Carlo Carrà and Virgilio Marchi, England's Christopher R. W. Nevinson, Germany's George Grosz, and the USA's John Marin and Frances Simpson Stevens.[147] Several additional futurist paintings demonstrate similarities to Maples Arce's other volumes of *estridentista* poetry (e.g. Boccioni's series "States of Mind" re: *Andamios Interiores*). Many of these works were shown at the Paris Exhibition over several years and received international attention. Similarity to another set of paintings should be noted: *Urbe* is much like a Diego Rivera mural in verse form.

Urbe is a difficult poem that allows many interpretations; only one (my own) has been presented here. Most previous studies have looked mostly at Canto I, have not examined the verses closely and in context, and have omitted attention to the dark, ominous, negative aspects of the work. These aspects are important to the understanding of the poem itself and its place in Maples Arce's *obra completa*. As Maples has said, it is a poem "en que latía la esperanza y la desesperación" and the contrasts are due

---

[147] See Anne d'Harnoncourt and Germano Celant, *Futurism and the International Avant-Garde*, catalogue from the exhibition at the Philadelphia Museum of Art, 26 October 1980-4 January 1981. The specific works referred to above are: Boccioni's "Agitated Crowd Surrounding a High Equestrian Monument" (1908), "The City Rises" (1910), "The Riot" (c. 1911), and "The Street Enters the House" (1911-12); Carrà's "Funeral of the Anarchist Galli" (1911); Marchi's "Vision of a Futurist City" (1919); Nevinson's "The Arrival" (c. 1913-14); Grosz' "The City" (1916-17); Marin's "Brooklyn Bridge, No. 6 (Swaying)" (1913); and Stevens' "Dynamic Velocity of Interborough Rapid Transit Power Station" (c. 1915); all included in the exhibition catalogue noted above.

to "circunstancias amargas que aniquilaban la alegría."[148] We have seen that the modern city has been presented in *Urbe* not only as a place of dynamism and progress, and a place of inevitable tumult and conflict, but also the place where a transcendence may be achieved in the continuing struggle for unity and permanence on the part of the protagonist.

---

148 Soberana Juventud 147-149.

Chapter Four: Poet in the Transitory World, *Poemas Interdictos*, 1927

> Cantar.
>   Cantar.
> Todo es desde arriba
> equilibrado y superior.
>   Maples Arce
>   "Canción desde un aeroplano"

> Art ... survives time and death... I shall make life for both of us.
>   Michelangelo

Poemas Interdictos, including poems written from 1923 to 1927, was the most well-received by critics of Maples Arce's three *vanguardista* volumes. Its images are fresh, unusual, often very striking, and well developed in cohesive poems. They give the sense of a poet maturing in his craft. Luis Mario Schneider has called *Poemas Interdictos* "uno de los poemarios más relevantes de la vanguardia en castellano."[149] It is in this volume that Maples Arce best illustrates the role of the poet in the world he has previously described to us—a world of impermanence and separation, as well as of dynamism and machines, seen in *Andamios Interiores* and *Urbe*. Now we see the protagonist out in the world, moving through it, acting upon it, rather than

---

149   Luis Mario Schneider, *El Estridentismo* 188.

quasi-passively observing it from his balcony. He has gone a step beyond the sympathetic solidarity with the masses of *Urbe* to the active role of modern man moving of his own will through his environment and, at the same time, to artisan moving toward new poetic heights. We have previously been presented with the basic union/separation, permanence/transitoriness problem (*Andamios*) and the world in which it exists (*Urbe*); *Poemas Interdictos* gives us the poet daring to exert his volition in order to overcome or outwit the problem in that world. The typical Maplesian vocabulary appears in this volume, expressing the usual problems, but now the poet works on one of the suggested possible courses of action (cf. Chapter Three) to solve the problem of time and impermanence: try to prolong the moment, to make it last as long as possible, to strive for timelessness through action and motion—endless dynamism.

The poems of *Poemas Interdictos* can be divided into three groups, the first being comprised of "Canción desde un aeroplano," "T. S. H." and "80 H. P." These are principally concerned with modernity and take place in the city and its environs. They are the most Cubist of all of his poems. "Canción desde un aeroplano" is one of the happiest poems Maples wrote, and *Poemas Interdictos* perhaps the most positive of his books. The second group is composed of "Primavera" and "Puerto." These two poems are set in seaports, and emphasize *Estridentópolis* as a place of contact with the rest of the world, an important dimension of communication. The third group contains "Revolución" and the poems of the subgroup titled "Poemas de la lejanía" ("Partida," "Ruta," "Paroxismo," "Evocación" and "Saudade"). These usually take place in the countryside, where the protagonist is sad and lonely and misses the woman he loves. The point of view has changed somewhat: it seems that now, when goodbyes are said in the train station, it is he who is leaving (not she). He is on the train in the narrative present of many of the poems, and in others he is out in the countryside after having travelled some distance. In fact, in most of the poems of *Poemas Interdictos*, he is in the process of travelling, in motion across the land, in a train, automobile or airplane. Thus the idea of dynamism is paramount, and there is nationalism in the sense of identity with the land and specific places. The new sense of Mexican identity and connection with the land brought on by the Revolution is still present here, and is linked with the technological advances of the modern age. The trips range from afternoon jaunts out to local towns, with a feeling of adventure, to distant treks as a soldier of the Revolution. Still present are the ideas of union and separation, memories, nostalgia, insomnia, and the autumnal vocabulary, but now taken out into the open air, poet confronting his world. As stated at the beginning of "Canción desde un aeroplano," he is in all of the poems of *Poemas Interdictos*, "a la intemperie de todas las estéticas."

"Canción desde un aeroplano"

Estoy a la intemperie
de todas las estéticas;
operador siniestro
de los grandes sistemas,
tengo las manos
llenas
de azules continentes.

Aquí, desde esta borda,
esperaré la caída de las hojas.
La aviación
anticipa sus despojos,
y un puñado de pájaros
defiende su memoria.

Canción
florecida
de las rosas aéreas,
propulsión
entusiasta
de las hélices nuevas,
metáfora inefable despejada de alas.

Cantar.
                    Cantar.
Todo es desde arriba
equilibrado y superior,
y la vida
es el aplauso que resuena
en el hondo latido del avión.

Súbitamente
el corazón
voltea los panoramas inminentes;
todas las calles salen hacia la soledad de los horarios;
subversión
de las perspectivas evidentes;
looping the loop
en el trampolín romántico del cielo,
ejercicio moderno
en el ambiente ingenuo el poema;
la Naturaleza subiendo
el color del firmamento.

Al llegar te entregaré este viaje de sorpresas,
equilibrio perfecto de mi vuelo astronómico;
tú estarás esperándome en el manicomio de la tarde,
así, desvanecida de distancias,

acaso lloras sobre la palabra otoño.

Ciudades del norte
                      de la América nuestra,
tuya y mía;
          New-York,
          Chicago,
          Baltimore.

Reglamenta el gobierno los colores del día,
puertos tropicales
del Atlántico,
azules litorales
del jardín oceanográfico,
donde se hacen señales
los vapores mercantes;
palmeras emigrantes,
río caníbal de la moda,
primavera, siempre tú, tan esbelta de flores.

País donde los pájaros hicieron sus columpios.
Hojeando tu perfume se marchitan las cosas,
y tú lejanamente sonríes y destellas,
¡oh novia electoral, carroussel de miradas!
lanzaré la candidatura de tu amor
hoy que todo se apoya en tu garganta,
la orquesta del viento y los colores desnudos.
Algo está aconteciendo allá en el corazón.

Las estaciones girando
mientras capitalizo tu nostalgia,
y todo equivocado de sueños y de imágenes;
la victoria alumbra mis sentidos
y laten los signos del zodíaco.

Soledad apretada contra el pecho infinito.
De este lado del tiempo,
sostengo el pulso de mi canto;
tu recuerdo se agranda como un remordimiento,
y el paisaje entreabierto se me cae de las manos.

The opening piece, "Canción desde un aeroplano," has a word-play throughout between poem/poet and flight/pilot: "Estoy a la intemperie" –flight– "de todas las estéticas" –poem. The poet/pilot is the "operador" ("siniestro" perhaps in the sense of "subversivo"), he is in control and has the world at his hands.

> Estoy a la intemperie
> de todas las estéticas;
> operador siniestro
> de los grandes sistemas,
> tengo las manos
> llenas
> de azules continentes.

He is Altazor, the *poeta-mago-pequeño dios*, in his flight from zenith to nadir in life and literature. His "proezas aéreas" (as Altazor says) –here "looping the loop" –are, in writing, an "ejercicio moderno / en el ambiente ingenuo del poema." The reason for the flight is the option, in the face of transitoriness, to live the moment to the fullest, to try to make it last as long as possible, a momentary stay against disintegration and time. "Aquí, desde esta borda, / esperaré la caída de las hojas"–up above, in the plane, on the other side of the sky, he will wait out the time he has left, filling it with aerial adventures. The poet's role is to record the experience, to re-create it in writing. His poem is a "Canción / florecida / de las rosas aéreas:" airplane flight is directed by the compass rose ("la rosa de los vientos") and poetry is inspired by the rose flower. This combination of the traditional poetic image of the rose with the modern realm of the airplane symbolizes the protagonist's technique and his inspiration. He says he is impelled by a new muse: the plane's propellers (modernity, mechanization, dynamism, man overcoming his natural limitations) which, inexplicably and wondrously, hold him up, make him fly even though he has no wings. The flight is his poetry. This poem is in fact almost an *ars poetica* for Maples Arce at this stage in his career, and it appropriately opens *Poemas Interdictos*.

The sections of "Canción desde un aeroplano" are connected semantically to glide one into the next though separated by space. As the poet sings the praises of mechanical flight, the use of short verses in the first four strophes imitates the zig-zagging of the airplane, and the alternation of short and long verses in strophe five reflects the looping the loop maneuvers, swooping and turning, that the section discusses. He says that "Todo es desde arriba / equilibrado y superior"—up in the air life seems timeless, safe, balanced. He is in control, at the helm, not at the mercy of some other force or chaos (cf. "¿Quién está en el manubrio?" from "Al margen de la lluvia"). He feels total integration between himself and the plane. The sound of the engine is like the heartbeat of the plane, which becomes his own heartbeat as well.

This auditory image of the heartbeat ("latido") at the end of strophe four foreshadows the "corazón" image of strophe five, where the poet/pilot does a loop the loop and the panorama is apparently turned upside-down. This sudden movement produces an effect in the protagonist's heart similar to that which one feels when ascending or descending rapidly in an elevator. In the poem, emotion propels these aerial manuevers. This time, the surge of energy comes from feeling so at one with the airplane; usually it comes from thinking of his beloved.

> Súbitamente
> el corazón
> voltea los panoramas inminentes;
> todas las calles salen hacia la soledad de los horarios;
> subversión
> de las perspectivas evidentes;
> looping the loop
> en el trampolín romántico del cielo,
> ejercicio moderno
> en el ambiente ingenuo del poema;
> la Naturaleza subiendo
> el color del firmamento.

As the panorama flips, the poet/pilot heads farther up into the sky, leaving the streets back in the world of time and transitoriness ("todas las calles salen hacia la soledad de los horarios"). It is "subversión" because he is defying the general rule of existence in the world below. The visual effect of looping the loop is "subversión / de las perspectivas evidentes": Cubism. The idea is: let's look at the world from a different point of view, from above, while swooping, while rising and falling, make it fresh, make it new; this is what his writing is doing, "ejercicio moderno / en el ambiente ingenuo del poema." Maples Arce has said that, more than merely including the airplane as a modern phenomenon (as the Italian Futurists did), the experience of flying in it in a poem was what mattered. It gave a new way of looking at the world and a new feeling. It is not just the inclusion of a modern object that counts, but rather the poetic expression of how it feels to fly and how the world looks from the sky. It was something very new.

> El aeroplano, por ejemplo, en Marinetti es artefacto de la industria moderna, pero las palabras no la alcanzan para incorporarle una superioridad de objeto ideal; para mí es una posibilidad de expresión, de

sentir el mundo, de penetrar en otras perspectivas. Desde las primeras palabras de mi poema 'Canción desde un aeroplano' entramos en una atmósfera que indica una nueva concepción del mundo, un nuevo orden mental.[150]

The effect on the poet/pilot is in part one of renovation, making the world look more vivid, more intense mid-swoop: "la Naturaleza subiendo / el color del firmamento." He wants to share that feeling with others—a hint at union, communion: "Al llegar te entregaré este viaje de sorpresas." There follows a reaffirmation of "Todo es desde arriba / equilibrado y superior," saying in strophe six that the trip is "equilibrio perfecto de mi vuelo astronómico," contrasted sharply with the mad condition of the world below where his lover waits—"tú estarás esperándome en el manicomio de la tarde." She awaits him there, feeling faint from the distance separating them, melancholic, neurasthenic ("acaso lloras sobre la palabra otoño"); he wants to bring to her the feeling of having transcended time and space limitations.

This sense of liberation from time and space constraints leads into the next section, in which he lists distant cities of North America ("New-York, / Chicago, / Baltimore")–distant but he calls them theirs, his and hers, with a sense of the continent as a whole. They are modern, fashionable places somehow claimed and brought close by radio programs and high-speed travel. It is as if he could bring them to her via his plane ride. He has overcome his previous spatial limitations—as he says in the first strophe, "tengo las manos / llenas / de azules continentes."

The next section (strophe eight) describes the tropical

---

150 Manuel Maples Arce with Emiliano Quiroz, "Manuel Maples Arce por él mismo: entrevista de Emiliano Quiroz," *La Cultura en México* [Sup. de *Siempre*] 12 mayo 1971: III.

ports of the Atlantic, closer to the protagonist's home. We see the colors of the nations' flags flying at the ports, the blue of the ocean, and the green of the palm trees. These colors are connected to the last line of the strophe, in which the woman is equated with springtime and beauty and flowers. In these beautiful tropical ports merchant ships greet each other, and the protagonist imagines himself a traveler, perhaps on one of those ships or another boat. He sees the palm trees that line river and ocean shores as if they were moving rather than he ("palmeras emigrantes") This is a phenomenon that recurs in several parts of *Poemas Interdictos*—which is the feeling that a traveler has, as if one were sitting still and the landscape were rushing by, just as when the airplane does a loop the loop it seems that the panorama does a flip-flop. The river seems to carry things along rather than boats moving across the water by the force of powered motors, faster than the current.

The identification of the woman with the colors of the ports and of springtime, as well as with elements of nature, connects with the next strophe (nine), where the woman is a metaphor for Mexico. The protagonist sings her/its praises: she is "País donde los pájaros hicieron sus columpios. / Hojeando tu perfume se marchitan las cosas"—everything else pales next to her. The images of color and nature continue throughout this strophe, adding the sparkle of the Mexican sun (in the woman's smile and eyes), as he promotes her in political metaphors, images fresh with influence of the historical period. She is his "novia electoral" and he will launch the candidacy of her love. The uplifting energy and sense of kineticism or dynamism are maintained here with words such as "columpios," "hojeando," "destellas," "lanzaré," "la orquesta del viento," and especially "carroussel de miradas." All nature rests on her words, is at her command. He realizes he is falling in love with her ("Algo está aconteciendo allá en el corazón") and the emotion he feels while thinking of her makes the plane swoop, leading to the next section.

In the next-to-last strophe of the poem the protagonist describes the feeling of that swooping. "Las estaciones girando / mientras capitalizo tu nostalgia," echoes the earlier loop the loop and the Cubist subversion of traditional perspective, plus the aforementioned dizziness, the vortex and the carrousel ("todo equivocado de sueños y de imágenes.") He feels he has been victorious in his campaign, his senses are alive, and he thinks it is fate: the protagonist and the woman were destined for each other, it was in the stars.

This mention of destiny and the zodiac ends the strophe, and suddenly reminds the protagonist of his ultimate fate (death) and his more immediate fate (loneliness) if he loses her. The last strophe begins: "Soledad apretada contra el pecho infinito." This remembering of time's course and of human mortality impels the protagonist to keep the flight going, to try to prolong the moment as much as possible, to live it to the fullest. He says, "De este lado del tiempo, / sostengo el pulso de mi canto"—or to paraphrase: in life, I'm in control of my actions, I control my poems, my flight; I will keep the pulse high, keep it going. It is as if the protagonist realizes the risk but says "go for it." He thinks of his beloved again and the plane swoops off once more, the landscape suddenly turning topsy-turvy as before.

> Soledad apretada contra el pecho infinito.
> De este lado del tiempo,
> sostengo el pulso de mi canto;
> tu recuerdo se agranda como un remordimiento,
> y el paisaje entreabierto se me cae de las manos. (p. 59)

The ending of the poem is ambiguous, however, because in the last two lines the protagonist says that the thought of the woman swells like a regret, and the landscape falls from his hands. This could mean that he feels he has already lost her, and has lost control of his flight as well as his life. Nevertheless, it is more likely that the emotion he felt (when suddenly thinking of the possibility of losing the woman and of the eventual inevitability of his own death) was very great, momentarily frightening. There are no real antecedents to support a negative ending to the poem, where he would definitely lose the woman's love. The last two lines of the poem communicate a lover's insecurity, they are a sentimental projection into the future, imagining how he would feel if he were ever to lose her. The lines could simply mean he wishes he were with her now. "Remordimiento" belongs with "el manicomio de la tarde" and "la palabra otoño" as emblems of the temporal, unbalanced world below. These words hint at the protagonist's fear that love will be as transitory as everything else in the world. There could also be a veiled reference here to Maples Arce's father, who had recently died, but the poem lacks any other use of that situation. In any case, the protagonist opts to stay in adventurous flight, where "todo es ... equilibrado y superior." And, as the epigraph to *Poemas Interdictos* indicates, "El estremecimiento es la parte mejor de la humanidad" (Goethe). What counts is the emotion: live it, feel it, be alive, *carpe diem*.

"T.S.H."

Sobre el despeñadero nocturno del silencio
las estrellas arrojan sus programas,
y en el audión inverso del ensueño,
se pierden las palabras
olvidadas.

        T. S. H.
        de los pasos
        hundidos
        en la sombra
        vacía de los jardines.

El reloj
de la luna mercurial
ha ladrado la hora a los cuatro horizontes.

        La soledad
        es un balcón
        abierto hacia la noche.

¿En dónde estará el nido
de esta canción mecánica?
Las antenas insomnes del recuerdo
recogen los mensajes
inalámbricos
de algún adiós deshilachado

        Mujeres naufragadas
que equivocaron las direcciones
trasatlánticas;
y las voces
de auxilio
como flores
estallan en los hilos
de los pentagramas
internacionales.

El corazón

me ahoga en la distancia.

Ahora es el "Jazz-Band"
de Nueva York;
son los puertos sincrónicos
florecidos de vicio
y la propulsión de los motores.

Manicomio de Hertz, de Marconi, de Edison!

El cerebro fonético baraja
la perspectiva accidental
de los idiomas.
Hallo!

        Una estrella de oro
        ha caído en el mar.

The second poem of the volume is "T. S. H.," the abbreviation for "telefonía sin hilos," an early term for radio. The poem was printed in *El Universal Ilustrado* on April 5, 1923 in an issue dedicated to radio, and it was recited by Maples Arce over in the first radio broadcast emanating from Mexico, May 8, 1923.[151] Like "Canción desde un aeroplano" and "80 H. P.," "T. S. H." presents a phenomenon of modern technology, the protagonist's fascination with it, and its effect on human life. As Maples Arce has said, "En este poema no hay propiamente una descripción, porque, evidentemente, en él traté de buscar una equivalencia lírica de lo que era la radiofonía de aquellos días."[152]

As usual, the verses of this poem are built around com-

---

[151] Also participating in this historic radio broadcast were Carlos Noriega Hope, editor of *El Universal Ilustrado*, Sr. Azcárraga from La Casa del Radio, there was music from Andrés Segovia, Manuel M. Ponce, M. Barajas, Sra. Wilson de Chávez, and the Director General de Telégrafos spoke. (Felipe Gálvez, "Cincuenta años nos contemplan desde las antenas radiofónicas: entrevista con Manuel Maples Arce," *Comunidad* [México: Universidad Iberoamericana] VIII.46 (dic. 1973): 732-742.)

[152] Gálvez, 734.

binations of 7, 14 or 11 syllables, with some variations; similar to *Urbe*, the variations are usually not significant but are rather examples of a creative lineation that attempts to mirror the content of the poem. Here, many offset (surrounded by white space) short verses and strophes help to communicate the idea of distance, isolation and loneliness. For a poem written to celebrate the invention of radio, it is overwhelmingly sad and dark, emphasizing the incompletion of human-to-human communication rather than the improvement of it (although we do see the contrast between before radio and after). We become aware that they are one-way broadcasts shot out into the dark space of night, bringing an awareness of distance, unlike a shortwave radio conversation which would bridge the gap and provide solace to one's loneliness in the night. Still, the modernity of it all and the fascination with the new technology is present in the use of modern images and new words in the poem to form a lyrical impression of the phenomenon of radio: ("el audión inverso del ensueño," "el reloj / de la luna mercurial," "las antenas insomnes del recuerdo," "los mensajes / inalámbricos," "los hilos / de los pentagramas / internacionales," "la propulsión de los motores," "el cerebro fonético"). "T. S. H." was written in 1923, one year after the publication of *Andamios Interiores*, before *Urbe*, and four years before the publication of *Poemas Interdictos*. The fact that "T. S. H." was written just after *Andamios Interiores* explains the similarity to the poems of *Andamios*, in its treatment of melancholy, loneliness and the yearning for communication with the outside world. The innovation is primarily in the images and word combinations, the *imagen equivalentista* with modern-world expressions, as seen in the list above.

In addition to the effectiveness of those images, the new "telefonía sin hilos" triumphs in the end over the darkness and loneliness so evident in the poem, and the work comes full-circle as it closes. Prevalent in the poem are a series of downward-moving, sinking images (typically Maplesian): "despeñadero," "pasos hundidos en la sombra vacía," "mujeres naufragadas," "me ahoga," "una estrella ... ha caído en el mar," "arrojan." To these are added a number of haunting, negative images: an allusion to a dog barking at the moon (an omen of death), "soledad," "se pierden," "insomnes," "olvidadas," "deshilachado," "equivocaron las direcciones," "voces / de auxilio ... estallan," "vicio," "manicomio." The major subjects of the poem are falling stars, the sea, nighttime, the moon, silence and sound. There are several expressions about being lost, forgotten, or leaving, as well as being sunk, sinking or shipwrecked (*naufragio*, a recurring image in Maples' poems, seems to be a metaphor for his inner life), and there is a sense of vast distances. During the protagonist's nights of insomnia, memory plays an important role in spanning that temporal and spatial distance before the advent of radio. Darkness and silence tend to intensify the narrator's loneliness when he cannot sleep. Memories of a cherished past may comfort him in those moments; or they may only serve to increase his loneliness–his awareness of being separated from that past. There is a hint in the poem of a romantic involvement lost or distanced: "El corazón / me ahoga en la distancia," "algún adiós deshilachado." He is lonely and is sympathetic to others' cries for help. He can't sleep, he looks out at the silvery moon as the hours pass, accompanied solely by his memories–until radio is invented. Radio broadcasts in the '20s were heard in Mexico only at night. They were programs from English-speaking countries, principally the United States—thus the references in the poem to a "Jazz-Band" program from New York, and to "los pentagramas / internacionales" of modern machine-age port cities, and the "Hallo!" in English. The protagonist wonders where some of the programs originate, from what city they are broadcast ("¿En dónde estará el nido / de esta canción mecánica?"). In the middle of the poem there is a reference to the sinking of the Titanic,[153] an event still very present in the public memory of those days. The Titanic's tragic accident occurred before ships had radios. The protagonist in "T. S. H." is haunted by the idea of women in that overturned, sinking transatlantic ship, calling out for help, in vain. In this poem we can almost feel the cold silence of the huge iceberg looming at them in the ocean night. The narrator wonders, what if their voices could have been heard? The next lines of the poem, separated by spaces, are "El corazón / me ahoga en la distancia," showing his sympathy and sadness, and echoing their tragic end.

    The lines "mujeres naufragadas / que equivocaron las direcciones" recall the verses from T. S. Eliot's "Love Song of J. Alfred Prufrock" –"In the room the women come and go, / talking of Michelangelo"– in which they actually wander with no sense of direction or coherent connection with the rest of the poem. The Eliot lines are written in parody of rhyme and meter, and form part of a larger treatment in "Prufrock" of three problems in the twentieth century: the lack of true communication between people, the inability to act (or to put thoughts into action), and a hesitation to act–thinking mistakenly that there will

---

153 Gálvez, 735.

be more time. The women on the Titanic call out but are not heard, we speak but are not understood, words seem senseless, Prufrock is afraid to talk or act ("Do I dare? Do I dare?") but wants desperately to communicate. Because the Titanic was overturned, passengers probably became disoriented, and they drowned because they hesitated, were lost, did not know which way to go. There was no "Time to turn back and descend the stair" (Eliot).

In the next section of the poem, Maples again refers to radio programs like "Jazz-Band," coming from New York. In the busy port cities life is full of modern inventions ("la propulsión de los motores"). However, the international transport business between ports, enabled by those inventions, produces a sharing only of vice, the protagonist says, and not true communication ("son los puertos sincrónicos / florecidos de vicio / y la propulsión de los motores.") The next line exclaims "Manicomio de Hertz, de Marconi, de Edison!" As in Prufrock's situation, there are numerous wonderful technological inventions, many having to do with the communication of sound and words (telegraph, phonograph, radio...), yet 20th-century man cannot communicate his feelings. Then the protagonist, listening to the radio while looking out at the night sky (one recalls the falling stars from the first strophe) sees a falling star at the same moment that he hears a distant, foreign-language call on the radio ("el cerebro fonético"): "Hallo!," and it is as if he hears the star calling out to him. It is now not the silence of the falling stars at the beginning of the poem nor the unheard voices of the women on the Titanic; it is, rather, a cry for help which he hears. And he hears it thanks to radio. It is a lone star at night, not unlike him at his window, a star falling from sky to sea, from zenith to nadir, and he hears its "grito náufrago" (cf. "Prisma"). He cannot stop the star's fall, but true communication is achieved, he does hear its cry, sounding like the last words of Altazor. Unlike Altazor, we know that the star is not alone now, that a connection has been made between it and the protagonist, and that the word made sense, even though foreign (Spanish does have a similar word, "aló"). Due to radio, the possibility for communication between two souls across distance (again, the transcendence of spatial limitations in *Poemas Interdictos*) has been opened. It is a beginning.

"80 H.P."

Pasan las avenidas del otoño
bajo los balcones marchitos de la música,
y el jardín es como un destello rojo
entre el aplauso burgués de las arquitecturas.

Esquinas flameadas de ponientes.

   El automóvil sucinto
   tiene a veces
   ternuras
   minerales.

   Para la amiga interferente
   entregada a las vueltas del peligro;

he aquí su sonrisa equilibrista,
sus cabellos boreales,
y sobre todo, el campo,
desparramado de caricias.

Países del quitasol

                        nuevo
    —espectáculo   mundo
    exclusivo-   latino
                       de sus ojos.

    En el motor   ⎰ El corazón apretado
    hay la misma canción.   ⎱ como un puño)

A veces pasan ráfagas, paisajes estrujados.

                y por momentos
                el camino es angosto como un sueño.

            Entre sus dedos
            se deshoja
            la rosa
            de los vientos.

Los árboles turistas
a intervalos
regresan con la tarde.
Se van
quedando

atrás
los arrabales
del recuerdo

        —oh el alegre motín de su blancura!-

            Tacubaya,   ⎰
            San Ángel,   ⎱ Pequeños
            Mixcoac.   ⎱ alrededores de la música.

Después
sólo las praderas   del tiempo

Allá lejos
    ejércitos
            de la noche
                    nos esperan.

"80 H. P." is the third poem of group one (as I have grouped them). This poem deals with modern machines, dynamism, and the desire to overcome spatial limitations and postpone temporal limitations. In essence, "80 H. P." is a description of the visual and kinetic sensations of a high-speed (for 1927) automobile ride.[154] The scenery is shown as if it were rushing by rather than the car by it, and the attempt to convey the kinetics produces an almost cinematic quality in the visual images in the poem. There is a joy in the dynamic quality of modern life, in man's inventions, his machines, the most positive aspect of the vortex. There is also a feeling of the poet as creator, as he, Adam in the twentieth century, gives names to everything he sees. Still, this adventure is ephemeral, passes by too quickly, with nothing left afterward. There is the typical Maplesian nostalgia for permanence, and anguish over not being able to retain anything through time. However, in "80 H. P." as in "Canción desde un aeroplano," the poet opts to live in the present moment and to try to prolong that as much as possible. The writing of the poem holds that moment indefinitely. Inside the dynamic moment there is a kind of eternity; in the re-creation of the ride by subsequent readers that moment is eternalized in another way.

Rubén Bonifaz Nuño suggests that the perspective of the landscape rushing by the car, rather than the reverse, communicates the sense of the transitoriness of things which is felt by the protagonist: "... la sensación terrible de lo que se va sin reparación posible, lo que de continuo

---

[154] A car with 80 horsepower could conceivably have a top speed of 80 or 90 miles per hour. This would have seemed very fast and powerful in 1927, considerably more than the performance of a typical car of that time.

se pierde para siempre... Así, nos deja ver una imagen de viaje en la cual el que se mueve no es el viajero sino el camino por donde transita."[155]

Like the other trips described in *Poemas Interdictos*, this automobile ride takes place in the late afternoon/early evening, during sunset ("el jardín es como un destello rojo;" "esquinas flameadas de ponientes")–the violet hour (when there are magical visions and things are more clearly understood). As the brilliant sunset enlivens the cityscape, so does the car ride excite and animate the protagonist's life. As Bonifaz Nuño suggests (p. 26), the beginning of the poem presents Maples Arce's world-view–of things in decadence, represented by the autumnal images. This is part of the issue of the ephemeral and transitory, the lack of permanence through time: "Pasan las avenidas del otoño / bajo los balcones marchitos de la música." But the automobile and its dynamism bring new life to that stage. More than the Italian Futurists, who merely exalted the power of the machine (for example, Luigi Russolo's painting "Dynamism of an Automobile," c. 1912-13,[156] focuses on the power of the car as machine, rather than on the effect of riding in it), Maples Arce gives us the sensation of the automobile ride, felt by the protagonist, the personal human interpretation of the effect of that machine on his life (cf. "Canción desde un aeroplano"). This is much like Stephen Spender's call to modern poets (see Chapter One), not to spell out or explain Einstein's Theory of Relativity in poems, but to understand and show its effect on human life. In "80 H. P." the automobile is presented not so much as a powerful engine

---

155 Bonifaz Nuño, 26.
156 d'Harnoncourt, fig. 63.

but as the agent of the protagonist's renewed joy in life, and it takes on human qualities at times: "El automóvil sucinto / tiene a veces / ternuras / minerales." This leads to the first mention of the woman riding with him in the car, equally an agent of his enjoyment of life at that moment. She is a true *mujer estridentista*, daring and bold, "entregada a las vueltas del peligro." She rides next to the protagonist in the small car, her smile is "equilibrista" (like the effect of the ride itself). As their car speeds along the road, her hair blows in the wind and reflects the colors of the sunset, and thus she forms an integral and integrated part of the whole scene. The description of her leads to one of the landscape, carrying on the idea of *ternura* and of the woman: "y sobre todo, el campo, / desparramado de caricias." Then it is as if the world were new to the protagonist; he is seeing it from a new perspective and with a renewed sense of identity. He is also showing the world to the woman from a new point of view.

Países del quitasol

                    nuevo
—espectáculo   mundo
exclusivo-   latino
                    de sus ojos.(p. 63)

This is the first point of climax in the poem, and appropriately, as the revelation happens in one instant, the verses are written side-by-side to communicate the idea of simultaneity, energy, and emotion. It also provides a feeling of freedom, as well as the visual effect of riding by places at high speed. Bonifaz Nuño explains:

> Ahora es ya la plenitud del viaje, en la cual se irán mezclando y alternando los estímulos de la mujer y del

camino al aire descubierto. Y, como otro Cristóbal Colón, el poeta descubrirá un mundo desconocido para todos, que esos estímulos irán revelando solamente a él, afortunado como nadie:

'Países del quitasol / nuevo / mundo / latino / de sus ojos.'

Allí está la idea, nace allí para él la sensación del descubrimiento. En los ojos de ella, todo un mundo desconocido, pero lleno de antiguas tradiciones y culturas propicias.[157]

As he felt at one with the airplane in "Canción desde un aeroplano" (the same heartbeat), here the protagonist identifies with the automobile:

| En el motor | { (El corazón apretado |
| hay la misma canción. | como un puño) |

He feels the thrill of the ride, the excitement of the adventure, Goethe's *estremecimiento*.

There follows a metaphor for life as the protagonist and the woman continue along the road: "A veces pasan ráfagas, paisajes estrujados, / y por momentos / el camino es angosto como un sueño." It may not always be an easy ride, but there is here a sense of freedom: "Entre sus dedos / se deshoja / la rosa / de los vientos." Again Maples uses the double meaning of the compass rose, instrument which guides the traveler, and nature's rose, poetic symbol of love and constancy. He wants something of both of these. Bonifaz Nuño suggests that the plucking of this "rosa de los vientos" signifies not loss but conquest, "la conquista de una inmensidad"[158] –riding with the protagonist, the woman has plucked apart the indicator of all directions, paths that lead to all places. This brings a tremendous

---

157 Bonifaz Nuño, 27.
158 Bonifaz Nuño, 28.

sense of freedom, and a transcendence of spatial limitations, not only through movement but through an opening of possibility regarding direction. "Abierto así mágicamente el camino, la alegría de asirse del momento presente ocupa al poeta."[159]

There follows a recapitulation of the evidence of decadence and transitoriness in the world. However, now that the protagonist has realized that the answer to this problem is to grasp the present moment and live it to the fullest, make it last as long as possible and thus try to overcome his temporal limitations, the images of transitoriness are not quite so negative as at other times. They are stronger, more beautiful and have a feeling of comprehension and almost contentment. Two such images are: "los árboles turistas / a intervalos / regresan con la tarde," and the lovely image "Se van quedando / [inserting a space to indicate distance and time] atrás / los arrabales / del recuerdo." Then, as he contemplates those images, we get the second climax of the poem, which is also the second moment of illumination and understanding: "–oh el alegre motín de su blancura!–" followed by a list of three small towns outside Mexico City (at the time), Tacubaya, San Ángel, Mixcoac.

Thus the idea is to live fully now, because later all that is left is time and death.

> 'Después / sólo las praderas del tiempo.' Ese tiempo voraz, aliado de la muerte que aguarda.
> Tiempo y muerte, confundidos en su conciencia e identificados con la hostilidad multiplicada de las horas nocturnas, le dan los últimos versos: 'Allá lejos / ejércitos / de la noche / nos esperan.'

---

159   Bonifaz Nuño, 28.

> Es la última esperanza: que el instante actual se prolongue, que la pérdida, las filas destructoras del tiempo, la oscura muerte, estén lejos. Que tengan que esperar todavía largamente.[160]

The poem gives a feeling of youth and joy, of freedom and possibility. It is a clear expression of *carpe diem*, one of the suggested solutions to the lack of permanence, made possible by the inventions of the modern city.

Each of the three poems of group one ("Canción desde un aeroplano," "T. S. H." and "80 H. P.") tells of the wonders of the airplane, radio or automobile, and in each case the protagonist is modern man, speaking in a new language, but still embracing life and the essentially human in life.[161] This human quality characterizes all of Maples Arce's poetry. Indeed it is a profoundly human quality in the midst of a mechanized society which is outstanding in Maples' work, and it is just this quality that critics so often miss while seeing only the machines.[162] The deep humanity of the later *Memorial de la Sangre*, noted by all critics of Maples Arce's poetry, is not so surprising when one looks closely at the earlier collections.

"Primavera"

> El jardín alusivo se envaguece de esperas
> y el corazón despierta a las últimas cosas.
>
> Un soplo de radiolas
> avienta hacia nosotros
> sus rumores de vidrio.

---

160 Bonifaz Nuño, 29.
161 Schneider, 188.
162 With the notable exceptions of Bonifaz Nuño and Schneider.

Los poetas comentan la renuncia del día.
Las calles vagabundas regresan del exilio.

Una tenue esperanza me llevó a sus caricias;
su imagen repentina me estremece en lo hondo;
anida su blancura en la tarde latente,
y mientras que desciñe su busto de suspiros
los árboles alumbran nuestro secreto cósmico.

La ausencia es el perfume que me deja en el pecho.
La pierdo en la espesura
de la vida moderna,
y nuevamente vuelvo,
al campo de deportes con sus lunas auténticas.

Apuesto a su sonrisa en el juego de pókar,
lecturas de la música anegadas de lágrimas.

Cuando pongo en sus manos
el cheque de mi adiós,
los expresos sonámbulos
despiden nuestras sombras,
y el mareo de los puertos dentro del corazón.

(Solfea la primavera
sus lecciones.)

De pronto el desenlace obscuro de la célula.

Transaré con los pájaros su recuerdo sangrante.

The second group into which I have divided the poems of *Poemas Interdictos* is composed of "Primavera" and "Puerto." "Primavera" is probably one of the earlier-written poems of this volume: it has a very regular structure and lineation, with verses of fourteen syllables with a caesura between the two heptasyllables virtually every time, a few separated lines (heptasyllables) noting major points, and only one irregularity, indicating the most important statement of the poem. It would almost fit in *Andamios Interiores*, except for the lack of anguish over separation—it is the attitude of the narrator here, rather than the structure or content, that makes this a *poema interdicto*. The place and situation are the same as always, and the attitude is live for today, seize the moment, and don't regret it; it's alright to remember the moment later, but don't get too sentimental about it. The protagonist is a bit of a don Juan here, and the poem is basically about the awakening of love and infatuation that springtime brings. Thus the title, and the key line of the poem, "(Solfea la primavera / sus lecciones.)" "Sus lecciones" is the only aberration of syllable count, and it stands out starkly; this is a poem about a brief affair, notable, but momentary and nothing promised. Like spring, love and youth don't last forever, so take advantage of them while you can. The setting of the poem is late afternoon/early evening, the hour of sunset, as usual; people have returned home from work, and the protagonist decides to visit a woman to whom he is attracted. Their love tryst is their "secreto cósmico." He leaves her and returns to the city nightlife. He bets her smile in a poker game, sad love songs being sung in the background, perhaps in a cabaret that has a back room for poker. Later he tells her goodbye to end the affair, and feels a pang of emotion as they separate. But a series of new words serve as reminders that he is a modern man in a modern city ("vidrio," "cósmico," "la espesura de la vida moderna," "campos de deportes," "lunas auténticas," "pókar," "cheque," "los expresos," "puertos," "célula") and springtime chimes in with its admonition, like a radio commercial or a flashing neon sign advertising lessons about life and love. Time's winged chariot looms on the horizon, a reminder of our mortality: "De pronto el desenlace obscuro de la célula." Nevertheless, the protagonist says he will keep a fond memory of the woman and their sunset-colored evenings, and these will form part of the landscape of his life.

"Puerto"

Llegaron nuestros pasos hasta la borda de la tarde;
el Atlántico canta debajo de los muelles,
y presiento un reflejo de mujeres
que sonríen al comercio
de los países nuevos.

El humo de los barcos
desmadeja el paisaje;
brumosa travesía
florecida de pipas,
¡oh rubia transeúnte de las zonas marítimas!
de pronto, eres la imagen
movible del acuario.

Hay un tráfico ardiente de avenidas
frente al hotel abanicado de palmeras.

Te asomas por la celosía
de las canciones
al puerto palpitante de motores
y los colores de la lejanía
me miran en tus tiernos ojos.

Entre las enredaderas venenosas
que enmarañan el sueño
recojo sus señales amorosas;
la dicha nos espera
en el alegre verano de sus besos;

la arrodilla el océano de caricias,
y el piano
es una hamaca en la alameda.

Se reúne la luna allá en los mástiles,
y un viento de ceniza
me arrebata su nombre;
la navegación agitada de pañuelos,
y los adioses surcan nuestros pechos,
y en la débil memoria de todos estos goces,
sólo los pétalos de su estremecimiento
perfuman las orillas de la noche.

The poem "Puerto" returns to a more typical meter for *Poemas Interdictos*—irregular but with a sense of balance in the strophes, still dominated by seven-syllable verses. In addition to the man (the protagonist) and the woman, other major participants in the action of this poem are music, the sea, ships and various elements of a large commercial port on the Atlantic. The most important features of the poem are the large number of sensorial images, the use of personal pronouns, a dream sequence, and the use of a positive / negative contrast. At the beginning of the poem, the protagonist seems to be walking down to the wharf of the port in the late afternoon with the woman, indicated by "*nuestros* pasos." He is escorting her to the ship on which she will travel. Going down to the piers to watch the ships is a popular thing to do, and the protagonist expects to see other women there. At the piers, smoke from the ships' smokestacks clouds the view, and suddenly the woman has boarded a ship and is off on her trip. As in the poems of *Andamios*, the woman is the traveler, not the protagonist, and there has been a goodbye scene and separation of the couple at a place of modern transport. The protagonist returns to his hotel, through the traffic-filled, palm-lined city streets. Back at the hotel, he thinks about his beloved as he looks out over the port city. Her image is evoked in the music he hears and in the colors of the sunset-filled sky he sees. This idea is expressed in an interesting way, giving her a more active role in the images, thus making her seem more present: "Te asomas por la celosía / de las canciones / al puerto palpitante de motores / y los colores de la lejanía / me miran en tus tiernos ojos."

As evening moves into night and sunset into darkness, it is inferred that the protagonist falls asleep, and the next strophe is a dream sequence. A victim of insomnia, it seems that when he does sleep, he is plagued by nightmares, as seen in *Urbe*. These nightmares present a negative image at the beginning of the dream sequence, but the lover reaches out to him in the dream and saves him, with the images changing to positive.

> Entre las enredaderas venenosas
> que enmarañan el sueño
> recojo sus señales amorosas;
> la dicha nos espera
> en el alegre verano de sus besos;
> la arrodilla el océano de caricias,
> y el piano
> es una hamaca en la alameda. (p. 65)

The use of personal pronouns (often confusing references in Maples' poems) is important here in two ways: first, the "tú" (you, familiar) referring to the woman in previous strophes changes now to "su" (her). The reference to her in the third person indicates her physical absence (the previous strophe, where he imagines that he sees her in the sunset and in the songs, is a sort of buffer zone or transition phase, until he realizes that she really has left) and this use of the third person continues to the end of the poem. More importantly, there is the direct-object pronoun "nos" (us) in the middle of this dream sequence, the second of only three instances of a variant of "nosotros" in the poem, after "nuestros" in the first line, when they (the lovers) were walking together down to the wharf. As a symbol of union, "nos" indicates a transcendence of their physical separation in real life, and occurs in the dream, which can be equated to the poem.

Thus, as in the poems of *Andamios Interiores* and in so many others, the protagonist achieves a solution to his problem of separation and impermanence through the writing of the poem. It is a suddenly very happy and affirmative image of union after the woman has reached out to save the protagonist from his nightmares, and indicates as well a future for them together: "la dicha nos espera / en el alegre verano de sus besos." This is the point of climax, and the next part of the dream illustrates its effect: his continued desire for her, plus relaxation and comfort, reassurance. It begins with a beautifully erotic dream-image of her being seduced by the ocean (or by a metaphorical "sea of caresses"): "la arrodilla el océano de caricias." The concluding image of the dream sequence is "y el piano / es una hamaca en la alameda," the idea of comfort and relaxation in a pleasant, non-threatening atmosphere. The "hamaca" recalls his sleep, and the "alameda" recalls the palm trees that line the street by his hotel in the port city. The piano connects with the "canciones" of the previous strophe, the transitional stage when he imagined she was still there, before he fell asleep. Music seems almost always to be positive in Maples Arce's poems, and is usually the agent that evokes a memory of his beloved.

In the last strophe, it seems that he awakens and goes

out on the balcony, and the poem states the dénouement, almost a recapitulation of the previous action. It is negative at first—he sees the moon up in the sky, among the ships' masts, and the wind snatches the woman's name away from him (much as the ship took her away): "y un viento de ceniza / me arrebata su nombre." This unusual and striking image conveys the negativity through "ceniza," which also recalls the smoke of the ships' smokestacks at the time of her departure, now more definitive and distant as "ceniza." The next image recalls the goodbyes and the deep effect on the couple: "y los adioses surcan nuestros pechos"—but here is the third instance of a variant of the pronoun "nosotros," meaning the union of the two people, not the separation, as again the writing of the poem triumphs over the apparent reality. Thus the strophe is brought out of negativity and back to the positive. The memory of the woman, and of the protagonist's relationship with her, though admittedly weak, remains, and her essence fills the night for him. It is expressed in a lovely final image: "sólo los pétalos de su estremecimiento / perfuman las orillas de la noche."

The character of the protagonist's memory of his beloved is illustrated throughout the poem by a number of nicely achieved sensorial images: the sound of their footsteps while walking together; the sound of the water lapping underneath the piers; the reflection in the water of women's smiles as they watch the ships; the way the smoke from the ships' smokestacks fills the air and makes it hard to see the surroundings—illustrating the dominance of the ships—agents of separation—over the rest of the landscape. The busy movement of people boarding the ship is linked metaphorically to the movement of fish in the water.

The use of kinetic images continues in the poem as the protagonist returns to the hotel and observes the traffic in the busy street, the hotel's palm trees swaying, and the "puerto palpitante de motores" in the transition scene (strophes three and four). Related to the kinetics and their implied rhythm is a reference to music (*canciones*). The sunset provides a rich colorful background to the other visuals, and is especially nice when the protagonist imagines it reflecting in his beloved's eyes as he looks at her: "y los colores de la lejanía / me miran en tus tiernos ojos." There are dark threatening colors in the "enredaderas venenosas" of the nightmares and the "viento de ceniza." Tactile images include her kisses and the ocean's caresses, the fanning of the palm trees, and the feeling of lying in a hammock. We can almost smell the smoke and ash, and the strongest olfactory image is metaphorically inferred in the last two lines ("sólo los pétalos de su estremecimiento / perfuman las orillas de la noche"), which are visual as well. All of these images serve to indicate a rich sense of awareness on the part of the protagonist, as awakened by his being in love–the emotion factor so important in all of Maples Arce's poems. Also evident is a strong sense of place, as the choice of title indicates, making this an appropriate poem for *Poemas Interdictos*, so concerned with the idea of space and movement through it in the modern world.

"REVOLUCIÓN"

El viento es el apóstol de esta hora interdicta.
Oh épocas marchitas

que sacudieron sus últimos otoños!
Barrunta su recuerdo los horizontes próximos
desahuciados de pájaros,
y las corolas deshojan su teclado.

Sopla el viento absoluto contra la materia
cósmica; la música
es la propaganda que flota en los balcones,
y el paisaje despunta
en las veletas.

Viento, dictadura
de hierro
que estremece las confederaciones!
Oh las muchedumbres
azules
y sonoras, que suben
hasta los corazones!

La tarde es un motín sangriento
en los suburbios;
árboles harapientos
que piden limosna en las ventanas;
las fábricas se abrasan
en el incendio del crepúsculo,
y en el cielo brillante
los aviones
ejecutan maniobras vesperales.

Banderas clamorosas
repetirán su arenga proletaria
frente a las ciudades.

En el mitin romántico de la partida,
donde todos lloramos
hoy recojo la espera de su cita;
la estación
despedazada se queda entre sus manos,
y su desmayo
es el alto momento del adiós.
Beso la fotografía de su memoria

y el tren despavorido se aleja entre la sombra,
mientras deshojo los caminos nuevos.

Pronto llegaremos a la cordillera.
Oh tierna geografía
de nuestro México,
sus paisajes aviónicos,
alturas inefables de la economía
política; el humo de las factorías
perdidas en la niebla
del tiempo,
y los rumores eclécticos
de los levantamientos.
Noche adentro
los soldados,
se arrancaron
del pecho
las canciones populares.

La artillería
enemiga, nos espía
en las márgenes de la Naturaleza;
los ruidos subterráneos
pueblan nuestro sobresalto
y se derrumba el panorama.

Trenes militares
que van hacia los cuatro puntos cardinales,

al bautizo de sangre
donde todo es confusión,
y los hombres borrachos
juegan a los naipes
y a los sacrificios humanos;
trenes sonoros y marciales
donde hicimos cantando la Revolución.

Nunca como ahora me he sentido tan cerca de la muerte.
Pasamos la velada junto a la lumbre intacta del recuerdo,
pero llegan los otros de improviso
apagando el concepto de las cosas,

las imágenes tiernas al borde del horóscopo.

Allá lejos,
mujeres preñadas
se han quedado rogando
por nosotros
a los Cristos de Piedra.

Después de la matanza
otra vez el viento
espanta
la hojarasca de los sueños.

Sacudo el alba de mis versos
sobre los corazones enemigos,
y el tacto helado de los siglos
me acaricia en la frente,
mientras que la angustia del silencio
corre por las entrañas de los nombres queridos.

Group three is composed of the last six poems of the book: "Revolución" plus the five poems of the section titled "Poemas de la lejanía." "Revolución" repeats the themes and images of *Urbe*, but now the protagonist is a more active participant in the battles of the Revolution, and not just a sympathetic bystander in the city during the political upheaval afterward. He is there, out in the *sierra* with the soldiers, a direct observer/participant (like Mariano Azuela, who was a medic, writing *Los de abajo* in the midst of the action on scraps of paper with rocks for a table). There is an intense feeling of the closeness of death, the silence of the unknown and of darkness, an awareness of time's course and fate. The protagonist says "Nunca como ahora me he sentido tan cerca de la muerte," an echo of Dante in the *Inferno* and of T. S. Eliot as a World War I air-raid warden near London Bridge in *The Waste Land*.

Arturo Sotomayor calls this awareness, as expressed in the images of "Revolución," "plástica tremenda, plástica espiritual categórica."[163] Sotomayor continues, referring to the line quoted above ("Nunca como ahora ...") and its strophe: "Imagen pura, sugerencia honda que nos hace sentir un estremecimiento conjunto de miedo ante lo desconocido, de ímpetus de combate, de una suerte de ternura inexplicable por lo que vive en nuestro recuerdo y puede ser borrado por la mano de la implacable."[164]

The poem "Revolución," like *Urbe*, is initially set in the city, and begins by explaining the situation and the causes of the Revolution. One-third of the way through the poem, the protagonist departs for the *sierra*, going off to fight in the Revolution. This setting is what places "Revolución" in group three: where the protagonist is the traveler, not through the city and its suburbs, but out into the country, and travel is by train.

The first third of the poem is a compact synthesis of *Urbe*. We see the same images: "el viento" as the foreboding catalyst of revolutionary change; a sense of the end of an era (strophe one); propagandistic music; the multitudes of workers ("las muchedumbres / azules / y sonoras") marching and protesting for equal rights for the proletariat, which provokes sympathy in observers; the brilliant red and orange colors of the factories and of the sunset in the late afternoon; the empathetic reaction of the elements of nature ("árboles harapientos / que piden limosna en las ventanas")—involvement of all elements of the sky and the land that are México; and synaesthetic images such as "Banderas clamorosas."

---

163   Arturo Sotomayor, "Manuel Maples Arce, Poeta Estridentista," *Sombras bajo la luna* (México: Porrúa, 1943) 178.
164   Sotomayor, 179.

There follows a typical goodbye scene at a train station but, as in most of the poems of *Poemas Interdictos*, it is the protagonist who is leaving and the woman who stays behind. She faints from emotion—with similar effect as the verse "sus palabras mojadas se me echaron al cuello" in "Prisma" —"y su desmayo / es al alto momento del adiós" (lines six and seven of strophe six here). Now, while the train stretches out into the distance, he thinks about her ("Beso la fotografía de su memoria").

On the train trip, moving across Mexico towards the *cordillera*, the protagonist views the landscape with fondness. They are "paisajes aviónicos" because from the mountains the land below looks like it does from an airplane. He feels the influence of the new socialist cause, the workers' factories, and the political uprisings. Then at night, having arrived at their destination, the rebel soldiers, perhaps sitting around a campfire, sing heartfelt popular songs. "Noche adentro / los soldados, / se arrancaron / del pecho / las canciones populares." The use of very short lines in this part gives a feeling of a slower pace, having ended the train trip, now sitting and waiting in the dark.

In the next strophe (eight), the poet effectively communicates how a soldier feels when he knows the enemy is watching him from nearby, perhaps just around the corner, and every little noise the soldier hears (a stone falling, a twig breaking) startles him, makes his heart leap. The pronoun "nos" in this strophe reinforces the fact that the protagonist is an active participant in the Revolution, one of the soldiers. "La artillería / enemiga, nos espía / en las márgenes de la Naturaleza; / los ruidos subterráneos / pueblan nuestro sobresalto / y se derrumba el panorama."

The following section shows military trains (packed

with soldiers, as we have seen in film clips and photos, especially of Pancho Villa's troops in the north) heading in all directions off to war. War is a "bautizo de sangre / donde todo es confusión," and where drunken men play at cards and at human sacrifice. This is the image-complex of trains going off to war, "trenes sonoros y marciales / donde hicimos cantando la Revolución."[165]

Next is the line where the protagonist feels closer to death than ever before; it is nighttime again, the soldiers have stayed up all night, wary, protected only by their memories. But the enemy attacks suddenly, wiping out those memories of the past and bringing closer the fate of the future. Back home, the protagonist says, pregnant women pray for the souls of those soldiers. After the battle ends, it is ghostly quiet again, and the nearness of death fills their dreams. An effective image in this part is: "Después de la matanza / otra vez el viento / espanta / la hojarasca de los sueños."

The protagonist remembers his poetry as hope against an unhappy fate: "Sacudo el alba de mis versos / sobre los corazones enemigos"—always the answer in Maples Arce's work. The poem ends as he sits there in the dark, vigilant, fearing death ("y el tacto helado de los siglos / me acaricia en la frente"), knowing that back home loved ones also live in anguish, not knowing if he is still alive or not. This is the real day-to-day reality of revolution, of war.

The last five poems of the book are placed together under the subtitle "Poemas de la lejanía." They will be grouped with "Revolución" in the third subdivision of this

---

[165] *Poemas Interdictos* is proof that the protagonist is not just a direct autobiographical persona of Maples Arce. The protagonist participates actively in the Revolution in these poems. Maples Arce did not fight in the Mexican Revolution (he was a child at the time).

discussion because they too deal with the protagonist travelling out, away from the city, as the subtitle indicates. Of particular interest is the manner in which they attempt to transcend space and time limitations, separation and transitoriness. All five poems of the subgroup "Poemas de la lejanía" can be seen as parts of one voyage. The titles support this interpretation, as they illustrate successive stages of the trip: "Partida," "Ruta," "Paroxismo," "Evocación," "Saudade."

"Partida"

Yo soy una estación sentimental
y los adioses pitan como trenes.
Es inútil llorar.

En los contornos del crepúsculo,
ventanas encendidas
hacia los rumbos
nuevos.

Palpita
todavía
  la alondra
    vesperal
      de su pañuelo.

"Partida" is a short poem of verses of eleven and seven syllables (some separated by lineation that reflects the content), with one exception of nine syllables. That exception, "En los contornos del crepúsculo," can be seen as a summation of the main point of the poem and its function as a defier of separation. The major spatial components of the poem are a train station, a train, the sky, and a handkerchief. As the title indicates, the situation is a departure. The first line implies that this is perhaps a metaphorical departure—maybe just a goodbye, a separation without a geographical voyage, as the protagonist says "Yo soy una estación sentimental / y los adioses pitan como trenes." He feels sentimental, but he says it is useless to cry, perhaps because the departure is inevitable. As the train takes off and heads for new routes, new adventures, the train windows are brilliantly illuminated by the colors of the sunset. But in those same "contornos del crepúsculo," he can still see his beloved waving her handkerchief goodbye to him from the station, this image now metaphorized into a lark winging through the sky that connects him with her. Thus what they share is the larger space across which they both move. Sky and nature ("la alondra"), which endure through time, connect them. An effective use of lineation is found in the last verse, which visually imitates the bird winging its way in flight and/or the waving of the handkerchief:

>   Palpita
>   todavía
>   la alondra
>   vesperal
>   de su pañuelo.

"Ruta"

>   A bordo del expreso
>   volamos sobre la irrealidad del continente.

La tarde apagada en los espejos,
y los adioses sangran en mi mente.

El corazón nostálgico presiente
a lo largo de este viaje,
literaturas vagabundas
que sacudieron las plumas
de sus alas
en los fríos corredores del paisaje.

Van pasando las campiñas sonámbulas
mientras el tren se aleja entre los túneles del sueño.

Allá de tarde en tarde,
ciudades
apedreadas de gritos y adioses.

Ríos de adormideras
que vienen del fondo de los años,
pasan interminablemente,
bajo los puentes,
que afirmaron
su salto metálico
sobre las vertientes.

Después, montañas, silenciosos ejércitos
aúllan a la muerte.

Entre las rendijas de la noche
me atormenta el insomnio de una estrella.
Trenes que marchan siempre hacia la ausencia,
un día,
sin saberlo,
nos cruzaremos
en la geografía.

The next piece, "Ruta," is another step in the voyage, perhaps the best poem of this subgroup. The protagonist is on board the express train, which he says is flying "sobre la irrealidad del continente," the irreality perceived is possibly due to the speed with which they are moving. Night has fallen, and he is recalling the goodbyes ("La tarde apagada en los espejos, / y los adioses sangran en mi mente"). An interesting image follows:

> El corazón nostálgico presiente
> a lo largo de este viaje,
> literaturas vagabundas
> que sacudieron las plumas
> de sus alas,
> en los fríos corredores del paisaje. (p. 69-70)

Riding at night alone is a natural catalyst for contemplation of one's life and of the country through which one is travelling. In this section the protagonist recalls other writers who have done the same and have recorded their impressions. He may also remember that travel away from home has often been the practice and inspiration of many great writers. The train continues on through the night, and as the protagonist is falling asleep, he sees the countryside passing by as if it were sleepwalking ("Van pasando las campiñas sonámbulas / mientras el tren se aleja entre los túneles del sueño"). This effective image not only conveys the feeling of travelling at night but also connects the inner and outer worlds: his own "túneles del sueño," the movement of the train with him on it, and the countryside through which it travels ("los fríos [nighttime] corredores del paisaje"), as well as the feeling that the train is gradually entering his dreams. The use of corridors and tunnels here gives a sense of the speed and dynamism of the train, the shape of the train, and also the deepening entrance into sleep and into the recesses of the mind and of dream. In all, it is an interesting psychological image-complex.

Other afternoons during the trip, the train passes

through cities and the protagonist witnesses goodbye scenes at the train stations. The train travels through immense, ancient fields of poppies—a lovely image that conveys the beauty and expanse of the countryside ("Ríos de adormideras / que vienen del fondo de los años, / pasan interminablemente, / bajo los puentes, / que afirmaron / su salto metálico / sobre las vertientes"). The second half of the strophe adds references to modern times, images that are also evidence of the recent presence of man in those ancient fields. Then the train travels through mountains; there silent armies howl at death. This last image is either an indication that the protagonist is off to war, as in "Revolución," or a tribute to the agelessness of the mountains, their existence spanning all known time. These images of great expansiveness make the protagonist think about time, infinity, and existence across space. An emblem of distance and of infinity, the twinkling of a star in the night sky haunts him: "Entre las rendijas de la noche / me atormenta el insomnio de una estrella" (cf. "Prisma"). Perhaps the infinity of nature brings a recollection of mankind's mortality: "Trenes que marchan siempre hacia la ausencia." A very human wish ends the poem, longing for union with those he is far away from: "un día, / sin saberlo, / nos cruzaremos / en la geografía." It would be chance, unknowing, but still a connection through space and time. This wish recalls Thoreau's thought while looking at a twinkling star in the night sky, that his friend Emerson, who was on a trip to England at the time, might be looking up at that same star at that same moment, and thus the two would be connected ("coincidimos").[166]

---

[166] Henry David Thoreau, *The Heart of Thoreau's Journals*, ed. Odell Shepard (New York: Dover Publications, Inc., 1961) 33; journal entry from 1847.

"Paroxismo"

Camino de otros sueños salimos con la tarde;
una extraña aventura
nos deshojó en la dicha de la carne,
y el corazón fluctúa
entre ella y la desolación del viaje.

En la aglomeración de los andenes
rompieron de pronto los sollozos;
después, toda la noche
debajo de mis sueños,
escucho sus lamentos
y sus ruegos.

El tren es una ráfaga de hierro
que azota el panorama y lo conmueve todo.

Apuro su recuerdo
hasta el fondo
del éxtasis,
y laten en el pecho
los colores lejanos de sus ojos.

Hoy pasaremos junto del otoño
y estarán amarillas las praderas.

¡Me estremezco por ella!
¡Horizontes deshabitados de la ausencia!

Mañana estará todo
nublado de sus lágrimas,
y la vida que llega
es débil como un soplo.

The poem "Paroxismo" tells of another goodbye scene, in *alejandrinos*, heptasyllables and hendecasyllables. The protagonist recalls the affair with his lover ("una extraña aventura / nos deshojó en la dicha de la carne"), and now while travelling, his thoughts alternate between her and the loneliness of the trip. He remembers how she broke into tears at the train station, and all night long in his dreams he hears her laments and her pleading that he not leave her. The kinetics of the rapidly-moving train speeding across the panorama stir his emotions—it is an exciting phenomenon—and seem to intensify his thoughts about his beloved. The next strophe is an interesting metaphor for the intensity of his feelings for her: "Apuro su recuerdo / hasta el fondo / del éxtasis, / y laten en el pecho / los colores lejanos de sus ojos." He fills himself with the thought of her as with a drink, and his resulting quickened heartbeat is like the way one feels after quaffing a strong drink. A renewed awareness of the trip and of their separation follows, and his loneliness finds an objective correlative in the landscape, described with typical Maplesian autumnal imagery: "Hoy pasaremos junto del otoño / y estarán amarillas las praderas." He exclaims, "¡Me estremezco por ella!," and the surroundings are filled with the awareness of her absence: "¡Horizontes deshabitados de la ausencia!" He says that tomorrow will be clouded by her tears, and life ahead without her "es débil como un soplo." There seems to be no solution, and his reaction is almost the same "paroxismo" as her tearful goodbye. However, they are at least linked by emotion, which is the essential quality of life. The lines of the poem that stand out because of their slight irregularity (through lineation; they do combine to form the typical seven or eleven syllable-length verses) or as unpaired heptasyllables are: "una extraña aventura," "y el corazón fluctúa," "escucho sus lamentos / y sus ruegos," "Apuro su recuerdo / hasta el fondo / del éxtasis, / y laten en el pecho," and "¡Me estremezco por ella!" These lines all refer to that emotion and intensify it in the structure of the poem. Also irregular is line seven, containing the verb "rompieron," thus emphasizing the act of separation.

"Evocación"

Al final de este viaje
he inclinado mis sueños
sobre la barandilla de su nombre.

El agua turbia de la sombra
ha metido la noche
hasta los corazones.

    —Muchedumbres inmóviles
    están asediando el horizonte.-

He apretado su imagen
contra mi desconsuelo
y la luna, apoyada en los cristales,
es el frío
deshielo
de su frente.

Un perfume imprevisto
la enciende en mi memoria;
tiene el "filing" latino
su actitud de dulzura.
Oh su carne platónica,
inocente
geometría que descansa en su seno!

La sonrisa es la flor del equilibrio orgánico,
y el campo
la estremece,
bajo mi abrazo

panorámico.

Pero a pesar de todo,
el otoño
inquilino
regó de hojas secas su recuerdo.

Oh mi novia lejana,
humareda romántica
de los primeros versos.

The next poem, "Evocación," is a good example of the way in which Maples Arce uses the elements of nature perceived during the protagonist's travels in combination with recollected visions of his beloved, together with emotion, to form not direct representation but Cubist images that give an original and complex portrait of his thoughts. In this way he, she, the inner and outer worlds are united into a whole. The images here are tight, striking, and effective.

It seems that the protagonist has arrived at his destination in the countryside, away from the city. As the poem opens, he is standing at the railing of a bridge, looking over into the water below, perhaps looking for her reflection, though the image works perfectly well as a metaphor without need for his actually being there (he may just be thinking about her): "Al final de este viaje / he inclinado mis sueños / sobre la barandilla de su nombre. / El agua turbia de la sombra / ha metido la noche / hasta los corazones." However, the murky water doesn't allow him to see her image there, and he feels that the landscape is conspiring against him. He says that he has pressed her photograph against his heart in moments of despair ("He apretado su imagen / contra mi desconsuelo"), and he imagines that the feeling of the silvery moon's reflection resting on the windowpane is like the feeling of his lover's cool forehead on his, soothing him. This image ("la luna, apoyada en los cristales") is similar to his own "he inclinado mis sueños / sobre la barandilla de su nombre." A sudden waft of perfume reminds him of her also. He uses the popular Spanglish word "filing" (feeling) while saying that her sweetness is very *latino*. He emphasizes her innocence while remembering her physical beauty ("Oh su carne platónica, / inocente / geometría que descansa en su seno!"). He says that her contentment ("equilibrio orgánico") makes her smile. The poem continues with an image that effectively combines the present landscape with the protagonist as actor, and also implies the woman's presence: "y el campo / la estremece, / bajo mi abrazo / panorámico." In spite of this, she is gone, along with everything else he has left behind ("Pero a pesar de todo, / el otoño / inquilino / regó de hojas secas su recuerdo"). Typical autumnal images here imply decadence and the loss of things over the course of time. The poem concludes with a fond, romantic memory of her as the inspiration for his early poems: "Oh mi novia lejana, / humareda romántica / de los primeros versos." He knows that she is in his poetry, and in it they have transcended the effects of time and space that have caused their separation.

Structurally, "Evocación" contains two metrically irregular verses or verse pairs which neither alone nor in combination reach a syllable count of 7, 11 or 14. As previous poems have shown, this fact signals important verses. The line about the murky water, "El agua turbia de la sombra," has nine syllables. Having the verse stand out as it does emphasizes the murkiness of the protagonist's memory of the woman (i.e. he doesn't have a clear picture of her, can't see her reflection in the water)–a foreshadowing in line four that is confirmed near the end of the poem, in lines 27-30 ("Pero a pesar de todo, / el otoño / inquilino / regó de hojas secas su recuerdo"). The other metrical irregularity is found in lines 25 and 26, a verse pair of five and four syllables, combining to form a phrase of nine syllables ("bajo mi abrazo / panorámico"). This verse pair significantly unites all three major components of the poem: the protagonist, his beloved, and the countryside. The strophe of which they are a part is the climax of the poem: the three are united in a happy embrace ("La sonrisa es la flor del equilibrio orgánico, / y el campo / la estremece, / bajo mi abrazo / panorámico.") The embrace not only evokes (cf. title) the spirit of the woman, but also produces in her the *estremecimiento* lauded by Goethe and Maples Arce in the epigraph to *Poemas Interdictos*. One supposes that the protagonist feels it, too, and this is the highest point of the poem. It is significant that the word "equilibrio" (indeed, "equilibrio *orgánico*") is part of this strophe, indicating that in the union a balance has been achieved. This heightened emotion combined with an integral stability is part of the ideal condition toward which the protagonist strives.

"Saudade"

Estoy solo en el último tramo de la ausencia,
y el dolor, hace horizonte en mi demencia.

Allá lejos,
el panorama maldito.

¡Yo abandoné la Confederación sonora de su carne!
Sobre todo su voz,
hecha pedazos
entre los tubos
de la música!

En el jardín interdicto
                    –azoro unánime–
el auditorio congelado de la luna.

Su recuerdo es sólo una resonancia
entre la arquitectura del insomnio.

¡Dios mío,
tengo las manos llenas de sangre!

Y los aviones,
pájaros de estos climas estéticos,
no escribirán su nombre
en el agua del cielo.

"Saudade," the Portuguese word for the painful, melancholy, lonely feeling of missing a person or place you love, is a curious poem. It is the final work of this subgroup and of *Poemas Interdictos*. The title is a good description of what the protagonist has felt throughout the book. Here, however, the feeling is carried to the extreme of desperation, madness and violence. "Estoy solo en el último tramo de la ausencia, / y el dolor, hace horizonte en mi demencia." There is a feeling of reproach toward the countryside and the distance that have separated the protagonist from his lover ("Allá lejos, / el panorama maldito"), but he admits that it was he who left her: "¡Yo abandoné la Confederación sonora de su carne!" He hears her voice in music, places seem ghostly vacant and cold, and all that is left of her for him is "una resonancia / entre la arquitectura del insomnio." This totally anguished awareness of her absence and of their separation due to his departure, brings him to the harsh and violent exclamation that "¡Dios mío, / tengo las manos llenas de sangre!" It is as if by having left her that he had killed her, certainly at least as a part of his life.

The last strophe brings in some modern images (feeling almost out of place here) to describe the definitiveness of the situation, that he has no way to hold on to her identity or eventually even to remember her: "Y los aviones, / pájaros de estos climas estéticos, / no escribirán su nombre / en el agua del cielo." If that act had been done, it would have united the extremes of space–zenith and nadir–expressed here in "en el agua del cielo," a typical sky / sea image combination, and thus would have provided a type of transcendence. But it will not happen. Appropriately, because it deals with dementia, there seems to be no definite metric pattern to the poem, but a mixed bag of verse lengths. While the protagonist is going crazy hearing voices and imagining ghosts or ghostly visions, he can't organize his thoughts smoothly on paper. Perhaps the writing of the poem was an attempt at that, since he knew it was a viable last resort. At the least, he has the words and thoughts of her on paper, and he can hold on to that, vague as it may be. His dementia is certainly a *poema interdicto*.

Poemas Interdictos was well received by the literary public. "Revolución" and "Primavera" were translated into English by Sherry Mangan in 1935 in a small Socialist magazine called *Poems for a Dime*.[167] The whole book was

---

167 "CHANTS by David P. Berenberg, And Two Poems by Maples Arce," *Poems for a Dime* 4 & 5 (Boston: John Wheelwright, 7 June 1935).

translated into French in 1936 by Belgian poet Edmond Vandercammen, as *Poèmes Interdits*. The original publication of *Poemas Interdictos* includes a symbolic portrait of Maples Arce by fellow *estridentista* Leopoldo Méndez, which can be related to the content of the poems. It looks deceptively simple at first, Maples seated and looking rather proper in suit and tie, hands folded on a table in front of him, in the background at the left is the top landing of a stairway, a railing, and a door open to the room where he is. However, looking closely, on the right are train tracks–four in concentric semi-circles, two trainyard light poles with signals and flags—one mid-way back and one immediately behind him which is large and partially hidden. Most interestingly, there is another set of (steel gray) railroad tracks, the fifth circle leftmost, which go from the track side of the painting into the room where Maples Arce is seated, and straddle him, that is, envelop him in their field. This is a wonderful mixing of inner and outer, of the two spaces. It is a good choice of portrait for this book, since *Poemas Interdictos* presents the poet in the moving world, the poet travelling, often by train, the poet going out and confronting the world, moving through it, and the poet as craftsman describing that world in his art.[168]

Maples Arce sums up his own view of *Poemas Interdictos* in *Soberana Juventud*:

> En 1927 publiqué, bajo la advocación de Goethe, *Poemas Interdictos*. La vida moderna, los viajes, la ausencia, la ansiedad, el amor, son los temas preferentes. La modernidad se expresaba más que en el

---

[168] Note the etymology of the word "poet": "Poet–from the Greek *poietes*, maker, poet, from *poiein*, to make, create." (*Webster's Ninth New Collegiate Dictionary*, 1987 ed.)

tema en la confrontación de éste con el yo, en un justo equilibrio entre la técnica y la emoción poética. Realidad sentida a través de sensaciones líricas y de una evocación múltiple. El poema inicial, 'Canción desde un aeroplano,' es al mismo tiempo una declaración de principios y una síntesis de mi ambición poética... En otros poemas procuré dar al lenguaje un potencial emotivo capaz de suscitar una impresión intensa y vivaz. Juventud, deporte, delicia amorosa, nostalgia, ironía, bañan la atmósfera de esos poemas que proyectaba mi sensibilidad. Imágenes y transposiciones constituían la clave del enigma poético...[169]

* * *

Arturo Sotomayor says of the lasting effect of *Estridentismo* (including Maples Arce's *Andamios Interiores*, *Urbe*, and *Poemas Interdictos*), "El tiempo pasa y lo que generó el Estridentismo ha dado sus frutos: la poesía actual, profunda, sugerente, emotiva, hecha de frases nuevas, que tiene acentuado sabor humano, en lo que tiene lo humano de más intenso y escondido."[170]

As for the style of these three *vanguardista* works, there has been discussion above regarding Maples' original *imagen equivalentista*, the affinities to Futurism, and those to Cubism. As has been indicated, Maples Arce's *estridentista* work is part of the avant-garde (including Futurism, Dada and Cubism) that dominated Western arts in the 1920s. It was the machine age, the jazz age, the age of Art Deco and of utopian architecture, fascination with the city, fascination with motion and speed, an age of revolution. It was a time of social and political protest and a time of

---

169   Maples Arce, *Soberana Juventud* 196-197.
170   Sotomayor, 184.

dreaming about an ideal future. To be modern was the "in" thing. Nevertheless, there was a psychological dimension behind the style and chic: artists felt a "poetic anguish in the face of inhuman technology."[171] The Futurists were fascinated by the dynamism of the machine, but when modern technology produced and used the war machines of World War I, other avant-gardists saw the inhuman side of the machine age, and an increasing sense of alienation was felt. The Dadaists exposed the nihilistic absurdity of the war, and expressed the incomprehensibility of the destruction —of human lives and human psyches— brought on by the war. The avant-garde as a whole captured the complexity of life in the 20s: "No [other] phase of modern art showed such profound doubts about the present, or threw off such febrile dreams about the new social orders."[172]

Maples Arce's work in this period emphasizes the confrontation of human emotion and technology. The themes of alienation, revolution, communication, dynamism, emphasis on the "new," and the search for the ideal are also treated in his work, as we have seen. The style Maples uses to convey these themes in his *estridentista* volumes is principally Cubist.

We have seen that Maples Arce's brand of Cubism in these books involves the restructuring of the object of attention into novel image combinations with other elements, and the manipulation of the structure of lines in some of the poems, plus an experimentation with perspective as related to movement through space. As further explanation of such a use of Cubism in poetry, it is useful

---

[171] Robert Hughes, "Putting a Zeitgeist in a Box" (review of the Montreal Museum of Fine Arts' exhibition "The 1920s: Age of the Metropolis") *Time* 7 October 1991: 66-67.
[172] Hughes, 66.

to note Gerald Kamber's summary of the general principles of the first phase of the Cubist technique, which can be applied to literature as well as to art:

> (1) a pulling to pieces of the object; (2) a rebuilding of the pieces into an independent composition; (3) a placing together of objects (or parts of objects) from an unrestricted range of observations; (4) a shifting of emphasis from the 'reality' of the object to the 'reality' of the esthetic surface. It seems plausible that Jacob, in his Cubist poetry, is furnishing a literary counterpart to each of these features.[173]

Leland Guyer relates Kamber's ideas to the poetry of Portuguese writer Fernando Pessoa, explaining that there are really no fixed guidelines for Cubism, that it was more of an approach to reality. It allowed a freedom of expression that artists were searching for at the time:

> To try to express what we know exists, free from the limited perspective and scope of the static camera eye, is to attempt to gain a fuller view of reality, deformed as it may appear to one who is accustomed to a limited perspective. In time this fundamental ideal of Cubism often either became somewhat hidden or entirely lost in much of what we now call Cubist works, but the shift of emphasis on the object to emphasis on the *idea* of the object persisted.[174]

In a 1921 interview by Maples Arce for the magazine *Zig-Zag*, Diego Rivera expressed his view of the future trajectory of art as follows:

> ... creo que debe ser aquella que encuentre la forma de equilibrio, perdida en el siglo XIX. Cezanne la en-

---

173 Gerald Kamber, *Max Jacob and the Poetics of Cubism* (Baltimore and London: The Johns Hopkins Press, 1971) 28.
174 Leland Guyer, "Fernando Pessoa and the Cubist Perspective," *Hispania* 70 (March 1987): 74.

contró, pero sus discípulos no supieron comprenderlo. La reconstrucción es la labor del cubismo. Un andamiaje para volver a adquirir la noción extraviada de la forma.[175]

This idea of balance and form is integrally connected to Maples Arce's search for a triumph of union over separation, of permanence over transitoriness, of humanity over time and space. The experimentation with a variation of Cubism and other avant-garde techniques was his attempt at that transcendence in his poetry during the period of *Estridentismo*.

As was mentioned in Chapter One, the *estridentistas* were forced to break up in 1927 with the fall of General Heriberto Jara's government in Jalapa; it was almost actually an opportune moment, propitious, since the members of the group were each starting to reach out in new directions individually at that time. Maples Arce studied art briefly in France and worked in government in Mexico for a few years, and then moved to Europe to work in the Mexican Diplomatic Corps. Chapter Five will examine his next published book of poetry, written while in Europe.

---

175 Maples Arce, "Diego M. Ribera [sic]," *Zig-Zag* 28 julio 1921: 34.

Chapter Five: The Search for Permanence, *Memorial de la Sangre*, 1947

> Fui a Egipto y sentí todo
> el peso del tiempo.
> > Borges, Dickinson College
> > April 7, 1983
>
> Ver en la muerte el sueño, en el ocaso
> Un triste oro, tal es la poesía
> Que es inmortal y pobre, la poesía
> Vuelve como la aurora y el ocaso.
> > Borges, "Arte poética"

Memorial de la Sangre continues Maples Arce's search for permanence in the transitory world. This volume is the work of a mature poet (written over several years, 1927-47, published at age 47) who had, since the publication of his previous book of poetry, lived and worked in Europe and witnessed the Spanish Civil War and World War II. *Memorial de la Sangre* is no longer avant-garde or Cubist but instead philosophical, reflecting the prevailing thought of the times. The destruction-creation cycle we have seen in Maples Arce's earlier books becomes predominant in *Memorial de la Sangre* and is of key importance in the kind of permanence-amid-the-transitory that these poems discover. *Memorial de la Sangre* examines more universal problems than the previous books (the personal situations of separation and transitoriness are expanded to societal dimensions), and this increased depth of thought causes a stylistic change in the poems. In *Memorial de la Sangre*, Maples Arce enters into mythical and existential concerns, questions of time, endurance, eternity, and memory; he confronts life and death and the idea of continuation into a future generation. At times in *Memorial,* he achieves poetic heights comparable to the mature work of Octavio Paz and T. S. Eliot, especially in his "Memorial de la sangre," "Fundación del olvido," "Elegía mediterránea," "Cántico de liberación," and "Elegía paterna." Living in Europe during the Spanish Civil War and World War II and visiting Greece, Egypt and Italy affected the poet profoundly and, (parallel to the evolution of the century's philosophy) together with his own maturation, those experiences account for the change in tone from the previous collections.

In *Memorial de la Sangre*, Maples Arce expands his preoccupation with time and the destruction/creation dichotomy (separation/union, absence/presence) to larger expanses of time and space, across whole periods of history, making connections between the New World and the Old World. There is a growing concern with destruction (separation, loss), and his fear of it, but the answers he finds in humankind's creative power span generations. This volume has a very human quality and emotional intensity. The style is refined and controlled. The title poem, "Memorial de la sangre" was written on the occasion of the birth of Maples Arce's first child, Manuel. Essence and identity persist and escape destruction through time by means of reproduction, re-creation. The poet's son carries on his essence, his identity. Blood is the life force, the creative force, the energy that is passed on from generation to generation. The poem, of course, is also the poet's child, his artistic creation.

"Cántico de liberación" is written in praise of this creative force, as it is manifested in art. "Fundación del olvido" looks for a persistence of human essence and identity similar to "Memorial de la sangre," but in entire races, across generations and centuries. Pyramids and ancient statues in marble and bronze contain something of the magic and mystery of the persistence of this essence through time. The protagonist says at the end of "Fundación del olvido": "¡Que el olvido descienda por las linfas del sueño! / Ya la creación imprime sus dedos en mi frente / y alzan su voz ardiente / de otras razas sonoras las sirenas, / y recitan mi vida, mi fábula, mi ausencia!"

"Elegía mediterránea" is a poem to the Mediterranean Sea, to Helen of Troy, perhaps in part also to Boticelli's Venus. The protagonist is becoming more preoccupied with "ausencia" and "olvido," but finds in great natural beauty and great works of art an essence that persists mysteriously even in material absence and remains unchanged by the years. He describes these works with the qualities of light, gold, bronze, marble, diamond. At the end of this elegy he says: "Oh! cuerpo incorpóreo sin mirada y sin eco, / soplo espantoso que propagas las fiebres inmortales / y levantas del polvo la multitud del olvido!"

The protagonist lives only by the energy he receives from these images of the creative, artistic force. At the end of "Cántico de liberación" he says of this force: "Oigo, oigo el furor astral de tu presencia, / tus labios persuasivos como un canto de bronce."

This secret power of metamorphosis from the world of time into that of timelessness within time is held by all of the subjects of the poems in *Memorial de la Sangre*. The poet writes in "Fundación del olvido," " ¿Qué espanto absoluto / brota de los anales de la piedra? / Potencias del silencio nos abisman / en el misterio de las metamorfosis. / Yo abro espacios de fuerza hacia la noche / donde se pierden las tribus del recuerdo / que persiguen los gritos famélicos del tiempo." As a poet, Maples Arce searches for the key to solve the mystery of this metamorphosis through time, and with this key he hopes to save essence and identity from the seemingly omnipresent death and destruction (separation, absence). Again, the answer becomes both the poem itself and the power of art in general to transcend time and space.

The evolution of Maples Arce's experience of the city as the place to achieve transcendence (earlier manifestations have been discussed in previous chapters) continues in *Memorial de la Sangre*. The reader travels with the protagonist to Mediterranean cities that were once capitals of great ancient civilizations, where marvels of art and architecture remain and are seen as elements of continuity with the past in which essence and identity remain across time, a union of epochs and minds. It is a logical progression and there are no inexplicable changes from Maples Arce's avant-garde phase to the *Memorial de la Sangre* phase, contrary to what most critics have said. He moves from the immediate to wider spheres of time, in search of eternity. In the city and in art, Maples Arce "ha buscado y encontrado la posibilidad de ser."[176]

While Estridentismo as a movement has received the

---

[176] Bonifaz Nuño, Estudio Preliminar, 30.

most critical attention (historical, biographical, some on the art) the actual poems of *Memorial de la Sangre* have received more attention from literary critics than the vanguardista poems, both upon the publication of *Memorial* (1947) and over time, and the reasons for this are many: their less hermetic quality, their lyrical perfection, Maples Arce's post-World War II reputation as a highly respected diplomat, his connections with the literary community in several countries from 1935 on, the publication of several of the poems of *Memorial* in various international journals, and easier access to published texts than was possible decades before. The poems have been reviewed and analyzed thematically, the most in-depth studies being Enrique Ruiz Vernacci's "Maples Arce, poeta universal" and "Los valores humanos en la lírica de Maples Arce," by Rogelio Sinán.[177] Other critics who have addressed this work include José María González de Mendoza (El Abate de Mendoza), Francisco González Guerrero, Ermilo Abreu Gómez, Ricardo A. Latcham, Edmond Vandercammen, Lionello Fiumi, Andrew Debicki, Luis Leal, Luis Mario Schneider, Juan Cervera, José Emilio Pacheco, and Cristina Pacheco. These critics have emphasized the humanism and lyricism of the poems, and have mentioned the high regard expressed in them for art and for the achievements of the great civilizations of the Classical period; most is general impressionistic criticism of style. Not to duplicate those essays, this chapter will concentrate

---

[177] Enrique Ruiz Vernacci, *Tres ensayos* ("Meditación en torno a 'El celoso extremeño,'" "Ricardo Miro, o la capacidad poética," "Maples Arce, poeta universal") (Panamá: Imprenta Nacional, 1948). Rogelio Sinán, *Los valores humanos en la lírica de Maples Arce* (México: Ediciones Conferencia, 1959), previously published in the magazine *Conferencia* [México] II.10 (abril 1958): 251-262. From a conference first given in Lima, Peru in May of 1948.

on explaining how *Memorial de la Sangre* fits in to the scheme of Maples Arce's complete work as expressed in this study. In my analysis, I will employ a comparison to works by Octavio Paz and T. S. Eliot, and examine the structure of Maples Arce's poems.

A thematic overview of the major long poems of *Memorial de la Sangre* has been given above. The problem of separation, the question of a discontinuity with the past, and the search for a sense of permanence beyond the ephemeral appearance of all things, are examined in these poems in the context of the social struggles of the present and the aesthetic achievements of history's great civilizations, as well as the endurance of humanity from generation to generation. In his search for permanence, the poet finds a persistence of essence through time. There results a convergence of multiple places in the spatial plane and a convergence of past, present and future in the temporal plane. Transcendence of spatial and temporal limitations is seen as possible through man's ability to create, especially in the triumph of creation over destruction (destruction as represented by war, death and decay). In *Memorial de la Sangre* there is not only a creation-destruction-creation cycle in life and art, but an enduring persistence and triumph of the creation element. *Memorial de la Sangre* affirms a link to the past and hope for the future, the "something we can hang on to" for which the protagonist has yearned.

The poems of *Memorial de la Sangre*, in their search for permanence and union to vanquish transitoriness, separation, and the limitations of time and space, have affinities with Friedrich Nietzsche's theory of the eternal return as expressed in *Zarathustra*, with T. S. Eliot's *Four Quartets*, and with several poems by Octavio Paz, such as "Viento entero" and "Blanco"—all well-regarded works of literature and philosophy. These writings, in turn, can provide insight into Maples Arce's poems. In my discussion of *Memorial de la Sangre*, I will make reference to these works by Nietzsche, Eliot and Paz (without attempting to explain them in detail) as touchstones that may provide clues to the meaning of Maples Arce's poems.

Joan Stambaugh, in her explanation of Nietzsche's theory of the eternal return, states: "If finitude is understood to mean impermanence, eternal return is that which gives permanence to Becoming, in the sense that the Same recurs again and again, thus constituting a kind of interrupted, periodically recurring duration."[178] Nietzsche's "Will to Power," or the "will to be more,"[179] is similar to the creative force evoked in several of the poems of *Memorial de la Sangre*. The Will to Power (or "increase") and its relation to eternal return (or the "Same") can be likened in Maples Arce's work to humankind's creative ability or the creative force, as related to the act of creating and the presence of the thing created. Both processes are very affirmative in character. This is not the Wasteland or nihilism ("nothingness"—meaninglessness—eternally)[180] but the opposite: it is desired attainment of the Same in each moment of the process, continual affirmation of the Same. Nietzsche says that eternal return (the transition) takes place in the instant, or moment—compare Eliot's still point, and Maples Arce's use of a similar moment of illumination in the poems of *Andamios Interiores*.

---

178 Joan Stambaugh, *Nietzsche's Thought of Eternal Return* (Baltimore and London: The Johns Hopkins University Press, 1972) 13.
179 Stambaugh, 14.
180 Stambaugh, 17.

Maples Arce's concern for continuation into the future recalls Nietzsche: "It should be pointed out here that, apart from his emphasis on the presence of the moment, Nietzsche's secondary emphasis with regard to eternal recurrence is on the future, on the anticipatory experience of recurrence, not on the past."[181] Eliot's and Maples Arce's preoccupation with a dissociation from the past finds some resolution in Nietzsche's idea of the moment drawing all past things and all that is to come through the "gateway" of eternal return:

> "Observe this moment! From this gateway, moment, a long, eternal lane runs *backward* : behind us lies an eternity. Must not whatever *can* run its course of all things have already run along that lane before? Must not whatever *can* happen have happened, have been done, have passed by before? And if everything has been there before—what do you think, dwarf, of this moment? Must not this gateway, too, have been there before? And are not all things knotted together so firmly that this moment draws after it *all* that is to come? *Therefore* —itself too? For whatever *can* run its course of all things—also into this long lane *outward* , *too* —it *must* run it once more! And this slow spider which crawls in the moonlight, and this moonlight itself, and I and you in the gateway, whispering together, whispering of eternal things—must not all of us have been there before? And return and run in that other lane before us, in that long, dreadful lane—must we not eternally return?"[182]

This concept implies a union of past, present and future, and it happens in the moment or in Eliot's still point. Eternity, in the words of Stambaugh (regarding Nietzsche), is:

---

181 Stambaugh, 27.
182 Stambaugh [quoting Nietzsche] 37.

the 'purely vertical' experienced with a kind of vertigo which results from the sudden release from the horizontal connection of successive time ... the literal *release* (in the sense of *solvere*) *into* that enigma itself.[183]

It is an incredibly radical experience, an experience so radical that Nietzsche himself was unable to maintain the purity of the dimension we have described here as the 'vertical.' He sought 'to will back all things which have ever been,' thus dispersing this vertical dimension back into the horizontal, back into the realm of 'all things knotted so closely together,' back to the causal chain of mechanistically conceived things and events 'in time.' It is not time that is a circle, as the dwarf would have us believe; it is eternity which is the ring of rings, the ring being thought of here as the absolute rejection of mechanistically *or* teleologically conceived time. There is no teleology involved in the ring, and there is no mechanistic determinism either. The ring of rings circles back into itself; its whole being is return. There is no substance, no 'God' in the Christian sense. There is 'God' only as the highest *power* from which 'follows' the world. Nietzsche was able to glimpse eternity as sheer occurrence, not as static persistence. Eternity *is* eternal return of the Same. The Same is not a thing or a person recurring in endless cycles of absolute time. The Same *is* return. Return can 'occur' only in the moment.[184]

Thus we see the importance of the poem/work of art/consciousness in the process of eternal return. In Eliot's *Four Quartets* and in Paz's "Viento entero," there is union of time and also union of place (union of places across time as well). Eliot unites four places: Burnt Norton, East Coker, the Dry Salvages and Little Gidding, known at various points in his life, and achieves a union of past,

---

183 Stambaugh, 106-107.
184 Stambaugh, 107.

present and future in the moment of illumination or still point. Paz unites in his poem "Viento entero" several places from his past and present in the Near and Far East and in Mexico, in the course of one "day" (morning, afternoon, night). In both works, there is a union of thought and spirit from the various times and places. For Paz and Maples Arce, there is also union of self with other (in Paz, most directly the protagonist and his lover; in Maples, the protagonist and his son, his father, his lover, and / or various civilizations, depending on the poem). For them (Eliot, Paz, Maples Arce), this union happens in the poem. What is of utmost importance is not the poem or painting or statue as artifact but the creative power that made it possible. The implied problem for Maples Arce of crumbling statues, fading paintings, and disintegrating civilizations, is resolved in Nietzsche's view of eternal return as process, movement, activity. This would concur with the supremacy of dynamism in the work of art in the vanguardista days. Stambaugh explains that, for Nietzsche, time is not form, it is process, it is how. What occurs or recurs in eternal return is not the content ("what") of such a form but rather the process, the "how." "The 'how' in this case is not the inexorable form of time, but the powerfull freedom of possibilities of being."[185] Thus in the question of the object of art, the statue eventually disappears but "art" remains, the creation of it remains, and the creative force continually affirms itself. " 'One is an artist at the price of experiencing that which all non-artists call 'form' as *content*, as 'the thing itself.' Then one, of course, belongs to a *transformed world*, for from then on content

---

[185] Stambaugh, 127.

becomes something merely formal, our life included.'"[186] Maples expresses this concept in his affirmation of the power of the creative force and in his demonstration of the triumph of creation over destruction.

Zarathustra's ascent in spite of the spirit of gravity sitting on his shoulder and drawing him downward is akin to the victory of timelessness within time at the still point at the center of the turning world, and the triumph of creation in the midst of destruction. Nietzsche says that the only true philosopher is the yea-sayer. This is what Zarathustra learns; it also describes Sisyphus' triumph of will over destiny, and the creation of a "new" world through refreshed perception in the prose passages of William Carlos Williams' *Spring and All*.

The experience of the thought of eternal return is new for each person; the same is true in the poem "Memorial de la sangre," where the protagonist tells his son that he cannot tell him what life is like, he has to live it for himself. Paz says that all poems are basically the same poem (or myth) repeated; it is a new experience for each reader. The reader re-creates the poem, renews the experience, likened to that of the author but fresh and different enough to be unique to each reader.

When Nietzsche's Zarathustra says "'My abyss *speaks*, my lowest depth have I turned over into the light!'"[187] we hear an echo of Eliot's "the way up is the way down" (from San Juan de la Cruz, Dante, others). Similarly in Maples Arce's "Memorial de la sangre," the poet's creation—the poem or the poet's son—rises up from the depths, in an affirmation of existence and of the creative force. Stambaugh

---

186 Stambaugh [quoting Nietzsche] 127.
187 Stambaugh [quoting Nietzsche] 43.

says, "once this thought has emerged from the depths, it will remain awake eternally."[188] Like Zarathustra's experience, part III of all four of Eliot's quartets shows the protagonist reaching the lowest point of despair, getting very close to the moment of illumination (for Nietzsche, the "vision"), and falling into a deathlike paralyzed state–which is part IV of the quartets. This is analogous to Maples Arce's "desierta obscuridad" and "la noche de la angustia" in the poem "Memorial de la sangre," as well as to the reference to society succumbing to wars, and to the following passage, which implies his own death:

> Cuando oprimiendo el pecho por donde cruzan las pasiones
> sólo tenga el gesto indefenso del silencio,
> cuando la tierra en mí se haya callado
> y despierte la luz en otros ojos,
> cuando un tacto de metal me arranque
> la voz, y sólo sea
> un sollozo de piedra reprimido
> o una fecha de pájaros,
> ¡que sea mi voluntad este deseo que crece!

In addition, Eliot says that once you have experienced the moment in the rose garden, you know and you remember what it was. It is too intense an experience to stay in it for long, both Nietzsche and Eliot agree, but one can recall the experience and hope for more in the future. This, in a sense, is the knowledge that Maples Arce's protagonist can hang on to, while affirming that the creative force exists and that it is a continually recurring process.

The abundant nature images in the poem "Memorial de la sangre" are related to the bird in Eliot's first quartet, "Burnt Norton," and to the animals in *Zarathustra*. When Zarathustra's animals talk, the world is as a garden to him

---

188 Stambaugh, 43.

(cf. Eliot's rose garden). Words and tones (the animals' chatter) are rainbows and " 'seeming bridges between the eternally separated.' "[189] The elements of nature can sense what is going on, but words cannot fully express Zarathustra's experience. This problem of communication is expressed in each part V of Eliot's quartets, especially in "Burnt Norton": "... Words strain, / Crack and sometimes break, under the burden, / Under the tension, slip, slide, perish, / Decay with imprecision, will not stay in place, / Will not stay still." But poetry, music, art, are the only modes by which one can hope to try to express the moment of illumination. In the same section, Eliot explains:

> Words move, music moves
> Only in time; but that which is only living
> Can only die. Words, after speech, reach
> Into the silence. Only by the form, the pattern,
> Can words or music reach
> The stillness, as a Chinese jar still
> Moves perpetually in its stillness.
> Not the stillness of the violin, while the note lasts,
> Not that only, but the co-existence,
> Or say that the end precedes the beginning,
> And the end and the beginning were always there
> Before the beginning and after the end.
> And all is always now.[190]

Art leads to a quality of timelessness within time. Eliot's Chinese jar echoes W. B. Yeats' "Lapis Lazuli," where the manipulation of words and use of syntactic delay also achieve a powerful affirmation. Poetry recreates the experience, in the ineffable phenomenon caused by form placed onto words in conjunction; the words to-

---

189 Stambaugh [quoting Nietzsche] 44.
190 T. S. Eliot, *Four Quartets* (New York: Harcourt, Brace & World, Inc., 1943) 19.

gether create the illumination, it happens (again and again, with each reader) inside the poem; "How can we know the dancer from the dance?"[191] Octavio Paz says that poetry "es la resurrección de las presencias, / la historia / transfigurada en la verdad del tiempo no fechado."[192]

For Eliot, there is the problem of how to get from *The Waste Land* to the *Four Quartets*; for Maples Arce the question is how to get from *Urbe* to *Memorial de la Sangre*. Nietzsche notes that an awareness of the idea of nihilism (endlessly recurring meaningless monotony) paralyzes man. "For this reason Zarathustra's fate becomes that of the teacher of eternal return, for which he must find and communicate another meaning."[193] This is perhaps the role of the poet. As for William Carlos Williams in *Spring and All*, the path for each poet is from endless doom to endless affirmation. This is made possible by the Will to Power, the creative force, which allows "giving structure to possibilities that recur anew constantly."[194] For Maples Arce, there is "un abismo de letras, un cuerpo de silencio," lying in wait for the creative force to act upon it.

In the title poem, "Memorial de la sangre," we sense that the protagonist feels a need for continuation of self, of his own essence and identity, just as he desires continuation of other things in the rest of the poems of the volume. This essence (identity) and regeneration are seen in Nietzsche's concept of the eternal return as Self and the Same,

---

[191] W. B. Yeats, "Among School Children," *Chief Modern Poets of Britain and America*, Vol. I: Poets of Britain, eds. Gerald DeWitt Sanders, John Herbert Nelson, M. L. Rosenthal (New York: MacMillan Publishing Co., Inc., 1970) 131-132.

[192] Frances Chiles, *Octavio Paz: The Mythic Dimension* (New York: Peter Lang Publishing, Inc., 1987) [quoting Paz from *Pasado en claro*] 210.

[193] Stambaugh, 45.

[194] Stambaugh, 51.

respectively.

> Self is the core of the experiencing subject which persists through the multiplicity of that experience. The Same is the substance of the object persisting throughout the change of qualities or attributes. It is the principle of the identity of the object... Self refers explicitly to a person, whereas the Same could be used to refer to anything self-identical, including a person.[195]

The child in "Memorial de la sangre" parallels the third and ultimate stage in Nietzsche's "Metamorphosis of the Spirit," in which the freedom needed for original creativity is attained: the first stage is the camel, load-bearing, his motto is "You shall;" second is the lion, master of himself, "I will;" third is the child, innocent, a new beginning, "I am," yea-saying, "the Innocence of Becoming." The union of self and other (or the individual and the universal) can be seen to arise then in the eternal return when "the dichotomy between 'one' and 'every' disappears because the quality of no end of each moment allows every moment to arise."[196]

Maples Arce sees the power and presence of the creative force not only in regeneration of self, but also in art. As in the poems of the previous volumes discussed in this study, union and permanence are achieved in the work of art. Eliot, Paz and Nietzsche would concur.

> Art is for Nietzsche the highest form of human activity ... for him art is not restricted to a particular sphere of human life, is not a collection of aesthetic objects and works; rather, it is the innermost nature of the world itself: 'The world as a work of art that gives birth to itself.' Nietzsche's 'aesthetic' is based on the artist himself, not on the observer. It thus illuminates the nature of artistic activity rather than that of the aesthetic product. Art is understood in the broadest

---
195 Stambaugh, 71-72.
196 Stambaugh, 114.

possible sense as a transfiguration and an affirmation of human existence... In his reflective remarks about art in *The Birth of Tragedy*, Nietzsche again states that art is the authentic task of life, the *metaphysical* activity of life. Art is what makes life possible; it is the greatest stimulus to life. Only through art can all the tendencies of life-denial (religion, science) be overcome.

It is hardly possible to overestimate the importance of 'art' in Nietzsche's thought. Art is not an isolated sphere of superfluous human activity originating in periods of leisure after the basic needs have been taken care of. Art is life, is the Will to Power in its full form.[197]

For Octavio Paz, the experience of (both writing and reading) poetry liberates man. What Paz calls "transparencia" (transparency)[198] is very similar to what we have referred to as transcendence in Maples Arce's poems and the still point or moment of illumination in T. S. Eliot's poetry. This liberation occurs in the poet's mind, outside of time and historical place. It is achieved by the creative force operating on language, in order to liberate words from having attachment solely to their traditional representational meanings. Part of what transparency brings, for example in Paz's poem "Blanco," is union of self and other, a heightened consciousness and self-knowledge, multiple associations of images, and a liberation towards one's inner reality ("inner freedom of 'la mirada' (the inner glance) over *lo mirado* (what is looked at, exterior reality").[199]

The poem "Viento entero" (from *Ladera este*) is similar and adds the union of past, present and future time, along with union of space (simultaneous multiple places). In

---

197 Stambaugh, 20.
198 Jason Wilson, *Octavio Paz* (Boston: Twayne Publishers, 1986) 112.
199 Wilson, 111.

"Blanco" time becomes, by the end, a *fluir*, shown in several images. "*Fluir* (to flow) is a metaphor of time and liberation... All is harmonious, one: body / world / spirit, for transparency (the mental experience of liberation from opacity) abolishes all differences."[200] This idea recalls Nietzsche's eternal return. In this *fluir*, language becomes "magnetized" and words / images are joined together. These are all elements of union and transcendence that Maples Arce is striving for in his poems. The disparities he finds and for which he suggests a solution in *Memorial de la Sangre* are similar to this process in Paz's work.

> The new poetics liberates the poet from the pressures of his age: 'La irrealidad de lo mirado / da realidad a la mirada...' For reality lies in the mind, but the mind's reality dissolves language, thought, and culture and can perceive the world as it is and was from the start.[201]

In light of this idea, what is learned in "Memorial de la sangre," "Fundación del olvido" and "Cántico de liberación," for instance, can be carried over to "España, 1936" and "Este día de pasión," which speak to the tragedy and senselessness of the Spanish Civil War and World War II.

The attempt to overcome present difficulty and return to a more Edenic past of a certain civilization, as Maples Arce does regarding Spain, Europe in World War II, and the Mediterranean countries which seem to have lost their classical splendor, is also present in Paz's poem "El regreso":

> 'El regreso' is a kind of parodic pilgrim's progress

---

200 Wilson, 113.
201 Wilson, 113.

in which the speaker undertakes an imaginary journey back to Eden in an attempt to overcome lineal, historical time, or at least render it more meaningful in the context of personal existence in this world... The central theme is of course another variation of the quest myth or the myth of the eternal return in which archaic man periodically abolished his profane temporal condition by ritually going back to the mythical time of perfection and bliss that was 'in the beginning.' The quest and labyrinth motifs are plain in the speaker's pilgrimage through desolate city streets, and later through ruins, plains, and deserts to the sea. Each stage of the journey corresponds to a progressive transformation of his psychological state, symbolized by the natural elements and cycles... [202]

Chiles notes in her discussion of Paz's "Cuento de dos jardines" the typical Pazian use of a garden. "Its prevailing message is that a garden need not be a place as such; the only real gardens are after all the ones within us, in which we may suddenly find ourselves at home at any time or place:"

> Una casa, un jardín,
> no son lugares:
> giran, van y vienen.
> Sus apariciones
> abren en el espacio
> otro espacio,
> otro tiempo en el tiempo.
> Sus eclipses
> no son abdicaciones:
> nos quemaría
> la vivacidad de uno de esos instantes
> si durase otro instante.[203]

Paz's garden in Mixcoac (at his childhood home) is much like Eliot's rose garden in "Burnt Norton," and the

---

202 Chiles, 67-68.
203 Chiles, 81-82.

revelation there for Paz is akin to Eliot's moment of illumination in the rose garden. These relate not only to Maples Arce's use of the still point but also to the abundant use of nature imagery in most of his poetry, and especially to that in *Memorial de la Sangre*. The garden is a place and a feeling that become internalized and which can be used later as a touchstone.

The way that time is transcended within the moment of illumination (regardless of where it takes place) is seen in Ivar Ivask's commentary on Paz's "Piedra del sol":

> 'llévame al otro lado de esta noche,
> adonde *yo soy* tú somos nosotros
> al reino de pronombres enlazados,
> puerta del ser ...'

A poem without end ... A poem of cyclical becoming which joins, strangely, in its last two strophes, *all* the principle key words; a synthesis poem, ... where creation and destruction, union and solitude alternate exactly, according to the rhythm of all human adventure, according to an exemplary process... [204]

Ivask's words echo our previous discussion of poems such as "Prisma" ("tú y yo coincidimos," ausencia/presencia, the creation-destruction cycle), and Nietzsche's "process" of eternal return.

Chiles notes from Paz that poetry "es la resurrección de las presencias, / la historia / transfigurada en la verdad del tiempo no fechado," and observes that:

> Places and things as such disappear in time and become history, but their reality as it was in the past remains intact in our memory and can be experienced anew in another place and in another timeless time. Finding himself again

---

204 Ivar Ivask, *The Perpetual Present: Prose and Poetry of Octavio Paz* (Norman: Oklahoma Press, 1973) 105.

at home where he had started from, but which was no longer as it used to be, the poet concludes as he had earlier in 'Cuento de los jardines' that
'El espacio está adentro
no es un edén subvertido
es un latido de tiempo
los lugares son confluencias
aleteo de presencias
en un espacio instantáneo.' [205]

Chiles goes on to note that Paz's vision of sunlight on a stone and moments of illumination with the fig tree in the garden at Mixcoac, from earlier times, return and bring similar moments. The passage from Paz that she quotes is an apt description of the still point, and recalls both Eliot's moment in the rose garden and Maples Arce's moment of transcendence:

'En quietud se resuelve el movimiento.
Insiste el sol, se clava
en la corola de la hora absorta.
Llama en el tallo de agua
de las palabras que la dicen
la flor es otro sol.
La quietud en sí misma
se disuelve. Transcurre el tiempo
sin transcurrir. Pasa y se queda. Acaso,
aunque todos pasamos, ni pasa ni se queda:
hay un tercer estado.'

The third state he speaks of is the weightless time-out-of-time, Eliot's still moment in a turning world or Wordsworth's spots of time; it is Mallarmé's void, plenitude, no-thingness; it is the bodiless, momentary god, appearing and vanishing even as the poet attempts to in-

---

[205] Chiles, 210-211.

carnate it with 'un nombre solar'... [206]

The connection between this use of the still point or moment of illumination in Paz, Eliot and Maples Arce, and the role of art as the vehicle, the only salvation, in *Memorial de la Sangre*, (and its importance to Nietzsche), is clarified by this passage from Chiles regarding Paz:

> ... the poem itself once written becomes a historical text. But at the same time, as Paz points out, all literary texts rest upon a structure that is constant and ahistorical. In a sense, all poems, though unique in themselves, are, to paraphrase Paz, 'cuentos distintos de la misma cuenta' (different accounts from the same account)... As in the telling or re-enacting of a myth, a text that is similarly historical and ahistorical, the composing of the poem by the poet and its re-creation by the reader reproduce the original time without dates. For it is in the poem that
>
> > 'being and desire come to terms for an instant, like the fruit and the lips. Poetry, momentary reconciliation: yesterday, today, tomorrow; here and there; you, I, he, we. All is present: will be presence.[207]

We may relate to "Memorial de la sangre" and "Elegía paterna" Chiles' statement that for Paz, "poetry, along with love in all of its forms, remains a means of reconciling the body and the non-body, of recovering our otherness in the renunciation of selfhood and the dissolution of pronouns, and confronting our mortality in going beyond ourselves."[208]

---

206 Chiles, 211-212.
207 Chiles, 212. [Also Chiles quoting Paz from *Children of the Mire*, trans. Rachael Phillips (Cambridge: Harvard University Press, 1975) 152-153, 161-164, and Paz, *The Bow and the Lyre*, trans. Ruth L. C. Aims (New York: McGraw-Hill, 1975) 262.]
208 Chiles, 212-213.

> El presente es perpetuo
> Los montes son de hueso y son de nieve
> Están aquí desde el principio
> El viento acaba de nacer
> Sin edad
> Como la luz y como el polvo
> ...
> Juntos atravesamos
> Los cuatro espacios los tres tiempos
> Pueblos errantes de reflejos
> Y volvimos al día del comienzo
> El presente es perpetuo.[209]

Near the end of "Viento entero" (a word play could shift it to "viento eterno"), "se acarician / Shiva y Parvati". Shiva is the Hindu god of destruction and rebirth. Parvati is the goddess of fertility, love, beauty, bravery, harmony, marriage, childbirth, devotion, divine strength and power. Their caress, the dance, represents, in the context of our study, the union of self and other in a timeless moment ("Cada caricia dura un siglo / Para el dios y para el hombre / Un mismo tiempo / Un mismo despeñarse"). It is also the meeting of destruction and creation–Maples Arce's cycle, occurring and uniting in the still point (the dance, as in Yeats' "Among School Children" and the men on the Chinese vase in his "Lapis Lazuli," mentioned above). That is, the transformation from destruction to creation takes place (cf. Paz, the transforming power of the poet)[210] in the work of art (which endures) during the still point (timelessness); it is made possible by the power of the creative force, and is experienced by the poet and that expe-

---

[209] Octavio Paz, "Viento entero," in Eugenio Florit y José Olivio Jiménez, *La poesía hispanoamericana desde el modernismo* (New York: Appleton-Century-Crofts, 1968) 466-468. [From *Viento entero* (Delhi, India, 1965), later collected in *Ladera este (1962-1968)* (Mexico City: Joaquín Mortiz, 1969).]

[210] Wilson, Chapter Four.

rience is recreated by the reader (a sort of eternal return), hence a permanence that vanquishes the transitory sense of the daily world.

"Memorial de la sangre"

En la desierta obscuridad en donde brota la sangre,
la noche de la angustia rompe
la forma maternal que un gemido desflora:
misterio ensangrentado de tu cuerpo,
primer deslumbramiento, lo azulinismimado.
¡Oh lúcida experiencia!

Como un sueño arraigado
en la luz vegetal, que se extiende en la tarde
yo soy el pensamiento de un ausente
a orillas de un estío rumoroso de árboles,
la pura desnudez de la memoria abierta
al jardín inmortal de los amantes,
¡un grito que se eleva sobre el pedestal de la tarde!

Tú no estabas anunciado en los libros,
ni en los calendarios de piedra,
pero yo te presentía
en la fuente original que se derrama en el pecho.
Los ríos ancestrales del tumulto
conducen hasta ti, parecido al silencio
golpeado de mi pulso:
tú eres la promesa eterna de la sangre.
Cuando oprimiendo el pecho por donde cruzan las pasiones
sólo tenga el gesto indefenso del silencio,
cuando la tierra en mí se haya callado
y despierte la luz en otros ojos,
cuando un tacto de metal me arranque
la voz, y sólo sea
un sollozo de piedra reprimido
o una fecha de pájaros,
¡que sea mi voluntad este deseo que crece!

Más allá de nuestro amor—transpuesto océano—,
un país de ardientes jeroglíficos te espera.
Ante ti su esplendor de piedras descifradas.
La estrofa secular de las pirámides
te arranca un grito ensangrentado
de belleza.

El pueblo persuadido de símbolos atlánticos
profiere la unidad cerrada de los puños.
Tú ves el trabajo humano
y la repartición de tierras.
¡Ah el día geométrico de las altiplanicies
y la gran primavera inaccesible de los lagos!

Escucha, fuerza creadora,
el grito de distancias que afluye hasta mis labios;
la naturaleza despierta sorprendida en tu rostro,
que surge desde el fondo pálido del agua.

Mis ríos, mis cataratas, mis rumores de bosques,
todo lo que me sonoriza y me afirma,
un día, invisible,
revivirá en la voz de mi regreso.
Por eso canto lo real, el fuego
fértil que devora la ausencia,
la evidencia de existir contra los ídolos,
la libertad terrestre de los sexos.

Tú llegas en la hora
en que una tempestad de acero
sopla sobre lejanas poblaciones,
y otros van a confundirse
en un abrazo sangriento de naciones.
¡Oh! tú, hecho de mi sangre y de mi fuerza,
tú de forma mortal, tú que no rezas,
absoluta presencia que sube de las profundidades.
Tú traes el germen
de la rebelión que desciende al mismo tiempo
que la energía secreta de las venas:
entrañable momento de las formas

o clamor encendido en el espacio vehemente.

Sopla un viento de arpas
que infunde al otoño sus más antiguos recuerdos,
y todo recomienza en el poder profundo de un latido.

¿Qué es lo que perdura del poema?
¡Ah! la esperanza obscura de la metamorfosis.
Un abismo de letras, un cuerpo de silencio.

With these guidelines in mind, we turn now more specifically to the texts of Maples Arce's poems. "Memorial de la sangre," as mentioned above, was written in 1937, the year that Maples Arce's first child was born. The poem abounds in nature imagery and an important connection is made between nature, the human body, emotions, memory and consciousness. Cycles of time and nature, their processes, are connected to human events, emotions and the senses. Blood is metaphorically related to rivers. There is a contrast throughout between darkness and light, and silence is contrasted with sound. Under the surface floats a message of the ages which must be deciphered and passed on from generation to generation. Human society's connection with the land and nature is seen, in part, as vital to work and survival, and there is a reference to Mexico's agrarian reform ("la repartición de la tierra"). There is an image complex (which includes the ocean, the desert, gardens or fields, riverbanks and pyramids) that suggests expansiveness, vast expanses of space. The most important image of the poem comes from this expanse: the face of the protagonist's son rises out of it, up from the depths of space and time.

Escucha, fuerza creadora,
el grito de distancias que afluye hasta mis labios;

> la naturaleza despierta sorprendida en tu rostro,
> que surge desde el fondo pálido del agua.

Here the poet first mentions the "fuerza creadora," the creative force, which will be the agent that enables continuance, transcendence, a way toward permanence, in all the poems of this book. The *grito* is a sign of life, the baby's cry at birth, and part of the sound/silence dichotomy found throughout the poem. It signals the son's arrival, along with the image of his face, which also brings in the concept of identity. The river (water traditionally is a symbol of life and could also relate to existence in the womb) is a conduit here from the son to the poet and from the distance/expanse of space to the immediate space where the protagonist is. The *grito*, which also represents creation or the creative force, reaches the protagonist, flows to his lips: the connection here is made between the potential creative force and the poet, and between poet, poem, words, communication. The protagonist's creation is not only the child but the poem as well. The child/creation enlivens nature ("la naturaleza despierta sorprendida"). The face rises up from the depths through the clear water, and just as the Lady of the Lake rises up to empower Arthur by returning his magic sword Excalibur to him, the son/creative force rises up to empower the protagonist. He is given the key, the power to create and overcome destruction.

In the next strophe, the nature elements are directly connected to the poet; now they belong to him, they are "*mis* ríos, *mis* cataratas, *mis* rumores de bosques," and they give voice to him (the power to communicate), give him life, and affirm his existence. Self and nature are joined and the protagonist's existence is made evident.

This connection brings about, or metamorphoses into,

a union of self with other and also a union of past, present and future time, in the eternal return: "todo lo que me sonoriza y me afirma, / un día, invisible, / revivirá en la voz de mi regreso." The future tense of *revivirá* and the word *regreso* signal eternal return. *La voz* is part of the image complex of sound (in the sound/silence dichotomy) and represents life, in the person of his son (cf. *grito*) or in the form of the poem he will create (*grito* = sound, communication). What is past and what is present will roll into the future and occur again. "Por eso canto lo real"—*canto* stands for sound/song/life, the poem, and *lo real* is concrete existence in the present. Then, "el fuego / fértil que devora la ausencia, / la evidencia de existir contra los ídolos, / la libertad terrestre de los sexos" finishes this strophe. Usually fire destroys but here it is fertile and life-making; it is movement, action, transformation, a life-source as in the metaphorical use of *fuego* to mean spirit, energy. *Devora* is also used in an unusual way in this poem, but what is devoured is absence, so it is a positive, presence-enabling action. There is an affirmation of self, of life and existence, and eternal return implies the continuation of it. The fire might be compared to Eliot's purifying, purgative fire in "Little Gidding" at the end of the *Four Quartets*. "Los ídolos" suggests some higher forces, sometimes believed to be in control, traditionally relied upon —but in Maples' poem it is "existir *contra* los ídolos" ("ídolos" implies that they are false idols rather than gods), and traditional religious systems which tout a better life after death are rejected in favor of life on Earth, in the here and now. It is "la libertad terrestre de los sexos" —*libertad* representing freedom, lack of death or of end, regeneration, future, and connected with "los sexos" it would symbolize reproduction, continuation of the species. This idea is reinforced in the next strophe by another reference to the arrival of the child.

The child arrives at a time of war, death and destruction. His life, the creation of it, signals a hope for the continuation of life, a victory over the death and destruction of the present historical moment. The use of the personal pronoun later in the strophe ("tú, hecho de *mi* sangre y de *mi* fuerza") indicates a vanquishing of death and destruction not only on the societal level (war) but on a personal level as well; the two senses occur simultaneously. The child is a hope for the future for both society now in the midst of war and for the protagonist, who in strophe four imagines the moment of his death and sees the child as "la promesa eterna de la sangre":

> Cuando oprimiendo el pecho por donde cruzan las pasiones
> sólo tenga el gesto indefenso del silencio,
> cuando la tierra en mí se haya callado
> y despierte la luz en otros ojos,
> cuando un tacto de metal me arranque
> la voz, y sólo sea
> un sollozo de piedra reprimido
> o una fecha de pájaros,
> ¡que sea mi voluntad este deseo que crece!

In strophe nine, there is another affirmation of the human and earthly and a rejection of any supernatural beings ("tú de forma mortal, tú que no rezas, / absoluta presencia que sube de las profundidades"); the son rises up from the vast unknown (interior and exterior) to the known and concrete.

There is an echo of Paz and Nietzsche in the statement that the child carries the seed of rebellion (against destruction) which is planted (in order to grow and take form) at the same time as is the creative power of man ("la energía secreta de las venas"). With "o clamor encendido en el espacio vehemente," the poem reiterates the new presence of sound (life) and light (fire and empowering energy) in the same place (Earth) as the social struggles (war).

Strophe ten shows the positive, life-giving power of movement and music/sound ("Sopla un viento de arpas"), which rejuvenates the moribund and unites past, present and future in an eternal return ("que infunde al otoño sus más antiguos recuerdos, / y todo recomienza"), all occurring with the birth of the child ("en el poder profundo de un latido.") The child's heartbeat ties together the idea of blood/river as transporter, the blood that by heredity ties generations together and is the continuance of past generations into future ones, the heartbeat as sign of life, and the image-group of sound (the heartbeat) as indicator of life in the sound/silence dichotomy.

The last strophe of the poem summarizes the possibility of transcendence that has been discovered through contemplation of the creative force and the birth of a new being. It asks, "¿Qué es lo que perdura del poema?"–*poema* in the literal sense and also perhaps the poem that is life– and answers with marvel and knowing, "¡Ah!," that what endures is "la esperanza obscura de la metamorfosis": regeneration, transformation, eternal return, permanence. The last verse describes this metamorphosis of the "poem": that it happens within or in the midst of "un abismo de letras"–language, lying in wait to be transformed into poetry, art. It is the possibility of life, waiting to be created; "un cuerpo de silencio," waiting, now silence but ready to be changed by man's creative power into sound, which will cry out as it rises up from the depths and begins a new life.

This is very similar to Octavio Paz's frequent use in poems about writing (and in "Blanco") of "an invocation of the poetic word as the *logos*, still concealed in silence, a potency on the verge of blossoming into life."[211]

The connections throughout the poem between human events and cycles of nature and time suggest that this process of creation and rebirth occurs in ever-widening concentric circles of space, from the protagonist and his family, to the European countries at war, across the ocean to Mexico, from ancient history (*pirámides, jeroglíficos*) to infinite future, across the expanses of space. The word *memorial* in the title is effective in that it simultaneously reaches back to the past (what is remembered), brings it alive in the present, and reaches forward to the future, to keep the memory alive. The title itself represents a connection and continuation across generations of life and identity, in which essence remains. This extending back in time while also extending ahead to the present or future is echoed in several of the verses: "Los ríos ancestrales del tumulto / conducen hasta ti," "parecido al silencio / golpeado de mi pulso," "la pura desnudez de la memoria abierta / al jardín inmortal de los amantes," "yo soy el pensamiento de un ausente / a orillas de un estío rumoroso de árboles," "un país de ardientes jeroglíficos te espera," "Ante ti su esplendor de piedras descifradas." A similar process is evident in strophe ten.

There are several words and phrases in the first two strophes that indicate an action of change, a new beginning, or location on the brink of change: "brota," "rompe," "desflora," "deslumbramiento," "se eleva sobre el pedestal de la tarde," "a orillas de." These are linked

---

[211] Chiles, 168.

with the ideas of birth, death, transformation, rebirth, eternal return, and relate to Eliot's theme "in my end is my beginning."

In addition to this movement back and forward in time or the spatial/action sense of being on the brink of change, many of the images of this poem have unusual depth and dimension: "En la desierta obscuridad en donde brota la sangre," "Como un sueño arraigado / en la luz vegetal," "yo te presentía / en la fuente original que se derrama en el pecho," "los ríos ancestrales del tumulto," "y sólo sea / un sollozo de piedra reprimido / o una fecha de pájaros," "el grito de distancias que afluye hasta mis labios." Many of the images also have a quality of mystery or presentiment. Along with the movement, shape and direction of these images, the subtle yet effective use of rhythm is important in this poem. There is no set rhyme, but vowel sounds predominate. The verses are of various syllable counts, but the hendecasyllables (11) and many of the *alejandrinos* (14) are very nicely achieved, and the seven-syllable phrase or line is still a natural rhythmic unit for Maples Arce—it is a strong repeating rhythmic theme. The repetition echoes the idea of cycles and the images of flowing rivers, ocean waves, the pulse of blood flow, the heartbeat—all of continuous, endlessly repeating rhythm. There is an almost mythic feeling to it, faintly reminiscent of the chanting in ancient rites. The rhythm could even be considered parallel to that of love-making and that of contractions and the birth process. All of these images mentioned as being part of the rhythm of the poem involve something similar to what Paz has called a sense of the interior reality —" 'la mirada' (the inner glance)"[212]— our in-

---

212   Wilson, 111.

terior selves, our self that is larger than the confines of our body. This vision or sense is realized with *transparencia* (the moment of illumination), and is also what a poem or any work of art attempts to achieve.

"Memorial de la sangre" is most concretely about the birth of the poet's son. However, the fact that he discovers the power of the creative force in many senses and speaks of it at the conclusion of the poem in the context of poetry, is another indication that for Maples Arce in his search for union and permanence, the only answer is art, or any aesthetic creation by man in a general sense. Art is a way to overcome transitoriness and temporality. "Poemas y mitos coinciden en trasmutar el tiempo en una categoría temporal especial, un pasado siempre futuro y siempre dispuesto a ser presente, a *presentarse* ."[213] Katherine Anne Porter said that the arts are the most enduring element; they outlast politics and government, and when the winds of war die down, art is what remains. "From a certain point of view, we may say that every great poet is *remaking* the world, for he is trying to see it as if there were no Time, no History."[214]

"España, 1936"

Voici le temps des assassins.
Rimbaud

La mañana resuena atacada en lo alto de motores,
espejos sepulcrales rompen sus imágenes

---

[213] Chiles, 16 [quoting Paz from his *Claude Levi-Strauss o el Nuevo Festín de Esopo* (México: Joaquín Mortiz, 1969) 57.]

[214] Chiles, 161 [quoting Mircea Eliade, *Myths, Dreams and Mysteries* (New York, 1967).]

y despedazan las risas de los niños,
mientras la sombra golpeada de los árboles
cae inerte al fondo de las fosas.

Yo siento la agonía de los suplicios
y los llantos agrietan mi memoria.
¡Oh España negra de sangre y de sollozos!

Voy a la multitud en que el día me transforma:
tú estás aquí traspasada de hierro,
pero no veo tu rostro.
Sólo el grito palpable de tus venas.
Estás toda cubierta de heridas,
surcada de arrugas corrosivas,
la primavera de tu cuerpo se mezcla a los metales
y un furor de potencias te amenaza con su aliento enemigo.

Desconozco los sitios alterados de pájaros.
Los perfumes baleares dudan en mi recuerdo,
y la carne gimiente de azucenas oprimidas,
implora, retorcida de angustia, en los crueles arrodillamientos.
Yo he visto volar los buitres del escombro,
arrasar los hospitales y las maternidades,
marchitar la rosa escolar de las declinaciones
y aniquilar el pulso confiado de los hombres.

Los agentes del crimen excavan el silencio,
siembran agujeros de muerte y de humo en las ciudades,
introducen venenos amarillos en los párpados,
injurian con saliva de nitratos
el recuerdo de Goya y de Velázquez
y riegan de terrores el sueño de las muchedumbres.

¡Sangre, sangre de libertad mancha tus imágenes
y el sudor de la muerte envenena tus piedras!

De pronto, marca un paso de acero tu evidencia,
la voz reminiscente de sirena,
la mirada de fuego de las fábulas,
transformada de ira en la matanza,
luchas contra la bestia africana que aúlla ensangrentada

tras un bosque colérico de armas.

Un viento de barrotes duramente esculpido
sopla contra los pechos ampliados de fronteras.
Tu instinto inextinguible no quiere que sucumbas.
Se oye un clamor potente de horizontes vengativos,
y te levantas, en el gran día que comienza,
palpitante, deslumbrada el mundo,
con un escalofrío de cementerios.

"España, 1936" and "Este día de pasión" present two cases of "the winds of war." "España, 1936" is about the Spanish Civil War. Highly evident are images related to identity, especially the face ("espejos sepulcrales rompen sus imágenes / y despedazan las risas de los niños"). Other images referring to the human body are connected metaphorically to the elements of nature ("la sombra golpeada de los árboles / cae inerte al fondo de las fosas," "la carne gimiente de azucenas oprimidas"). The people and the land of Spain are under attack, and the damage to them is so bad that they are almost unrecognizable now ("tú estás aquí traspasada de hierro, / pero no veo tu rostro," "Desconozco los sitios alterados de pájaros. / Los perfumes baleares dudan en mi recuerdo"). There are several images of deep rifts, very violent in character, illustrating both the invasion of the land and the physical wounding of the people, and as well the profound, lasting effect this will have on Spain (plus the impression made on the poet): "los llantos agrietan mi memoria," "tú estás aquí traspasada de hierro," "Estás toda cubierta de heridas, / surcada de arrugas corrosivas," "excavan," "siembran agujeros." Violent images of death and destruction are infused into all parts of the poem. The greatest sadness, perhaps, is found in the verses that tell of the killing of children: "despedazan las risas de los niños," "la primavera de tu cuerpo se mezcla a los metales," "yo he visto ... / arrasar los hospitales y las maternidades, / marchitar la rosa escolar de las declinaciones."

Strophe five is a surrealistic vision of the enemy surreptitiously invading in the night and implanting death and destruction upon Spain as it sleeps:

> Los agentes del crimen excavan el silencio,
> siembran agujeros de muerte y de humo en las ciudades,
> introducen venenos amarillos en los párpados,
> injurian con saliva de nitratos
> el recuerdo de Goya y de Velázquez
> y riegan de terrores el sueño de las muchedumbres.

The exclamation at the end of strophe two, "¡Oh España negra de sangre y de sollozos!," expresses two of the most prominent recurring images of the poem: blood and sound in the form of weeping, screaming, crying, echoes and the noise of war machines. There is so much bloodshed that it is permanently staining the face of Spain and seeping poisonously into the earth ("¡Sangre, sangre de libertad mancha tus imágenes / y el sudor de la muerte envenena tus piedras!")

The sound of airplane motors is the first sign of the attack; it is associated in strophe one with the shooting. In strophe seven the tanks that moved up from Africa with Franco are "la bestia africana que aúlla ensangrentada."

The cries of wounded and dying people echo in the poet's memory ("Yo siento la agonía de los suplicios / y los llantos agrietan mi memoria," "no veo tu rostro. / Sólo el grito palpable de tus venas," "y la carne gimiente de azucenas oprimidas, / implora, retorcida de angustia, en los crueles arrodillamientos.")

Even though this crying and screaming are connected with pain and dying, they are actually the last outcry of life, and if we recall that strophe five shows the enemy attacking during the silence of night, the sound/silence as life/death dichotomy seen in "Memorial de la sangre" operates here as well. Indeed, it is this outcry of life, the instinct for survival, sound as sign of life and initiator of action, that is the salvation factor of the poem, the hope for survival (continuation), as seen in strophes seven and eight (especially the first two lines of strophe seven and the first three lines quoted here from strophe eight):

> De pronto, marca un paso de acero tu evidencia,
> la voz reminiscente de sirena,
> la mirada de fuego de las fábulas,
> transformada de ira en la matanza,
> luchas contra la bestia africana que aúlla ensangrentada
> tras un bosque colérico de armas.
> ...
> Tu instinto inextinguible no quiere que sucumbas.
> Se oye un clamor potente de horizontes vengativos,
> y te levantas, en el gran día que comienza,
> palpitante, deslumbrada del mundo,
> con un escalofrío de cementerios.

There is a sense of national identity and essence (here, "tu evidencia") that awakes, takes hold and in the "paso de acero" implies the slogan "no pasarán." The mention of "sirena" and "las fábulas" suggests that the collective persona of the *republicanos* consciously or unconsciously finds strength and inspiration in the mythical past and wants to carry the national identity or essence into the future. Strophe six says the bloodshed is "sangre de libertad" and it is this value, this desire for freedom that impels the *republicanos* to rise up and defend themselves and the country ("un clamor potente de horizontes vengativos"). The combination of this positive sound, movement, and "el gran día que comienza" gives hope for the future, even though it is qualified in the last verse by "un escalofrío de cementerios," because it is war, after all, and more deaths will be added to those already suffered.

"Este día de pasión..."

Este día de pasión a través de multitudes,
de hierro traspasadas las entrañas,
la fiebre de las manos deja escapar el grito
con que la libertad despide sus pájaros de octubre.

Este día de pasión en las plazas febriles
el corazón sacude sus sueños seculares
y oye que se desploma una muralla
de voces. La infamia militar estalla
y deja su marca lívida en las carnes del pueblo.

Este día de pasión y de acontecimientos,
abandonad el antro de los sueños,
dominad vuestra angustia de belleza
y no temáis la ira que deslumbra vuestros huesos.

Este día en que un orden de mármol se derrumba,
los hombres a quienes la jornada imprime
su martirio de hierro,
vienen desde la soledad nocturna de la hulla
de los obscuros fondos del castigo,
de las callejuelas de la desgracia y del crimen,
de las praderas antiguas de la noche,
errantes, borrosos por las deportaciones,
sin edad y sin rostro,
por un tiempo cargado de huelgas
punzados por la miseria y por los clavos.

Este día de pasión y de lamentaciones,

mientras sangra todo pecho, toda carne, todo overol humano,
los niños extraviados lloran en los quicios de las puertas
y las mujeres de luto siguen los entierros
con los párpados enrojecidos por el olor de las farmacias.

Este día de eternidad y de derrumbes,
un espasmo de orgullo agita a los tiranos
y llena de estragos y de angustias
las ediciones sangrientas de la tarde.

¿Qué significa el misterio del hombre?
En este día de ejecuciones y sentencias
se forman torbellinos de basura en los barrios
y el pueblo se amotina en los mercados,
y las madres preguntan por sus hijos
y una sombra ecleswástica ensombrece las ciudades.

En este día de holocaustos
pasa un soplo fúnebre anunciando
sequías de la belleza, rebeliones de hambre.
En un solo día ¡cuántos pájaros
abatidos por el odio!
¡Cuántos cuerpos mutilados por las represalias!

Se oyen lamentos de dolor en un huerto.
El ojo de la fuerza nos asedia
entre las zarzas devastadas.
Cae un cuerpo pesado entre las hojas.
Ya el óxido de la guerra se extiende en las praderas
y el yodo del otoño mancha los cadáveres.

Con un solo pensamiento, en este día de violencia,
salimos al encuentro de la injuria,
a estrangular la garganta de los días obscuros
en las prisiones donde se pudre el olvido.

Este día de pasión en que las explosiones
despiertan el furor de las arterias
y martillea la cólera, anónima en la sangre,
sudamos resplandores de acero
en un silencio angustiado de cabellos.

¡Oh, tú resucitado a imagen de mi violencia,
memoria de lodo y sangre de las fundaciones
hasta donde mi planta posa el sufrimiento!
¡Oh, tú a quien creen sin defensa, extinguido,
pero que todavía respiras
y marchas de pie, sangrante, por los barrios fatídicos!
Hay una razón de suprema esperanza:
hablemos con los puños de la resolución extrema,
preparemos las armas nuevas en la fuerza del silencio.

"Este día de pasión" is similar in content to "España, 1936," but is about World War II ("una sombra ecleswástica ensombrece las ciudades"). The phrase "este día de pasión" is repeated in almost every strophe, usually at the beginning, with variations, the repetition giving the effect of a litany. The third-to-last strophe, just after what is perhaps the lowest moment of the poem, brings a feeling of solidarity with the cause and a move to action: "Con un solo pensamiento ... salimos al encuentro de la injuria, / a estrangular la garganta de los días obscuros..." Before this point the victims in the poem have been largely passive; now they rise up to defend themselves. It is a delayed response to the call for strength and courage found in strophe three: "Este día de pasión y de acontecimientos, / abandonad el antro de los sueños, / dominad vuestra angustia de belleza / y no temais la ira que deslumbra vuestros huesos."

Strophe seven begins with a question that finds its answer only later and vaguely, in the last strophe of the poem (twelve). The question is, "¿Qué significa el misterio del hombre?" The last strophe is an exclamation, an invocation to an unidentified "tú," who represents memory and the strength and courage of the past resuscitated and brought into the present (eternal return) to lead the effort at self defense. The mystery of man is the will to go on, the instinct to survive, the desire for continuance of self. The culture was founded with the determination and solidarity that will help it to survive and endure.

> ¡Oh, tú resucitado a imagen de mi violencia,
> memoria de lodo y sangre de las fundaciones
> hasta donde mi planta posa el sufrimiento!
> ¡Oh, tú a quien creen sin defensa, extinguido,
> pero que todavía respiras
> y marchas de pie, sangrante, por los barrios fatídicos!
> Hay una razón de suprema esperanza:
> hablemos con los puños de la resolución extrema,
> preparemos las armas nuevas en la fuerza del silencio.

"Cántico de liberación"

> Hacia otras perdurables realidades despierto
> buscando ardientemente tus promesas;
> los frutos engañosos del sueño se corrompen
> y en el fragoso corazón te siento:
> brillante fuerza que doblegas selvas
> y del alto silencio arrobamiento.
> ¿Quién eres tú que un palpitar dichoso
> al evocar la juventud, trasciendes,
> análoga de lirios en la sombra?
> Tú mueres y renaces intacta de los éxtasis.
>
> Por ti yergue la luz columnas de hermosura
> y al blanco mármol
> te confía desnuda,
> pero tú no eres eso, ni tampoco la nube, ni la ola, ni el árbol.
>
> El violento presagio que atormenta al poeta
> rompe cárceles eternas de repente;
> una llama sin labios resiste en las tinieblas
> y un segundo mortal agólpase en las venas

tras el adiós agónico de los sexos supérstites.

Yo quiero detener tu tránsito de siglos
de la antigua memoria de los bosques
a las limpias claridades que en la frente reposan,
y aprisionar con todos los sentidos
tu apariencia, insinuada en los latidos
del otoño que llega por el campo
persiguiendo las potencias frutales
o en la contemplación purpúrea que obscurece la cólera.
Y contra certidumbre de bárbaros horrores,
vienes y enigmática, al instante, huyes,
dejándome un combate de atroces sujeciones.
Y en las horas radiantes en que mayo
cribado de esplendores,
en el alma penetra
y se diluye,
a través del mirífico fulgor de los follajes,
empedernidos ruiseñores
desalteran su sed de impaciente belleza.

La muerte abre su surco y deposita su germen negro.
Y cuando las estrellas y los ríos de la fiebre
y el vientre de las mujeres y el hacha de los verdugos
y el cielo y la existencia mutilada
despeñen mi silencio,
tú de futura vida,
estremecido, por la fuerza insonora de mi canto,
proclamarás la dura voluntad de mi estrofa,
y al soplo irresistible que del eterno mar te invoca,
volverá a florecer quemante y viva
la voz que aquí dejaron mis labios calcinados.

Me desborda un deseo de ignotas maravillas.
La turbadora brisa
el alma me satura de frescas pubescencias:
nostalgias de jardines esclarecen sus élitros,
y de la fiel semblanza superpuesta de pétalos
la obscuridad borra su imagen
y entre mis manos
queda sólo el tremor de un acto.

¿Eres tú el arcano latido de la sangre?
¿Un útil secreto que exalta y nos libera?
¿Sublime perfección de arduos imposibles
o el progreso ardiente que se eleva
en el hombre?
Al curso inteligible
del tiempo da mi nombre
demudada de ausencias y estupores silábicos.
Razones son de ti el peso de las maternidades,
palidez, sueños,
ceniza, adiós, bosque, mirada,
mar, viento, eternos elementos,
la irrupción de la música en la piedra,
la verdad misteriosa que en sus ojos avanza.

Mi destino es vivir volcanes de belleza.
Del seno impenetrable de la noche
nacerá la avidez incisiva de los pájaros.
¿Quién eres tú que a mí llegas
alcanzando,
por múltiples, transportes
de ala hasta mi frente
con un ruido de hierro,
como un vértigo cruento
entre las sombras adversas de la época?
Oigo, oigo el furor astral de tu presencia,
tus labios persuasivos como un canto de bronce.

"Cántico de liberación" returns to ponder the mysteries and identity of the creative force. The poem is both a look inward—the protagonist's feelings about life and his own existence—and an inquiry as to the exact nature of the phenomenon we have been calling here the "creative force." Two key focal points in the personal dimension are found in strophes four and five, at the center of the poem. At the beginning of strophe four the protagonist wants to grasp all there is to life at once and live it to the fullest, while stopping the onward course of time, bringing all past and present awareness together: "Yo quiero detener tu tránsito de siglos / de la antigua memoria de los bosques / a las limpias claridades que en la frente reposan, / y aprisionar con todos los sentidos / tu apariencia ..."

In strophe five the protagonist faces the fact of his mortality, and invokes the "tú" from "Memorial de la sangre" (a variation on the use of "tú" in the rest of "Cántico de liberación"), which we recall was both his human creation (his child) and his artistic creation (poetry), together with the power of the creative force. This creation will take over when the protagonist dies, and will continue his voice, his essence, his art:

> tú de futura vida,
> estremecido, por la fuerza insonora de mi canto,
> proclamarás la dura voluntad de mi estrofa,
> y al soplo irresistible que del eterno mar te invoca,
> volverá a florecer quemante y viva
> la voz que aquí dejaron mis labios calcinados.

Interspersed among the verses extolling the wonders of life and those sensing the horrors and inevitability of death, are questions regarding the identity of the creative force: the poet wonders just what this power is:

> ¿Quién eres tú que un palpitar dichoso
> al evocar la juventud, trasciendes,
> análoga de lirios en la sombra?
> Tú mueres y renaces intacta de los éxtasis.
> Por ti yergue la luz columnas de hermosura
> y al blanco mármol
> te confía desnuda,
> pero tú no eres eso, ni tampoco la nube, ni la ola, ni el árbol.
> ...
> ¿Eres tú el arcano latido de la sangre?
> ¿Un útil secreto que exalta y nos libera?

> ¿Sublime perfección de arduos imposibles
> o el progreso ardiente que se eleva
> en el hombre?
>
> ...
>
> Razones son de ti el peso de las maternidades,
> palidez, sueños,
> ceniza, adiós, bosque, mirada,
> mar, viento, eternos elementos,
> la irrupción de la música en la piedra,
> la verdad misteriosa que en sus ojos avanza.
>
> ...
>
> ¿Quién eres tú que a mí llegas?

The final strophe of the poem combines all of the above currents plus the historical concerns seen in the previous two poems: the protagonist's avid and explosive love of art and of life, his quest to know the mystery of the creative force, and the social turmoil in his contemporary world.

> Mi destino es vivir volcanes de belleza.
> Del seno impenetrable de la noche
> nacerá la avidez incisiva de los pájaros.
> ¿Quién eres tú que a mí llegas
> alcanzando,
> por múltiples, transportes
> de ala hasta mi frente
> con un ruido de hierro,
> como un vértigo cruento
> entre las sombras adversas de la época?

The combination of these elements is followed by an affirmation in the last two lines of the poem of the existence and presence of the creative force in the protagonist's life, in a powerful image: "Oigo, oigo el furor astral de tu presencia, / tus labios persuasivos como un canto de bronce." Present here are images characteristic of the rest of *Memorial de la Sangre*, the contemplation of the creative force, and the search for permanence: sound/song as sign of life, a sense of expansive space, a spanning of time from ages past to the present with a sense of moving on into the future, a sense of duration and permanence (*bronce*), the feeling of a tremendous power rising to the surface of awareness, and the connection of the protagonist to all of this—perhaps poet as witness and as expressive agent for society. The poem leaves the reader with a feeling of reassurance, hope, and a sense of the huge power of the creative potential and its triumph over death and destruction.

"Fundación del olvido"

Desde el silencio azul del horizonte dicto
rumbos de soledad hacia lo incierto;
la memoria transcurre con tiempo favorable
y apenas si la brisa da señales de pájaros.

Resuena el mar con ecos forestales de espuma
——las olas desenrollan sus órdenes orales——
de pie en los corredores de fábricas marítimas
os presiento criaturas de lejanos umbrales.

A veces por pulsantes caminos de latidos
atravieso los ríos torrenciales del odio;
me detengo en ciudades de nostalgia y de estruendo
donde la fría imagen de la luna no llega.

Llamamientos urgentes me vuelven multitudes
y el trino del motor las fuentes suplantando.

¿Qué espanto de absoluto
brota de los anales de la piedra?
Potencias del silencio nos abisman
en el misterio de las metamorfosis.
Yo abro espacios de fuerza hacia la noche
donde se pierden las tribus del recuerdo

que persiguen los gritos famélicos del tiempo.

Con una voluntad de altiplanicies
que apaga la fiebre de los soles aborígenes
salto de las palabras a los puños del alba.
Las mañanas irrumpen con un grito de alas
entre las juventudes jubilosas del aire:
hermosura inmortal que me tiende los brazos
más allá de los bosques, del deseo, de las rejas.

A través de fronteras que diseña la sangre
mis sentidos descubren silentes claridades:
esfinges, simetrías, ofrendas, signos,
entretejidas viñas a la más pura gloria.
Me estremecen las formas apacibles del mármol
y vuelan de los párpados enigmas de las fábulas.

Mi corazón escucha, oh tardes laboriosas
de suspensos rumores,
al hombre que se enjuga el sudor religioso
mientras sueñan las vírgenes exultantes mensajes
y los altos otoños
en sus senos deshojan sus ramajes de oro.

Me acerco a la vida elemental de los sexos,
a la muerte de acero que irradia del trabajo;
mi rostro alucinado se pierde entre otros rostros,
extranjero, en un pueblo
que flagela la muerte.

Camino en las ciudades con una sed amarga
y me devora un fuego de blasfemias;
miro los esplendores del orden,
las estatuas ecuestres,
las cenizas votivas y los dientes
orificados de la fuerza.

Leyes de violencia dominan
las propiedades cómplices del día
y un viento fúnebre de escorias
que presagia los males de la ciencia

barre de estragos y dudas la memoria.

Leo proclamas del sol que nos prometen
las herencias del sueño, los tiempos luminosos
(demagogias de abril) oh bíblicas jóvenes
que os alejáis por los floridos viales.
Poblado el aire terso está de vuestro gozo.

Siento el hálito seductor de vuestros labios,
la libertad como un soplo entre las frondas.
Crecer, cambiar como la vida de la tierra,
pasar un tiempo de amor
y deslumbrantes trigos en silencio,
y despertar un día de la fluvial memoria
de los siglos, a la sombra
del árbol milenario,
—oh inefable delicia de los deltas—
confiado en la cálida pubertad de las rosas.

¡Que el olvido descienda por las linfas del sueño!
Ya la creación imprime sus dedos en mi frente
y alzan su voz ardiente
de otras razas sonoras las sirenas,
y recitan mi vida, mi fábula, mi ausencia!

"Fundación del olvido" can be divided into sections alternating between a) idyllic visions of the harmony, beauty and eternal quality of nature (strophes one and two, five and six, and a variation in strophes eleven and twelve), and b) a witnessing of the contemporary social conditions and the war in Europe, along with inquiry about history, prophecies, false hopes, and the woes of our existence (strophes three and four, seven through ten, with a conclusion in strophe thirteen). In the nature sections, there is a union of past and present time and of far and near spaces. In the societal sections there is a discontinuity with the past, a contrast between what was before and what is now, between the ancient and the modern, an inability to remember.

The first "a" (nature) section is very peaceful, which is reflected in the metrics: the only change from the fourteen-syllable line (with regular hemistichs) pattern is the second line, an hendecasyllable, which refers to the uncertain future. Otherwise there is union of time and space; only the protagonist stands out from the cosmos, in his "rumbos de soledad." Even though alone, he seems to feel a communion with the surroundings and with his place in time. However, his wanderings lead him into the first "b" (war/society) section, where he confronts human calamity and war. He is overwhelmed by the outcries of people, and the noise of machines and motors seems a fraudulent impersonation of nature. Strophe four asks what terrible secrets history holds, and why do we forget, why don't we learn from history—it is frightening that we forget and do not change mistakes and bad practices as time goes by (there are still wars, for example). The protagonist says he tries to make a connection and remember the past ("Yo abro espacios de fuerza hacia la noche / donde se pierden las tribus del recuerdo / que persiguen los gritos famélicos del tiempo.") The metrical pattern of the first strophe of this section is very regular, but along with the confusion and questioning and fear of losing the past in strophe four, there is a break in the metrical pattern, now 7, 11, 11, 12, 11, 12, 14 syllables.

Strophe five starts the next "a" section, when the protagonist, apparently weary of writing and of contemplating the world's ills, leaves his writing and goes outside to breathe the morning air ("Con una voluntad de altiplanicies / que apaga la fiebre de los soles aborígenes / salto de las palabras a los puños del alba.") The feeling of cool, open spaces, fresh air and the "hermosura inmortal" of nature calm the protagonist and free him from the previous troubling, restrictive thoughts. Now contemplating the same nations as before but in this frame of mind, in strophe six he sees some timeless truths ("mis sentidos descubren silentes claridades: / esfinges, simetrías, ofrendas, signos, / entretejidas viñas a la más pura gloria") and is struck by the enduring quality of pieces of art ("Me estremecen las formas apacibles del mármol") and senses the eternal return of mythic vision ("Y vuelan de los párpados enigmas de las fábulas.") Again the metrical pattern of this "a" section is quite regular, mostly fourteen-syllable lines, with only one hendecasyllable beginning strophe five and one twelve-syllable line at the middle of strophe six.

The next "b" section (strophes seven through ten) starts out with quite regular metrics (with two isolated hemistichs) as the poet considers the faith that some people have in religion, the promised sweeter afterlife. They seem to be at first in tune with nature, but as we recall the negative quality of *otoño* and *deshojan*, typical Maplesian images, we see the pattern of declination and false hope. After the observation and questioning intensify ("la muerte de acero que irradia del trabajo") and begin to affect the protagonist more ("mi rostro alucinado se pierde entre otros rostros") and as he feels more alienated ("extranjero, en un pueblo / que flagela la muerte"), the metrical pattern breaks up in strophes nine and ten, where he is saddened, embittered, horrified, and feels a terrible gap between before and now, between ancient civilizations and the modern world.

Camino en las ciudades con una sed amarga

> y me devora un fuego de blasfemias;
> miro los esplendores del orden,
> las estatuas ecuestres,
> las cenizas votivas y los dientes
> orificados de la fuerza.
> Leyes de violencia dominan
> las propiedades cómplices del día
> y un viento fúnebre de escorias
> que presagia los males de la ciencia
> barre de estragos y dudas la memoria.

This lowest point of the poem is followed by an "a" section with variations: now the idyllic picture is seen with a more cynical, world-wise eye. This passage refers back to strophe seven. Now the promises are seen to be false promises ("demagogias de abril"), deception. Amid the images of sunlight and springtime and dreams, they thought it would be so easy, but now the protagonist realizes that it is not: "Leo proclamas del sol que nos prometen / las herencias del sueño, los tiempos luminosos / (demagogias de abril) oh bíblicas jóvenes / que os alejáis por los floridos viales." Strophe twelve goes on to say that the idea of freedom being as easy as "un soplo entre las frondas" is very seductive. The protagonist longs for a life akin to the long, enduring, secure, eternally recurring cycles of nature,

> Crecer, cambiar como la vida de la tierra,
> pasar un tiempo de amor
> y deslumbrantes trigos en silencio,
> y despertar un día de la fluvial memoria
> de los siglos, a la sombra
> del árbol milenario,
> –oh inefable delicia de los deltas–
> confiado en la cálida pubertad de las rosas.

Nevertheless, this strophe reminds us that there must

be a continuity with the past, we must remember and the memory must go on into the future, or the result will be the "b" passages: war, social turmoil, endless repetition of civilization's woes and absurd destructive impulses (Nietzsche's nihilism). Of key importance here are "la fluvial memoria de los siglos" and "el árbol milenario." The poem must be considered as a whole, the "b" sections contrasted with the "a," taking care not to isolate only certain lines for analysis. Strophe thirteen offers a somewhat perplexing first verse, which may be interpreted in various ways: "¡Que el olvido descienda por las linfas del sueño!" Taken out of context, this seems to be a desire on the part of the protagonist to procure whatever he means by "el olvido," perhaps escape from reality through sleep and dream. Seen in the context of the entire poem, however, we must recognize that "el olvido" is a negative element, especially considering strophes four, nine and ten, and the whole dichotomy between past and present set up in the poem. The affirmative sections are those in which we find a union of past and present, a flowing harmony between them. The discordant, negative passages are those in which we find a striking discontinuity between present and past, which horrifies the protagonist. He sees the danger in blindly dreaming for a sweeter future without learning lessons from the past and remembering them (strophes seven through eleven). His desire in strophe thirteen (the conclusion) is not to enter into "el olvido," not to forget, but that "el olvido" go the way of deceptive dreams and false promises, that it be carried off with them. We may contrast here the good things carried by *sangre* which rise up rather than descend, "descienda" being a negative directional image. He has seen the truths, the "silentes claridades" in "las formas apacibles de mármol" and the "enigmas de las fábulas." The creative force is already beginning to work through him, bringing up to the surface of his present consciousness the mythic voice of other civilizations, ancient races, who tie together their past and his present, their lives and his life, and the future beyond his life: "Ya la creación imprime sus dedos en mi frente / y alzan su voz ardiente / de otras razas sonoras las sirenas, / y recitan mi vida, mi fábula, mi ausencia!" There must be a union of past, present and future in order to transcend the realm of time, to reach timelessness, the still point. There must be memory of the past in order to achieve continuity and eternal return. Maples explains in "Fundación del olvido" how the mistaken pattern starts, the seduction of false promises that put blinders on people who then are deceived into looking only to the future, while the world lives its daily present in ignorant destruction. In order to achieve timelessness or eternal return, all past, present and future must be brought together into the moment (dragged along through Nietzsche's gate). This is much like what Eliot writes in "Little Gidding," the last of the *Four Quartets*, even though Maples Arce does not share Eliot's religious beliefs and that dimension is excluded from the similarity. Still the basic sense is the same, there must be a continuity in order to get out of time, or rather to timelessness within time:

> ... This is the use of memory:
> For liberation–not less of love but expanding
> Of love beyond desire, and so liberation
> From the future as well as the past. Thus, love of a country
> Begins as attachment to our own field of action
> And comes to find that action of little importance
> Though never indifferent. History may be servitude,

History may be freedom. See, now they vanish,
The faces and places, with the self which, as it could, loved them,
To become renewed, transfigured, in another pattern.
...
... A people without history
Is not redeemed from time, for history is a pattern
Of timeless moments. So, while the light fails
On a winter's afternoon, in a secluded chapel
History is now and England.
...
We shall not cease from exploration
And the end of all our exploring
Will be to arrive where we started
And know the place for the first time.
Through the unknown, remembered gate
When the last of earth left to discover
Is that which was the beginning...[215]

"ELEGÍA MEDITERRÁNEA"

De recuerdos impuros disipada en el tiempo
tu antigua armonía se ha derrumbado;
la luz vigila inmóvil sus ruinas de silencio
y el mar nos estremece con lejanos fragmentos
de homéricos rumores.

¡Oh, ternuras sangrientas que abrasan los ojos y la frente
y abren hondos sollozos en el pecho del hombre!
Diáfana sed de insaciable justicia.
Agrieta el sol las rocas de cristal y penetra
en los muros de hiedra y de sangre.
La claridad me roba toda sombra de signos.
¡Oh, belleza nimbada como un sueño,
delicia sin palabras, bañada por los golfos!

---

215 Eliot, *Four Quartets*, 55-59.

Su cuerpo dejó impreso en la ausencia
el olor sin memoria de las cosas extintas,
marmóreas formas que ignoran la caricia
una ráfaga de siglos destruyó su mirada
y del milagro, ciega,
la arcaica primavera con su exangüe sonrisa,
a iluminar su rostro de embriagada ausencia, llega,
y así esperas el día de gloria de los dioses.

¡Qué lejos de tu éxtasis, Helena,
cuando la cólera inefable agitaba a los hombres,
y esparcías el delirio cruel en los corazones!
Tu soledad desfallecida es la única prueba de otras épocas.

Hoy todavía la paz que te circunda alteras
y remueves la tierra de zozobras mortales,
un cráter se presiente tras barrotes de odio
y la memoria acaba su agonía,
aquí, donde cesa de respirar el silencio.
Oh! días corrompidos de miseria y de lodo,
que excavó de horror la tiranía;
contra el alma conspiran augurios de tristeza.
Sólo cumbres fatales
de la antigua belleza
me retienen.

De su abrupto recuerdo el fuego crepitante,
la culpable cabellera ondea
al pie de la violencia,
las bestias fabulosas husmean en su garganta de nieve
el olor sofocante que invade sus caminos
y el esplendor amortiguado de su sexo duerme
entre los pliegues profundos de la muerte.

Oh, Mar Mediterráneo que arrullaste las épocas de oro,
mar de viajes ardientes y cadencia eterna,
espuma entre columnas, discípulas del tiempo,
tu razón de diamante purifica mis sueños!

Si la toca el repentino hielo de los siglos
la sangre sin color suspende su latido,

forma pura, el milagro visible arde en mis ojos;
reconozco su espíritu lejano
que surge incorruptible de los años.
¿Para qué revivir la luz de los sentidos?
Vivo sólo del brillo de tu ausencia,
y la llaga que me abre un ruiseñor efímero
me impide ver la flora del sueño en sus entrañas,
y cantar es esta fuerza mortal que me destroza.

Duerme, duerme, aparente de rosas,
como un cálido río de caricias,
que yo sienta correr bajo tu pulso
la verdadera vida.
El sol, los árboles, el cielo,
claridades primeras de tu mente,
firmamento de márgenes y mármoles las fuentes.
El estío fecunda tu presencia
oculta entre jardines y mágicos crepúsculos
mientras se enfría el amarillo de las viñas,
y me arranco del pecho despoblado de pájaros
arroyos tumultuosos de rumores obscuros.

Tú reflejas los deseos, los sueños
contagiosos. En tus ojos eternos nada cambia:
tu evidencia carnal es igual a mi nostalgia
cuando pasó ya la tempestad, la metralla, el espasmo.

Mi dolor se concentra en tu azul abismo
y tu misma sospecha de acero es mi tormento.
¿Quién volverá a verte deslumbrada de siglos?
Oh! cuerpo incorpóreo sin mirada y sin eco,
soplo espantoso que propagas las fiebres inmortales
y levantas del polvo la multitud del olvido!

"Elegía mediterránea" begins with a statement of the basic problem: "De recuerdos impuros, disipada en el tiempo / tu antigua armonía se ha derrumbado." Visiting the Mediterranean countries today, the protagonist sees that the quality of the ancient civilizations (here, especially ancient Greece) has not remained, has been corrupted by modern problems ("Oh! días corrompidos de miseria y de lodo, / que excavó de horror la tiranía; / contra el alma conspiran augurios de tristeza.")

As the protagonist contemplates this Mediterranean region, he recalls "lejanos fragmentos / de homéricos rumores" —Homer's *Iliad* and *Odyssey*, possibly also Virgil's *Aeneid*— literary classics of the mythical-historical past. The Mediterranean Sea is inextricably bound up in the essence of these stories, the beauty of the place, and man's sense of the timeless enduring presence of nature—as such, the Mediterranean inspires the protagonist. In the last lines of strophe two, there are images of bright, intense light. We sense the light sparkling on the water, and in fact it surrounds all the panorama, almost blindingly, giving a halo effect that seems like a dream. Also inspirational are the ancient ruins and marble statues, which, though damaged by the ravages of time, still retain their essence. The picture of those ruins and statues is indelibly imprinted in the world's mind—it is the essence of the creative force, of art, that remains over the centuries, and endures in our consciousness.

Beginning in strophe four, the protagonist recalls Helen of Troy, and from that point on she shares the "tú" persona of the poem with the Mediterranean region and/or the Mediterranean Sea, and at times she is the sole referent of the pronoun. It was Helen who inspired the soldiers of the Trojan War—according to legend, her abduction by Paris provoked the war ("cuando la cólera inefable agitaba a los hombres, / y esparcías el delirio cruel en los corazones")—and the memory of her remains an inspiration to the protagonist, now so distant from that golden age of the Mediterranean. Today it appears that the region has forgotten that golden age, though the sea remains ("y la memoria acaba su agonía, / aquí, donde cesa de respirar el silencio"), and the protagonist almost loses faith, "Sólo cumbres fatales / de la antigua belleza / me retienen." This thought recalls Helen's beauty (there is also a hint of Boticelli's "The Birth of Venus" in this sixth strophe, as well as in strophe ten) and the mythic dimensions of the Mediterranean's history.

In strophe seven we see that the protagonist finds in the Mediterranean Sea an example of permanence and endurance: "Oh, Mar Mediterráneo que arrullaste las épocas de oro, / mar de viajes ardientes y cadencia eterna, / espuma entre columnas, discípulas del tiempo, / tu razón de diamante purifica mis sueños!" This use of "diamante" is a typical Maplesian metaphor in *Memorial de la Sangre*, the image of durable precious gems or strong metals and stones, especially those used in art (bronze, gold, marble, diamond, and the like), to represent the quality of permanence, endurance through time. Maples once used the phrase "el bronce de la inmortalidad" in an interview.[216]

Even if the sea were to freeze and its mysterious eternal movement cease, its spirit would still be "incorruptible de los años" and the protagonist would still live by its inspiration, as is true about the statues in strophe three, and here in strophe eight: "Vivo sólo del brillo de tu ausencia." Trying to write poetry (metaphorized as "cantar") is impossible for him without the aid of this mysterious life force, "the rhythm of the groundswell that 'is and was from the beginning,' the eternal rhythm of the universal

---

216 Emiliano Quiroz, "Manuel Maples Arce por él mismo: entrevista de Emiliano Quiroz," *La cultura en México* [Sup. de *Siempre*] 12 mayo 1971: V.

order."[217] In strophe nine, Maples invokes this life force, this creative force, to sleep as "un cálido río de caricias" so that he could feel "correr bajo tu pulso / la verdadera vida." Nature is again seen to have the most evidence of this eternal life force, and as its presence fills him, the protagonist is infused with creative power, "y me arranco del pecho despoblado de pájaros / arroyos tumultuosos de rumores obscuros," verses.

The "tú" of the poem (Helen/the Mediterranean Sea) is eternal, outlasting history ("cuando pasó ya la tempestad, la metralla, el espasmo.") As he ponders the depths of the sea, the protagonist fears what could happen in the future if this force is forgotten (strophe eleven)–and perhaps fears as well what future wars/conflicts the sea may also inspire, as it fires man's spirit. What lasts is this energizing force, movement, inspiration–to whatever effect, good or bad, violent or creative–this dynamic evidence of the universal life force, and it is to that force that the elegy is dedicated.

"Elegía paterna"

> Por los tránsitos mortales de la sangre, llego,
>   padre de tierra.
>   El capricho de un trino
>   colma el claro sosiego.
>   ¿En dónde están las sombras familiares?
>   ¿Dónde las voces seculares
>   que el dolor soterra?
>   Un soplo repentino
>   la flor de vuestro esfuerzo aterra
>   y las horas no lucen ya su brillo divino.

---

217 Audrey T. Rodgers, "The Mythic Perspective of Eliot's 'The Dry Salvages,'" *Arizona Quarterly* 30.1 (Spring 1974): 84.

La luz bate sus alas en las logias de estío
      y a los esquivos senos se retira.
      La tierra, el aire, el mar bravío
      insinúan una virtud gentil.
      Es una vid la sangre en que se mira
      mi sueño florecido. Un deseo vago suspira
          por las cimas de abril.

      Gira el tiempo en su pura geometría
      y en el ayer perfecto nos reposa:
          El mar trémulamente
como un romance antiguo entre el pinar se oía.
      Siento aún la mordente maravilla
      y yo apoyado en la viril mejilla
      buscando por la sombra ardiente
          el carro de la Osa.

Los años más hermosos pasan en vana espera
      desdeñando en soledad señera
          los vientos del favor;
en el pecho socaba su nostalgia la onda
mientras el mar marmóreo corre entre la fronda
          con el mismo furor.

          De dudas y deseos entretejida
          contemplé en los desnudos
          ramajes del invierno
          la claridad de vuestra vida
              declinar.

¿Por qué impetuosos cauces de misterio eterno
serpea la sangre y rompe sus terribles nudos?
Me esclaviza la fuerza de ese obscuro anhelar.
          Se extingue lentamente
la memoria de un día antiguo y fuerte
que borra al duro afán mortales huellas.
En su rostro se ha helado la verdad de la muerte;
ninguna nube cruza por su pálida frente,
          la voz yerta y silente
      la semblanza alta de estrellas.

¡Oh signos argentados! ¡oh mágicos tributos!
un tardo rayo alumbra la artera
gracia que os evoca, espíritu que elevas
los gloriosos frutos
sobre el poder tranquilo de las glebas.

Como en áspera cumbre
la altiva primavera
brota y esplende
de su triste veste
una fúnebre llama mi dolor enciende.

¡Oh frágiles criaturas! ¡Oh padres de ceniza!
Un abrazo glacial en polvo os eterniza
y ante el sueño desierto que duerme la creación
la viva soledad de vuestra ausencia siento
mientras un viento
incierto
como de mar y huerto
turba mi expectación.

Mis obscuros ausentes,
dormid en vuestra orilla,
al pie de los baluartes que escande el oleaje.
El incólume azul del mediodía
en mí clava sus garras relucientes
y arde el suplicio estéril de la arcilla.
Sobre reliquias rotas
que devastó el ultraje
del tiempo, cedro y palma
cernidos de gaviotas
epigrafía—
–blanca y fugaz
el silencio perlúcido se astilla
y con su grito
entra en el alma
el infinito
de la marina paz.

"Elegía paterna," the closing poem of this section of the volume, the last of the longer poems, complements the opening poem, "Memorial de la sangre," as it contemplates now not birth but death, and more specifically not the birth of one's child but the death of one's parents, and how that relates to the cycle of generations, of creation and destruction, life and death, the transitory and the eternal. The protagonist writes here about the loss of his father, about mortality, aging, family and *sangre*, the fleeting quality of time and the ephemeral quality of life, the definitiveness of death. He stands in the cemetery, which is peaceful, quiet, with a blue sky above, occasional birds, sturdy trees, bright sun, and cold definitive tombstones in front of him. It seems a world apart from the daily familiar activities. His father, who was once part of that world of daily *sombras* and *voces*, now has been cut off. The traditional use of the seasons of the year to symbolize the ages of man is employed in this poem, as are the parts of the day (the protagonist is at *mediodía*, mid-life). Nature images symbolize what endures through time. The protagonist recalls scenes from his childhood, tender moments spent with his father, and realizes now how quickly time passes, and that youth is gone before we know how to take advantage of it (strophe four), always anxious as we are to grow up and live the future ("Los años más hermosos pasan en vana espera / desdeñando en soledad señera / los vientos del favor.") He says that he watched his parents grow old, saw their life fading, and he wonders about the mysterious thing that is the cycle of life and the secret of its beginning and ending. "¿Por qué impetuosos cauces de misterio eterno / serpea la sangre y rompe sus terribles nudos? / Me esclaviza la fuerza de ese obscuro anhelar."

His father's youth now seems so long ago, his absence so definite, and the emotions involved in missing him very painful. The protagonist seems to implore an answer from the stars (the alternation of groups of long and short lines in this poem approximates visually the shape of a cross, or perhaps the blinking of the stars), for some comfort for his grief, but receives only more intense pain. The death of his father is definitive; he misses him. At the same time, he feels uncertain and insecure about the future: "la viva soledad de vuestra ausencia siento / mientras un viento / incierto / como de mar y huerto / turba mi expectación." But with the beginning of a new strophe, he wishes him peace, tranquil sleep on the other shore, and sees himself as still safe, at mid-life, the noontime of his day. Nature images provide relief and hope at the end of the poem, and the span of time is more calmly and acceptingly understood. Ancient ruins destroyed by the conquest and by time provide the backdrop and lie beneath living palm and cedar trees—green, alive. Suddenly a flock of white seagulls lands on the trees and then flies off ("epigrafía blanca y fugaz") and the silence of the cemetery scene is broken by the birds' call. This fleeting but intense moment strikes the protagonist as the answer that he needs, a reminder of life (sound/silence as the life/death dichotomy; movement, the flight of the birds as contrasting to the stillness of the tombstones, also indicates life) and of the infinite cycles of nature. This and the endless movement of the sea and the continuing quality of nature, bring solace to the protagonist saddened and confused by the ephemeral quality of human life: there is a sense of the eternal return: "el silencio perlúcido se astilla / y con su grito / entra en el alma / el infinito / de la marina paz."

As in the work of Paz, Eliot and Nietzsche, in Maples Arce's *Memorial de la Sangre* the use of a sense of myth and the idea of eternal return function as unifying thematic and structural controls in each poem and in the volume as a whole. Audrey Rodgers explains this use of myth as it occurs in Eliot's *Four Quartets* as a quest for revelation:

> In the hands of the imaginative artist, then, myth could be used as a unifying structural control. In this interest, he could draw upon an existing myth, create his own, or adopt the mythic perspective—without benefit of 'story' —as a device for harmonizing all the disparate elements of his experience. For myth, as Ernst Cassirer defined it decades ago, 'is distinguished by the assumption that the world it posits is unified, indivisible, and self-contained,' and as R. W. B. Lewis noted, need not apply to '... the more familiar sense of *story* — say, about the life, death and rebirth of some god. It is a myth in the alternate but no less valid and traditional sense of *revelation*: a revelation in the form of what Whitman called a national and original literary archetype. The story, such as it is, consists in the poet's journeying effort to arrive at such a revelation...' "[218]

Rodgers explains that the revelation Eliot searches for is "the apprehension of an enduring, immutable reality;" the moment of illumination brings "the abolition of time and space in the contemplation of lasting values."[219] The same occurs in Maples' *Memorial de la Sangre*, though with original Maplesian characteristics.

Enrique Ruiz Vernacci has called the ten short poems of the "La memoria y el viento" section at the end of *Memorial de la Sangre* pieces of chamber music, following the

---

[218] Rodgers, 74 [and quoting R. W. B. Lewis, *The Poetry of Hart Crane* (Princeton: Princeton University Press, 1967) 255.]
[219] Rodgers, 93.

symphony of the long poems of the first part of the book.[220] They are short, neat poems, some (the first few) written on Maples' 1929-30 visit to Paris, others added closer to the year of publication.[221] "Metamorfosis" speaks of the rose, anxiously awaited with the arrival of spring, whose concrete existence is brief apogee, fragile, ephemeral, and in the end it is the memory of that moment, echo, which inspires poetry. Essence endures through expectation, culmination, echo, so that the idea of the rose's perfect beauty remains after the flower itself has expired.

"Plenitud," ten hendecasyllabic verses, joyfully affirms peak, plenitude, noon, summer, midlife, concrete fullness here and now and enjoyment of it. Love and life in that present moment are strong ("la mejilla de mármol contra el viento") and it is implied at the end that, in years to come, their echo will remain.

The *sirena* of "Cita" is the protagonist's inspiration, a wild, sonorous, exotic, sensual spirit. The iconoclastic poetry (cf. Maples Arce's early work and the antics of *Estridentismo*) that she inspires is contrasted to the stiff, boring traditional rules of the Academy and the poetry of the establishment. The train departure in strophe two recalls Maples' earlier poems; he says he sees the *sirena* (his inspiration) and hears her voice not only in the sea but also in the busy city streets—she (Poetry/the creative force) is able to make that transition unharmed, unspoiled. Strophe two is a defense of the poetry of the modern city. But in strophe three he also senses her in nature settings; she inspires his creation of poetry and she is all his world, his concentration.

---

220   Ruiz Vernacci, *Tres ensayos*.
221   Some dates are, "Metamorfosis," New York 1929; "Plenitud," Paris 1930; "Mensaje," Lisbon 1942.

A similar inspiration is found in a modern-day version of Boticelli's Venus in the next poem, "Venus prospecto." She has apparently been taken from the Louvre by the protagonist and transported to busy city life. Planes and trains announce her arrival, echo her image, her face, smile, voice, her long flowing hair (long train whistles and trails of smoke). Newspapers and business transactions react to her presence. Telegrams arrive for her, train tracks lead to her, airplanes fly to her, as do memories. She is somewhat abstract, eccentric, other-worldly, very graceful, and full of the rhythms of the modern world, repeating vertiginous neologisms through the night to the pace of flashing neon signs. Finally at the end of the day she sleeps, exhausted by her precipitous transfer from the wall of the Louvre to the poet's busy city life; she sleeps in the protagonist's arms, not remembering her previous life. Here is the modern poet, possessor of the creative force, holding poetic inspiration captive in his loving arms, as its spirit trembles with life and energy ("toda trémula de vida"), all his, here and now.

"Oceánida" is thematically much like the poems of *Andamios Interiores*, though the setting is at oceanside rather than in a city. The color blue dominates, from the open expanses of sea and sky in the protagonist's view. This panorama, as well as the departure of his lover who had been in his company there, inspires the creation of a poem. The two contexts gradually merge, the woman's handkerchief waving goodbye from the boat echoed in the image of a swallow flitting by, the sound and movement of the ocean waves echoed in the protagonist's heartbeat. The blue of sky and sea and map blend together and make all places seem one, thus the ocean becomes a unifying agent that brings the departed lover closer to the protagonist, "y mi silencio afronta su presencia de espuma." As usual, we find here the desire for union to overcome separation, and the poem is the place where it is achieved.

"Verbo" presents words as part of the sound-as-life image complex (in the sound/silence dichotomy). The possibility of language rises up from the depths to potentiality and then to action, sound, realization. The possibility and potentiality are present before the actualization (as the creative force empowers the poet to write and then the poem is created): "La palabra principia su rumor de Universo". In actualization, there are many types of sounds and words: the various hurrahs in sports, the mythical mermaid or siren's song to sailors, a bird's call, shouting... Radio and record players have increased the dimension of sound production, and radio, in particular, carries the word to almost unimaginable far-off places. The protagonist has a feeling of great power in the transmission of his word (verb as action word adds to the dynamicity and energy of the act), and lets out a shout, symbolic of his writing, "con fuerzas ferroviarias," and receives an echoed response of precise diction, perfect reproduction, from as far away as the exotic and distant Soviet Union, the word multiplied on the wind to furthest extreme of comprehension, to the masses. The desire to communicate and the joy in doing so are most evident here, as the young poet delights in his craft and the energy of his inspiration.

"Renacimiento" discusses both the eternal beauty of a work of art (here, a statue at some ancient ruins) and the ravaging effects of the passage of time. The damage done to artifacts of the past by time and the elements is lamented as unjust, but at the same time the protagonist feels that those works of art are strong, have lasted and will continue to do so, "eternidad petrificada."

"Verano" paints a beautiful picture of tropical summer, all light and sound and bright color, fresh air, fresh breeze, waves breaking at the shore. In the ocean there is a sense of the infinite and of eternal cycles. Its rhythm extends to the life of the port city. The sense of its continuance dominates over any transitory occupation on the shore, and makes one ("tú") happy as it has forever, although the last two lines remind us that its pleasure, though eternally present, can be experienced only concretely ("sólo responde por el tacto") in the here and now. Thus youth and energy correspond to the summertime and the height of sensorial experience.

"Transfiguración" seems to be the memory of a summer night's seduction and love scene, recalled in a moment of solitude. The transfiguration is the seduction, echoed in a transformation from darkness to light and in the metaphor of a rose being picked–"mortal" but giving a "sueño de jardines." The protagonist's *soledad* vanishes in the richness of the memory and in the poem.

"Mensaje" was written in Lisbon, Portugal, after the birth of Mireya, Maples Arce's second child, and is dedicated to both of the children. The "message" is not so much advice to his children but an expression of the gift that is the arrival of his children, who bring him happiness and peace. It is also an explanation of who he is, what his life as a poet is like. As much as a reference to the children, the poem is also an invocation of the creative force, "belleza inefable que a mí llegas sonriente," both arriving after loneliness, solitude and false mirage/image. He explains the inspiration he receives at the still point, the moment of illumination. The vision brought about by the contemplation of the mystery of life and the beauty of nature, causes a mixture of emotions in him bringing with them energy and a desire to create, to write about that vision. The creative empowerment is invoked in order to guide him, enable him, and to calm his desire, just as the children inspire and calm him. It is a poem about his inspiration and his reason for writing.

The poems of "La memoria y el viento," as we have seen, treat the same basic themes as the longer poems of the first part: the creative force, eternity, continuance, beauty, art, artistic inspiration, nature, eternal return, permanence, and a triumph of union over separation, as well as a heightened awareness of the importance of the present moment. The next chapter will examine how these recurring themes in Maples Arce's work continue in the poems at the end of *Las semillas del tiempo*.

Chapter Six: Self-Portrait with Memories,

Poemas No-Coleccionados, 1919-1980

> Mirar el río hecho de tiempo y agua
> Y recordar que el tiempo es otro río,
> Saber que nos perdemos como el río
> Y que los rostros pasan como el agua.
> Borges, "Arte Poética"

> Step by step you go into the darkness.
> The movement is the only truth.
> Ingmar Bergman, *The Magician*

Placed at the end of *Las semillas del tiempo* are fifty poems, grouped by theme, that were not previously published in book form (some had appeared individually in periodicals). These heretofore uncollected poems span Maples Arce's career, but the majority of them were written in his later years and constitute an examination of the poet's life, a self-portrait through poems dedicated to his friends, his loves, his favorite works of art and literature, places he admired, and his treasured Tuxpan River. Because of the length and the lack of a total cohesion of the assortment, this chapter will discuss only those poems (some from each of the seven groups) that relate directly to the themes of this study: Maples Arce's contemplation of the transitoriness of life, his search for union, permanence, and timelessness through time. Thus we will see how these preoccupations progress in the years after *Memorial de la Sangre*, and on through his final years, when the nature of death becomes the dominant question.

Included in the first group, called "Personas y retratos," is "Elegía a Ignacio Millán," a lengthy poem dominated by fourteen-syllable lines and having the feel of prose. Maples Arce relates his friendship with Millán from adolescence through adulthood, speaks of Millán's character and his concerns, and of the poet's sadness at the passing of his friend. They were kindred spirits from youth; "ahondábamos nosotros en el ser y lo eterno." Contemplating the loss of his friend, the poet feels both anxiety over the finality of death and anguish over the absence of Millán. Death took this good man away unfairly and the poet wants him back.

> Lector ¿alguna vez tuviste tú un amigo?
> ¿Conociste, por gracia, la amistad verdadera?
> ¿No es acaso una estrella, una alta esperanza,
> una fuerza tangible que tiene nuestra barca
> confiada contra el viento que azota la ribera?
> Millán tendía su brazo, su corazón verídico
> en generosa ayuda, pero falta de pronto,
> la obscuridad le cubre los ojos para siempre,
> y nos hunde en la noche de un tiempo desvalido.
> ¡Ay! mi llanto
> corre por el silencio que esconden las ciudades.
> Regrésame su sombra, aunque esté más oscuro
> que el mismísimo Fausto ¡él tan claro!
> y permite que venga
> a respirar conmigo el aire del poema. (p. 106)

The poet recalls similar mourning in all of tragic literature, and senses that Millán's spirit has gone into that realm, called by *las sirenas,* as the ocean waves repeat Millán's name. Maples tells himself that at least now Millán has no troubles, is not suffering. But the poet suffers—"tú ya no tienes penas, ni yo tengo sosiego." He closes the elegy wishing his friend tranquil sleep, and concludes, "La vida es lo que huye, y su furor, la nada." The fear of *la nada* becomes increasingly present in the later poems.

"Estrofas para un amigo" is a group of eleven poems dedicated to Germán List Arzubide on his eightieth birthday. Though they are a birthday felicitation, the poems contain some rather brazen criticisms (that only a true friend and confidant would be allowed to make) of List Arzubide, and imply the need for greater modesty and truth-telling. At the same time, they examine the nature of the two men's friendship over the many years, and promise eternal faithfulness, "ser amigo sin fin." Some things the poet criticizes are his friend's penchant for self-aggrandizement, stretching the truth, womanizing, generalizing, frivolity, and radical political views. Maples also defends himself (in "Confrontaciones") against some earlier attacks from List, asserting that his (Maples Arce's) only masters or teachers are "Don Quijote, Hamlet y el Mago Simón" (p. 108).

To a certain extent, List Arzubide is a metaphor for Mexico or the Mexican man in the criticisms raised by Maples Arce in "Estrofas para un amigo." This metaphor brings the poems out of a personal realm into art and social commentary. Examples of this are found in "Encuentros" ("caíste en la quimera de creerte Don Juan;" "Tú esperabas entonces que alzaran el telón: / el aplauso y el público fueron tu perdición"); "La máscara" (where the poet talks about the *máscara*—a false, protective façade—and also criticizes the 1968 murder of students at the Tlatelolco protest against government spending for the Olympic Games); "Interrogaciones" (mentioning people and events in Mexico's history; corruption and indifference); "El vals del peyote" (in which he warns against *sueño, espejismos, engaño, un arsénico dulce*—as in the effects of peyote—and speaks of the false image Mexico puts on publicly: it isn't the truth); and "Destellos" ("¡Que el mundo de la mentira y la farsa haga crac!;" "¡Desastre mexicano! ¡Diana de la victoria!"). Many of the poems of this series talk about false appearances, false promises, corrupt behavior, false self-importance, lying, exaggeration—not only as personal character flaws of Maples' friend List Arzubide, but problems of Mexico as a country.

In the poems of "Estrofas para un amigo," the poet works with fixed rhyme schemes quite often; they seem a bit forced or self-conscious at times, though not always. As in the other sections of "Personas y retratos," "Estrofas para un amigo" demonstrates what being a true friend meant to Maples Arce, and who his real friends were. The eleven poems of the series can be briefly summarized as follows: 1) "La Plaza Dorada," a sonnet, serves as an introduction to the group, especially in lines 4, 9, 10 and 11: "el tiempo y la historia están frente a mí;" "Tengo pocos amigos, la mayor parte han muerto, / estoy casi solo como el desierto, / y resuena en mi pecho un lejano fragor." 2) "Confrontaciones" is an attack against List Arzubide's / Mexico's weaknesses, and a defense of himself. 3) "Encuentros" contains advice and criticism, and mentions another friend of Maples and List, Germán Cueto. 4) "La Máscara" asks for a confession of List Arzubide's true self ("Sácate la verdad de lo más entrañado. / Confiesa ante tu amigo"). The poem tells about the time when Germán List Arzubide and Leopoldo Méndez showed up at the Maples house after a fight at a protest and Maples Arce's mother tended their wounds. It ends saying that the quashing of demonstrations back in those days was relatively tame, far from the violence with which the army countered the 1968 protest at Tlatelolco (students protested the use of excessive government monies to host the Olympic Games rather than to care for the poor, hungry and homeless in Mexico), causing it to be viewed as an international tragedy. 5) "El País de la U" refers to List Arzubide's trip to the USSR–"a Moscú saludaste" –combined with another jab at his *donjuanismo* ("Ser Don Juan es tu tic"). 6) "Interrogaciones" finds the poet asking, from his residence in Europe, if things are still the same back in Mexico, or if they have changed. 7) "El vals del peyote" warns List Arzubide and Mexico against false promises, illusions, mirages, says to heed the old idea that "las apariencias engañan." The poet refers to Mexico's economic problems, false appearances, chimeras; he says you can't always believe what you see on the surface. He advises belief, however, in the lessons of Don Quijote and Sancho. 8) "Alarma" speaks to the threat of nuclear war. 9) "Bifurcación" discusses going to heaven versus going to hell, and how one should live life. 10) "Ars Poética" talks of literary preferences and the value of poetry. 11) "Destellos" affirms and promotes youth, says down with the old ways, down with falseness; it contains an element of nostalgia, and says to live life to the fullest while you can. This poem is a final tribute to List Arzubide, just as he is, good points and bad points, his best quality being "ser amigo sin fin." This poem ends the series.

Most related to the themes of this study are "Destellos," "Bifurcación," "Confrontaciones," and "Ars Poética." Combining a *carpe diem* approach to life in old age with a nostalgia for the past, a desire for eternity, and a respect for love and friendship, the mid-section of "Destellos" says:

> Olvida tu cadáver, que nada te atormente,
> y bébete conmigo, melancólicamente,
> los últimos raudales de un día acariciador.
> ¡Porque nunca desertes la amistad y el amor!
> Y aun, que en muchos años, lo mismo que en la escuela,
> cuando oigas tu nombre, puedas decir ¡presente!
> La vida se marchita con el tiempo que vuela
> bajo el veredicto de la luz mortecina.
> Tú, vive en mi poema de confeti y carmín. (p. 117)

"Bifurcación" notes that the two friends will soon have to part, one headed for hell (List) and the other (Maples) either headed for heaven, back to the river of his youth, or to wander with Hamlet. The poem affirms the importance of living life to the fullest while one can: "Ser –ahí es lo importante; no estar tumbado. / ... Quisiera marcharme, pero antes desalterarme, / y a borbotones beberme el mar."

The last strophe of "Confrontaciones" asserts the value "to thine own self be true," especially when facing up to one's mortality.

> En las brumas del yo, ser yo es esencial.
> Mi crítica comienza a partir de mí mismo,
> y no es importante que esté cerca el abismo.
> Asumo lo fatal.
> ¡Ya resuenan los cascos de los temidos potros!
> Miro dentro de mí. Me aparto de los otros.
> ¡Que los perros se pongan a ladrar!
> La caravana pasa sin siquiera voltear. (p. 108)

"Ars Poética" ends affirming the power of poetry to live on eternally, stating once again that art is the only salvation, the only possible transcendence of man's time and space limitations.

> La poesía es lo que vive más que una sepultura.
> Es la pura excepción. Un soplo de altura.
> La flor invulnerable a la espada temida.
> El último reducto que nos deja la vida.
> Es angustia, horizonte, anhelo del confín. (p. 117)

After the group of poems dedicated to his friend List Arzubide, Maples Arce places next in *Las semillas del tiempo* a poem about himself, his "Autorretrato con paisaje."

"AUTORRETRATO CON PAISAJE"

No todo en mí es cuerpo, apariencia y figura:
la voluptuosidad enciende mi vivir,
y aunque el sol de mis días ya casi no fulgura
aún me queda un hondo y doliente sentir.

Extraño el ancho mundo de los antiguos viajes.
Contemplo, reflexiono, dramatizo. Sonrío
a mi juventud y al brillo de sus mirajes:
al fondo una atalaya y la cinta de un río.

No vivo del decir sino de lo que hago.
Morir viviendo en la poesía es halago
como brisa que surca un recuerdo naval.

A veces en el alma me prende un sueño vago,
que me deja en un éxtasis, y presiento el amago
de alguien que me mira con un mirar letal.

This self-portrait with landscape is appropriately in verse rather than painting, since it begins "No todo en mí es cuerpo, apariencia y figura." He says that even though he is old, he still has feelings, is emotionally moved by the "voluptuousness" of the world and life, and memories of his rich past bring a sense of melancholy to him. The strophe of memories includes his manner of thinking about his past:

> Extraño el ancho mundo de los antiguos viajes.
> Contemplo, reflexiono, dramatizo. Sonrío
> a mi juventud y al brillo de sus mirajes:
> al fondo una atalaya y la cinta de un río.

Similar to the effect of reading Maples' complete poetry as collected in *Las semillas del tiempo*, this strophe ties together the various periods of his life, here in reverse chronological order: his travel around the world while working in the diplomatic corps, his adventurous avant-garde youth and young-adulthood, and the ever-present image of the river that was so much a part of his childhood in Tuxpan. The strophe is almost a summary of Maples Arce's three-volume autobiography, *Mi vida por el mundo* (maturity), *Soberana Juventud* (youth and young-adulthood) and *A la orilla de este río* (childhood).

The following strophe is a philosophy of life, a summary and self-justification of what he has done, and also includes a sense of contentment at the end of the road, almost akin to Amado Nervo's "En paz."

> No vivo del decir sino de lo que hago.
> Morir viviendo en la poesía es halago
> como brisa que surca un recuerdo naval.

The last verse of this strophe echoes the previous image of the river, itself a metaphor for life. The second tercet of this *alejandrino* sonnet (returning to the verse syllable count of *Andamios Interiores*), repeats the rhyme scheme of the first tercet. The total scheme is ABAB, CDCD, EEF, EEF. The rhyme repetition in the second tercet, by its emphasis, reinforces the philosophy of life affirmed in the first tercet. In addition, the form reflects the content in that the only verses with *encabalgamiento* end in words significant to the message and to what his life has been: line three, *fulgura* (the point of strophe one, as in *voluptuosidad*); line six, *sonrío* (the point of strophe two, looking back on what he has done and feeling happy about it); line ten, *halago* (pleasure, contentment with the way of life described in strophe three); and line thirteen, *amago* (a threat or threatening posture, the principal idea of strophe four, which is the second tercet). This final tercet introduces the thought that haunts the poet in his later years, a presentiment of death (and as we see in later poems, a fear of *la nada*).

> A veces en el alma me prende un sueño vago,
> que me deja en un éxtasis, y presiento el amago
> de alguien que me mira con un mirar letal.

The repetition of the rhyme scheme from the previous tercet and the emphasis on *amago* indicate a fear of the loss of the life that was affirmed in tercet one. In addition, the only *agudo* verses end in words whose meaning summarize both the poem and the poet's thoughts on his life: *vivir, sentir, naval, letal*. The first two are verbs that emphasize the active quality of early life, the second two are adjectives that reflect the contemplation typical of the later years. The fact that the pairs rhyme reinforces their association, and that the protagonist's way to *vivir* is by a profound *sentir*, that the river / life metaphor in *naval* is threatened by "un mirar letal," the haunting image of the mythical *peregrina* approaching the moribund. The only significant *agudo* words in the poem progress as: *mí, vivir, sol, sentir, juventud, decir, morir, naval, mirar, letal*. The *agudo* stress of *letal* as the last word of the poem gives it heavy emphasis and makes a lasting impression on the reader. (The *llano* verses can be similarly compared and paired: *figura / fulgura, sonrío / río, hago / halago, vago / amago*, though less dramatically.) The consonantal rhyme of all of the verses adds a sense of continuity across the stages of life contemplated here, as well as an echo that brings past into present. Like the complementary or balancing effect achieved by placing spaces of the same color across different parts of the canvas of a painting, and the use of a particular brushstroke technique with which to paint the images, the sound and structure technique in this well-wrought poem—appropriately titled *autorretrato*—work to reflect and reinforce the semantic content.

Twenty-seven of the fifty poems included in "Poemas No Coleccionados" are sonnets. Of those that are not, one is the *pieza teatral* and ten are in the "Estrofas para un amigo" section; the other twelve are spread across the collection. In his later years, Maples Arce clearly had a serious interest in the sonnet, a form which had not appeared in his earlier volumes. Perhaps the form provided a challenge to the mature poet secure in his craft and increasingly interested in the nuances of perception. Maples Arce also works with rhyme in these poems more than ever before. The rhyme may at times sound somewhat artificial in the non-sonnet poems of this collection, but it is natural and effective in the sonnets. As we saw in *Andamios Interiores*, Maples Arce was able to achieve a creative originality and effective innovation within the traditional fourteen-syllable *alejandrino* line; in the sonnets of the "Poemas No Coleccionados" he takes on the challenge of freedom and dexterity within the traditional poematic structure. There seems always to be a tension between presence and absence, between traditional place or role and the non-traditional, in Maples Arce's poetry. The titles of his volumes attest to this: *Andamios Interiores*, *Poemas Interdictos*, and ironically the "Poemas No Coleccionados" which are now *coleccionados*. This is, of course, yet another Maplesian subversion in the form of poetry of the separation / union dichotomy, timelessness within time, unexpected combinations, and so on.

"A Puebla"

¡Oh! Puebla de barroca arquitectura
a quien Mayo engalana de banderas,
tienes un don feliz de primaveras
que en mi memoria para siempre dura.

Los sones de campanas por la altura
van volando a morir entre las eras,
donde se alzan las cúpulas señeras
que aposentan la luz de tu hermosura.

Pasa el tiempo, con él también la vida,
el alma queda en soledad transida
y es tan sólo rescoldo el sentimiento;

por eso al recordar mi juventud y amores,
a tus plantas, igual que un haz de flores,
pongo la estrofa de mi rendimiento.

Of the group "Tres Ciudades," "A Puebla" relates best to the themes discussed in this study. The poem is a sonnet with a regular rhyme scheme. The image evoked is one of Puebla on a fresh spring day, perhaps the main square of the city, surrounded by baroque architecture, cathedral bells tolling, flags blowing in the breeze. The spring breeze carries the sound of the bells off into the distance where it gradually fades among the occasional peaks of buildings on the outskirts of town, with sunlit towers standing as guardians of the city's beauty. This image is presented in the two quatrains. The tercets are contemplative, the first lamenting the passage of time and the approach of death, the second reaffirming the memory of life and the creative power of poetry.

The first tercet says that time passes and with it so does life, leaving the soul beset with loneliness, and sentiment / feeling is now only like dying embers. A semicolon leads to the next tercet, which begins "por eso." To paraphrase, "as I remember my youth and loves, I place at your feet (Puebla's), like a bouquet of flowers, this poem of my making." Significantly, the first line of the last tercet, "por eso al recordar mi juventud y amores," has fourteen syllables, making this verse stand out from all the rest, which have eleven. The memory of the narrator's youth and his loves, metaphorized in Puebla's eternal spring, vanquishes the first tercet's image of temporality, loneliness, separation and imminent death. This vanquishing is achieved by the writing of the poem dedicated to these themes; they are now preserved in the work of art.

The group "El poeta y el río" has an epigraph from the *modernista* poet Manuel José Othón, one of Maples Arce's favorite lines from poetry, "... y una eterna nostalgia de esmeralda," reminiscent of the mature narrator's sentiment towards his youth. This section is composed of nine sonnets, each taking its title from its first line.

"Evocando del tiempo..."

Evocando del tiempo en la distancia
el río de mi edad amanecida,
aspiro el alto don de su fragancia
y proclamo mi pasmo ante la vida.

Como en un espejismo de mi infancia,
miro el confín. El alma, desasida
del mundo y de su ansia,
tiene un leve temblor de despedida.

Volveré a tus riberas, claro río,
a retemplar mi espíritu en tu brío,
antes de andar la última jornada.

Al ocaso arderán las viejas fraguas
del sol, mientras tus aguas
corren hacia la mar y hacia la nada.

"Evocando del tiempo" has two irregularities in the form: line seven and line thirteen have only seven syllables rather than eleven. This variance from the norm serves to emphasize the image of the river (line thirteen and its strophe) and the liberating effect that the memory of it has on the poet (the mirage or daydream evoking his childhood by the river frees him from the cares of the world of his present-day reality, in lines six and seven). These two short lines synthesize the principal message of the poem, and illustrate two worlds—that of the river and peaceful contemplation, and that of hectic urban life and anxiety. Strophe one is the evocation of the image and then his wonderment at it. Strophe two, as mentioned above, recounts the liberating effect of the image/memory /illusion. Strophe three is the protagonist's vow to return to the shores of his river once again before the end of his days (death), to revive his spirit. Strophe four paints the picture of that day when he will return, a flaming sunset on the western horizon, the river's waters endlessly flowing toward the sea and toward "la nada," nothingness, here perhaps seen as infinity. Thus we have in this poem another example of Maples Arce's use of the eternal qualities of nature as contrasted to the transitory quality of man's life. The difference between the two, man's apparent inability to achieve eternity, is bridged by memory and by concretizing the recollection in the form of this poem.

"Cuando en pensarme..."

Cuando en pensarme y en pensarte quiero,
apoyada en la mano la mejilla,
miro el agua correr desde la orilla
igual que en tiempos de mi amor primero.

Tú fuiste el paraíso tempranero
en que colmé las ansias de mi arcilla,
y en mi pecho encendiste la amarilla
brasa del trópico altanero.

Ya cristalino o empañado espejo,
a medida que avanza tu corriente,
hundidos sueños por el cause viejo

suman las sombras de aquel tiempo ausente,
y me parece ver en tu reflejo
los años que pasaron por mi frente.

In "Cuando en pensarme," the protagonist sits at the river's edge, watching the water flow by, and recalls the times spent by that river in his youth, his formative years. It seems to him that the dreams he dreamed in youth are still carried along by the timeless current of the river. As he looks into the water he can see images from those years of his life in the past. Structure reinforces content in the two tercets, where intertwining rhyme (CDC, DCD) reflects intertwining past and present, and the final words of each line contain the major images involved in bringing past dreams and events to the present through the river (*espejo, corriente, viejo, ausente, reflejo, frente*). In this way, past and present are united in the poems.

"Contigo van..."

Contigo van mi alma y mi albedrío,
mi afán, mi vida y mis desvelos,
mientras que los marmóreos cielos
duermen al fondo de tu cauce frío.

Por el mar las banderas del hastío
se agitan ya entre revueltos vuelos
encrespados, y vagan mis anhelos
en la marina azul del tremolío.

Olvidando el fluir de tus cristales
alcanzas los tumultos litorales
en un pacto sellado con la suerte;

que retratadas queden en tu historia
transparente—mi vida y mi memoria—,
redimidas del sueño de la muerte.

The next sonnet, "Contigo van," presents the sky / sea

dichotomy (seen in some of the poems earlier in Maples Arce's career) as united–that is, combined, in the reflection of the sky in the sea. The union of opposites was typical of *vanguardismo*; here we see it as representative of the union of past and present and the abolition of differences–the reconciliation of conflicting elements. This idea continues in strophe two as images of boredom now stir with a yearning for adventure. In strophe three the river swells, rises to meet the shore, and introduces a metaphorical link of past and present with the future or destiny (*suerte*), revealed in the "pact" of the last tercet: that the river will hold the protagonist's life and memory in its crystalline-watered and endlessly flowing current, thus saving them from temporality and death. Again, transitoriness is transcended in the work of art (poem), and the agent is nature.

"Oigo el pulso latir..."

Oigo el pulso latir de tus riberas
que la vida y la muerte me enseñaron;
forastero, crecí junto a tus eras,
y tus aguas al mundo me llevaron.

De tus frescas muchachas tempraneras,
la belleza y la gracia me elevaron,
aliadas de tus fuerzas y banderas.
¡Que el texto de tus aguas sea alabado!

¿Qué es lo que me aguarda cuando muera?
¿Mi carne es sólo un fruto magullado
que se pudre al sol de las praderas?

Cuando acabe el favor de la mentira,
despliega el rumor de tus palmeras
y mira con amor a quien te mira.

"Oigo el pulso latir" continues in a similar vein, but has the protagonist feeling more anxiety about death than in the previous poems of this group. Now the pact is not so certain; he wonders what awaits him when he dies, whether his body is merely like a bruised piece of fruit that falls from a tree and then rots in the sun. In the last tercet, he asks the river to help him out when his time comes, asks that it unfold the comforting sound of the breeze through the palm trees, and that it look kindly on the person who is looking at it now. The river and the land taught him lessons of life and death when he was young, and helped carry him off to later adventures (strophes one and two). There is a clear identification with nature in the two tercets, but the protagonist would prefer, rather than the "returning back to the earth" cycle of the piece of fruit, that he be carried on in the eternal movement of the wind and of the river.

"De la ausencia devuelto..."

De la ausencia devuelto a estas orillas,
dragón verde que guardas mi tesoro
(el ídolo, el mago y lo que lloro),
¡que tu claro satín corten mis quillas!

El poema labrado y sin astillas,
la caoba y el cedro que deploro,
lucen en ti el cielo con que brillas,
las arenas, las estrellas de oro.

Tras los trances del mar y sus murales
avanzas de las áreas sepulcrales,
y despacioso pasas por mi puerta

cantando tus baladas de marino,
mientras que yo contemplo mi destino
y los despojos de mi vida muerta.

"De la ausencia devuelto" is an unusual poem, more mysterious and sinister than the other poems of this group, due probably to the fact that it is apparently a nighttime scene. After some absence, the protagonist has returned to the river. He calls it a green dragon, keeper of his treasure. It is night, and the moonlight on the river makes it look like satin. The protagonist is either on a boat or wishes to be, watching the keel plying through the smooth water. The water reflects the moon (which is also the agent of its illumination: "lucen en ti el cielo con que brillas, / las arenas, las estrellas de oro") and the stars—another instance of sky / sea imagery united—and shines on the sand, which is also reflected in the water. (Considering this unifying projection and reflection between extreme spaces, a traveler passing through the scene would surely feel "at one" with the surroundings, achieving a sense of union.)

In the first half of the poem, the movement described has been that of the poet (in a boat) moving through the water of the river. In the second half (the tercets), there is a change, and the movement is that of the river moving through the darkness toward the protagonist (we recall the green dragon image). It has moved from the perilous sea, past fortresses, and advanced on through the darkness, and now slowly passes by the protagonist's door (presumably now in a house, not in the boat—a dream?). The image recalls the legendary *peregrina* searching out the next to die. As the river passes by, it sings sailors' ballads (presumably of love and death), while the protagonist contemplates his fate, "y los despojos de mi vida muerta" (the curious last verse). The phrase "vida muerta" does not seem typical of Maples Arce if it is meant to be a wasted life, wondering what scraps remain of it. However, the expression suggests "despojos mortales," mortal remains, and would hint at a contemplation of whether the soul has a life after the death of the body. In addition, "vida muerta" unites the opposites, life and death, much as the sky / sea imagery earlier overcame separation, in the river. This phrase also expresses the reality of the moment of contemplation, when the protagonist is alive but feels death approaching and it is heavy on his conscience. There is an increasing anxiety about death on the part of the protagonist as the *Poemas no coleccionados* series advances.

"COMO LEOPARDI MIRO..."

Como Leopardi miro el infinito
de la antigua colina de mi infancia;
el lejano cristal en la distancia
corriendo va a la mar de ronco grito.

El reflejo del tiempo indiferente
—esencia de las cosas que pasaron—,
se parece a las tramas que llevaron
mi fortuna y mi ansia a tu corriente.

Vosotras aguas hondas y sumisas,
apariencia de cosas verdaderas,
tan sólo sois las sombras tornadizas

de la vida, los juegos temporales,
la malla, el pensamiento, las quimeras
del hombre y sus duelos ancestrales.

"Como Leopardi miro" continues contemplation of the

river and introduces the idea that the images seen in the water are merely reflections, not the real thing. The last strophe also points out that life is complicated, not solely idyllic adventures of childhood: "los juegos temporales, / la malla, el pensamiento, las quimeras / del hombre y sus duelos ancestrales."

"Esperaré paciente..."

Esperaré paciente en la ribera
que a mí llegue el tiempo prometido:
siento ya que se acerca a mi latido
la amarga broca de la edad postrera.

Contemplando en tus aguas de esmeralda
mi nostalgia y tu eterna primavera,
una vez más la parda sementera
dará su fruto escarlata y gualda.

¿Por qué en su afán la carne florecida
junta al goce la pena de la vida?
Como el pájaro oculto entre las brumas

que lanza al aire su dolido grito,
envío mi mensaje al infinito,
sobre el sueño del mar y las espumas.

"Esperaré paciente" has the protagonist saying he will wait patiently on the riverbank for his time (of death) to come. He thinks of the cycles of nature; spring, planting, rebirth and growth dominate the second strophe. The third strophe adds the idea of the coexistence of pleasure and pain in life. He cries out to the heavens, pondering this duality: "Como el pájaro oculto entre las brumas / que lanza al aire su dolido grito, / envío mi mensaje al infinito,

/ sobre el sueño del mar y las espumas."

This notion of duality is present in the sense of mystery and the unknown in "Preludio en la montaña," another nighttime scene, as we saw in "De la ausencia devuelto."

"Preludio en la montaña..."

Preludio en la montaña del encino,
¿qué misterio te lleva, linfa pura,
para bajar curiosa a la llanura
y volcarte en el mar de tu destino?

Las antorchas alumbran el camino
que va al puerto; velera arboladura
finge a la noche leve veladura
y fuegos de San Telmo en lo marino.

A través de las sombras de abalorio,
la luna de ámbar como un ostensorio,
silenciosa resbala en la arboleda.

Yo conduzco a mi pueblo, peregrino,
entre votivas piedras y adivino
cerca el mar de la sal y la alborada.

The protagonist wonders what mystery propels the river along its course; there is a light/dark, fire/night-sky image complex playing off illumination as knowledge or the familiar and darkness as the unknown. The port is veiled in fog; glassy, colored shadows are described; silence fills the area. The protagonist, "peregrino," returns home to his town in this scene, as if in a promise to return before dying, and he senses in the darkness that the sea is near, as is the dawn. This last image, the imminent dawn, provides a sense of security and contentment as the poem closes. After the mysterious, long dark trip related in the poem, this final image adds a more positive note to the contemplation of death. There is comfort in returning home.

"¡Oh tiempo! ¡oh río…"

¡Oh tiempo! ¡Oh río de la existencia!
Voy en la entraña de tu ser fluido,
marcho por el caudal de tu experiencia
que atrás dejó mi último latido.

Heráclito, conozco tu sentencia:
nadie, nadie remonta lo vivido,
ni dos veces bañó su diferencia
en las aguas del tiempo que es olvido.

Río de cristal, sí, adiós te digo,
con las mismas palabras de un amigo
que como yo vagó por los océanos,

mientras miro en tus fondos y ramajes
los sangrientos derrumbes tramontanos
que son de nuestra vida los mirajes.

"¡Oh tiempo! ¡Oh río…" concludes the group of poems called "El poeta y el río." Here the river is expanded to larger metaphorical proportions, now "¡Oh río de la existencia!" It seems to be the moment of death or afterwards, as the protagonist says, "Voy en la entraña de tu ser fluido, / marcho por el caudal de tu experiencia / que atrás dejó mi último latido," as he is carried along by the river. He mentions Heraclitus, and asserts that no one can live twice, that one cannot go back and do it over. He bids the river farewell, and as he goes (similar to the popular belief that one's life passes before one's eyes upon dying) he sees in the water the reflections of what his life has been.

In the group "El poeta y el río," then, we have seen the river as companion; confidant; teacher; keeper of the images of one's life; eternal presence; motionlessness (ever-presence) within motion (the current) or timelessness within time; natural bridge between past, present and future; inspiration; messenger; self-portrait. In the poems of this section, and in other mention of the Tuxpan River in Maples Arce's poetry (directly related to the first volume of his autobiography, *A la orilla de este río*), we have seen the creation of a myth about the river in relation to the protagonist's life and his existential dilemmas. Advancing in age, the poet contemplates death with increasing frequency, and finds no comfort for his fear of "la nada" except in this particular river, the cradle of his youth, which is a symbol of the eternal cycles of nature, a timelessness-within-time bridge between past, present and future, and of whose history his life has formed a part. There are parallels here to the role of nature in the eternal return discussed above in Chapter Five. In the river, the protagonist has found a constant within the transitory world. The mature adult, facing imminent death, returns to his origins, to the security of his childhood, base, home, and attaches those qualities to the salient image of his youth, the river, an image that has always stayed with him. Memory can associate ideas, find patterns. The objective world (things) and the subjective world (the mind) mix to form the expression of the perception of things in word (the poem). Things are dispersed in the mind (memory), and the mind also is dispersed in things. William Carlos Williams described poetry as imposing a design on experience in order to find a meaning. It can be a liberating experience once a pattern is found and the pieces fall into place. For Maples Arce, the vision of this river of mythical powers and eternal return, as expressed in his poems, provides an anchoring point in his search for permanence, in his quest to transcend separation and transitoriness and achieve unity and continuance. The form chosen for these poems also gives meaning, and is generated by the content: the sonnet form in the "El poeta y el río" section adds to the notion of steadiness, structure, tradition, continuation through time, constancy. There is very little subversion of form in these poems. Here what the poet is looking for is not the "new;" it is not brash youth subverting the establishment, but rather the (somewhat foundering) aged person looking for meaning, pattern and comfort, constants in what has been his life.

"Otoño"

I

El otoño ha acampado su cortejo dorado
y difunde vibrantes leyendas de metales,
mientras yo sueño que unos ojos suavemente imantados
de soledad, alivian mis vigilias mortales.

Pasa el viento accionando su discurso amarillo.
El agua confidente aclara sus escalas
y el sol, que luce apenas con apagado brillo,
ensaya sus esgrimas en las dormidas salas.

Otoño, encantamiento de la leve pintura,
me miro en ti y recorro tu triste agrimensura
buscando en el retiro de la tarde velada,

del vino de tus viñas la ardiente certidumbre,
pero hallo sólo el imperio de la herrumbre,
y en lugar del prodigio la carne desahuciada.

II

Yo tuve del amor la seducción triunfante
y de los días vacantes espléndidos destellos,
el dulce rendimiento de su gracia fragante
y la sonata ardiente del viento en sus cabellos.

Yo penetré al jardín de un verdor susurrante
una noche radiante de silencio y de estrellas,
y gusté del festín las primicias más bellas,
pero el encanto dura lo que dura un instante.

¿Qué se hicieron sus risas y el reino milenario
que yo puse a sus plantas? ¿Qué se hizo el salario
de sus besos? ¿Qué las áureas bonanzas

del otoño y el arte? Todo desvanecido.
La sombra ha descendido a mis tristes labranzas.
Y ahora sólo tengo las nieves y el olvido.

III

Cuando miro a través de los viejos jardines
de las vagas marinas el azul deslumbrante,
se enciende su recuerdo de gracia palpitante
al fondo de una fiesta de mágicos confines.

Yo respiré la Arabia de los tibios jazmines
que brota suavemente de su cuerpo fragante
tejido con el gozo de la hora radiante
y las rosas carnales a las diosas afines.

El viento terminó con visiones y halagos,
acumuló el otoño sus bárbaros estragos,
fue su paso un momento de breve claridad.

¡Oh gloria! ¡Oh anhelo! ¡Oh dulzura sumisa!

¡Qué tristeza pensar en su sonrisa
prendida al artilugio de la eternidad!

In the group "El oro de los días," the poem "Otoño" is composed of three *alejandrino* sonnets, each giving a variation on the themes of life, youth, love, aging, and transitoriness. Part I mixes beautiful images of nature in autumn with a possible historical backdrop of war and concern, and the soothing quality of a lover's soft, lonely eyes. Here the protagonist wishes to find in nature the latent power of transformation from the realm of time to timelessness, as found in the long poems of *Memorial de la Sangre*, but instead finds only rust, decay, hopelessness, the moribund. The war imagery may just be a metaphor for the protagonist's struggle with the idea of mortality versus eternity. His mind, in "vigilias mortales," wages a battle between mortality and eternity, echoed in the language chosen for the nature images: "ha acampado su cortejo," "difunde vibrantes leyendas de metales," "accionando su discurso," "aclara sus escalas," "ensaya sus esgrimas," also possibly "agrimensura" and "retiro." The lover's eyes, "suavemente imantados [re: 'leyendas de metales'] de soledad," seem somehow inherently aware of the ways of the world and the sadness of temporality. They are wise, yet calm, and they lend a sense of comfort to the protagonist that nature cannot give him at this point. Each of the three sonnets has only one line of irregular syllable count; significantly, that line in Part I (line three, sixteen syllables) is the one in which the narrator dreams of these eyes.

Part II recounts the joys and adventures of youth, especially those concerning love. At the end of the second quatrain, however, the protagonist says, "pero el encanto dura lo que dura un instante." The tercets then lament the loss of youth, the disappearance of laughter, of apparent endlessness ("el reino milenario"), of reward and prosperity. What has happened to them? All has vanished, he says. Now he is aging and feels he is losing the past. "La sombra ha descendido a mis tristes labranzas. / Y ahora sólo tengo las nieves y el olvido" (p. 130). The irregular-count line in Part II (line eleven, eleven syllables) includes the questions about what happened to love's reward and prosperity.

Part III continues the themes of life, youth, love, aging and transitoriness, in the form of memory and nostalgia. The past, as seen in this section, has a magical charm to it, and recalls certain words from the previous parts: *leyendas, sueño, encantamiento* (I); *encanto, el reino milenario* (II). Part III includes "una fiesta de mágicos confines," "la Arabia de los tibios jazmines," "las diosas afines," "visiones y halagos." The two quartets are filled with sensorial images of colors, textures, perfumes, shapes, flowers, fresh coolness and radiating warmth, and give a sense of the exotic to the past. Then the first tercet brings an abrupt end to the *encanto*: "El viento terminó con visiones y halagos, / acumuló el otoño sus bárbaros estragos, / fue su paso un momento de breve claridad." The images of the quatrains were associated with the woman (whose eyes were a key part of sonnet I), and in the second tercet both she and the glorious past are first praised. Then the thought of them both being connected to time and temporality, transitoriness (leading to separation rather than union), is lamented. The thought of her smile being lost to the realm of time and the past is the irregular syllable-count verse of this section (line three, eleven syllables). Thus, emphasis makes her smile a lasting image in the mind of the reader, and as such it is another instance of poetic structure vanquishing separation and transitoriness in the concrete form of the written poem. The protagonist has managed to save that image from oblivion by placing it as he does (and emphasizing it) in the poem he writes.

"Post scriptum"

Mi vida por el mundo quedó hecha pedazos,
pero mi corazón no deja de palpitar.
Cuando llegue el final de mis hondos ocasos
¿durarán aun siquiera el rumor de mis pasos,
los barruntos del mar?

¡Que un llanto contenido me premie cuando muera!
¡Que atruene el océano su estrofa de cristal!
¡Que en tus ojos esplenda la antigua primavera
y dé mi polvo para ti un rosal!

"Post Scriptum," a nine-line poem, says that the protagonist's world travels have ended, but that his heart hasn't stopped beating; that is, he is retired but still alive. He wonders if, after he dies, the sound of his footsteps will remain, or if the north wind from the sea will still be felt. In the second strophe he wishes for some quiet weeping in reaction to his death, for a thundering crash of surf from the ocean, for his wife's eyes to shine with the splendor of springtime past, and for his ashes in the ground to help grow a rosebush for her (the rose was her favorite flower). This poem is both existentially intimate in the poet's broodings about whether he will be remembered after he dies, and personal in its implied reference to doña Blanca, her lovely eyes, and the roses the couple shared as a symbol of their love over the years. Though personal, the poem has transcending value, as it reiterates Maples Arce's deep concern over death and oblivion, his fear of entering into a fatal *nada*, and the loss of connection between him and the world.

In the group called "Aire de ausencia," we find principally poems about Maples Arce's childhood in Papantla and Tuxpan and adolescence in Jalapa, Veracruz. "Serenata pueril" is a long (seven pages) narrative poem of short verses (seven syllables) with a prose conclusion. In the verse section (a nocturnal vision or dream), characters from the poet's childhood are evoked and brought forth to play out a drama, in which the protagonist also becomes involved. Concerns are rivalries in a love triangle, the devil, emotional pain, life and death, magic, and spells. As the dream/drama ends and dawn breaks, the narrator says in the prose conclusion, "Siento una vaga nostalgia, sensación fabulosa de tiempo y de distancia." The dream/drama has brought about a union of time and space extremes. He praises the wonders and the abundance of nature. The coordinator of all this is the sea, "almirante de los milenarios, adelantado azul de las tierras contingentes." The narrator says to the sea, "Sobrellevas en tus cambios la medida de la contradicción humana. Los impulsos y sofrenos de tu mecanismo son la imagen de la eternidad." The end of the verse section had stated that the drama was just a dream at the edge of the sea: "Despejó la noche el ceño, / se desnubló mi pesar, / como en el viejo cantar, / todo fue tan sólo un sueño / a las orillas del mar." The prose conclusion contains a number of meetings of sky and sea, zenith and nadir, extremes of space and existence (e.g. "La inmensidad se esfuerza por alcanzar las huellas de mis pasos en la arena.") The sea holds the secrets of both life and death, and itself is eternal. The protagonist asks of it (using an avant-garde vocabulary in a numbers/checks/business document image complex of the second half of the prose conclusion, combined with images of the beauty of nature): "Mírate en el alinde de la estupefacción franqueada por noviembres de púrpura y refrenda nuestro pacto metamórfico endosando las eflorescencias de tu reino contra las últimas libranzas del sueño." This pact must be one of achieving eternity, of vanquishing "la contradicción humana." It is a "pacto *metamórfico*"–for change, evolution, transcendence. To paraphrase, he says, "Cash my check for eternity, accept my money order for timelessness, you who possess the secret, you who bridge expanses, extremes of space and time. Bring 'la voz blanca de Dios–alfa y omega, todo y nada,' as I regret the loss of the wonderful time of my precious childhood in the face of 'la honda inquietud de la transitoriedad de la vida!'" (p. 140). As in the long poems of *Memorial de la Sangre*, we see here the role of nature as arbiter between the transitory and the eternal. In his increasing anxiety over mortality and *la nada*, the protagonist both looks back to periods of his life that seemed timeless, and ponders the "eternal" elements of nature for the key to transcendence.

"El viajero"

En mi viaje por el mundo
perdí las ansias de ser.
Ya no soy el vagabundo
que todo lo quiso ver.

El tiempo como un fluido
se ha llevado mi querer;
presente apenas ya es ido,
¿qué queda de nuestro ayer?

Solo estoy con el gusano
que me comienza a roer;
él es hoy el soberano,
y algo va a acontecer.

"Historia personal"

De niño hacia las estrellas
por los tapancos miré,
y dije: iré hacia ellas,
por la escala subiré.

De joven por el camino
una muchacha me hallé,
y dije: es mi destino,
es ella a quien seguiré.

De viejo cuando en la nada
de la noche me encontré,
volví a cambiar de tonada:
¡a la tierra bajaré!

The first two poems of "Tres canciones existenciales"—"El viajero" and "Historia personal"—recount the protagonist's realization that death is approaching, and he faces his mortality. In the first poem he says that the wanderlust that led him around the world has now diminished. He feels that the flow of time and the loss of yesterday are too fast, and that he is already dying bit by bit, gnawed at by the *gusano*. He senses that "algo va a acontecer." The second poem traces directions of his life: the child wanting to climb up to the stars, the young man deciding that his destiny is to follow a certain young woman he met, and the elderly man facing death and *la nada* who realizes that it is into the earth and not up to the stars that he will go.

"Tiempo y eternidad"

> El tiempo que me acribilla
> me da mucho en qué pensar:
> es cosa que maravilla
> que siendo sólo arenilla
> se mezcle a la eternidad.
> La vida es la tarabilla
> que ahonda nuestra ansiedad:
> yo no voy tras lo que brilla.
> Yo busco la eternidad.
> El mundo de la mirilla
> se me ha vuelto obscuridad:
> fuera danza la gavilla.
> Yo marcho en la eternidad.

The third poem of the group is called "Tiempo y eternidad." Though still trying to face death and its consequences, he marvels at the concept of eternity ("es cosa que maravilla / que siendo sólo arenilla / se mezcla a la eternidad"), here accenting his marvel by contrasting vastness with minutiae. It is this eternity that he decides to pursue—not worldly treasures, not youthful adventure, but timelessness: "yo no voy tras lo que brilla. Yo busco la eternidad."

The final section of the "Poemas No-Coleccionados" is titled "Hamlet o el oscuro," and is composed of a *pieza teatral* of the same title, written in eight-syllable verses (36 pages long), and an *endecasílabo* (eleven-syllable) sonnet called "A Hamlet." (Perhaps Maples chose to use *arte menor* for the sarcastic conversational tone of the *pieza teatral* and returned to *arte mayor* for the much more somber tone of the final sonnet.) Together these two conversations with Hamlet form the climax of the "Poemas No-Coleccionados" section of *Las semillas del tiempo*. The play is a dialogue between Hamlet and the young poet ("el poeta adolescente"). Other characters are Death and a chorus of voices. The setting is a sawmill on the Tuxpan River. An epigraph reads, "Yo le doy mi moribunda voz," from the final scene of Shakespeare's *Hamlet* ("He has my dying voice").

The *pieza teatral* opens with the Poet meditating on several issues: first on having to face the fact of mortality, then on the existence of literature and art in the world, next on man and God, and back again to life and death. He invokes the spirit of Hamlet to visit him and end his anxiety over the question of the finality of death. With Hamlet's arrival, the tone, language and cockiness of hip modernity (a reprise of *Estridentismo*?) take over. Hamlet arrives on a tugboat and jumps down onto the dock, greeting the Poet with: "Hola, chico, andas de pinta" (You're playing hooky). The language continues in the vernacular, with playful exchanges and self-conscious rhyme. The modernity of style is reflected in part of the content, since while they discuss matters of mortality and eternity, the Poet and Hamlet argue and jab at each other about expression and language, their precision or lack thereof, appropriateness, references, style. Many literary references are included, not only as illustrations of content or story line but also in relation to the degree of autonomy of literary characters from their authors, which could be extended to that of man from God, and further, to that of creation (poem, for example) from creator (poet) (and perhaps that of these characters from Maples Arce?) Hamlet and the Poet also discuss the Poet's reading of Shakespeare's play, *Hamlet*, and why Hamlet behaved as he did.

Hamlet's behavior regarding his father's ghost leads to the first really significant exchange. Hamlet says, "Si amas realmente al arte / tendrás que reportarte / y ceñirte a lo veraz. / Tienes que 'ser', no 'hablar', / como esa gente que vuela / de un romance de vihuela / tras el aplauso banal." The Poet responds with questions that reveal his preoccupation with death as finality, as the end of existence in any form, death as *la nada*: "¿Y si fui ya no seré? / ¿Y si vivo moriré? / ¿Y si muero acabaré?" Hamlet says "Lo que pasó, ya pasó. / Es fuerte forzosidad." The Poet gets angry and attempts to leave, but Hamlet grabs him by the neck and pulls him back, saying, "Aguarda. Vas a entender / que para la eternidad / no importa la actualidad, / el fin es ser o no ser."

There follows more discussion and banter, on Hamlet's conduct in the play—virtually always having to do with matters of life and death, but also on imitation versus reality and what is the truth. There are some literary allusions and biographical references, and God and the Devil are mentioned. The conversation floats back and forth between the topic of death and that of literature, or more precisely, the writing of poetry (rhyme, the image of the moon, allusions to *sombra* and *sueño*). Hamlet asks the Poet why he worries so much about what is hidden, about the unknown, and tells him, "¿Qué te importa lo encubierto?

/ Tú piensa sólo en lo cierto, / lo precipuo es la cuestión. / Cuando te grite la parca / ya tu tiempo se acabó, / procura estar en la barca / y que tu 'yo' sea tu 'yo'"—when your time's up, it's up; then just go, don't miss the boat, and know who you are—to thine own self be true.

The literary references that follow (this alternation seems to be the pattern) are to the existentialist writers Unamuno, Sartre, Marcel (Proust?), Kierkegaard and Heidegger (see p. 160). Maples Arce, ever the existentialist in his later poems, says "A man's fate lies in his deeds." The references evolve into a series of exchanges about *la nada*, at first meaningful, revealing the basic philosophy or outlook of each of the two characters (including their views on fiction versus reality) and then, after the entrance of the character La Muerte (Death), they become self-conscious wordplay, though still meaningful. Some examples of the first part are:

> HAMLET: Sartre dijo: Soy la nada.
> POETA: Y yo digo, no soy él,
> pues lo falso está en la mente.
> ...
> POETA: La vida es sentimental.
> HAMLET: La vida es circunstancial.
> POETA: La vida tan sólo es una.
> HAMLET: Querrás decir que no es dada.
> POETA: El tiempo no vale nada.
> HAMLET: Hay patos en la laguna.
> POETA: Yo nado con la quimera. (pp. 160-161)

When Death enters, it says: "Fantoches de la tiznada / verán si la nada es nada, / nadie puede probar nada." After some more exchanges, the Poet soulfully says to his interlocutor, "Hamlet, Hamlet, cuán amarga / suena en mí tu reflexión. / Yo creía la vida larga, / de una eterna duración,

/ pero hoy sé que nos embarga / el roedor de la razón." Hamlet responds, "Mantente siempre en la brecha. / No aceptes la cosa hecha: / es parte de la cuestión."

This dialogue then leads to some autobiographical musings on the part of both speakers, then more questions about Hamlet's actions in Shakespeare's work, some relief from the serious topic by way of word play and contemporary references. Interestingly, their lives, through this dialogue, seem to become the creation of their respective literary manuscripts, and at the same time, the character has a life outside the manuscript (especially in the case of the "fictional" character):

> POETA: ¿Trajiste el manuscrito?
> HAMLET: Allí no está el finiquito
> de todo lo que pasó. (pp. 165-166)

In addition, Hamlet refuses to clarify many of the obscure details of the play to the Poet.

As mentioned above, in the dialogue between El Poeta and Hamlet, a discussion of death and *la nada* typically leads into a series of either autobiographical or contemporary references, which in turn lead back into more discussion about death. After an autobiographical passage about Hamlet and his actions in Shakespeare's play, obvious wordplay and allusion to Shakespeare's drama evoke references to art and to the contemporary world, and then the conversation returns to the theme of time and eternity: Hamlet says: "Hay algo que huele mal / en este reino letal" [i.e. something's rotten in Denmark]. "... Todo está en putrefacción. / Ya no se ve el cielo. / ... Todo está contaminado ..." (a reference to Mexico City).

Relating to our previous discussions of time in the writings of Maples Arce, Eliot, Paz, Nietzsche, and others, we find in this dialogue: "POETA: El pasado es el presente / y el presente es el futuro. / HAMLET: El tiempo no está enfrente, / tampoco detrás del muro. / Está, sí, precisamente / en el punto del momento, / no es cosa de conjuro / mas de tiempo simplemente." On this they seem to agree. But the Poet says that he is not interested in circular time, starting out and returning to the same point, but rather in duration, continuance. He does not want to return to the past, but rather to continue on to the future. "POETA: El tiempo con que yo cuento / no se parece al de ayer. / Si acaso queda un reflejo / de aquel tiempo en el espejo / quedaría algo por ver."

The Poet then speaks of the basic things of life, and later says, in answer to Hamlet's question "¿Qué me quieres sugerir?": "Que no todo es soñar, / que no todo es morir, / que no es todo acabar." There follows a series of phrases, each beginning "Hay que ... ," about life. Live it while you can, do it all, he says. Later Hamlet says "Solamente el absoluto / podrá decirme quién eres / y quién yo creo que soy. / Escoge: ser o no ser." After a digression by the Poet, Hamlet adds, "No te salgas del presente, / no abandones la cuestión."

> POETA: La cuestión es el futuro
> y el futuro sucesión.
> HAMLET: "To be or not to be."
> "Ser o no ser" eso es todo. (p. 176)

The Poet then basically says that we are each responsible for our own actions ("De tal hombre tal hazaña"), that all is not so occult but rather is clear, and "Corramos hacia el mañana." The Poet says that what may have been the way in the past, in Hamlet's time context, is not necessarily true for the Poet today in his world. Hamlet accuses him of being a traitor. He thought that his heart was in literature and that the Poet would defend him; now he realizes he is a "coautor." "HAMLET: Yo creía que tus anhelos / miraban a la poesía, / y que con ella tus duelos / y tu languor finirían. / Qué desengaño ¡ay de mí! / siempre, siempre lo temí. / Me heriste en el corazón." The Poet says, "La vida tiene rigores / que mudan el parecer, / los que ayer fueron albores / mañana sombra han de ser." Hamlet retorts, "Yo creía en tu poesía, / y sólo por cofradía / abandoné mi panteón"–Hamlet agreed to come down to talk when the Poet called for him, feeling a sense of solidarity with him as a poet. The Poet then recognizes Hamlet's pain and says, "Me acongoja tu pesar / y que todo tenga un fin. / Volvamos a lo ninguno, / a la nada, al Nahui Olin. / Por ti lo haré, lo haré por ti. / Votaré por Unamuno, por Dilthey, por Kierkegaard. / Por ti lo haré, lo haré por ti... Lo que quiero es tu amistad, / la gracia, la eternidad."

The last two pages of the play follow the above passage and return more specifically to the question of eternity vs. *la nada*, in keeping with the personal-biographical / philosophical-mortality alternation in a spiraling structure. The Poet asks, "¡Oh Hamlet!, nuestro futuro / ya no es nada prematuro... ¿Volveremos cual la ola / con su retorno eterno / o seremos arrumbados / en el más negado infierno? / ¿No somos los más pintados?" Hamlet says that we all die no matter who we are or what we do. He says that he will wait for the Poet in the cemetery, to meet before the Poet decays, and there the Poet will decide "si el falso panteón prefieres / con las glorias del montón / o el eterno verdadero / de la única cuestión." Hamlet cannot answer the Poet's question about death and *la nada*, but understands that the Poet's question and his own ("ser o no ser") are ultimately the same, the only true question that exists. The Poet says he is glad to be in it with him ("de estar contigo / en la última cuestión"). He says he will honor him in his own way, "a ti mi postrera voz" ("Shakespeare's "He has my dying voice")–these poems written to Hamlet. Hamlet asks, *"Remember me* es lo que pido." Throughout the *pieza teatral,* we hear the Poet expressing his own anxiety about the transitoriness of life, his fear of *la nada,* asking Hamlet if death is absolute finality, with Hamlet answering repeatedly, "to be or not to be," "ser o no ser," that is everything, and we hear Hamlet and Shakespeare's other characters repeating "Remember me," tell my story.

Long before the rest of the world heard about Xibalba, the Underworld, the Land of the Forgotten and the Land of the Remembered, they were part of Mexican consciousness since the time of the Mayas. Hamlet's father's ghost, after his long speech explaining how his brother killed him and took his queen and crown, asks Hamlet to seek his revenge, bids Hamlet adieu and says "Remember me." Later, Hamlet asks Horatio to tell his (Hamlet's) story and aright his cause. Referring to the presumed next leader, Fortinbras, Hamlet says "He has my dying voice." As the conversation between the Poet (Maples Arce) and Hamlet ends, the Poet says "I'll give you my final voice" ("a ti mi postrera voz", meaning these two poems). Hamlet replies, "'Remember me" is what I ask."

"'Remember me' es lo que pido." Maples Arce didn't want to be forgotten and he didn't want to forget. He wanted to remember and be remembered. We have seen that this preoccupation with presence and loss starts with the dichotomy of separation vs. union in his early poetry collections: fugacity, never being able to retain anything in his grasp, goodbyes, separation, and a consequent desire for union, harmony, continuation. This Modern problem of things being broken or absent, wanting to fix them and return to harmony, while simultaneously being fascinated by everything new, dynamic and of the moment, so prevalent for Maples Arce in the 1920s, grows to deeper proportions in the 30s and 40s regarding the creative force and existential questions, and continues in the later poems of the 60s and 70s on a more intimate level. Remembrance and oblivion, continuing and ceasing, presence and loss, creation and destruction, life and death, renovation and stagnation, like waves rolling in to shore, these fill Maples Arce's poetry.

At the end of the *pieza teatral*, voices in the background salute poets and decry *caciques*, and the Poet, in Shakespearian manner, ends the drama saying that if the public has enjoyed the work, he invites all to the Hamletian banquet, but beware that at this banquet "el que come es el gusano."

Although the *pieza teatral* ends on an ambiguous but not overly somber note, admitting mortality but praising the philosophical question and mystery, the sonnet that follows, titled "A Hamlet," works as a summary of the theater piece and sums up the protagonist's fears in a more ominous tone.

"A Hamlet"

¡Oh Hamlet, camarada de este sueño,
que has venido a buscarme hasta mi río,
mira conmigo en el destino umbrío

y líbrame de angustias con tu empeño!

¿Es mejor reposarse como un leño
que aguantar el horror de lo baldío?
¿O por la oculta voz del albedrío
volver la daga en propio desempeño?

Al punto de partir para lo eterno
mi temor a lo oculto es un infierno;
—flor, mi vida de ayer, sólo un momento,
sé que estoy en la última jornada,
pues de la muerte voy en seguimiento,
a las nadas de nada de la nada.

The first quatrain summarizes the premise of the play, that Hamlet's spirit comes to speak with the poet and settle his anxiety over "el destino umbrío." The second strophe, echoing Hamlet's famous "to be or not to be" soliloquy (III, i), asks if it is better not to worry about it so much, as stated many times in the play in reference to doubt and excessive preoccupation, and also asks if perhaps the answer to the anguish is to heed "la oculta voz del albedrío," exercising one's own free will rather than submitting to destiny, and commit suicide. The tercets are not separated from each other in this poem, but still work as separate semantic units. The first says that as the time of his death approaches, what torments him is the unknown. The third verse of the tercet alludes to the transitoriness of youth, recalled now late in life. The second tercet encapsulates the issue: he knows he is at the end of his life, that he will die soon, and that after death will be nothingness. This is his great fear; "sé que estoy en la última jornada, / pues de la muerte voy en seguimiento, / a las nadas de nada de la nada." The repetition in the last line drives the point home, reinforces the depths and darkness of the abyss.

Part of the answer offered in the other poems of *Las semillas del tiempo*, transcendence and timelessness as achieved in the poem / in the work of art, is included very subtly in this poem. First of all, Maples Arce has chosen a traditional form, the eleven-syllable sonnet, with a regular rhyme scheme and regular metrics, here perhaps to anchor in the strength of literature, something to hold on to. Better, the poem is addressed to Hamlet, his comrade in the "dream" just told in the *pieza teatral,* but also the protagonist of his favorite play. Most importantly, the fact that the sonnet is addressed to Hamlet, together with the appearance that it does not come to any overt poetic resolution (as many of the other poems have done), in effect reasserts the conclusion of the *pieza teatral*: what is primordial is the great question and that we all ask it. He also thinks it admirable that so much literature ponders that question, and enjoys pondering it. The questioning is endless and dynamic (rather than static). This questioning is, in essence, a metonymic expression of what life is. As such, the poem does achieve a transcendence over the topic of death. The title of the *pieza teatral*, "Hamlet o el oscuro," implies a choice between living the dynamic questioning (Hamlet) and giving in to *la nada* and finitude ("el oscuro").

Why is so much written about the question of mortality? Some critics believe there is a process of psychological self-healing involved in putting a problem into words and telling someone else about it. Expressing the problem in poetry (or other artistic form) has a liberating, alleviating effect. It also provides a medium for the contemplation of the problem. Understandably, mortality—finitude versus eternity—is a painful preoccupation and forms powerful literature. Speaking of T. S. Eliot's experiences during the war, Russell Elliot Murphy has said of him, "Eliot knew that all that progress meant nothing compared to the darkness and emptiness when the lights went out."[222] Maples Arce feared that darkness at the end of life. His poems, however, live on, and shine a bright light on his rich, full life. "*Remember me* es lo que pido."

---

222 Russell Elliot Murphy, Conference paper, T. S. Eliot Centennial conference, University of Maine at Orono, 18-20 August 1988.

Chapter Seven: Conclusion, The Seeds of Time

> Ver en el río o en el año un símbolo
> De los días del hombre y de sus años,
> Convertir el ultraje de los años
> En una música, un rumor y un símbolo.
>   Borges, "Arte Poética"

> To me, literature is a calling, even a kind of salvation. It connects me with an enterprise that is over 2,000 years old. What do we have from the past? Art and thought. That's what lasts.
>   Susan Sontag
>   New York Times Magazine
>   August 2, 1992

What we have seen in "A Hamlet" and the other poems of Chapter Six —the protagonist pondering his own life versus death, his own mortality— is the ultimate and most personal extension of the destruction/creation dichotomy and the search for union and permanence. The connections made with nature, time, myth and the river make the concentric circles of the destruction-creation cycle grow ever wider, while at the same time anchoring in the most basic and essential elements of life. Like Hamlet's endless questioning, "To be or not to be," Maples Arce's career as a poet is a continual questioning of the essence of both life and art. Maples Arce was not only the *estridentista* poet of the 1920s, but also the man who continued writing poetry that grew and evolved for more than fifty years after the *estridentistas* broke up. He insisted on the poet's right, indeed duty, to continue to progress, change, and evolve—like Hamlet, to continue questioning. Maples Arce's work matured as he did, in pace with the twentieth century.

The trajectory of Maples Arce's poetry, spanning more than sixty years, begins with *Estridentismo*'s manifestos and innovative, rebellious experimentation combined with art as a "happening." *Andamios Interiores* presents the themes of separation vs. union, destruction vs. creation, and transitoriness vs. permanence, which continue to dominate all subsequent volumes of Maples Arce's poetry. These themes are seen in *Urbe* as Maples Arce considers the state of his country and the process of revolution. *Poemas Interdictos* continues the same themes as it examines dynamics and time-space relationships. *Memorial de la Sangre* goes deeper into the themes by exploring the essence of literature and art and meditating on the course of life from birth to death. Still considering these dichotomies, the *Poemas No Coleccionados* recall memories of the poet's past (what his life has been) and ponder questions of mortality and the ominous presence of death in man's consciousness. Within these large themes, there is present a basic connection to the self, the individual. Maples Arce's work shows a preeminence of the sense of man's existence in the time and space context of the modern world, and a coetaneous dissociation from some ideal harmonious place and time. We have seen Maples Arce's poetic struggle to achieve union in order to overcome separation (space), and to find permanence in order to overcome transitoriness (time). Structurally and philosophically, he finds in poetry a way to achieve harmony in a disharmonious situation. That desire for harmony, or continuance, relates again to Hamlet's question, "ser o no ser." In the chapters of this study, I have illustrated the concrete way that these abstract issues work in Maples Arce's poems.

Maples Arce's poetry progresses in maturity as follows, expressed in his own words:

> Al vanguardismo emotivo, radical y psicológico de mi juventud, siguieron otras formas de expresión y de experiencia. Con el tiempo, mi poesía avanzó de una manera esencial y no puramente técnica. La duración existencial, el pulso de los días jugó en ella un papel primordial, imprimiéndole un movimiento de fuerza vital. No tiende ya a plasmar la fugacidad de los acontecimientos, sino a buscar la permanencia del ser en su total realidad: es el fruto de una diferente intencionalidad.
>
> Por supuesto, la metáfora no desaparece, con su significado múltiple y sintética, pero el poema no reposa en ella exclusivamente. La continuidad temática es mayor, más apretada, más coherente y acaso deja pasar percepciones y sensaciones más complejas, y no únicamente por una cuestión de estilo, sino de la concepción misma de la poesía y del lenguaje que transmite algo profundo de mi subjetividad.[223]

As Maples Arce explains in the above quotation, there is a subtle switch in emphasis between his *estridentista* poems and those of *Memorial de la Sangre* and after. The later poems deal with the same issues as the early ones, but from a slightly different point of view. Instead of trying to illustrate and overcome the problem of transitoriness (as

---

223   Manuel Maples Arce, "¡Italia! ¡Italia!," *Plural* [special issue on *Estridentismo*] Segunda Época XI-III.123 (dic. 1981): 28. [From third volume of MMA autobiography, *Mi vida por el mundo*, Chapter Three, 72.]

did the early work), the later poems search for permanence. The two approaches are like opposite sides of the same coin. Maples Arce also notes that there is a change from more emphasis on style in the early volumes to more emphasis on theme and on the concept of poetry itself in the later work. So too, is life: youth is discovery, vivid experiencing of the here and now, self-expression and self-affirmation, identification of problems, facing conflict. Maturity has long been familiar with the problems, and speaks with the voice of wisdom and experience. Age sees life in a wider context, from a more ample perspective, and is able to delve more deeply into the heart of things, below the surface. Age ponders the meaning of life and the human expression of it. Age confronts the issue of death. This is a normal process of maturation, and is an entirely appropriate progression for a poet's work. This is how William Carlos Williams progressed from *Spring and All* to *Paterson*, how T. S. Eliot moved from *Prufrock* through *The Waste Land* and to the *Four Quartets*. Maples Arce's *obra completa* is a poematic symphony, each successive movement building on the themes of the previous one, variously weaving and intertwining motif and rhythm–in a style appropriate to its own stage in the process–as it grows and approaches its conclusion.

Throughout this study, I have illustrated the destruction-creation cycle in Maples Arce's poetry. In his poetry, we have seen how the traditional poetic image has been challenged, how the union of apparent opposites has created new, multi-dimensional images, and how the union of those elements has often overcome a contextual separation. (In this regard I have referred to Cubism, William Carlos William's use of imagination and Dadaist theory to destroy the old in order to create the new, Mário de Andrade's image work in *Paulicéia Desvairada,* and Ezra Pound's motto "Make it new!") We have seen how the structure of the poem has managed, in a literary way, to vanquish the thematic problems of separation and transitoriness. The actual creation of the poem, its subsequent concrete existence as a document, and its re-reading/re-creation on the part of the reader, becomes a way to overcome the negative or destructive issues spoken of in the poem, in a positive, constructive ("creative") manner. We have seen allusions to art (of any form, including literature) as the only salvation for man in his existential dilemma, allowing the eternal return: art persists across time and space, goes beyond their apparent limits. We have seen innumerable assertions of life, living and dynamism. In the later poems we have seen an increasing preoccupation with death and nothingness, as the poet reached old age and contemplated his fate; in these poems we have witnessed an affectionate recollection of his life and people and places he knew and loved, asserting the positive and the power of art and the creative process in the context of Hamlet's question, "To be or not to be." I have compared Maples Arce's work to that of several well-regarded twentieth-century poets (T. S. Eliot, William Carlos Williams, Mário de Andrade, Hart Crane and Octavio Paz), with favorable results.

Seen as a whole, Maples Arce's complete poetry has remarkable cohesiveness of theme and progression of style. Critics who have considered only isolated lines, poems or volumes have not put the entire picture puzzle together. The epigraph to *Las semillas del tiempo* comes from Shakespeare's *Macbeth,* asking that he who thinks he can tell which seeds will grow and flourish in the future (who can say?) not attack prematurely: "If you can look into the seeds of time, / And say which grain will grow and which will not, / Speak then to me, who neither beg nor fear / Your favors nor your hate."[224] This is perhaps a jab at critics who mocked *Estridentismo* and berated Maples Arce's place in the history of Mexican poetry too early, before examining the totality of his work. Rubén Bonifaz Nuño, one of the growing number of critics who now recognize the value of Maples Arce's work, has written a sensitive and serious introduction to *Las semillas del tiempo*. In the introduction, or "Estudio preliminar," he observes that from the first to the last of his volumes of poetry, Maples Arce maintains a unified, coherent sense and tone. Maples Arce's concept of humanity, values and man's function in the world gives shape to his poems, which Bonifaz Nuño also considers to be of admirable form. Maples Arce worked to renovate the existing state of poetry in Mexico, and in his writing he tried to glean from the chaos of life some sense of permanence. Bonifaz Nuño says that Maples Arce's volumes of poetry were short, but sufficient to shake the Mexican literary world and contribute elements which still remain, including increased freedom, directness, energy, clarity, rigor, wisdom and humanity. Bonifaz Nuño acknowledges that, in the end, Maples Arce did manage to wake up the sleeping literary circles of Mexico. Early on, Maples Arce did not receive the critical praise he deserved, perhaps due to bad feelings about the destructive part of his revolution. In recent years, however, Mexico has begun to see the creative side of that revolt.[225]

---

224 William Shakespeare, *Macbeth*, act I, scene III, 58-61 (epigraph to MMA, *Las semillas del tiempo*.)
225 See Rubén Bonifaz Nuño, "Estudio preliminar," *Las semillas del tiempo*, 33-34.

Manuel Maples Arce's poetry illustrates a literary career truly worthy of recognition. In a time when scholars are re-evaluating the traditional literary canon, I believe that new anthologies of Latin American poetry should include Maples Arce as a poet of significant importance in the twentieth century, on a par with Vicente Huidobro, César Vallejo, and Mário de Andrade, for example. Maples Arce's work had an effect on Mexican poetry at least equal to that of those authors in their countries. Maples Arce was the standard-bearer for the application of the Mexican Revolution to literature, and he brought the avant-garde to Mexico. Beyond waking up the *postmodernista* literary community and transporting Mexican poetry to modern times, Maples Arce explored in his work "la honda inquietud de la transitoriedad de la vida."[226] In his five volumes of poetry, he consistently asserted man's humanity in the face of an often inhuman world, and at the same time, he affirmed the value and importance of art in life. Maples Arce believed in the immortality and endurance of art ("una obra auténticamente bella, y por lo mismo, imperecedera").[227] Even during his years as a diplomat, Maples Arce considered his principal career to be that of poet, and poetry for him was the vanquisher of separation and transitoriness. It provided him with a route to union and permanence, a prismatic light in the dark, lonely night. Near the end of his life, Maples Arce wrote:

> A la hora de las postrimerías hay que decidirse... ¿Tiempo o Eternidad? ¿Historia o Absoluto? ¿Plenitud o Lobreguez? ... La idea seductora para mí es la Supervivencia, la Poesía, según Valéry. Una ilusión

---

226 Manuel Maples Arce, *Mi vida por el mundo* (Xalapa, Ver.: Centro de Investigaciones Lingüístico-Literarias, Universidad Veracruzana, 1983) 374.
227 Maples Arce, *Mi vida por el mundo* 320.

más que no he perdido. Por ella afirmo mi identidad de poeta, testigo, inflictivo, significante e interiorizante, hasta el final, cuando caiga como *corpo morto cade*.[228]

We can learn from Maples Arce's poems; they are quintessentially human, they are universal in scope and application, and they illustrate the trajectory of humanity moving through the twentieth century. Maples Arce's writing (poetry and essay) is a treasure trove as yet barely explored. The publication of *Las semillas del tiempo* in 1981 put back into circulation texts that were difficult to find, and the reprint in 2013 put *Semillas* back into circulation. One hopes that future anthologies will conscientiously include Maples Arce's work and give it the attention it most certainly deserves.

---

[228] Maples Arce, *Mi vida por el mundo* 379.

Works Cited*

Abreu Gómez, Ermilo. "Sala de Retratos: Manuel Maples Arce." [Revista Mexicana de Cultura, Sup. de El Nacional? c.1946-1947]: 3, 8.

Andrade, Mário de. *Hallucinated City: Paulicéia Desvairada*. Trans. Jack E. Tomlins. Kingsport, TN: Vanderbilt University Press, 1968.

Baciu, Stefan. "Un estridentista silencioso rinde cuentas." *La Palabra y el Hombre II* (julio-sept 1968): 453.

Beaujean, Alfred. *Jacket notes*. Waldszenen, op. 82. By Robert Schumann. N.p.: n.d.

Bonifaz Nuño, Rubén. "Estudio preliminar." *Las semillas del tiempo*. By Manuel Maples Arce. México: Fondo de Cultura Económica, 1981.

Boucourechliev, André. *Schumann*. London and New York: John Calder Ltd. and Grove Press Inc., 1959.

Bustos Cerecedo, Miguel. *La creación literaria en Veracruz, II*. Xalapa: Editora del Gobierno, 1977.

Cano Ballesta, Juan. *Literatura y Tecnología: Las letras españolas ante la revolución industrial*, 1900-1933. Madrid: Editorial Orígenes, 1981.

Caws, Mary Ann. *The Poetry of Dada and Surrealism: Aragon, Breton, Tzara, Eluard & Desnos*. Princeton, NJ: Princeton University Press, 1970.

---

* Unfortunately, many of the newspaper and magazine clippings in the Maples library made available to me by doña Blanca did not include publication information (newspaper name, article title, author, date, page). As much information as possible is given here.

"'Chants' by David P. Berenberg, "And Two Poems by Maples Arce." *Poems for a Dime* 4 & 5. Boston: John Wheelwright, 7 June 1935.

Chiles, Frances. Octavio Paz: *The Mythic Dimension*. New York: Peter Lang Publishing, Inc., 1987.

Chissell, Joan. *Schumann*. London: J . M. Dent and Sons, Ltd., 1948.

Chumacero, Alí. "Una antología." Tierra Nueva I.6 (nov.-dic. 1940): 353-56.

Cuesta, Jorge, ed. *Antología de la poesía mexicana moderna*. México: Contemporáneos, 1928.

Debicki, Andrew, ed. *Antología de la Poesía Mexicana Moderna*. London: Tamesis Books Limited, 1977.

d'Harnoncourt, Anne, and Germano Celant. *Futurism and the International Avant-Garde*. Exhibit catalogue. Philadelphia Museum of Art. Philadelphia, 26 October 1980-4 January 1981.

Díez-Canedo, Enrique. "Poetas en Antología." *Letras de América. Colección Estudios Literarios 3*. México: El Colegio de México y Fondo de Cultura Económica, 1944. 251-257.

Duque de Fréneuse [Manuel Maples Arce]. "Pinceladas de colores: los cabarets." [See Maples Arce, Manuel.]

Eliot, T. S. *Four Quartets*. New York: Harcourt, Brace & World, Inc., 1943.

——————. "Love Song of J. Alfred Prufrock." *"The Waste Land" and Other Poems*. New York: Harcourt, Brace & World, 1934. 1-9.

Faulkner, William. *The Sound and the Fury*. New York: Random House, 1929.

Florit, Eugenio, and José Olivio Jiménez, eds. *La poesía hispanoamericana desde el modernismo*. New York: Appleton-Century-Crofts, 1968.

Francastel, Pierre. "The Destruction of a Plastic Space (1951)." *Art History: An Anthology of Modern*

Criticism. Ed. Wylie Sypher. New York: Vintage Books, 1963.

Frank, Waldo. "Introduction" (1932 ed.) *The Bridge*. By Hart Crane. New York and London: Liveright, 1970.

Gálvez, Felipe. "Cincuenta años nos contemplan desde las antenas radiofónicas: entrevista con Manuel Maples Arce." Comunidad [México, Universidad Iberoamericana] VIII.46 (dic. 1973): 732-42.

Gómez Robelo, R. "Las Pirámides." Irradiador 1 (sept. 1923), 2 (oct. 1923): n. pag.

Guyer, Leland. "Fernando Pessoa and the Cubist Perspective." Hispania 70 (March 1987): 73-78.

Harper Dictionary of Modern Thought. Eds. Alan Bullock and Oliver Stallybrass. New York: Harper & Row, 1977.

Hemingway, Ernest. *The Short Stories of Ernest Hemingway*. New York: Charles Scribner's Sons, 1966.

Hoffmann, Frederick J. *The 20's: American Writing in the Postwar Decade*. New York: The Free Press, 1962; London: Collier MacMillan Publishers, 1965.

Huerta, Efraín. "Una antología de forcejeos." Taller XII (enero-feb 1941): 68-70.

Hughes, Robert. "Putting a Zeitgeist in a Box." Rev. of exhibit "The 1920s: Age of the Metropolis." Montreal Museum of Fine Art. Time 7 October 1991: 66-67.

Ivask, Ivar. *The Perpetual Present: Prose and Poetry of Octavio Paz*. Norman: Oklahoma Press, 1973.

Janson, H. W. *History of Art*. Englewood Cliffs, NJ: Prentice-Hall, Inc.; New York: Harry N. Abrams, Inc., 1971.

JEP [José Emilio Pacheco?]. "Manuel Maples Arce (1900-1981) (Segundo y último artículo)–'Así en la paz como en la guerra.'" Proceso 13 julio 1981: 48.

Kamber, Gerald. *Max Jacob and the Poetics of Cubism*. Baltimore and London: Johns Hopkins Press, 1971.

Kenner, Hugh. *The Pound Era*. Berkeley and Los Angeles. University of California Press, 1971.

"Kurt Schwitters (Merz-Dada)." Exhibit. Museum of Modern Art. New York, 10 June-1 October 1985.

Leal, Luis. *Panorama de la literatura mexicana actual*. Washington DC: Unión Panamericana, Secretaría de la OEA, 1968.

Leblanc, Oscar. "¿Qué opina Ud. del estridentismo?" El Universal Ilustrado 8 marzo 1923: 33-34.

"Lieder" from the Spanish and from "Myrtle." By Robert Schumann. Jacket notes. Deutsche Grammophon LPM18655, Octoher 1960.

López y Fuentes, Gregorio. Rev. of *Andamios Interiores* by Manuel Maples Arce. El Heraldo 16 marzo 1923: 3.

Lyons, James, ed. *The American Record Guide*. Jacket notes. *Arabeske, Nachstücke, Romanzen, The Prophet Bird*. By Robert Schumann. Pianist Guiomar Novaes. Vox PL11.990, 1961.

Maack, A. "Huidobro, Picasso, y la correlación de las artes." El Sur [Concepción, Chile] 19 agosto 1984, II: n. pag.

Malespine, Emile. "La audición colorida y las sinestesias en los ciegos." *Irradiador 3* (noviembre 1923): n. pag.

Maples Arce, Manuel. *Actual No. 1: Comprimido Estridentista de Manuel Maples* Arce. Mexico, 1921.

_____. ed. *Antología de la poesía mexicana moderna*. Roma: Poligrafia Tiberina, 1940.

_____. "Diego M. Ribera [sic]." Zig-Zag 28 julio 1921: 34.

_____. "El movimiento estridentista en 1922." El Universal Ilustrado 28 dic 1922: n.pag.

_____. "¡Italia! ¡Italia!" Plural [México], Segunda época, XI-III.123 (dic. 1981): 28.

_____. "La Sistematización de los Movimientos Literarios." El Universal Ilustrado 10 julio 1924: 57.

_____. *Las semillas del tiempo*. México: Fondo de Cultura Económica, 1981.

_____. *Mi vida por el mundo*. Xalapa, Ver.: Centro de Investigaciones Linguístico-Literarias, Universidad Veracruzana, 1983.

_____. [El Duque de Fréneuse]. "Pinceladas de colores: los cabarets." Zig-Zag 14 abril 1921: 32-33.

_____. *Soberana Juventud*. Madrid: Editorial Plenitud, 1967.

_____. Typescript notes for an interview [c. 1971] [20pp.] Maples library.

Marín Loya, Luis. *El meridiano lírico*. [Manuel Maples Arce, Arqueles Vela, Diego Rivera.] México: n.p., 1926.

Martins, Wilson. *The Modernist Idea*. Trans. Jack E. Tomlins. New York: New York University Press, 1970.

Mejía, Eduardo. "Más allá del Estridentismo." La guía [Sup. dom. de Novedades] 24 (14 marzo 1982): 3.

Melgar, Luis. *Historia de la Literatura Mexicana*, #11: Las Vanguardias. México: Cultura/SEP/Editorial Somos, [1982].

Monahan, Kenneth C. *Manuel Maples Arce and "Estridentismo."* Diss. Northwestern University, 1972. Ann Arbor. Michigan: UMI, 1973. 73-10,260.

Morales, Miguel Ángel. "Viva el Mole de Guajolote." Diorama [Sup. de Excelsior] 6 dic. 1981: n. pag.

Movius, Geoffrey H. *The Early Prose of William Carlos Williams*, 1917-1925. New York and London: Garland Publishing, Inc., 1987.

Murphy, Russell Elliot. "T. S. Eliot, Poet of the Waste Land." Conference paper. T. S. Eliot Centennial conference. University of Maine at Orono, 18-20 August 1988.

New Lexicon Webster's Dictionary of the English Language, Encyclopedic Edition. New York: Lexicon Publications, Inc., 1987 ed.

Osorio, Nelson. "El estridentismo mexicano y la vanguardia literaria latinoamericana." *El estridentismo: memoria y valoración*. Ed. Esther Hernández Palacios. México: Fondo de Cultura Económica, 1983: 49-61.

Paz, Octavio. *Poesía en movimiento: México 1915-1966*. México: Siglo Veintiuno Editores, 1974.

―――――. "Viento entero." Florit & Jiménez 466-468.

Pérez Firmat, Gustavo. *Idle Fictions: The Hispanic Vanguard Novel 1926-1934*. Durham, NC: Duke University Press, 1982.

Quiroz, Emiliano. "Manuel Maples Arce por él mismo: entrevista de Emiliano Quiroz." La Cultura en México [Sup. de Siempre] 483 (12 mayo 1971): I-IV.

Rodgers, Audrey T. "The Mythic Perspective of Eliot's 'The Dry Salvages.'" Arizona Quarterly 30.1 (1974): 74-94.

Ruiz Vernacci, Enrique. *Tres ensayos*. Panama: Imprenta Nacional, 1948: 99-117.

Rutter, Frank. "La estética cubista en 'Horizon carre' de Vicente Huidobro." Bulletin Hispanique 80 (1978): 129-31.

Salazar Mallén, Rubén. "Maples Arce: Las semillas del tiempo." Excélsior 13 marzo 1982: 7A.

Schneider, Luis Mario. *El Estridentismo: o una Literatura de la Estrategia*. México: Ediciones de Bellas Artes, 1970.

_____. *Mele* (Carta Internacional de Poesía/International Poetry Letter) Ed. Stefan Baciu. [Special issue on *Estridentismo*] agosto 1980: 10-11.

_____. *Ruptura y continuidad: la literatura mexicana en polémica*. México: Fondo de Cultura Económica, 1975.

Schwartz, Sanford. "Eliot and the Objectification of Emotion." Conference paper. T. S. Eliot Centennial conference. University of Maine at Orono, 18-20 August 1988.

Shakespeare, William. Macbeth, I, iii: 58-61. *William Shakespeare: The Complete Works*. Gen. Ed. Alfred Harbage. Baltimore: Penguin Books, 1969: 1110-35.

Sinán, Rogelio [Bernardo Domínguez Alba]. *Los valores humanos en la lírica de Maples Arce*. México: Ediciones Conferencia, 1959.

Sotomayor, Arturo. "Manuel Maples Arce, Poeta Estridentista." *Sombras bajo la luna*. México: Porrua, 1943: 173-84.

Spender, Stephen. *The Making of a Poem*. London: Hamish Hamilton, 1955.

Speratti-Piñero, Emma Susana. *El ocultismo en Valle-Inclán*. London: Tamesis Books Limited, 1974.

Stambaugh, Joan. *Nietzsche's Thought of Eternal Return*. Baltimore and London: Johns Hopkins University Press, 1972.

Stevens, Wallace. "The Idea of Order at Key West." *Chief Modern Poets of Britain and America, Volume II: Poets of America*. Eds. Gerald DeWitt Sanders, John Herbert Nelson, M. L. Rosenthal. London: MacMillan, 1970: II-145.

Thoreau, Henry David. *The Heart of Thoreau's Journals*. Ed. Odell Shepard. New York: Dover Publications, Inc., 1961.

Torres Bodet, Jaime. *Perspectiva de la literatura mexicana actual 1915-1928*. México: Ediciones de Contemporáneos, 1928.

Vallejo, César. "Piedra negra sobre una piedra blanca." Florit & Jiménez 293-94.

Vela, Arqueles. "Los 'Andamios Interiores' de Maples Arce." *El Universal* 31 agosto 1922, segunda edicion: 8.

—————. "El estridentismo y la teoría abstraccionista." *Irradiador 2* (oct.1923): n. pag.

—————. "Manuel Maples Arce, Poeta de la Revolución." [Unidentified magazine, n.d., n.pag.]

Vogler, Thomas A. Introduction (1970 ed.). *The Bridge*. By Hart Crane. New York and London: Liveright, 1970.

Webster's Ninth New Collegiate Dictionary, 1987 ed.

Whitaker Peters, Sarah. "Georgia O'Keefe and Photography: Sources and Transformation." Lecture. Memorial Art Gallery. Rochester NY, 8 March 1988.

Whitman, Walt. "A Broadway Pageant," "Drum Taps," "Passage to India." Leaves of Grass. Eds. Harold W. Blodgett and Sculley Bradley. New York: W. W. Norton & Co., Inc., Comprehensive Reader's Edition, 1965.

Williams, William Carlos. *The Collected Poems of William Carlos Williams,* Volume I, 1909-1939. Eds. A. Walton Litz and Christopher MacGowan. New York: New Directions, 1986.

Wilson, Jason. *Octavio Paz*. Boston: Twayne Publishers, 1986.

Yeats, W. B. "Among School Children." *Chief Modern Poets of Britain and America*, Vol. I: Poets of Britain. Eds. Gerald DeWitt Sanders, John Herbert Nelson, M. L. Rosenthal. New York: MacMillan Publishing Co., Inc., 1970.

Other References

Abate de Mendoza [José María González de Mendoza]. "Una crónica estridente de El Abate de Mendoza." *El Universal Ilustrado* 9 sept. 1926: 41, 64.

──────────. "La Leyenda de Guillaume Apollinaire: Una Crónica Sutil." *Revista de Revistas* 14 feb. 1926: 17, 46.

Abreu Gómez, Ermilo. "Desde México: La voz mexicana del poeta Maples Arce." [Unidentified Mexican newspaper, c. 1947]

──────────. "El libro de hoy: Cuentos, Novelas, Memorias y Crónicas." *Revista Mexicana de Cultura* [Sup. de *El Nacional*] 5 julio 1964: 7.

──────────. "Los libros y otros engaños: El Grupo 'Nosotros' y el Estridentismo." *Revista Mexicana de Cultura* [Sup. de *El Nacional*] 3 feb. 1963: 7.

──────────. "Los libros y otros engaños: Manuel Maples Arce." *Revista de Cultura* 8 sept. 1963: 4.

──────────. "Maples Arce." Rev. of *A la orilla de este río* and *Soberana Juventud* by MMA [Unidentified Mexican newspaper, late 1960s.]

──────────. "Maples Arce y la Poesía." *Revista Mexicana de Cultura* [Sup. de *El Nacional*] 13 enero 1952: 1.

———. "Sala de retratos." [Unidentified Mexican newspaper, c. 1947: n. pag.]

———. "Sala de retratos: Manuel Maples Arce." [*Revista Mexicana de Cultura?* Sup. de *El Nacional*] 8 sept. 1963: 4.

Abril, Xavier. *César Vallejo, o la teoría poética.* Madrid: Editorial Tauros, 1963.

———. *Dos Estudios, I: Vallejo y Mallarmé* ("La estetica de *Trilce* y *Una jugada de dados* jamás abolirá el azar.") Bahía Blanca, Argentina: Universidad Nacional del Sur, Cuadernos del Sur, 1960.

Acevedo Escobedo, Antonio. *Letras de los 20s* México: Seminario de Cultura Mexicana, 1966. 87, 179.

Ades, Dawn. *Dali and Surrealism.* New York: Harper and Row Publishers, 1982.

Aguilar Zinser, Carmen. "El Estridentismo... 50 Años Después." *Excélsior* 10 feb. 1972: B1-2.

Alegría, Fernando. *Literatura y Revolución.* Mexico: Fondo de Cultura Económica, 1971.

Allen, Roy F. *German Expressionist Poetry.* Boston: Twayne Publishers, 1979.

Al-Nahar (El Día). Beirut, 28 March 1964. Typescript of French translation of newspaper article in Arabic (3 pp.). Maples library.

Anaya, Marta. "Recuerdos de Germán List Arzubide: Ruidosamente, el Estridentismo Surgió en Puebla, en 1922, con Manifiesto Explosivo." *Excélsior* 9 julio 1981: 2.

Anderson-Imbert, Enrique. *Historia de la literatura hispanoamericana II: época contemporánea.*

México: Fondo de Cultura Económica, 1954.

_____. *Spanish American Literature: A History*. Detroit: Wayne State University Press, 1963.

"Apollinaire y Huidobro: dos extranjeros en París." *Revista Bibliográfica de Ciencias y Letras* 291: n. pag.

Appendini, Guadalupe. "Salvador Gallardo Dávalos no es únicamente estridentista." *Excélsior* 3 oct. 1981: 1+.

Araya, Juan Gabriel G. "Huidobro y el cubismo." *El Sur* [Concepción, Chile] 5 agosto 1984: n. pag.

Arrellano, Jesús. "Las ventas de Don Quijote: Revisión de algunos nombres de la literatura mexicana: Maples Arce: Estridentista." *Nivel, Gaceta de la Cultura* 46 (25 oct. 1962): 5.

Argos. "El Café de Nadie," "On Dit." *El Universal Ilustrado* 27 mayo 1926: 46.

Arnheim, Rudolf. *The Reach of Reality in the Arts*. [University of Michigan] V: 13-14: 97-106.

Arp, Jean, and Marcel Jean, eds. *The Documents of 20th-Century Art*. New York: Viking Press, 1963.

Ashbery, John. "The Glory of Picasso." *New York* 12 May 1980: 27-33. [See also Pete Hamill, "Picasso: The Man," 34-38.]

Baciu, Stefan. *Antología de la poesía surrealista latinoamericana*. México: Joaquín Mortiz, 1974.

_____. *Jean Charlot: Estridentista Silencioso*. México: Editorial "El Café de Nadie," 1982.

_____. ed. *Mele* (Carta Internacional de Poesía/International Poetry Letter) [Special issue on *Estridentismo*] XV (agosto 1980): 10-11.

_____. "Un movimiento literario de América, de

balance positivo: 'Estridentismo, medio siglo después'–German List Arzubide contesta doce preguntas de Stefan Baciu." *El Imparcial* [Guatemala] 29 nov. 1975: 5.

——————. "Palabras en libertad: Actualidad del Estridentismo." *Guángara Libertaria* [Miami FL] III.9 (invierno 1982): n. pag.

Balakian, Anna. "Latin American Poets and the Surrealist Heritage." *Surrealismo /Surrealismos: Latinoamérica y España*. Philadelphia: Congreso del Instituto Internacional de Literatura Iberoamericana, 1975.

——————. *The Symbolist Movement: A Critical Appraisal*. New York: Random House, 1967.

Ballman, Jacqueline. "Sous le ligne du Mythe et de la poésie trois cents de quarante deux pays etaient presents a la Ve Biennale de Knokke." [Unidentified Belgian newspaper, 1959]: 5, 8.

Bardack Kiess, Emily, Larry Rinder and Philip Yenawine. *Cubism*. New York: Museum of Modern Art, n.d.

Barr, Alfred H., Jr. *Cubism and Abstract Art*. New York: Arno Press, 1966.

Barreiro Tablada, Enrique. "El 'joven maestro' se ha vuelto un burgués de la judicatura." *El Universal Ilustrado* [Jalapa] 2 julio 1925: 44, 90.

Barrios, Roberto. "Libros y revistas que llegan." Rev. of *Poemas Interdictos* by Manuel Maples Arce. *El Universal Ilustrado* XI.541 (22 sept. 1927): 55.

——————. "Urbe." Sec. "Libros y revistas que llegan."

El Universal Ilustrado 31 julio 1924: n. pag.

Bartolo Hernández, Juan, y Franciso R. Illescas. *Escritores veracruzanos: reseña biográfico-antológica.* Veracruz, 1945.

Beals, Carleton. *Mexican Maze.* Philadelphia: Lippincott, 1931 [Ch. 17: "The Noisemakers].

_____. "The Noisemakers: the 'Estridentistas' and Other Writers of Revolutionary Mexico." *The Bookman* LXIX (May 1929): 280-285.

Benítez, Fernando. "Conversaciones con Manuel Maples Arce." *Sábado* [Sup. de *unomásuno* 160 (29 nov. 1980): 3-4.

Bergsten, Staffan. *Time and Eternity: A Study in the Structure and Symbolism of T. S. Eliot's 'Four Quartets.'* Sweden: Berlmgska Boktryckeriet Lund, 1960.

Bierly, Rachel. "Mexican Avant-Garde: What is Estridentismo Mexicano," 2/6/2020. *https://www.panoramas.pitt.edu/art-and-culture/mexican-avant-garde-what-estridentismo-mexicano.* Accessed 10/15/21.

Bolaño, Roberto. "Tres estridentistas en 1976" (Arqueles Vela, Manuel Maples Arce, List Arzubide). *Plural* 62 (nov. 1976): 48-60.

Bonifaz Nuño, Rubén. "El primer Maples Arce." *La Gaceta,* nueva época, 128 (agosto 1981): n. pag.

Borges, Jorge Luis. "Acotaciones." "Los *Andamios Interiores* de Manuel Maples Arce." *Proa* I (dic. 1922): 120-123.

_____. Alberto Hidalgo y Vicente Huidobro, eds. *Índice de la nueva poesía americana*. México y Buenos Aires: Sociedad de Publicaciones el Inca, 1926.

Bourdon, David. "The Jewels of Venice." *Vogue* August 1986: 82+.

Bravo, Víctor. "Huidobro y la Vanguardia." *Revista de Literatura Hispanoamericana*. Venezuela: Universidad de Zulia Maracaibo, 1977: n. pag.

Brotherston, Gordon. *Latin American Poetry: Origins and Presence*. London, New York and Melbourne: Cambridge University Press, 1975.

Burns, Ken. "The Brooklyn Bridge." Film [1981]. PBS 29 Jan. 1992.

Bustos Cerecedo, Miguel. "Manuel Maples Arce." *Punto y Aparte* [Xalapa] 31 enero 1980: n. pag.

Cahiers Dada Surrealisme (Cahiers de l'association internationale pour l'etude de Dada et du Surrealisme) No. 2. France: Lettres Modernes, 1968.

Caillet-Bois, Julio. *Antología de la poesía hispanoamericana*. Madrid: Aguilar, 1965.

Cajero Vázquez, Antonio. "Manuel Maples Arce en Manomètre," *Literatura mexicana* 2010, Volumen 21, No. 2: 265-270.

Calder, Nigel. *Einstein's Universe*. New York: Viking Press, 1979.

Camargo B., Angelina. "Hará el IPN el primer Encuentro de Poesía Mexicana y Latinoamericana; Ocho Países." *Excélsior* 19 marzo 1981: n. pag.

Cansinos-Asséns, Rafael. *La nueva literatura, Vol. III: La evolución de la poesía (1917-1927): Colección de estudios críticos*. Madrid: Editorial Páez, 1927.

Cantú, Arturo. "Política de la Cultura: El desconocido Maples Arce." *Sábado* 67, 1978: n. pag.

Caracciolo Trejo, E. *La poesía de Vicente Huidobro y la Vanguardia*. Madrid: Editorial Gredos, 1974.

Cárdenas, Gilda, Carmina Chíchara y Armando Torres Michua. "Decían que el mural era de Diego." [Unidentified Mexican newspaper] 18 abril 1982: n. pag.

Carter, Boyd G. *Historia de la literatura hispanoamericana a través de sus revistas*. México, 1968.

_____. *Revistas literarias de Hispanoamérica: breve historia y contenido*. México, 1959.

Casan. "El Arte Africano y el Cubismo." *El Universal Ilustrado* 24 julio 1924: n. pag.

Castillo, Carlos de. [No title.] *Revista de Revistas* 14 feb. 1926: n. pag.

Castro Leal, Antonio. *Las cien mejores poesías mexicanas modernas*. México: Porrúa, 1939.

_____. *La poesía mexicana moderna*. México: Fondo de Cultura Económica, 1953.

_____. "La poesía mexicana moderna." Discurso leído ante la Academia Mexicana de la Lengua. México: Academia Mexicana de la Lengua, 1953.

Cervalán, Octavio. *Modernismo y vanguardia* (Coordenados de la literatura hispanoamericana del siglo XX). New York: Las Américas, 1967.

Cervera, Juan. "Manuel Maples Arce: Del Estridentismo al Humanismo." *El Nacional* 11 marzo 1980: n. pag.

Chareyre, Antoine, translator to the French of Manuel Maples Arce, *Stridentisme!* Paris: Le Temps des Cerises, 2013.

Chipp, Herschel B. *Theories of Modern Art: A Source Book by Artists and Critics.* Los Angeles: University of California Press, 1968.

Churchill, Allen. *The Literary Decade.* Englewood Cliffs NJ: Prentice Hall, Inc., 1971.

Coignard, Jerónimo [Francisco Zamora]. "Epístola estridentista." *El Universal Ilustrado* 17 abril 1924: 11.

Collazos, Óscar, Julio Cortázar y Mario Vargas Llosa, eds. *Literatura en la Revolución y Revolución en la Literatura.* México: Siglo Veintiuno Editores, SA, 1979.

Comunidad 46 [Mexico: Universidad Iberoamericana] VIII.46 (dic. 1973): n. pag.

"Conferencia sobre Maples Arce Pronuncia en Lima R[ogelio] Sinán." *La Estrella de Panamá* [Panamá] 4 mayo 1948: n. pag.

Constantine, Mildred. *Tina Modotti: Una Vida Frágil.* México: Fondo de Cultura Económica, 1979.

"Cordialité, Eclectisme et Prêtige." *Le Journal des Poètes* 8 (oct. 1961): n. pag.

Cortés Gaviño, Agustín, et al., eds. *Xilote* [México]. Primavera 1973. [Special issue on Estridentismo.]

Costa, René de. "Pablo Neruda's *Tentativa del hombre infinito:* Notes for a Reappraisal." *Modern Philology* 73.2 (Nov. 1973).

———. *Vicente Huidobro y el Creacionismo.* Madrid: Taurus Ediciones, 1975.

Costa Lima, Luiz. *Lira e Antilira.* Brasil: Editora Civilição Brasileira, 1968.

Cosío Villegas, Daniel, ed. *Historia general de México*. México: El Colegio de México, Centro de Estudios Históricos, 1976.

Crane, Hart. *The Bridge*. Ed. Thomas A. Vogler. New York and London: Liveright, 1970.

Crespo, Ángel, ed. *Antología de la Poesía Brasileña: Desde el Romanticismo a la Generación del Cuarenta y cinco*. Barcelona: Seix Barral, 1973.

Dante Alighieri. *The Divine Comedy*. Trans. C. H. Sisson. Chicago: Regnery Gateway, 1980.

_____. *Inferno*. Trans. Allan Mandelbaum. New York: Bantam Books, 1982.

Davidson, Morris. *An Approach to Modern Painting*. New York: Coward-McCann, Inc., 1948.

Debicki, Andrew P. *Poetas hispanoamericanos contemporáneos: punto de vista, perspectiva, experiencia*. Madrid: Gredos, 1976.

Delano, Luis Enrique. "Manuel Maples Arce." *El Día* 4 julio 1981: [Sección Opinión-Doctrina.]

DeWitt Sanders, Gerald, John Herbert Nelson and M. L. Rosenthal, eds. *Chief Modern Poets of Britain and America*. 2 vols. London: MacMillan Co., 1964.

Díaz-Plaja, Guillermo. *Vanguardismo y Protesta*. Barcelona: Libros de la Frontera, 1975.

Diehl, Gaston. *Picasso*. New York: Crown Publishers, Inc., 1977.

Díez-Canedo, Enrique. *Letras de America*. México: Fondo de Cultura Económica, 1944.

_____. *La nueva poesía*. México: Colección Siglo XX, Ediciones Encuadernables de *El Nacional*, 1941.

Díez-Echarri, Emiliano, y José María Roca Franquesa. *Historia de la literatura española e hispanoamericana.* Madrid: Aguilar, 1972.

d'Harnoncourt, Anne. *Futurism and the International Avant-Garde.* New Haven: Eastern Press, 1980.

Dos Passos, John. *Metropolis.* [Trans. of *Urbe* by Manuel Maples Arce.] New York: T. S. Book Co., 1929.

Drew, Elizabeth. *T. S. Eliot: The Design of His Poetry.* New York: Charles Scribner's Sons, 1949.

Duque de Fréneuse. [See Manuel Maples Arce.]

Durán Rosado, Esteban. "La historia de sí mismo." Rev. of *A la orilla de este río. Revista mexicana de cultura* [Sup. de *El Nacional*] 12 julio 1964: 10.

Eastman, Max. *The Literary Mind: Its Place in an Age of Science.* New York and London: Charles Scribner's Sons, 1935.

Echeverría del Prado, Vicente, y Ramón Gálvez. "Pausas literarias." Sup. dom. de *Novedades* 7 nov. 1948: n. pag.

Eliot, T. S. *To Criticize the Critic.* New York: Farrar, Straus and Giroux, 1965.

———. *"The Waste Land" and Other Poems.* New York: Harcourt, Brace and World, Inc., 1934.

"Una entrevista con el embajador Maples Arce." *México en Marcha,* 1951: n. pag.

"El Estridentismo contribuyó a modificar los conceptos artísticos tradicionales." *Gaceta UNAM,* n.d.

"El Estridentismo." Exhibit program. UNAM, Dirección General de Difusión Cultural. Casa del Lago. 23 abril 1983.

"El Estridentismo: Memoria y Valoracion." *Punto y aparte* [Jalapa, Ver.]. Sup. especial. 26 nov. 1981.

"Evocación del Movimiento Estridentista." Exposición 7 feb. 1972. Invitación y Programa. México DF: Sociedad Mexicana de Geografía y Estadística, enero 1972.

Escalante, Evodio. *Elevación y caída del estridentismo*. México: Conaculta, Ediciones Sin Nombre, 2002.

"Exposición German Cueto, 1893-1975. Homenaje a sus 60 años de labor artística: esmaltes, y otras técnicas." Programa. Museo de Arte Moderno [México], mayo/julio 1981.

Fernández Moreno, César. *Introducción a la poesía*. México: Fondo de Cultura Económica, Colección Popular #30, 1962.

Ferrand, Diógenes. "Crónicas Exclusivas de España: el Triunfo de un Poeta Mexicano en el Ateneo de Madrid." *El Universal Ilustrado* 9 marzo 1922.

Ferro, Hellén. *Historia de la poesía hispanoamericana*. New York: Las Américas, 1964.

Fitzgerald, F. Scott. *The Great Gatsby*. New York: Charles Scribner's Sons, 1925.

Fiumi, Lionello. "Al paese dei vulcani–ministri e ambasciatori scelti fra i poeti–Questo e il messicano Manuel Maples Arce." [Unidentified Italian newspaper, c. 1941: n. pag.]

_____. "Éste es el mexicano Manuel Maples Arce." Sup. de *El Nacional* [México], n.d.: n. pag.

———. "Panorama della poesia messicana." *Meridiano di Roma* 4 May 1941: 8.

Flores, Tatiana. "Clamoring for attention in Mexico City: Manuel Maples Arce's avant-garde manifesto Actual No. 1," *Review: Literature and Arts of the Americas*, Volume 37, 2004, Issue 2: 208-220.

Forster, Merlin. *An Index to Mexican Literary Periodicals.* New York and London: Scarecrow Press, 1966.

———. *"Letras de México:" Índice anotado.* México: Universidad Iberoamericana, 1972.

———. *La muerte en la poesía mexicana.* México: Editorial Diógenes, S. A., 1970

———. ed. *Tradition and Renewal: Essays on Twentieth-Century Latin American Literature and Culture.* Urbana, Chicago and London: University of Illinois Press, 1975.

Fowlie, Wallace, ed. *Mid-Century French Poets.* New York: Twayne Publishers, Inc., 1955.

Franco, Jean. *César Vallejo: The Dialectic of Poetry and Silence.* Cambridge, London, New York and Melbourne: Cambridge University Press, 1976.

Frank, Joseph. "Spatial Form in Modern Literature." *Sewanee Review* 53 (Spring, Summer, Autumn 1945). Reprinted in *Criticism: The Foundations of Modern Literary Judgement.* Eds. Schorer, et al. New York: Harcourt, Brace, n.d.

Fréneuse, el Duque de. [See Manuel Maples Arce.]

Frías, José D. "Un Manifiesto Literario." *Revista de Revistas* 8 enero 1922: n. pag.

_____. "El nido de avispas y la literatura mexicana." *El Universal Ilustrado* 5 feb. 1925: 48.

Friedrich, Otto. *Before the Deluge: A Portrait of Berlin in the 1920's.* New York: Avon Books, 1972.

"Fundó el movimiento estridentista—El diplomático Manuel Maples Arce, que nos envió México, opina que la poesía es absorbente; genio y figura." [Unidentified Chilean newspaper, 1949.]

"Futurism and Photography." Exhibit. Museum of Art, Pennsylvania State University. University Park. 7 July-26 August 1984.

"El Futurismo. La Última Palabra en el Arte." *Revista de Revistas* 31 agosto 1919: n. pag

Gallardo, Salvador. *9 Sonetos de amor.* Aguascalientes, 1950

_____. *El Pentagrama Eléctrico.* Puebla, Méx.: Ediciones Germán List Arzubide, 1925.

García Maroto, Gabriel. *Galería de los poetas nuevos de México.* Madrid: La Gaceta Literaria, 1928.

Godoy, Emma. *Sombras de magia: Teorías estéticas de Rabindranath Tagore.* [México, 1968]

Goic, Cedomil. *La Poesía de Vicente Huidobro.* Santiago de Chile: Ediciones de los Anales de la Universidad de Chile, 1955.

Golding, John. *Cubism: A History and an Analysis, 1907-1914.* New York: George Wittenborn Inc. 1959.

Golwarz, Sergio. "La simulación en el arte." *Estaciones* [México] II.5 (Primavera 1957): 71-93.

Gómez-Gil, Orlando. *Literatura Hispanoamericana: Antología Crítica, Tomo II.* New York, Toronto and London: Holt, Rhinehart, Winston, 1971.

González Casanova, P. "Las metáforas de Arqueles Vela." *El Universal Ilustrado* 29 mayo 1924: 42, 92.

González Guerrero, Francisco. "Memorial de la Sangre." *Los libros de los otros*. México: Ediciones Chapultepec, 1947: 57-65.

_____. "Manuel Maples Arce: 'Memorial de la Sangre.'" Rev. Sec."Autores y Libros," *El Universal Ilustrado* 27 julio 1945: 3, 8.

_____. Review. "Autores y Libros." *El Universal* 21 julio 1945: n. pag.

González Ramírez, Manuel, y Rebeca Torres Ortega. *Poetas de México*. México: Editorial América, 1945.

González Stephan, Beatriz. "La narrativa del estridentismo: *El café de nadie* de Arqueles Vela," *Nuevo Texto Crítico*, Año 1, Primer semestre de 1988: 133-149.

"El gran poeta mexicano Maples Arce habla de los rumbos poéticos de hoy: es el Lic. Maples Arce el Embajador de México en nuestra república." *El Panamá-América* 3 feb. 1945: 18.

Gray, Christopher. *Cubist Aesthetic Theories*. Baltimore: Johns Hopkins Press, 1967.

Gringoire, Pedro. "Niñez Provinciana de un Poeta." Rev. of *A la orilla de este río* by Manuel Maples Arce. Sec."Libros de Nuestros Tiempos." *Excélsior* 2 sept. 1964: 4.

Gullón, Germán. *Poesía de la Vanguardia Española*. Madrid: Taurus, 1981.

Hartley, Anthony, ed. *The Penguin Book of French Verse: the Nineteenth Century*. Baltimore: Penguin Books, 1965.

Hemingway, Ernest. *A moveable feast*. New York: Charles Scribner's Sons, 1964.

[Henestrosa, Andrés?] A. H. "Notas bibliográficas: literatura de guerrillas." *El Libro y el Pueblo* XIV (mayo-junio 1941): n. pag.

Hernández Palacios, Esther, ed. *Estridentismo: Memoria y Valoración* México: Fondo de Cultura Económica, 1983. [Proceedings from Nov. 1981 Homenaje a MMA in Jalapa.]

Hernández-Rodríguez, Rafael. "Whose Sweaty Men Are They? Avant-Garde and Revolution in México," *CiberLetras: revista de crítica literaria y de cultura*, No. 8, 2002.

Hess, Eva, ed. *New Approaches to Ezra Pound*. Berkeley and Los Angeles: University of California Press, 1969.

Hewes, Timothy. *Surrealism—a Celebration: Exhibition of Surrealist Art*. Exhibit program. University Park: Pennsylvania State University, 1974.

Hilton, Timothy. *Picasso*. New York: Oxford University Press, 1975.

Hirschfield, Susan B. *Kandinsky in Munich: 1896-1914*. Exhibit and program. New York: The Solomon R. Guggenheim Foundation, 1982.

Holman, C. Hugh. *A Handbook to Literature*. Indianapolis and New York: Bobbs-Merrill Co., 1972.

"Homenaje a Manuel Maples Arce, veracruzano distinguido." Programa. Xalapa, Ver., 25 nov. 1981.

"Homenaje al estridentismo mexicano." *Nivel, gaceta de cultura* 86 (25 feb. 1970): n. pag.

Horta, Manuel. "El 'Chauvre-Souris' mexicano: obras y

decorado para el (primer) teatro 'murciélago' de México." *El Universal Ilustrado* 5 junio 1924: n. pag.

———. "Introito sobre el pelo y el espíritu. *El Universal Ilustrado* 21 agosto 1924: 20-21.

———. "Puntos de vista." *El Universal Ilustrado* 7 agosto 1924: 16.

Hughes, Robert. "Futurism's Farthest Frontier." [USSR] *Time* 9 July 1979: 58-59.

———. "Gleams from a Gorgeous Twilight." [Vienna] *Time* 21 July 1986: 66-69.

———. "'Kill the Moonlight!' They Cried." [Venice retrospective of Italian Futurism] *Time* 4 August 1986: 66-67.

———. "The Show of Shows." [Picasso] *Time* 26 May 1980: 70-76.

———. "The Tintoretto of the Peons." [Diego Rivera] *Time* 9 June 1986: 78-79.

Huidobro, Vicente. *Obras completas, Vol. I: Poesía y Manifiestos*. Santiago de Chile: Zig-Zag, 1964.

J. C. O. "Antología de la poesía mexicana moderna." *Revista Portuguesa Mensal* XIV.41 (setembro 1941): n. pag.

Jiménez Rueda, Julio. *Historia de la literatura mexicana*. México: Ediciones Botas, 1942.

Kazin, Alfred. *An American Procession: The Major American Writers from 1830 to 1930–the Crucial Century*. New York: Alfred A. Knopf, Inc., 1984.

Kaufmann, Walter. *The Portable Nietzsche*. New York: Viking Penguin, Inc., 1982.

Kermode, Frank, ed. *Selected Prose of T. S. Eliot*. New

York: Farrar, Straus and Giroux, Inc., 1965.

Klich, Lynda. *The Noisemakers: Estridentismo, Vanguardism, and Social Action in Postrevolutionary Mexico.* Oakland, CA: University of California Press, 2018.

Kyn Taniya. [See Luis Quintanilla.]

Labastida, Jaime. "Los Estridentistas Hoy." *Plural* XI-III.123 (dic. 1981): n. pag.

Lafuente, Mireya. "Raigambre y Proyección del Arte." *Pro Arte* [México, n.d.: n. pag.]

Lamothe, Louis. *Los mayores poetas latinoamericanos de 1850 a 1950.* México: B. Costa-Amic, 1959.

Lamour, Felipe. "Poemas de Felipe Lamour." Trans. Manuel Maples Arce. *Crisol* III.5 (7 enero 1929): 418-426.

Last, Rex W. *German and Dadaist Literature: Kurt Schwitters, Hugo Ball, Hans Arp.* New York: Twayne Publishers, Inc., 1973.

_____. *Hans Arp, the Poet of Dadaism.* Chester Spring [MD?]: Sufour Editions, Inc., 1969.

Latcham, Ricardo A. "Manuel Maples Arce." *La Nación* [Santiago de Chile] 12 feb. 1951: n. pag.

_____. "'Memorial de la Sangre' de Manuel Maples Arce." Página Literaria, Sup. dom. de *La Nación* [Santiago de Chile] 4 mayo 1947: 16.

Leal, Luis. *Breve historia de la literatura hispanoamericana.* New York: Knopf, 1971: 179-93 [la Vanguardia].

LeBihan, Adrien. Rev. of *A la orilla de este río* by Manuel Maples Arce. *Cahiers du Sud.* [Marseille, France] 52.381: 139-40.

Leiva, Raúl. *Aproximación a la poesía*. México: Gráficas Menhir, 1968.

―――――. *Imagen de la poesía mexicana contemporánea*. México: Imprenta Universitaria, 1959.

―――――. "Manuel Maples Arce y el Estridentismo." *Revista mexicana de cultura*. [Sup. de *El Nacional*] 1 sept. 1957: 8-9.

Leredo, Pablo [Febronio Ortega]. "Libros y revistas que llegan." Rev. of *El meridiano lírico* by Luis Marín Loya. *El Universal Ilustrado* 25 marzo 1926: n. pag.

Levy, Roger. "Manifiesto." [Unidentified newspaper] 3 July 1924: n. pag.

"Libros y revistas que llegan." Rev. of *Urbe* by Manuel Maples Arce. *El Universal Ilustrado* [julio-oct] 1924: n. pag.

Lima, Robert. "Toward Gnosis: Exegesis of Valle-Inclan's *La lámpara maravillosa*." 8 pp. Typescript of a paper. From author's library.

List Arzubide, Germán. *Esquina*. México: Librería Cicerón, 1923.

―――――. "El Estridentismo ha muerto. ¡Viva el Estridentismo!" *Diorama de la Cultura* [Sup. de *Excélsior*] [nov. 1981]: 16.

―――――. *El movimiento estridentista*. Jalapa, Ver.: Ediciones de Horizonte, 1927 [31 dic. 1926-1 enero 1927].

―――――. *El movimiento estridentista*. México: Secretaría de Educación Pública, Cuadernos de lectura popular, 1967.

―――――. "Poemas de Germán List Arzubide." *El Universal Ilustrado* 5 dic. 1923: n. pag.

———. "Soberana Juventud." Rev. of *Soberana Juventud* by Manuel Maples Arce. *El libro y el pueblo* 39 (abril 1968): 38-39.

Lista, Giovanni, and Yolanda Tincerre. *Futurism and Photography*. Greenwale: Hillwood Art Gallery, 1984.

"Literatura mexicana contemporánea. 35 poetas." México: *El Nacional*, 1939.

Litvak, Lily. *A Dream of Arcadia (Anti-Industrialism in Spanish Literature, 1895-1905)*. Austin and London: University of Texas Press, 1975.

Lozano, Rafael. "El endemoniado 'Dada' se adueña de París." *El Universal Ilustrado* 3 feb. 1921: 28-29, 43.

———. "Marinetti y la Última Renovación Futurista: 'El Tactilismo.'" *El Universal Ilustrado* 3 marzo 1921: 19, 46.

Lucie-Smith, Edward, ed. *Primer of Experimental Poetry I: 1870-1922*. Indianapolis and New York: Bobbs-Merrill Co., 1971.

Magis, Carlos H. *La poesía hermética de Octavio Paz*. México, 1978.

Maidanik, Marcos. *Vanguardismo y revolución: metodología de la renovación estética*. Montevideo: Editorial Alfa, 1960.

Maldonado, Tomás. *Vanguardia y racionalidad: Artículos, ensayos y otros escritos: 1946-1974*. [Trans. of "Avanguardia e razionalita: Articoli, saggi, pamphlets: 1946-1974"]. Barcelona: Editorial Gustavo Gili, SA, 1977.

"Manuel Maples Arce (1900-1981)." Sec."Inventario," *Plural* 6 (junio 1981): n. pag.

"Manuel Maples Arce: Embajador de México." [Unidentified newspaper.] Beirut, Lebanon, 27 July 1964: n. pag.

"Manuel Maples Arce, en los Domingos Literarios del INBA." *Excélsior* 28 junio 1980: [5].

"Maples Arce, I." [Interview.] *Plural* nov. 1976: 53-56.

Maples, Manuel [Sr.]. "A José Martí." [Poem written in Veracruz in June 1895.] *Hero* [Cuba], abril 1910: n. pag.

Maples Arce, Manuel. *A la orilla de este río*. Madrid: Plenitud, 1964.

———. "Actual No. 1: Comprimido Estridentista" de Manuel Maples Arce. México: n.p., 1921.

———. "Alegría y queja de Panamá." *Cuadernos Americanos* [Mexico] XXXVI.1 (enero-feb. 1977: 185-195.

———. *Andamios Interiores: Poemas Radiograficos*. México: Editorial "Cultura," 1922.

———. *Anthology of Mexican Poets*. Trans. Edna Worthley Underwood. Portland, ME: Mosher, 1932.

———. *Antología de la poesía mexicana moderna*. Roma: Poligrafica Tiberina, 1940.

———. "Arqueles Vela." Discurso para el Homenaje a Arqueles Vela (leído en ausencia). Typescript [from Maples library: n.d.]

———. "Bajo el mito de las estrellas" [Prólogo a *Mi vida por el mundo*]. *Diorama de la Cultura*. [Sup. de *Excélsior*] 4 abril 1976: 10, 11.

———. "Bibliográficas de 'El Heraldo.'" *El Heraldo* 16 marzo 1923: n. pag.

_____. "¿Cuál es mi mejor poesía?" [Óscar Leblanc] *El Universal Ilustrado* 12 junio 1924: 38.

_____. "Cuando llegue el otoño." [Prose poem probably later included in *Rag*.] Sec. "Página literaria de los lunes." *El Dictamen* [Veracruz] XIX.2063 (30 abril 1917): 5.

_____. *El Dictamen* [Veracruz] 1 feb. 1917: n. pag. [Text of speech given in honor of arrival of Spanish poet Salvador Rueda to Veracruz.]

_____. "Diego M. Ribera [sic]." Entrevista. *Zig-Zag* 68 (28 julio 1921): 34.

_____. "Diorama Estridentista." *El Universal Ilustrado* 21 feb. 1924: 10.

_____. Discurso leído por Blanca V. de Maples. "Homenaje a Manuel Maples Arce." [Jalapa] nov. 1981. [Typescript of quotes from his work. Maples library.]

_____. *Ensayos japoneses*. México: Cultura, 1959.

_____. [El Duque de Fréneuse]. "Los Escaparates de Plateros: Directorio Sentimental de la Ciudad de México." *Zig-Zag* 68 (28 julio 1921): 35.

_____. "España 1936." Phonograph record. [Poem from *Memorial de la Sangre*.] Paris: Ediciones Fonoric, 1936.

_____. "El espíritu del plan educativo." Radio-conferencia dictado por la estación XEFO. México, 21 abril 1934. [Text.]

_____. "Esquemas y retratos de Chile." *El Nacional* [México: n.d., n. pag.]

_____. "El estridentismo valorado por Maples

Arce." *El Gallo Ilustrado* [Sup. de *El Día*] 643 (20 oct. 1974): n. pag.

_____. *Incitaciones y valoraciones*. México: Cuadernos Americanos, 1956.

_____. Interview notes. Typescript (20pp). [c. 1971. From Maples Library.]

_____. y Fermín Revueltas, eds. *Irradiador* 1, 2, 3 (sept., oct., nov. 1923) México, 1923.

_____. *Hommage a F. García Lorca*. Bruxelles, n p. [41, Rue Papenkasteel, UCCLE, Bruxelles], 1938.

_____. "Jazz XY" y "Manifiesto." *El Universal Ilustrado* 3 julio 1924: n. pag.

_____. *Leopoldo Méndez*. México: Fondo de Cultura Económica, 1970.

_____. Letter to the present writer, 20 May 1981.

_____. Letter to Sr. Don Porfirio Martínez Peñaloza (México). [On *Estridentismo*.] Oslo, 12 mayo 1960.

_____. Manifiestos (Actual No. 1, Manifiesto Estridentista No. 2). [Texts from Maples library. Also in Luis Mario Schneider, *El Estridentismo, México 1921-1927* [Anthology]. México: UNAM, 1985.

_____. *Memorial de la Sangre*. México: Talleres Gráficos de la Nación, 1947.

_____. "Memorias." *Revista de UNAM* XXI (agosto 1967): 19-27.

_____. *Metropolis*. Trans. John Dos Passos. [Trans. of *Urbe*, 1924.] New York: T. S. Book Co., 1929.

———. *Modern Mexican Art*. London: A. Zwemmer, 1944.

———. "El movimiento estridentista en 1922." *El Universal Ilustrado* 28 dic. 1922.

———. "El movimiento social en Veracruz." (Conferencia sustentada en la Cámara del Trabajo de Jalapa.) 1 mayo 1927.

———. "Nicolas Beauduin." Sec. "Los poetas de Francia." *Zig-Zag* 4 mayo 1922: 43.

———. "Oigan a Maples Arce." [Unidentified magazine] 34 (Primavera 1973): n. pag.

———. "El origen del vanguardismo en México." *La Cultura en México* [Sup. de *Siempre*] 276 (31 mayo 1967): I-VI.

———. "El paisaje en la literatura mexicana." [Unidentified Chilean? newspaper. Fragment from the essay for the University of Cambridge, England.] Primavera de 1944: n. pag.

———. *El paisaje en la literatura mexicana*. México: Porrúa, 1944.

———. "El pensamiento internacional de Bolívar." [Unidentified newspaper or magazine.]

———. [Duque de Fréneuse]. "Pinceladas de colores: los cabarets." *Zig-Zag* 14 abril 1921: 32-33.

———. *Peregrinación por el arte de México*. Buenos Aires, 1951.

———. trans. "Poemas de Felipe Lamour." *Crisol* III.5 (7 enero 1929): 418-426.

———. *Poemas Interdictos*. Jalapa: Ediciones de Horizonte, 1927.

———. "Poemas intuitivos." "Los nuevos poetas de Veracruz." *El Universal Ilustrado* 12 oct. 1922: 48.

———. *Poèmes Interdits*. Trans. Edmond Vandercammen. Bruxelles: *Les Cahiers du Journal Des Poètes*, 1936.

———. "La poesía mexicana en Bélgica." [Unidentified newspaper] 15 feb. 1948: n. pag.

———. "La poesía no es aceptada por el público mexicano porque nuestra educación es insuficiente: M. Arce." *unomásuno* 28 junio 1980: 19.

———. [*Rag. Tintas de abanico*. Veracruz: Catalán Hnos., 1920. Prose poems. Rejected by MMA; not available.]

———. "Remembranza de Gregorio López y Fuentes." *La Semana de Bellas Artes* 155 (19 nov. 1980): 15.

———. *Las semillas del tiempo*. México: Fondo de Cultura Económica, 1981.

———. ed. *Siete cuentos mexicanos*. Panamá: Biblioteca Selecta I.5 (mayo 1946).

———. "La sistematización de los movimientos literarios." *El Universal Ilustrado* 10 julio 1924: 57.

———. "Soberana Juventud." Typescript notes for a draft. Maples library.

———. *Soberana Juventud*. Madrid: Plenitud, 1967.

———. "Tres Poemas ('Metamorfosis,' 'Plenitud,' 'Mensaje'). *Revista de América* [Sup. de *El Tiempo,* Bogota) IV.12 (dic. 1945): 368-369.

———. "Two Poems," in "'Chants' by David P.

Berenberg, And Two Poems by Maples Arce." *Poems for a Dime* 4 & 5. Boston: John Wheelwright, 7 June 1935.

_____. *Urbe: Super-poema bolchevique en 5 cantos*. México: Andrés Botas e Hijo, 1924.

_____. "El verdadero Juárez y el falso Bulnes." *Voces sobre Juárez*. México: Procuraduría General de la República, Colección Libro Abierto No. 2, 1972: 41-63.

_____. "Viejo y nuevo Japón." Exhibit program. México: Sociedad Mexicana de Geografía y Estadística, marzo 1972.

"Maples Arce, poeta de México." *Pro Arte* [Santiago de Chile] II.62.10 (15 sept. 1949): 3, 5.

"Maples Arce: Renovó el estridentismo al movimiento modernista." *Punto y aparte* [Xalapa] 3.74 (enero 1980): 5.

Marinetti, F. T. *The Futurist Cookbook* [trans. of "La cucina futurista"]. Trans. Suzanne Brill. Ed. Lesley Chamberlain. San Francisco: Bedford Arts 1989.

Marín Loya, Luis. "Libros y revistas que llegan." Rev. of *Urbe* by Manuel Maples Arce. *El Universal Ilustrado* 31 julio 1924: II-III.

_____. "El meridiano lírico: Manuel Maples Arce." [Rev. of *Urbe* and some early poems later published in *Andamios Interiores*.] *Zig-Zag* II.77 (29 sept. 1921): 46.

Mariscol Acosta, Amanda. *La poesía de Jose Juan Tablada*. México: n.p., 1949.

Márquez Rodiles, Ignacio. Letter to Germán List Arzubide [on the revitalization of *Estridentismo*] 15 feb. 1982. From Maples library.

Martínez, José Luis. *La literatura*. México: Fondo de Cultura Económica, [c. 1960]. (Sobretiro de *México: Cincuenta años de revolución, IV: la cultura.*)

_____. *Literatura mexicana siglo XX 1910-1949, tomo 1*. México: Antigua Librería Robredo, 1949.

Martínez Bonati, Félix. "La estética de la recepción." *Reseñas* [Columbia University] IV.10 (1979): 103-106.

Materer, Timothy. *Vortex: Pound, Eliot and Lewis*. Ithaca and London: Cornell University Press, 1979.

Matthews, J. H. *An Anthology of French Surrealist Poetry*. Minneapolis: University of Minnesota Press, 1966

Mediz Rolio, Antonio. "¿Qué opina Ud. del estridentismo?" *El Universal Ilustrado* 8 marzo 1923: n. pag.

Mejía, Eduardo. "Más allá del Estridentismo." Rev. of *Las semillas del tiempo* by Manuel Maples Arce. Sec. "Libros." *La guía* [Sup. dom. de *Novedades*] 24 (14 marzo 1982): 3.

Mejía Sánchez, Ernesto. "El estridentismo mexicano." *Diorama de Excélsior* [Sup. dom.] 15 sept. 1963: 3.

"Memorial de la Sangre." Rev. of *Memorial de la Sangre* by Manuel Maples Arce. *La Prensa* [Buenos Aires] 11 mayo 1947: n. pag.

Méndez, Evar. "Doce poetas nuevos." *Síntesis* II [Buenos Aires] 1928: n. pag.

Méndez de la Vega, Luz. Intro. "Homenaje a Maples Arce." Guatemala: Universidad de Guatemala, Dpto. de Letras, 1980.

Mendoza, el Abate de. [José María González de Mendoza]. [See Abate de Mendoza.]

Michelena, Margarita. "Mensaje a Margarita López Portillo." [Unidentified Mexican newspaper, late 70s-early 80s.]

Millán, María del Carmen. *Literatura mexicana*. México: Editorial Esfinge, S. A., 1963.

Miller, Edwin, ed. *A Century of Whitman Criticism*. Bloomington: Indiana University Press, 1969.

Molina, Javier. "I: El movimiento se originó como una reacción al modernismo, dice Manuel Maples Arce." *unomásuno* 1 julio 1980: 16.

_____. "II: Un escritor no debe detenerse ante ningún momento de su vida, siempre debe ir más lejos: Maples Arce." *unomásuno* 2 julio 1980: 27.

Monahan, Kenneth C. "El Estridentismo y los críticos." *Cuadernos Americanos*, 1974: 218-233.

Monguió, Luis. "Poetas postmodernistas mexicanos." *Revista Hispánica Moderna* [La Habana, Cuba] XII (julio-oct. 1946): 239-266.

Monsiváis, Carlos. *La poesía mexicana del siglo XX (Antología)*. México: Empresas Editoriales, 1966.

Montgomery, Harper. "Facture and Gloss: Making the Woodcut Modern in Mexico City, 1924-1928."

Moody, A. David. "Eliot's Formal Invention." Keynote Address. T. S. Eliot Centennial conference. University of Maine at Orono, 18-20 August 1988.

Morales, Miguel Ángel. "Caballada Intelectual." *Diorama de la Cultura* [7] mayo 1980: 8.

———. "Nuevas estridencias." *Diorama* [Sup. de *Excélsior*] 20 sept. 1981: 4-5.

———. "¡Viva el Mole de Guajolote!" *Diorama* [Sup. de *Excélsior*] 6 dic. 1981: n. pag.

Morse, Richard M. "Triangulating Two Cubists: William Carlos Williams and Oswald de Andrade." *Latin American Literary Review* XIV (Jan.-June 1986): 175-183.

Motherwell, Robert, ed. *The Dada Painters and Poets: An Anthology*. New York: Wittenborn, Schultz, Inc., 1951.

"El movimiento estridentista." Mesa redonda y exposición biblio-iconográfica. Programa. México: Biblioteca Nacional UNAM, 1 dic. 1971.

"El movimiento estridentista." *La Palabra y el Hombre*. Revista de la Universidad Veracruzana. [Xalapa, Ver., México] [Special issue.] Nueva época, oct.-dic. 1981.

"El movimiento estridentista—poesía y pintura." Programa. México: Procaduría General de Justicia del Distrito Federal, [1982].

"El movimiento estridentista, su respuesta de renovación." *Gaceta UNAM*. Quinta Época, II.33 (16 mayo 1983): 20, 29.

Movimientos literarios de vanguardia en Iberoamérica: Memoria del undécimo congreso (Celebrado en Austin y San Antonio, TX, 29-31 agosto 1963). México: Universidad de Texas México, 1965.

Muñoz, José Antonio. "Ni están todos los que son ni son todos los que están." *El Universal Ilustrado* 5 julio 1926: 11.

Muñoz Cota, José. "En Memoria: Manuel Maples Arce."

Novedades 7 julio 1981: 4, 21.

_____. "Memorias de Maples Arce: 'A la orilla de este río.'" *Revista Mexicana de Cultura* [Sup. de *El Nacional*] 895 (24 mayo 1964): 1-2.

Musgrove, S. *T. S. Eliot and Walt Whitman*. Wellington: New Zealand University Press, 1952.

Nadeau, Maurice. *The History of Surrealism*. Trans. Richard Howard. Intro. Roger Shattuck. New York: MacMillan, 1965.

Nänny, Max. "The Meaning of Form in T. S. Eliot's Poetry." Conference paper. T. S. Eliot Centennial conference. University of Maine at Orono, 18-20 August, 1988.

Nash, J. M. *Cubism, Futurism and Constructivism*. New York: Barron's Educational Series, Inc., 1974.

Neck, Mónico [Antonio Ancona Albertos]. "Apuntes de actualidad: Maples Arce, el artista/Maples Arce, diplomático." *El Nacional* 16 julio 1945: n. pag.

_____. "Apuntes de Actualidad." *El Universal* 16 julio 1944: 8.

Neruda, Pablo. *Obras completas*. Buenos Aires: Editorial Losada, S. A., 1962.

Noriega Hope, Carlos. "La T. S. H." *El Universal Ilustrado* 5 abril 1923: n. pag.

"La nota cultural." *El Nacional* [México] 18 nov 1949: 3, 7.

Novack, George, ed. *Existentialism vs. Marxism*. New York: Dell Publishing Co., 1966.

Nuila, Luis G. Rev. of *Andamios Interiores* by Manuel Maples Arce. *El Universal Ilustrado* 24 agosto 1922: 9.

Obligado, Pedro Miguel. *¿Qué es el verso?* Buenos Aires: Editorial Columba, 1957.

"Las obras del embajador mexicano en Colombia Excelentísimo Señor Maples Arce." [Unidentified newspaper, Colombia, 1951: n. pag.]

Ocampo de Gómez, Aurora, y Ernesto Prado Velázquez. *Diccionario de escritores mexicanos*. UNAM: Centro de Estudios Literarios, 1967.

Olson, Paul R. *Circle of Paradox: Time and Essence in the Poetry of Juan Ramón Jiménez*. Baltimore: Johns Hopkins Press, 1967.

Onís, Federico de. *Antología de la poesía española e hispanoamericana: 1882-1932*. New York: Las Américas, 1961.

Ontiveros, José Luis. "El Estridentismo: Manuel Maples Arce." *El Heraldo de Chihuahua*. 27 dic. 1982: n. pag.

Ortega, [Febronio]. [See also Pablo Leredo.] *Hombres, mujeres*. México: Ediciones de Bellas Artes, 1966.

_____. "Nuestro Apóstol Creacionista Maples Arce." *El Universal Ilustrado* 24 agosto 1922: 29, 56.

_____. [y Arqueles Vela.] "Zig-Zags en la República de las Letras: Lo que dijo a nuestro enviado especial Díaz Mirón." *El Universal Ilustrado* 6 sept. 1923: 29-30, 52-53.

Ortiz, Juan. "Manuel Maples Arce: biografía, estilo, obras y frases." *https://www.lifeder.com/manuel-maples-arce*. Accessed 10/15/21.

"Pablo Picasso: A Retrospective." Exhibit. New York: Museum of Modern Art, 1980.

Pacheco, Cristina. "Con motivo de los 80 años de Manuel Maples Arce: Un extraño rumor de mariposas." *El Gallo Ilustrado* [Sup. dom. de *El Día*] 933 (4 mayo 1980): n. pag.

⎯⎯⎯⎯. "El estridentismo, 60 años después, visto por Maples Arce, su gran gurú." *Siempre* [México] 1388 (30 enero 1980): n. pag.

Pacheco, José Emilio. "In Memoriam: Manuel Maples Arce (1900-1981)." *Sábado* [Sup. de *unomásuno*] 194 (25 julio 1981): 2-7.

"Las palabras en libertad." *Revista de Revistas* 26 sept. 1920: n. pag.

"Las Palabras y las Ideas: Versos de Manuel Maples Arce." Rev. of *Memorial de la Sangre* by Manuel Maples Arce. *La Hora* [Panamá] 25 mayo 1948: 7.

Papel, Juan de. "Se está escribiendo un libro." *Jueves* [c. 1945-47]: n. pag.

Parodi, Claudia. "Fracturas lingüísticas: Los estridentistas," *Mexican Studies / Estudios Mexicanos*, Vol.22, NO.2 (Summer 2006): 311-329.

Paz, Octavio, et al., eds. *The Siren and the Seashell (and Other Essays on Poets and Poetry)*. Austin and London: University of Texas Press, 1976.

Pérez, Alberto Julián. "La renovación de la poesía postvanguardista en Hispanoamérica," *Hispania*, March 1992.

Picon, Gaeton. *Surrealists and Surrealism*. New York: Rizzoli International Publications, Inc., 1977.

Plural XI-III.123 (dic. 1981). [Special issue on *Estridentismo*.]

"Un poeta peregrina por el arte de México." *Revista de América* [Bogotá] 25 oct. 1951: 10.

Poulet, Georges. *The Metamorphosis of the Circle*. Baltimore: Johns Hopkins Press, 1966.

Pound, Ezra. *Selected Poems*. Ed. T. S. Eliot. London: Faber and Faber, 1948.

Prado, Roberto Luis. "Manuel Maples Arce, el embajador de la poesía." [Unidentified newspaper, n.d.: n. pag.]

Preston, Raymond. *'Four Quartets' Rehearsed*. London: n.p., 1946.

Prieto, Adolfo. "El Martinfierrismo." *Revista de Literatura Argentina e Iberoamericana* I.1 (dic. 1959): 9-31.

"¿Qué opina Ud. del estridentismo?" *El Universal Ilustrado* 8 marzo 1923: n. pag.

"¿Qué significa estridentismo?" *Antorcha* 5 (nov. 1929): n. pag.

"¿Quién es el poeta más grande de México?" *El Universal Ilustrado* 21 sept. 1922: 37.

Quintanilla, Luis [Kyn Taniya]. *Avión (Poemas 1917-1923)*. México: Editorial Cultura, 1923.

_____. *Pintura ¿Moderna?* México: Organización Editorial Novararo, 1968.

_____. *Radio (Poema inalámbrico en trece mensajes)*. México: Editorial Cultura, 1924.

Rashkin, Elissa J. "Allá en el horizonte. El estridentismo en perspectiva regional," *LiminaR* versión on-line Vol. 13 No. 1, San Cristóbal de las Casas, ene./jun. 2015.

_____. "La poesía estridentista: vanguardismo y compromiso social," *Intersticios sociales* No. 4, Zapopan, sept. 2012

———. *The Stridentist Movement in Mexico: The Avant-Garde and Cultural Change in the 1920s.* Plymouth, UK: Lexington Books, 2011.

Review of *Urbe. El Demócrata* 2 agosto 1924: 3.

Reyes Nevares, Beatriz. "El México de la 'Belle Epoque' en el recuerdo de Manuel Maples Arce." *Siempre* 1024: 42-43.

Richardson, John. "Picasso's Sketchbooks: Genius at Work." *Vanity Fair* May 1986: 74-95.

Ripoll, Carlos. "*La Revista de Avance* (1927-1930): Episodio de la literatura cubana." Diss. NYU, 1964. [Chapter VII on Mexico, pp. 82-90.]

Rivera Marín, Guadalupe. "Diego [Ribera]: El 'sapo-rana' más humano y genial del mundo." *Casas y Gente* 15 (1987): 37-47.

Rizzuto, Anthony. *Style and Theme in Reverdy's "Les Ardoises du Toit."* Alabama: University of Alabama Press, 1971.

R. M. Rev. of *Siete cuentos mexicanos* by Manuel Maples Arce. *El Panamá-América* [Panamá] 8 junio 1946: n. pag.

Rodríguez, Antonio. "El Dibujo en Fernando Leal." Exhibit and program. México: Difusión Cultural/UNAM, Dpto. de Humanidades, Palacio de Minería, mayo/junio 1982.

———. "Una vida al servicio de la cultura mexicana: Manuel Maples Arce, el poeta que sembró la rebeldía en la lírica, y el diplomático que difunde los versos de mexicanos por el mundo." [*Siempre?*] n.d. [1952?]: 34-35.

Rodríguez González, Alberto. "La equivalencia como principio de composición en el poema 11-

35 P.M. de Germán List," *Revista destiempos.com*, Año 4, número 20, 15pp. Universidad Metropolitana, Iztapalapa. Accessed 10/15/21.

Rodríguez Prampolini, Ida. "La cultura como identidad nacional" (fotografías por Juan Rulfo). *Siempre* 1431: II-VI.

Rojas Garcidueñas, José. "Estridentismo y Contemporáneos." *Revista de la Universidad de México*. [México: UNAM] VI.7 (2 dic. 1952): 11.

Rómulo, Carlos P. "El embajador de Filipinas en Panamá, al rescate del Canal." *Siempre* 1024: n. pag.

Rosales, Salatiel. "¿Cuál es su mejor poesía?" *El Universal Ilustrado* 8 mayo 1924: 18, 45.

Rose, Barbara. "The Future is Now." *Vogue* October 1986: 490-493, 550.

Ruffinelli, Jorge. "Las memorias (éditas e inéditas) de Manuel Maples Arce." *Sábado* 13 feb. 1982: n. pag.

Ruiz Vernacci, Enrique [ERV]. "Feria de ingenios." [Unidentified newspaper or magazine, Panama, n.d.: n. pag.]

_____. "Manuel Maples Arce, poeta universal." Rev. of *Memorial de la Sangre* by Manuel Maples Arce. [Unidentified newspaper or magazine, Panama, c. 1947: n. pag.]

_____. "Un nuevo libro de versos de Maples Arce." *Revista Americana de Cultura* [Sup. de *El Nacional*, Panamá] 11 mayo 1947: 16, 18.

Sáenz, Vicente. "Homenaje al Estridentismo Mexicano." *Nivel* 86 (25 feb. 1970): n. pag.

Salas García, Luis. "Lic. Manuel Maples Arce." *Juu Papantlan* [Papantla, Ver., México] (Apuntes para la historia de Papantla.) México: Industria Gráfica, Editorial Mexicana, n.d.: n. pag.

Salazar Mallén, Rubén. "Desagravio: Maples Arce y Nandino." *Últimas noticias* 8 oct. 1977: 4+.

_____. "Letras." Rev. of *Ensayos japoneses* by Manuel Maples Arce. *Mañana* 15 agosto 1959: 56.

_____. "Estridentismo: La muerte de Maples Arce." *Excélsior* 1 julio 1981: 7, 8A.

_____. "Maples Arce, ensayista." Rev. of *Incitaciones y valoraciones* by Manuel Maples Arce. [Unidentified Mexican magazine, sec. "Letras," c. 1956]: 59.

_____. "Maples Arce: *Las semillas del tiempo*." Rev. *Excélsior* 13 marzo 1982: 7A.

Sánchez, Luis Alberto. *Nueva historia de la literatura americana*. Buenos Aires: Editorial Guaranía, 1950.

Schmeller, Alfred. *Cubism*. New York: Crown Publishers, Inc., n.d.

Schneider, Luis Mario. *El Estridentismo: Antología*. México: UNAM, Cuaderno de Humanidades 23, 1983.

_____. *El Estridentismo, México 1921-1927*. México: UNAM, 1985.

_____. *El estridentismo o una literatura de la estrategia*. Diss. UNAM, 1968.

_____. *La literatura mexicana*. Buenos Aires: Centro Editor de América Latina, 1967.

———. *México y el surrealismo: 1925-1950*. México: Arte y Libros, 1978.

"Kurt Schwitters (Merz-Dada)." Exhibit. New York: Museum of Modern Art, 10 June-1 Oct. 1985.

Shaviro, Steven. "'That which is Always Beginning': Stevens' Poetry of Affirmation." *PMLA* 100.2 (March 1985): 220-34.

Shelden, Michael. *The Lost Generation: American Writers in Paris in the 1920s.* Modern Scholar Series, Audible Books.

Sheridan, Guillermo, ed. (Introducción, selección y notas.) *Antología de la poesía mexicana moderna*, ed. Jorge Cuesta [1928]. México: Fondo de Cultura y Secretaría de Educación Pública, serie Lecturas Mexicanas, 1985.

———. ed. *Homenaje a los Contemporáneos: Monólogos en Espiral. Antología de Narrativa.* México: INBA, Cultura SEP, 1982.

———. "México, los 'Contemporáneos' y el nacionalismo." [*Plural?*] n.d.: 29-37.

———. "La Vanguardia Literaria." El Saldo Convulso de la Revolución: de 1920 a 1929. Jornadas Vasconselianas. Lecture. México: Auditorio Principal del Palacio de la Antigua Escuela de Medicina, 27 junio 1982.

Short, Robert. *Dada & Surrealism*. London: John Calmann & Cooper Ltd., 1980.

Sierra Partida, Alfonso. "Los 'ismos' poéticos contemporáneos." *Suplemento Cultural* [1967]: 3.

"Siete cuentos mexicanos." Rev. of *Siete cuentos mexicanos* by Manuel Maples Arce. *La Estrella de Panamá* 11 junio 1946: n. pag.

Silva Castro, Raúl. "Vicente Huidobro y el Creacionismo." *Revista Iberoamericana* XXV.49: n. pag.

Sirias, Silvio. "El estridentismo visto desde '80 H. P.,' " *Chasqui*, Vol. 17, No. 1 (May 1988): 75-83.

Sotomayor, Arturo. "La capital histórica...y sus personajes: academias extraescolares." [MMA pp. 63-64.] [Unidentified Mexican magazine, n.d.: n. pag.]

_____. "Estridentismo; Tránsito de Maples Arce." *unomásuno* 26 junio 1981: 17.

_____. "Manuel Maples Arce. Poeta Estridentista." *Sombras bajo la luna*. México: Porrúa, 1943: 173-184.

Spanos, William V. "Modern Literary Criticism and the Spatialization of Time: An Existential Critique." *Journal of Aesthetics* n.d.: 89-104.

Sparrow, John. *Sense and Poetry: Essays on the Place of Meaning in Contemporary Verse*. London: Constable & Co., Ltd., 1934.

Spender, Stephen. *The Imagination in the Modern World*. Washington DC: Library of Congress, 1962.

Spitzer, Leo. *La enumeración caótica en la poesía moderna*. Trans. Raimundo Lida. Buenos Aires: Universidad de Buenos Aires, Instituto de Filología, 1945.

Stein, Gertude. *Picasso*. Boston: Beacon Press, 1967.

Stimson, Frederick S. *The New Schools of Spanish American Poetry*. Madrid: Editorial Castalia, 1970.

Strand, Mark, ed. *New Poetry of Mexico*, Bilingual Edition. (Original eds. Octavio Paz, Alí Chumacero, José Emilio Pacheco, and Homero

Aridjis.) New York: E. P. Dutton & Co., 1970.

Sypher, Wylie. *Art History: An Anthology of Modern Criticism*. New York: Random House, Vintage Books, 1963.

Tablada, José Juan. "Una bella carta inédita de José Juan Tablada sobre el movimiento estridentista." [Written to his nephew, Enrique Barreiro Tablada, 4 April 1927.] *El Universal Ilustrado* 26 enero 1928: 34.

——————. "Daguerrotipos." *El Universal Ilustrado* 29 enero 1925: 29.

Tibol, Raquel. "El estridentismo al ataque en Casa del Lago." *Proceso* 2 mayo 1983: n. pag.

Torre, Guillermo de. *Historia de las literaturas de vanguardia*. Madrid: Ediciones Guadarrama, 1965.

——————. "La imagen y la metáfora en la novísima lírica." *Alfar* [La Coruña] 45 (dic. 1924): n. pag.

Torres Bodet, Jaime. "Encuestas de 'La Antorcha': ¿Qué significa el estridentismo? ¿Cuáles son los caminos inmediatos de la poesía mexicana?" [Recopilación de Ortega.] *La Antorcha* (Semanario de José Vasconcelos) [México] I.5 (1 nov. 1924): 11-12.

——————. "Perspectiva de la literatura mexicana actual, 1915-1928." *Contemporáneos* sept., oct., nov., dic. 1928: n. pag.

Torres Michua, Armado. "Germán Cueto en la escultura mexicana." *El Gallo Ilustrado* (Semanario de *El Día*) 994 (5 julio 1981): 2-3.

Torres Rioseco, A. y Ralph E. Warner. *Bibliografía de la poesía mexicana*. Cambridge MA: Harvard University Press, 1934.

Trachtenberg, Alan. "The Brooklyn Bridge and the Mastery of Nature." *Massachusetts Review* IV.4 (Summer 1963): 731-741.

"Ultrafuturismo." *El Universal Ilustrado* 1 nov. 1923: n. pag.

Unger, Leonard. *T. S. Eliot: Moments and Patterns*. Minneapolis: University of Minnesota Press, 1967.

"Urbe." Rev. of *Urbe* by Manuel Maples Arce. Sec. "Libros y Revistas que Llegan." *El Universal Ilustrado* 31 julio 1924: n. pag. [41?]

Valdés, Héctor, ed. *Los contemporáneos: una antología general*. México: SEP/UNAM, 1982.

Valle, Juvencio. "Manuel Maples Arce." *El Día* 24 mayo 1969: 13.

Vallejo, César. *Trilce*. Buenos Aires: Losada, 1961.

Valverde, José María. *Estudios sobre la palabra poética*. Madrid: Ediciones Rialp, 1958.

Vandercammen, Edmond. "Homenaje a Manuel Maples Arce." Knokke: Bienal de Poesía, Academia Real de Bélgica, 1961.

_____. Letter to Maples Arce, 19 April 1977.

_____. trans. *Poèmes Interdits* by Manuel Maples Arce. Bruxelles: Les Cahiers du Journal des Poètes, 1936.

_____. "Poésie de Langue Espagnole." Rev. of *Memorial de la Sangre* by Manuel Maples Arce. *Le Journal des Poètes* 9 (nov. 1947): n. pag.

Vela, Arqueles. *El café de nadie*. Jalapa, Ver.: Ediciones de Horizonte, 1926.

⎯⎯⎯. "Estridentismo Automovilístico: Literatura Balloon." *El Universal Ilustrado* 26 nov. 1925: 50.

⎯⎯⎯. "Historia del Café de Nadie." *El Universal Ilustrado* 21 abril 1924: 57.

⎯⎯⎯. *Poemontaje*. México: Colección Espiral, 1968.

⎯⎯⎯. "La sonrisa estridentista." *El Universal Ilustrado* 24 dic. 1925: 24.

⎯⎯⎯. "La tarde estridentista. Historia del Café de Nadie." *El Universal Ilustrado* 17 abril 1924: 37, 57.

Velázquez, Jaime G. "Homenaje a Manuel Maples Arce, 'Un abismo de letras, un cuerpo de silencio'–De arrebatado muchacho a hombre de reposadas reflexiones y fina poesía." [Unidentified Mexican newspaper, 1981: n. pag.]

Vergara, Gloria. "La poética vanguardista de Manuel Maples Arce," *La colmena* 1996, Issue 11 (UNAM): 27-29.

Villaurrutia, Xavier. *La poesía de los jóvenes de México*. México: Antena, 1924.

Warner-Ault, Ann. "Manuel Maples Arce, Salvador Novo and the Origin of Mexican Vanguard Autobiographies," *Revista Hispánica Moderna*, June 2014, Año 67, No. 1: 91-108.

Williams, William Carlos. "An Essay on *Leaves of Grass*." *Leaves of Grass: One Hundred Years After*. Ed. Milton Hindus. Stanford CA: Stanford University Press, 1955: 22-31.

Xilote 34 (Primavera 1973). [México] [Special issue on *Estridentismo*.]

Xirau, Ramón. *Tres Poetas de la Soledad*. México: Antigua Librería Robredo, 1955.

Yúdice, George. "*Poemas árticos*: modelo de una nueva poética." Conference paper. "Vicente Huidobro y la Vanguardia," International Symposium. University of Chicago, 5-8 April 1978.

www.ingramcontent.com/pod-product-compliance
Lightning Source LLC
Chambersburg PA
CBHW021113300426
44113CB00006B/138